The Power to Divide

A VOLUME IN THE SERIES

Cornell Studies in Security Affairs

Edited by Robert J. Art, Robert Jervis, and Stephen M. Walt

A list of titles in this series is available at cornellpress.cornell.edu.

The Power
to Divide

*Wedge Strategies in Great
Power Competition*

TIMOTHY W. CRAWFORD

Cornell University Press

Ithaca and London

Cornell University Press gratefully acknowledges receipt of a grant from Morrissey College of Arts and Sciences, Boston College, which aided in the publication of this book.

First published 2021 by Cornell University Press

Library of Congress Cataloging-in-Publication Data

Names: Crawford, Timothy W., author.
Title: The power to divide : wedge strategies in great power
    competition / Timothy W. Crawford.
Description: Ithaca [New York] : Cornell University Press, 2021. |
    Series: Cornell studies in security affairs | Includes bibliographical
    references and index.
Identifiers: LCCN 2020031366 (print) | LCCN 2020031367 (ebook) |
    ISBN 9781501754715 (hardcover) | ISBN 9781501754739 (pdf) |
    ISBN 9781501754722 (epub)
Subjects: LCSH: Alliances—History—20th century. | World politics—
    1900–1945. | International relations—History—20th century.
Classification: LCC JZ1314 .C73 2021 (print) | LCC JZ1314 (ebook) |
    DDC 327.1/16—dc23
LC record available at https://lccn.loc.gov/2020031366
LC ebook record available at https://lccn.loc.gov/2020031367

For Orly, Tamara, and Abraham

Contents

CONTENTS

Acknowledgments

This book was "in the works" for about fifteen years. That adds up to a lot of debts to family, friends, colleagues, and institutions—including some that I have no doubt forgotten.

As the project evolved, many friends and colleagues commented on parts of it or otherwise shared ideas that pushed me along. Yasuhiro Izumikawa's scholarship on wedge strategies, and his perceptive commentary on mine, have helped me considerably. Even after enduring more hours of my talking about this project than almost anyone, Mark Sheetz agreed to review the longest version of the manuscript and provided extensive remarks. Two anonymous reviewers of the manuscript, a series editor, and a half-dozen other anonymous reviewers of precursor pieces supplied much—indeed, very much—constructive criticism. While I doubt that the finished product has remedied all of their concerns, I am certain that their critiques helped to make it better.

Many other colleagues provided substantial feedback and suggestions. Steven Lobell, Norrin Ripsman, and Jeffrey Taliaferro each did so individually and as a team. Stacie Goddard, Ron Krebs, Dan Nexon, and Evan Resnick all weighed in at points along the way. So too did Jason Davidson, Charles Glaser, Mark Haas, Michael Glosny, Eugene Gholz, Lewis Griffith, Robert Jervis, Alexander Lanoszka, Keir Lieber, Sean Lynn-Jones, T. V. Paul, Barry Posen, Jeremy Pressman, George Quester, Joshua Rovner, Robert Ross, Joshua Shifrinson, Jon Schuessler, Jack Snyder, Mark Stoller, Caitlin Talmadge, Keren Yarhi-Milo, and Christopher Williams.

I also benefited much from the comments of participants at research seminars hosted by the International Security Program at the Belfer Center for

Science and International Affairs at Harvard University; the Security Studies Program at the Massachusetts Institute of Technology; the National Security Seminar at the John M. Olin Institute for Strategic Studies at Harvard; the Institute for Security and Conflict Studies at George Washington University; the Research Program on International Security at Princeton University; the International Security Program at the University of Denver's Josef Korbel School of International Studies; the Denver Council on Foreign Relations; the Center for American Studies at Doshisha University; and the Graduate School of Asia-Pacific Studies at Waseda University. Special thanks are due to Yasu Izumikawa, Takeshi Lida, and Chikako Kawakatsu Ueki for arranging the latter two events. I must specially thank those who organized and participated in the book workshop at the 2016 Lone Star National Security Forum, where two chapters from an early draft of this book were put through the wringer. The S. Rajaratnam School of International Studies at the Nanyang Technological University generously sponsored a working paper related to this project.

Excellent undergraduate and graduate research assistants at BC helped me with the book: Raakhi Agrawal, Danielle Cardona, Mary Curley, Jonathan Culp, Alexandre Provencher-Gravel, Amanda Rothschild, Leor Sapir, Djuke Stammeshaus, Lara Steele, Paul White, and Gary Winslett.

I am most grateful for the editorial guidance provided by Roger Haydon and Ange Romeo-Hall at Cornell University Press, copy-editing by Anne Davidson, production by Mary Ribesky, and indexing by Lisa DeBoer.

Portions of chapters 4, 5, 7, and 8 contain material published in earlier forms in: "Wedge Strategy, Balancing, and the Deviant Case of Spain, 1940–41," *Security Studies* 17, no. 1 (Winter 2008): 1–38; "Powers of Division: From the Anti-Comintern to the Nazi-Soviet and Japanese-Soviet Pacts, 1936–1941," in *The Challenge of Grand Strategy: The Great Powers and the Broken Balance between the World Wars*, ed. Jeffrey Taliaferro, Steven Lobell, and Norrin Ripsman (New York: Cambridge University Press, 2012), 246–78; and "The Alliance Politics of Concerted Accommodation: Entente Bargaining and Italian and Ottoman Interventions in the First World War," *Security Studies* 23, no. 1 (March 2014): 113–47.

I am fortunate to have an academic home in the Boston College Political Science Department, where I have been surrounded by a vibrant and growing group of international relations colleagues, including David Deese, Jennifer Erickson, Jonathan Kirshner, Peter Krause, Lindsey O'Rourke, and last but not least, Robert Ross. To Bob Ross, I owe special thanks for unflagging encouragement throughout the long gestation of the project. Hats off as well to the Morrissey College of Arts and Sciences for granting two timely sabbaticals and a subvention.

From my parents and a legion of in-laws came love and support that helped keep me even-keeled. So too did the comradery of Ross Adams and

Bill Lind. Of course, my greatest debt is to my wife, Orly Mishan—a big-hearted woman with a potent intellect and career. She is the rock-steady builder of a happy life for me and our children, Tamara and Abraham. This book is dedicated to the three of them, for giving me so much to be thankful for while I struggled to finish it.

The Power to Divide

Introduction

The Power to Divide in Alliance Politics

> How to induce another power to make a separate peace or . . . detach
> it from a counter-coalition, is the first question of strategy.
>
> George Liska, 1962

Facing the fact or prospect of a hostile alliance, a state has a few basic strategic options. Whether its motive is defensive or offensive, whether it seeks to enhance or deplete balancing power, the menu does not change. If the state is not willing to surrender the primary values or goals the alliance would harm, it must try to reduce the alliance's potential to harm them. To do this, the state can try to build strength against the alliance, either by mobilizing internal resources and forces or by recruiting and pooling allied power.[1] Or it can try to weaken the opposing alliance by dividing it. That is where wedge strategies come in—they use diplomacy and statecraft to move or keep a potential adversary out of an opposing alliance.[2] Coercive ones rely chiefly on threats and punishment to influence the target state's alignment.[3] Accommodative ones emphasize inducements.[4] This book focuses on the accommodative kind.[5]

I call it "selective" accommodation because the state doing it (the "divider") does not conciliate indiscriminately.[6] It does so in a fashion calculated to achieve strategic effects against the constellation of opposing forces. The logic follows Frederick Hartmann's "cardinal principle" of the "conservation of enemies," which prescribes "deliberately holding down the opponent's number of allies by making policy adjustments that satisfy the requirements of third nations."[7] In short, selective accommodation extends inducements toward a specific state in the opposition (the "target"), in order to better isolate, deter, or coerce others. This book seeks to explain how selective accommodation works, when states try it, and what makes them succeed or fail.[8]

1

Why Study Selective Accommodation?

To understand such things is a matter of both practical and intellectual urgency. Their relevance to central problems of U.S. grand strategy is hard to overstate. The post–Cold War pattern of primacy is eroding. "Russia is back, and China is coming" in their regional neighborhoods.[9] As the White House's 2017 National Security Strategy (NSS) puts it, "Great power competition [has] returned."[10] This "long-term, strategic competition," as the U.S. Department of Defense (DoD) calls it, will define high politics for decades to come.[11] With that comes intensified efforts to divide U.S. alliances.[12] That such efforts have already begun is now a persistent refrain in official U.S. strategic outlooks: Russia "aims to . . . divide us from our allies and partners," is "stepping up its campaign to divide Western political and security institutions," and seeks "to shatter the North Atlantic Treaty Organization."[13] China "seeks to displace the United States in the Indo-Pacific region . . . and reorder the region in its favor," and to "drive a wedge between U.S. allies and partners to undermine the development of a unified, U.S.-led security architecture in the Asia-Pacific."[14] Whether and how China or Russia can use selective accommodation may thus impact the shape and cohesion of the U.S.'s alliances and the chances that great power competition will precipitate war.

There also looms the danger of increasing Sino-Russian alignment against the U.S. The U.S. intelligence community's 2019 global threat assessment warns that already, "China and Russia are more aligned than at any point since the mid-1950s."[15] In their military modernization efforts and growing cooperation in military affairs, their shared revisionism and "authoritarian capitalist" affinity, it is hard not to discern their potential to combine against the U.S.-led order.[16] While observers disagree about the extent to which their strategic partnership will deepen, and the gravity of threats it may pose, it undoubtedly constitutes a serious challenge to U.S. primacy and the system of alliances and strategic partnerships it maintains and extends through deep engagement. [17] Whether and how the U.S. uses selective accommodation to prevent or degrade a Sino-Russian alliance is thus a first-order problem of U.S. grand strategy.

For scholarship in the study of alliances politics, focusing on selective accommodation wedge strategies also accomplishes several important purposes. By zeroing in on a principal form of wedge strategy, it both advances the research program on that broader subject and redresses other important gaps in the study of alliances in international security.[18] As a motor of alliance division and thus alignment patterns, selective accommodation's role has been obscured in much alliance politics research. Though foundational and general works in international relations have often noted the importance of dividing adversaries, the main lines of alliance research have, in various ways, steered away from the subject.[19] At a high level, much theoretical effort has gone into understanding the politics of aggregating—the forming and managing of alliances.[20] Much less has gone into the politics of disaggregating—the dividing and weakening of *other* alliances. And though what I call selective accommodation has been recognized, it has not been studied systematically.[21] We know little about the conditions that encourage states to try it and that influence whether they succeed or fail.

Alliance studies that have addressed fragmentation have tended to search for causes in places well removed from the intended efforts of opposing states. The breakups, weaknesses, or failures to form alliances have thus been attributed to structural incentives of multipolarity, the general decline or restraint of threatening power, the prevalence of defense-dominant strategic beliefs, ideological incompatibilities or within-movement competition, heterogeneous levels of development, and domestic political turbulence, leadership turnover, and alliance design.[22] As illuminating as many of these perspectives are, they nevertheless obscure the extent to which alignment relations reflect actors' strategic choices about diplomacy and statecraft.

A kindred bias lies in the thriving research program in international relations (IR) on "alliance reliability."[23] These studies build on a bedrock concept of alliance theory that expects the quality of allies' cohesion to reflect the incentives on which their alliance is founded. Hence, in the search for what makes allies more or less likely to keep commitments, such studies often home in on the measures they adopt to shape *each other's* incentives to cooperate—for example, how they "design" alliance contracts, craft alliance institutions, or coordinate war aims.[24] But alliance reliability research does not grapple with the other half of the story: the extent to which incentives undergirding alliances are subject to change by forces *outside* alliances. And chief among those forces are measures opposing states can take to weaken or unwind the incentive structures that allies try to erect for each other.

Close study of selective accommodation also spotlights the influence approach (inducements) traditionally downplayed in security studies and pigeonholed in analyses of politics inside alliances.[25] Thus, we know much more about how states use side payments to manage their allies than about how they use them to attack *others'* alliances.[26] Indeed, when it comes to power politics between alliances, more careful thought has been given to the strategic uses of coercion, subversion, and brute force than to the uses of reward.

Consider the concept of "abandonment." Among the most important in alliance studies, it denotes one of the chief hazards of having an ally—being left in the lurch when crisis comes. Abandonment is alliance division actualized, fragmentation made manifest. In alliance studies, the conventional theoretical framing (of the "alliance security dilemma") implies that coercive pressure is the prime cause of abandonment. A gets B to abandon C by confronting B with the prospect of "entrapment" in a punishing war between A and C that B does not want to fight.[27] Though it is not hard to fathom that

A might entice rather than coerce B into abandoning C, that catalyst of abandonment has largely dropped out of alliance dilemma theory.[28] The study of selective accommodation thus ties back to one of the fundamental issues of alliance politics—what causes abandonment?—and forces one to consider the role of adversary inducements.

This study also sheds light on a political weapon *of*—not just against— alliances. Great power competition inevitably entails alliance competitions. And yet, whether one is focusing on defensive alliances meant to deter and repel aggressors or offensive alliances meant to enable them, how selective accommodation—as an enterprise *concerted* by allies—can further these purposes is easy to overlook. For defenders, it helps to weaken and deter the aggressive power by fragmenting it. For aggressors, it helps to dilute the counterbalancing resistance. Alliance studies have almost entirely ignored this external thrust of alliance diplomacy, and the inside politics of coordination necessary to carry it through. A better grasp of when states are likely to concert selective accommodation, and what shapes its prospects for success, thus improves understanding of political warfare between alliances.

Finally, concentrating on selective accommodation enables one to develop a theoretical construct high on the ladder of policy relevance. Many "midrange" IR theories are policy-relevant because they help to diagnose or explain problems of major concern to leaders, and more so when they trace the effects of variables that leaders can influence.[29] The edge of policy relevance sharpens in work that concentrates on things that leaders directly influence and routinely manipulate, foreign policy ends and means. Here one finds, for example, works that focus on a particular kind of policy goal (such as nonproliferation or human rights promotion) while examining the range of policy approaches and instruments that may be used to advance it, or, conversely, studies of the utility of a particular approach (such as economic or military coercion) in respect to a variety of policy goals.[30] My theory goes a step further up the ladder. It gains traction in policy relevance by narrowing the scope on both the policy approach and the policy objectives sides of the equation. It analyzes how a particular policy approach works to further a particular kind of policy goal, and the conditions for its successful use. Such a theory seeks to generalize about a "generic" kind of means-end influence attempt while "differentiating" cases in that genre, using "key variables thought to have a high leverage effect" on outcomes.[31]

Theory of Selective Accommodation: Framework for Analysis

The theory advanced here focuses on attempts to use inducements to prevent or break up opposing alliances. The emphasis on incentives means that it rests on a basic premise: state leaders bring a kind of "politically rational" and "sensible" goal-oriented approach to making statecraft and alignment choices that is sensitive to the likely political costs, benefits, and risks of alternatives.[32] The theory addresses three questions arising from this strategic context. First, what are the descriptive logics and causal mechanisms that define selective accommodation? Second, under what circumstances are states likely to attempt it? Third, what contingencies promote success or failure? These central analytical questions drive this book.

The theory's framework consists of two parts. The first contains a core "abstract conceptual" model that describes what a selective accommodation attempt looks like and its mechanisms of action—that is, how it should work when it works. It also suggests initial conditions that encourage states to attempt it and shape how they try to do it. The second adds key variables for describing the strategic context and actors, which identify conditions that may favor success or failure.[33] To be clear: the framework is not meant to provide comprehensive explanations of attempts and their outcomes, covering all of the relevant causes, in the cases to which it is applied. In every case, there will be other important situation-specific factors at work, brought to light through inductive analysis. Nevertheless, the framework's purpose is to concentrate on a few things that help to define the initial conditions of attempts, and key differences and commonalities in the resulting contexts and interactions, which should favor success or failure.[34] The theory will be fleshed out in the next chapter. Here I provide a rough overview.

The core model, describing the basic contours and mechanisms of attempts, comes first. With selective accommodation, inducements are the main levers that dividers manipulate to move or keep target states away from threatening combinations. Selective accommodation can accomplish this in three ways. The primary way is by rewarding specific targets for refraining from hostility. This implies a basic exchange process: success follows from giving or promising to extend benefits that are valuable enough to the target to win its compliance. This central logic of the core model constitutes the framework's baseline explanation of outcomes of selective accommodation attempts. Dividers well positioned to use reward power vis-à-vis a target are more likely to succeed than those that are not.[35] The next two ways are potential side effects of the first, which can in their own fashion advance the divider's goal. Accommodative bids can help to defuse common threat perceptions that might otherwise push the target to ally against the divider.[36] And they can introduce or elevate issues that sow conflict between the target and other foes.[37] When selective accommodation works, one may find one or both of these mechanisms also at work in the political sequence leading from the initial attempt to the successful result.

From the model's primary exchange logic, I also deduce two initial conditions that should hold when states try selective accommodation. The first concerns *motive*: the divider's leaders are likely to believe that the target's alignment carries high "strategic weight." That is, they expect that their grand strategic aims in peace or war will be seriously harmed if the target joins other opponents.[38] Because inducements, when they work, are inherently costly, and accommodating potential adversaries is risky business, states will rarely try to accommodate potential adversaries perceived to have low strategic weight. The second proposition concerns *means*: the divider's leaders are likely to believe that they are well positioned to use inducements to influence the target; they possess or control something the target values, which they can parlay to gain the desired alignment. If the divider's leaders do not believe this, they are also not likely to try selective accommodation. In sum, when states attempt selective accommodation, their leaders are likely to believe that the target's alignment carries high strategic weight and that they are able to use rewards to influence it.[39]

The second part of the framework consists of generalizations about other conditions that shape selective accommodation attempts and tend to promote success or failure. Here I won't detail the relevant variables behind these generalizations, but instead just give the main idea embodied by each.

The first concerns the degree of change in the target's alignment that the divider aims to induce. The intuition is that big alignment change is harder to obtain than small change. Moving a state from adversary to ally is a heavy lift; moving one from adversary to neutral requires less work; and keeping a potential adversary in a hedged or neutral position involves even less. Thus, the scale of the divider's alignment change goal impacts the prospects of success. The second generalization concerns alliance constraints on the divider's side that may handicap its attempts at selective accommodation, and circumstances that can aggravate or alleviate those constraints. This reflects a basic truth of alliance politics: to sow discord in the enemy's camp, one often needs to overcome discord in one's own camp. The key conjecture here is that dividers will have more trouble making selective accommodation work if they depend on allies that oppose the accommodative approach or do not agree about the target's high strategic weight.

In sum, these generalizations identify factors that may condition the divider's ability to convert inducements into influence over the target, and thus they help to explain how and why selective accommodation works in some cases and not others. Encapsulated, they address (1) how much change in the target's alignment the divider seeks, and (2) how much outside political support the divider has to induce it.

Applying the Theoretical Framework

I put the theory to work in two ways: in the study of historical cases, and in the analysis of contemporary scenarios. First, I will examine eight cases of great power diplomacy surrounding the two world wars, in which selective accommodation was tried, sometimes successfully, sometimes not. Given the historical import of the events involved, there is intrinsic value in understanding these cases better. But the case studies also speak to contemporary concerns, because they are situated in contexts of multipolar great power politics not unlike the one now emerging.[40] Great power competition today is intensifying and becoming more contentious in the alliance domain. While scholars may debate whether the international power structure will become bipolar (topped by the U.S. and China) or multipolar, it is today trending multipolar in the behavioral sense, with the U.S., Russia, and China treating each other as "important strategic actors" in a contest of "making and breaking coalitions."[41] Such was true even in the heyday of Cold War bipolarity—in the 1970s and 1980s—when the U.S. worked assiduously to cooperate with China (and vice versa) against the Soviet Union.[42] About these earlier competitions, Waltz observed, "Much .... centered on one side's trying to make and maintain coalitions while the other side tried to prevent or break them."[43] These contests of yesteryear are not so far removed from today's. This book revisits them to better understand our own.

Some of the cases are well known, such as Germany's efforts to avert U.S. intervention in World War I, and its bid, on the eve of World War II, to prevent an Anglo-Franco-Soviet alliance. Others are less so, such as Germany's efforts to detach Japan from the Entente in World War I, and to woo Turkey away from alliance with Britain in World War II. Each, nevertheless, will be brought into a new light as I apply the theoretical framework, along with evidence drawn from scholarly historical works and official sources, to describe what happened. I will also control the cases with comparative methods to assess how well parts of the theory help explain why selective accommodation succeeds or fails. In the context of each case, I will also address complementary and alternative explanations.

I also use the theoretical framework to analyze contemporary scenarios of alliance dividing involving the United States, China, and Russia. To a considerable degree, the initial conditions of these scenarios are already laid. China's power surge is stressing U.S. alliances in Asia, and Beijing's potential to use selective accommodation may determine the contours of the alliance system and whether it can deter China. I consider a scenario in which China tries to accommodate India ahead of a confrontation with the U.S. in Asia. The prospect of a Sino-Russian alliance against the U.S. is also bearing down. Whether and how the U.S. can use selective accommodation to prevent or degrade such a Sino-Russian alliance thus also demands a closer look. I consider how the U.S. might use selective accommodation to wean Russia away from its deepening alignment with China. In sum, I use the framework to prompt careful thinking, along lines one might otherwise overlook, about coming problems of great power politics and grand strategy. The first part helps to guide thinking about what might promote selective accommodation attempts in those contexts. The second part, which highlights conditions that make selective accommodation likely to succeed or fail, helps to discern the potential content and prospects of such scenarios.

Plan of the Book

Chapter 1 presents the theoretical framework outlined above. It also sets up the methods—of structured focus comparison and qualitative analysis—that organize the historical case studies. Chapters 2 to 9 cover those cases. Chapter 2 examines Germany's failed attempts during World War I to induce Japan to abandon the Entente. Chapter 3 examines Germany's successful attempts to keep the U.S. a nonbelligerent until early 1917. Chapter 4 analyzes the Entente's failed attempts (after the July Crisis of 1914) to prevent the Ottoman Empire from intervening on the side of the Central powers. Chapter 5 analyzes the Entente's successful attempt in 1915 to promote Italy's defection from and intervention against the Central powers. Chapter 6 assesses British and French efforts to prevent Italy from allying and fighting with Germany between 1937 and 1940. Chapter 7 assesses Germany's successful attempt to stop the USSR from allying with Britain and France in 1939. Chapter 8 explores Britain and the U.S.'s success in keeping Spain from joining the Axis in 1940 to 1941. Chapter 9 explores Germany's failure to induce Turkey to defect from the British alliance and join the Axis in 1941.

   With chapter 10, I synthesize the findings and address the question of what makes selective accommodation work, with cross-case comparisons that show the impact of conditions conducive to success. Chapter 11 concludes the study. In that chapter I first examine the two contemporary scenarios outlined above, then conclude with commentary for policy practitioners seeking to make selective accommodation work.

The Theory of Selective Accommodation

The theoretical framework comprises two elements. The first, the "core" theory, is an "abstract conceptual model" that identifies the "critical variables" of the strategy and the "general logic associated with [its] successful use."[1] It describes how selective accommodation works (when it works) and suggests conditions under which states are likely to attempt it (what I call "initiation" conditions).[2] The second consists of propositions about contingent conditions, and associated mechanisms, conducive to the success or failure of attempts. Like the initiation conditions, these are probabilistic. Combined, these elements offer an overarching framework to explain selective accommodation attempts and outcomes, one that is geared to the priorities of policy-applicable theory. It thus furnishes two kinds of "usable" theoretical insight: (1) a general conceptual model of the strategy of selective accommodation, and (2) generic knowledge about the conditions that favor its success.[3]

Because this framework does not cover all of the potential causes, actors, and interactions that may produce outcomes, and because its propositions are probabilistic, the theory's limits are worth noting. It cannot offer a parsimonious "covering law" explanation of outcomes across the range of cases. Nor can it identify, in the linkages between attempts and their outcomes, a master intervening variable that consistently determines success and failure. In different cases, different contingent conditions will weigh more heavily in shaping developments.[4] The framework thus anticipates "equifinality"— the possibility that "different causal pathways . . . lead to similar outcomes."[5] Moreover, even when the values of all of the elements of the theoretical framework are strongly congruent with the outcome of a case, this can only yield a "partial equilibrium" account. That is because the theory covers only a subset of the strategic interactions (involving the divider, target, and divider's allies) that combine to produce outcomes. Thus, in each case, actors and factors outside the theory's scope—such as the reactions of the target's alignment alternatives, or the quality of domestic politics within key actors—may augment the explanation.[6]

Given those limitations, one can expect from the theory the following: first, to direct attention in each case to initial conditions and patterns of calculation, observable through process tracing that elucidates the divider's decision to initiate selective accommodation; second, that the contingent conditions implicated in each case correspond to features of the policy and strategic context that are salient to decision-makers operating within it; and third, that those contingent conditions specified in each case, and the mechanisms they entail, have leverage—that is, they help explain decisions, moves, and interactions that are central to the chain of events leading to the outcome (i.e., success or failure) in each case.[7]

The Core Theory

The core theory contains the general conceptual model of selective accommodation and its basic influence formula—the use of positive incentives (e.g., promises, rewards, and concessions) to create divergent pressures on members or potential members of an opposing alliance. More specifically, the divider uses such inducements to accommodate a target "singled out for preferential treatment" in order to lure or keep it away from a more dangerous main enemy.[8]

This definition implies, indeed presumes, a broader theoretical domain—a bargaining arena in which the divider competes against others in a "bidding war" over the target's alignment.[9] Although rooted in that image of alliance competition, the core theory abstracts away from certain aspects of it. It does not specify the alignment goals the other bidders will seek, or which of them will bid higher, or why they will do so, or whether they can do so credibly. But it does stipulate that the target's alignment will be determined by its assessment of the *relative* attractiveness of the benefits offered, which will reflect both the content and credibility of the alternative bids.[10]

The techniques that dividers can use to accommodate vary in their costs and utility. The costliest is appeasement (by which I mean the sacrifice of a primary interest), which is rarely used to divide. Less costly and more often used are concessions and compensation (which entail sacrifices of secondary values) and endorsement (which means extending diplomatic support for a target's position that conflicts with that of other potential adversaries).[11] Whatever the form, the primary mechanism of influence is exchange: inducements are given or promised to a target in return for a desired change (or preservation) of its alignment. These accommodations will influence the target's choices by directly shaping its leaders' view of the relative attractiveness of compliance versus other alignment options, and/or by "catalyzing" domestic political shifts in favor of a decision to comply.[12] Either way, in the first instance, their relative value to the target is the driver.[13]

Though they can have these advantageous effects, accommodative bids are not generally cheap options—instead, they are costly and risky. Like all influence attempts involving positive incentives, when they work, the logic of exchange makes them costly.[14] That is, to win (or sustain) compliance, one has to give up something, either immediately or at a promised future point, or both. Along with that cost comes the risk that one's flexibility will convey weakness and invite more danger and demands.[15] Such downsides raise the question, when are states likely to try selective accommodation? The propositions discussed next answer it.

Initiation Conditions

That selective accommodation entails costly exchange suggests two important things about when states will tend to try it. These are the deductive bases for the initiation propositions. First, there is a motive calculus: the state must face a situation pressing or threatening enough to prompt its leaders to consider giving up some things to someone who wants them, in order to get a less dangerous pattern of hostile alignment. Second, there is a means calculus: the state must believe it possesses reward power relative to the target. Beliefs that such reward power is very limited depress the motivation to try selective accommodation. Thus, for a state to initiate a serious attempt, its leaders must think they have—or can control—some things that they can manipulate and dispense which are valuable to the target. These basic ideas are fleshed out next.

MOTIVE: BELIEFS ABOUT THE TARGET'S STRATEGIC WEIGHT

A divider's willingness to pay costs to influence the target is related to how much advantage it expects to gain by doing so.[16] The concept of strategic weight captures this. The divider's assessment of a target's strategic weight boils down to beliefs about the potential impact of the target's alignment on war and peace outcomes vital to the divider.[17] When it believes the target's alignment has high strategic weight, its motivation to influence the target successfully will be stronger, and so should be its willingness to make concessions to that end.

The determinants of strategic weight are varied and context-specific. They may figure in the divider's larger deterrence or coercive strategy. If its larger goal is to deter the main enemy, then it will rank the target as a strategic heavyweight if the enemy will be (1) likely to aggress if it has the target as an ally and (2) unlikely to if it does not. If the divider's goal is to coerce the main enemy on some issue, then it will rate the target's strategic weight highly if the enemy will be (1) likely to stand firm if the target is its ally and (2) likely to capitulate if the target is not.[18] Similarly, perceptions of a target's

11

strategic weight may reflect beliefs about the extent to which its alignment will delay or hasten the outbreak of war. Thus, for countries looking to "buy time" before they have to fight, keeping the target neutral or detaching it from the main enemy may be seen as a way to slow the latter down.[19] A target's strategic weight may also be reckoned in terms of how much its alignment will enable or impair the divider's plan to fight a war. If the divider has invested heavily in a war-fighting strategy that either depends on the target's neutrality for success or, much the same, becomes unworkable if the target joins the main adversary, then the divider will place high strategic weight on the target's alignment.

Especially in wartime, beliefs about strategic weight will focus on the target's "war-tipping" potential. These judgments may home in on the threats or opportunities posed by the target's capabilities per se—and the desire to deny them to the enemy or deploy them against it. They may also reflect a positional calculus, if the target is located in a place that will enable or obstruct operations with serious consequences for prosecution of the war effort. Finally, assessments of war-tipping potential may also turn on beliefs about the knock-on political effects of neutralizing or realigning the target. Thus, the divider may perceive the target to be a war tipper because it expects that a change in the target's alignment will trigger a series of alignment shifts that cumulatively will decide the war.[20]

For case analysis, I condense these variations into a simple categorical variable with two values. If evidence shows that the divider's leaders expect the target's alignment can swing their prospects against the main enemy in any of the ways just described, then the target has "High" strategic weight. If evidence shows that the divider's leaders do not believe that the target's alignment will have such effects, then the target has "Low" strategic weight. Table 1 summarizes the logic.

Table 1 Perceptions of the target's strategic weight

HIGH if the Divider's leaders do expect	The Target's alignment will:
LOW if the Divider's leaders do not expect	• Cause the main enemy to comply with or defy the Divider's deterrence or compellence policy. • Speed up or slow down how soon the main enemy goes to war. • Enable or impair the divider's peacetime plans to defend against the main enemy. • Add or subtract military capabilities from the main enemy's camp that can decisively tip the war against (or in favor) of the divider. • Give or deny to the main enemy, access to a location that can decisively tip the war against (or in favor) of the divider. • Trigger a chain of alignment shifts that can tip the war against (or in favor of) the divider.

MEANS: REWARD POWER RELATIVE TO THE TARGET

In the core theory, inducements are the main means for influencing the target's alignment. Here I identify the features of inducements that can (1) influence a target to comport its alignment in desired ways, and therefore (2) encourage a government that believes it can deploy them to try selective accommodation. When these features are present and strong, they do not guarantee success or translate into precise measures of the divider's relative influence over the target. But they do provide a rough gauge of the potential for success—indicating when and why states are likely to wager on selective accommodation—and suggest first-cut explanations of outcomes.

General bargaining logic implies three key qualities of reward power (see Table 2). First, the inducements should benefit the target in areas or on issues of major importance to it. The most obvious sign of such importance are the demands or desiderata conveyed by the target. In the first instance, then, reward power is reflected in one's ability to offer inducements that in some way correspond to what the target says it wants. Second, the divider should have an evident ability to control the inducements—either directly or indirectly, through its relations with others. Third, the inducement should not be easily substituted or outbid by those competing for influence over the target (i.e., its allies or potential allies).[21] When states, believing they can manipulate such sources of influence, face dangerous alignment patterns, they are likely to try selective accommodation in response.[22]

Behind these factors stands another important quality of relative reward power—credibility.[23] The power of promises—which are central to selective accommodation diplomacy—depends on their credibility.[24] Doubts about whether the divider can and will deliver promised rewards will lower the target's assessment of their expected value. It is not just the record of past negotiations and follow-through that matters here. Evident control over promised rewards, as noted above, clearly feeds into credibility. With uncertainty about such control, or other ambiguities around the content and timing of such rewards, credibility suffers. This happens when the promised payoffs have a long time horizon or depend for their fulfilment on a string of future developments in relations among other actors. Most importantly, how the divider handles surrounding commitments and conflicting interests when offers are made can bolster or undermine the influence of its relative reward power. As I will show next, the divider's alliance constraints are critical here, creating uncertainty for both the divider and the target about the content and deliverability of accommodative offers.

In sum, the core theory's conceptual model describes the primary policy approach and means of influence—selective accommodation of the target, using inducements to encourage it to keep or change its alignment. Basic principles of bargaining indicate what kind of resources and contexts give dividers the wherewithal and hope to try this. And the divider's strategic

Table 2 Divider's relative reward power—actual and perceived

ACTUAL	
HIGH	LOW
Divider controls (directly or indirectly) resources desired by Target. The resources impact areas or issues important to the Target. The resources cannot be easily substituted or outbid by others. The Divider can credibly promise to deliver the rewards if the Target complies.	Divider does not control resources desired by Target. It does control resources desired by the target, but those resources do not impact areas or issues important to the Target. It does control resources desired by the target, that impact areas or issues of major importance to the Target, but the resources can be easily substituted or outbid by others. It does control resources desired by the Target, that impact areas or issues of major importance to the Target, and the resources cannot be easily substituted or outbid by others, but the Divider cannot credibly promise to deliver the rewards if the Target complies.
PERCEIVED	
HIGH	LOW
The Divider's leaders express in official or private documents and statements beliefs consistent with the points above.	The Divider's leaders express in official or private documents and statements beliefs consistent with the points above.

weight calculus indicates its motivation to commit reward power to the effort. Combined, these deductions yield a scale of the likelihood of selective accommodation attempts. When both reward power and strategic weight are thought to be high, selective accommodation attempts will be *likely*. When one or the other is lacking, attempts will be *unlikely* (but still happen with some frequency). When both conditions are absent, attempts will be *rare*.

The outcomes of attempts are, nevertheless, ultimately determined by the reality of the divider's relative reward power—whether what it offers the target is enough to outbid its alternatives. Thus, beliefs about relative reward power may be mistaken—actual influence may not measure up to the hoped-for influence. The reactions of the target's existing allies or potential alternatives cannot be known in advance or estimated with much precision. But these will affect the relative attractiveness of the divider's offer. Likewise, if the divider has allies implicated in the relationship, this may add to uncertainty about its relative reward power, because their behavior can shape the content and credibility of what it can offer. Thus, it is not surprising that even "likely" attempts sometimes fail. For the core theory, this is not a flaw. Certainty of success is not a necessary condition for influence attempts—just a prospect of success reasonable enough to warrant the effort.[25] The contingent conditions developed next help to explain why they do or don't succeed. These capture two different big issues that can influence whether the divider's relative reward power is "enough" to secure compliance.

Contingent Conditions

The contingent conditions add to the ease or difficulty with which inducements can be parlayed into desired results. The first, *attempted alignment change*, conveys the idea that it is generally harder and costlier to induce big changes than little ones. The second, the *divider's alliance constraints*, conveys the idea that the divider's own alliance relationships can impact its ability to do selective accommodation, by shaping the content and credibility of relative reward power.

ATTEMPTED ALIGNMENT CHANGE

As a general rule, selective accommodation's prospects are shaped by the degree of alignment change it tries to induce. That degree is a function of the target's existing alignment and the position the divider wants it to take.

The exchange logic of selective accommodation implies that whether a target complies with the divider's bid will depend on its calculus of the costs and benefits. Will compliance make it better off than it can expect to be if aligned otherwise? Not just the expected benefits offered by the divider, but also the costs the target will likely incur by complying, must be considered. Thus, for a selective accommodation bid to work, the divider must offer rewards that the target believes will (1) exceed the expected value of its alignment position before the divider's bid and (2) *also* cover its alignment change costs. Degree of alignment change matters, then, because it generally costs targets more to make big alignment changes than little alignment changes— and those costs get passed on to a divider trying to induce compliance. Thus, it will generally be more costly and difficult for dividers to induce big changes than little changes.

Formal treaty alliances matter in international politics because they are costly to make and costly to break.[26] Defecting from alliances is therefore bad for states because doing so damages their alliance reputation, which makes it hard to find future alliances on reasonable terms.[27] This foundational idea of alliance theory helps to explain why targets' compliance costs can vary in connection with degrees of alignment change. To put it simply: the graver its betrayal, the greater the hit to the target's reputation. Defecting on an ally by going neutral will incur less reputational damage than joining the ranks of its enemies. Because it costs targets more to do the latter, dividers must pay targets more to get them to do it.

How does one gauge the degree of attempted alignment change? First, I identify the target's initial alignment position. Does it have a formal, broad, public treaty commitment to militarily support an ally? If so, breaking this "fixed" position explicitly will incur high costs. Moving away from that ideal, there is a spectrum of less committed and uncommitted positions, which are less costly to change. This includes various kinds of hedging and neutral postures—for instance, that of a state which holds politically contradictory public and secret commitments. Or that of a "defected neutral" who, when fighting starts, declares itself "nonbelligerent" and thus attenuates its fixed alignment—without denouncing or fully decoupling from its formal allegiances.[28] It also includes states that are formally neutral or otherwise free of alliance ties.

For simplicity's sake, I distinguish three kinds of alignment positions a target may hold. It is in a "fixed" position when it has a formal, exclusive, and active alliance tie. It is in a "hedged" position when it has adopted policies or relations that compromise, convolute, or contradict its primary formal alliance tie.[29] It is in a "neutral" position when its starting position is a more or less formal nonaligned posture.

Second, I also identify the target alignment the divider wishes to achieve. Here, I consider three main contingencies. First, the divider may try to *realign* the target—shift it out of an opposing alliance and into a friendly one. Realignment entails the greatest degree of alignment change, and thus the highest compliance costs for targets. Second, the divider may try to *dealign* the target—shift it out of a fixed alliance and into a hedged position or out of a hedged position into a more neutral position.[30] Dealignment entails less alignment change, and thus lesser compliance costs for targets. Third, the divider may try to *reinforce* the target's existing hedged or neutral position— keep it from moving closer to the opponent.[31] This entails the least alignment change, and thus the lowest compliance costs for the target.

Drawing together the two elements—the target's alignment position and the divider's alignment goal—yields a three-level scale (High, Medium, Low) for measuring degree of alignment change (see Appendix, Table 13). Attempts to realign a target in a fixed or hedged alignment position seek a High level of alignment change. Attempts to dealign a target in a fixed or hedged position seek a Medium level of alignment change. Attempts to reinforce the position of a target in a hedged or neutral position seek a Low level of alignment change. These degrees of alignment change correspond to different levels of difficulty involved in selective accommodation attempts. High change (realignment) is the hardest and most costly to induce; medium and low changes are, progressively easier and less costly. Thus, success is easiest to achieve when the goal is to reinforce a target's existing hedged or neutral position. It is harder when the goal is to dealign. And it is much more difficult when the goal is to realign. Table 3 below summarizes the key contingencies and implications.[32]

Table 3 Cost and difficulty of attempted alignment change

←LOW		MEDIUM		HIGH →	
Reinforce	Reinforce	Dealign	Dealign	Realign	Realign
Neutral	Hedged	Hedged	Fixed	Hedged	Fixed
Target	Target	Target	Target	Target	Target

To operationalize these values in case studies, I use secondary histories and official documents to describe the two underlying variables. For the target's alignment position, I use such sources to establish how the target's position was defined officially and understood by observers at the time. For the divider's alignment goal, I draw from internal documents and public statements expressing the intentions of the divider's foreign policy leaders, and secondary histories based on these sources.

DIVIDER'S ALLIANCE CONSTRAINTS

The divider's alliance relationships may also affect the quality of its selective accommodation bid. Those relationships can diminish the credibility of its diplomacy and curtail its willingness or ability to mobilize inducements in support of it.[33] An unaligned divider need not deal with such alliance constraints (though its isolation may itself limit the rewards it can offer). A divider *with* allies will be constrained by such ties if it depends on those allies and they have direct stakes in relation to the target. This is especially true if the divider needs allied support and sacrifices to generate inducements important to the target.

To get at these issues, my alliance constraints concept does two things: it distinguishes between dividers with low constraints and high constraints; and, for those with high constraints, it identifies additional mechanisms that conduce failure or success.[34] What determines the level of constraints is not merely whether the divider has allies, but also the nature of (1) its relationship with those allies and (2) *their* relationship with the target. High constraints exist when the divider depends on allies that have direct stakes in relations with the target.

To operationalize this logic, I do two things. First, I identify *relevant* allies. I ask: Does the divider have strategic partners possessing direct stakes in the relationship with the target or the inducements needed to sway it, which may impinge on its attempt to accommodate it? If the divider does have such allies, then I ask a second question: How much can the divider control them? To answer this, I consider the symmetry (or asymmetry) of the divider's relations with them. With greater symmetry of power and dependence comes greater alliance constraints. If the divider is relatively equal to the ally in terms of power and dependence, that will curtail the divider's ability to dominate the formulation and conduct of policy with regard to the target. If the divider is more powerful and less dependent than the ally, then intra-alliance bargaining over how to deal with the target will be settled close to its preferences.[35] I frame these propositions with conventional distinctions between an alliance of relative equals versus a "patron-client" alliance.[36] When the relevant ally is the divider's peer or patron, the divider will face High alliance constraints.[37] When the relevant ally is its client, the divider will face Low constraints. Figure 1 summarizes these deductions. (It takes as its starting point a divider with allies—dividers without allies, ipso facto, have low alliance constraints.)

When alliance constraints are high, selective accommodation's prospects will be influenced by the ally's policy in two important ways. The first turns on whether the ally agrees with the basic enterprise—that is, using accommodation to shape the target's alignment. If the ally rejects this approach, its opposition can more or less impair the divider's initiative through several possible mechanisms (see Figure 2). The divider may abandon the attempt, either in anticipation of the destructive effects of the ally's opposition or after those effects have been felt. If the divider instead proceeds, the ally's opposition will be most debilitating if it manifests in an observable policy that actively contradicts the divider's. This will weaken the credibility of the divider's inducements, if not spoil them outright. The ally's opposition will be less debilitating if—for the sake of presenting a common front—it coordinates its declaratory policy with the divider's (even while withholding substantial support in the form of concessions). This latter path of declaratory coordination dodges the destructive effects of open discord, but still handicaps the divider's reward power.

The second way turns on the ally's beliefs about the target's strategic weight. Here the logic from the core model extends to the allied context. If willingness to pay costs to accommodate a target increases in proportion to estimates of its strategic weight, then this relationship scales up to the group

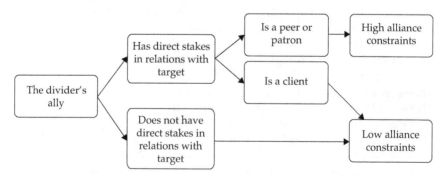

Figure 1. The divider's alliance constraints.

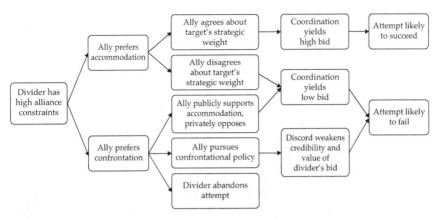

Figure 2. How high-alliance constraints affect prospects of success.

context, where states in concert seek to accommodate a target.[38] Thus, when the ally's sense of the target's strategic weight aligns with the divider's (at a high level), the ally should coordinate deeply with the divider's initiative and pay costs to help advance it. Two mechanisms of such coordination can be observed through process tracing. First, the allies—in order to bolster the accommodative effort—make concessions to the target on important interests. Second, the divider and allies strike side bargains with each other in order to offset and thereby facilitate the sacrifices they make to further the common policy.[39] Such coordination will drive up the value of the bid they can offer the target, increasing the likelihood that they will successfully influence it. By contrast, when the divider's ally sees little strategic value in accommodating the target, the quality of its coordination diminishes, reverting to the pattern described earlier, in which the ally publicly endorses the selective accommodation effort, but makes no substantial concessions to advance it.

Summary of Initiation and Contingent Conditions

INITIATION CONDITIONS

When facing a potential or actual combination of adversaries, a state will be likely to attempt selective accommodation when its leaders believe that (1) the target's alignment has high strategic weight, and (2) they have reward power relative to the target. The outcome of these attempts (success or failure) will reflect the state's actual relative reward power, which may (or may not) measure up to its leaders' hopes and expectations.

CONTINGENT CONDITIONS

The following conditions make success or failure more likely by shaping the scope, viability, and relative competitiveness of the divider's reward power.

- Attempted Alignment Change: Attempts to reinforce a target's existing (hedged or neutral) position are more likely to succeed than attempts to dealign a target, which are more likely to succeed than attempts to realign a target.
- Alliance Constraints: When alliance constraints are Low, prospects for success turn on the quality and credibility of the divider's relative reward power and the degree of attempted alignment change. When alliance constraints are High, failure is likely unless the divider and its relevant allies reach strategic consensus on (a) the accommodative approach and (b) the target's high strategic value.

Cases and Methods

I use qualitative methods to assess the theory in eight case studies. Here I provide a brief overview of the cases, outcomes, and condition values they cover, and some general observations concerning their selection. Then I explain the methods of analysis.

The eight cases occurred in the run-ups to and during World Wars I and II, comprising nine distinct selective accommodation attempts.[40] On the primary outcome of interest—success or failure—there is a roughly even distribution, as shown in Table 4 below.

These cases capture the full range of variation in both the initiation and contingent conditions. In each case study, the condition values are assigned and described qualitatively. Here I will stipulate them, in order to summa-

Table 4 Selective accommodation attempts and outcomes

World War I	Outcomes
1. Germany tries to detach Japan from the Entente, 1914–16	Failure
2. Germany tries to keep the U.S. neutral, 1914–17	Success
3. The Entente tries to keep Ottoman Empire neutral, 1914	Failure
4. The Entente tries to realign Italy, 1915	Success

World War II	
5. Britain and France try to divide Italy from Germany, (a) 1936–39; (b) 1939–40	Failure (a), (b)
6. Germany tries to divide the USSR from Britain and France, 1939	Success
7. Britain and the U.S. try to keep Spain neutral, 1940–41	Success
8. Germany tries to realign Turkey from Britain, 1941	Failure

rize the range covered by the cases and highlight the kinds of observations and inferences they permit.

VARIATION OF INITIATION CONDITIONS

The most uniformity is in the initiation conditions: the divider's beliefs about the target's strategic weight and its relative reward power. The theory posits that low values on both conditions make failure very likely, and thus these attempts are rare. The case selection is therefore limited to cases with a high value on at least one of the two initiation conditions, and skewed toward cases with high values on both (see Table 5). Six of the cases (nos. 2–7) hold constant high values for both conditions. In the two remaining cases (nos. 1 and 8), either the target's strategic weight or relative reward power are perceived to be low or lacking. These latter two ("unlikely") attempts allow one to investigate the expected implications of such offsetting values for the way a case plays out.[41]

VARIATION OF CONTINGENT CONDITIONS

There is also substantial variation across the cases for the two major contingent conditions. With attempted alignment change, the full spectrum is represented (see Table 6). There are two cases of attempted realignment; two of attempted dealignment; and five of attempts to reinforce.

As the table shows, there is a strong pattern of clustering on two sides of the spectrum. Four attempts are right of the center line, in the Medium High

Table 5 Initiation conditions

	World War I				World War II			
	1. Germany-Japan	2. Germany-U.S.	3. Entente-Ottoman Empire Initiator: Russia	4. Entente-Italy Initiator: Britain	5. Britain & France-Italy Initiator: Britain	6. Germany-USSR	7. Britain & U.S.-Spain Initiator: Britain	8. Germany-Turkey
Motive: Perceived Strategic Weight of Target	High	High	High	High	High	High	High	Low
Means: Perceived Reward Power of Divider	Low	High	High	High	High	High	High	High

Table 6 Attempted alignment change

LOW		MEDIUM		HIGH	
Reinforce Neutral Target	Reinforce Hedged Target	Dealign Hedged Target	Dealign Fixed Target	Realign Hedged Target	Realign Fixed Target
Germany-U.S. WWI	Entente-Ottoman WWI		Germany-Japan WWI	Entente-Italy WWI	
Britain & France-Italy WWII (a)	Germany-USSR WWII		Britain & France-Italy WWII (b)	Germany-Turkey WWII	
	Britain & U.S.-Spain WWII				

Table 7 Attempted alignment change across cases (compressed)

LOW	HIGH
Entente-Ottoman WWI	Germany-Japan WWI
Germany-U.S. WWI	Entente-Italy WWI
Britain & France-Italy WWII (a)	Britain & France-Italy WWII (b)
Germany-USSR WWII	Germany-Turkey WWII
Britain & U.S.-Spain WWII	

to High range. The other five attempts are on the left, in the Low range. Between the two clusters is a gap—the lower Medium cell. This makes it possible to simplify the variable space, "compressing" it into a High-Low dichotomy. This yields five Low difficulty/cost attempts and four High difficulty/cost attempts, as shown in Table 7.

As for the divider's alliance constraints, the distribution is tilted toward greater difficulty—there are three Low constraint and six High constraint cases (see Table 8). In the six High constraint cases—where allies considered or adopted a concerted approach to the target—I designate the ally that led the combined effort as the "initiator." I identify the initiator inductively, through process tracing focused on who moves first to accommodate the target and leads any concerted effort that develops. Across the six High constraint cases, the level of strategic consensus among the initiator and allies varies in roughly equal proportion. There are two Low ("no") consensus cases, two High ("yes") consensus cases, and two that are "mixed," with those values alternating within the cases.[42]

Table 8 Alliance constraints and strategic consensus across cases

LOW	HIGH
Germany-Japan WWI	Entente-Ottoman Empire WWI (Initiator: Russia) (consensus-no)
Germany-U.S. WWI	Entente-Italy WWI (Initiator: Britain) (consensus-yes)
Germany-USSR WWII	Britain/France-Italy WWII, a & b (Initiator: Britain) (consensus-mixed)
	Britain/U.S.-Spain WWII (Initiator: Britain) (consensus-yes)
	Germany-Turkey WWII (Initiator: Germany) (consensus-no)

CASE SELECTION AND GENERAL CONTROLS

The portfolio of cases covered in this study provides some control over several big factors in international politics that shape alignment patterns, and thus helps concentrate analysis on the traction of the theory. It also provides a platform for conclusions relevant to the kinds of great power alliance competitions likely to play out in the years ahead.

First, because all of the cases occurred in or on the eve of the world wars, and all of the main players were strategically implicated in those wars, it may be assumed that a high level of security competition and geopolitical pressure runs across them. Students of international relations distinguish between periods in which power politics are more "permissive" or "restrictive"; when "systemic imperatives" of security competition are less or more constraining.[43] Because all of the cases occurred in close proximity to the most compelling circumstances imaginable—major systemic wars—it is unlikely that the alignment shifts that happened in some of the cases were due to the "slack" of a low-level threat environment and political concerns unrelated to external incentives and constraints.

Second, the cases' world-war context makes it possible to control for two kinds of multipolarity in the system that tend to pull on alignment dynamics. The first is a multipolar distribution of power—which realists expect to generate alliance uncertainty, rigidities in intra-alliance management, and tight competition for the allegiance of wavering or unattached powers.[44] Because all of the cases occur under such multipolarity—and involve states that constitute poles in the system—one can assume that they are all exposed to the same pressures toward alliance compression generated by multipolar power structure. Hence, that structure won't explain the "process-level" variation in alignment outcomes that interest us. The second kind of multipolarity is ideological—among the competing powers, there were at least three ideological groups represented in and across the alliances.[45] In World War I, these included European liberal democracies, authoritarian monarchies, and an Islamic caliphal empire (the Ottoman Empire).[46] In World War II, the groupings were liberal democracies, communist dictatorships, and fascist dictatorships. Following Haas, in such circumstances, it is expected that alliance formation will be sluggish, cohesion will be weak, and buck-passing will be prevalent. These tendencies are especially pronounced when systems are multipolar in *both* power and ideological terms because the systemic conditions encourage mismatched rankings of power and ideological threats among major states.[47] In sum, the cases all occur in roughly the same systemic context, in which two different kinds of multipolarity, with *contradictory* tendencies for alliance behavior, offset each other. With these high-level factors thus controlled, the assessment of the theory's explanations for outcomes becomes more tractable, as does the appraisal of alternative accounts specific to each case.

QUALITATIVE METHODS

Three kinds of qualitative analysis are applied in the cases. The first is basic descriptive inference. In each case, I use historical sources to establish that it is an instance of selective accommodation and to describe the presence and strength of the initiation and contingent conditions.[48] The second kind are "within-case" techniques—congruence procedures and process tracing.[49] In each case, then, I use congruence procedures to assess the relationships between the initial conditions of the attempt (or changes in them), and the contingent conditions (or changes in them), and the outcomes. Here, within the confines of the case, my concern is with patterns of consistency between the values of the assigned conditions and the expectations of the theoretical framework. Process tracing goes deeper, examining the key decisions, moves, and interactions in the chain of events in a case, to determine whether these reflect the causal mechanisms anticipated by the theory. This latter stage of assessment includes trying to weigh the impact of conditions that conjointly point to the same outcome, and to discern processes that dominate when specified conditions point in contrary directions, and interact, within the same case.

The third method is paired comparison, which I employ in chapter 10. With this technique, I use the logic of "most similar" case comparison to highlight the alternative operations of key mechanisms.[50] This means isolating pairs of cases that are controlled by similarities in initiation and contingent conditions, but differ in respect to one "framed" condition and the outcome. This procedure throws into relief the alternate causal processes expected to flow from the different values of the framed conditions. It is important to emphasize that with these kinds of paired comparisons the intent is *not* to establish that the different outcomes deterministically follow from the expressed values of the framed conditions. That is not possible because the conditional propositions are probabilistic, and the cases are retrospectively matched. Rather, the purpose is to show the working out of the causal mechanisms expected to unfold when the framed conditions and the probable outcomes do hold.

The case studies unfold along the lines of a structured, focused comparison.[51] The narratives trace the inception, implementation, and outcomes of selective accommodation diplomacy, keying in on five big questions:

1. How did perceptions of the target's strategic weight motivate the divider (or initiator)?
2. How did the divider perceive its reward power relative to the target?
3. How much change in the target's alignment did the divider try to achieve?
4. Was the divider constrained by allies with direct stakes in the relationship with the target?
5. If so, to what extent did its allies agree on the approach and share its perceptions of the target's strategic weight? Did they support (or fail to support) the initiator's bid?

Many of the cases also address other explanations for the alignment outcomes observed, not covered by theory. There are two kinds of these. Complementary explanations work in tandem with the theory's account and provide a fuller picture of the development of the outcome. As noted earlier, because the theory is a partial equilibrium framework, it anticipates the importance of such additional explanations. By contrast, alternative explanations conflict with the thrust of the theory's account. Here, the logic and evidence supporting the competing alternatives are considered, as well as the extent to which they undermine confidence in the theory and findings. The point of both kinds of assessments is not to settle disagreements between general competing theories, but rather to gauge the force of key alternatives specific to each case. The appraisals feed into conclusions about the leverage the divider's policy (and constraints on it) exerted on events, and a richer understanding of conditions outside the scope of the theoretical framework that contributed to success or failure.

Germany Fails to Detach Japan, 1915–16

Even if we are at war with Japan, it does not prevent me from saying
that . . . Kiaochow would have permitted both of our peoples to reach
a just and appropriate understanding.

Theobald von Bethmann, chancellor of Germany,
March 1917

As soon as it becomes obvious that no separate peace can be concluded, the whole swindle is of no importance.

Wilhelm II, emperor of Germany,
May 1915

On 23 August 1914, nineteen days after its British ally, Japan declared war
on Germany.[1] By November it had conquered Tsingtao (the fortified base
for Germany's East Asia Squadron) and the surrounding Kiaochow Bay
concession on the Shantung Peninsula that Berlin had leased from China in
1898. Japanese forces also occupied German bases in the Pacific Ocean
north of the equator, on the the Marshall, Mariana, and Caroline Islands.
After that, direct fighting between Japan and Germany was finished.[2] Over
the next two years (1915–16) Germany tried twice to induce Japan to break
from the Entente and make a separate peace. Its primary levers in these efforts were offers to cede German territory in the Far East and Pacific that
Japan had captured, to support Japan's ambitions for an enlarged sphere of
control in the region (at the expense of Russia and Britain), and to construct
rewarding postwar commercial and strategic relationships.

Although Berlin's initiatives were encouraged by the Japanese government, they were never successful. The theoretical framework identifies two
major reasons. In brief: Germany's alignment change goals were high, while
its inducements were relatively weak, especially in the context of a bidding
war over Japan's allegiance. Berlin's efforts enabled Tokyo to repeatedly convert German overtures into better bargains with its allies. Thus, Japan obtained from its existing alignment values that largely matched what Germany
offered in exchange for a costly defection.[3]

Initiation Conditions

PERCEPTIONS OF TARGET'S STRATEGIC WEIGHT

German officials believed that neutralizing Japan through a separate peace would help them shape the larger war's contours to favor German victory and war aims. The goal of separate peace with Japan, wrote Foreign Ministry State Secretary Gottlieb von Jagow, was to "receive benefits [from Japan] which are of use to us *during the war* in exchange for concessions from our side."[4] In calculating such benefits, they ascribed war-tipping strategic weight to Japan's alignment. In the first months of the war, Berlin worried that Japan might send troops to the western front, which might help prevent a French collapse, and that inspired them to first consider how to avert this through a mutual understanding. But it soon became clear that Japan was unwilling to engage forces in Europe and fears that it might do so ceased to drive German perceptions of Japan's strategic weight.[5] German motivations to detach Japan then shifted to broader conceptions of wartime advantages. The German Admiralty, for example, hoped that turning Japan into a neutral state—and thus breaking the Anglo-Japanese alliance—would impel Britain to allocate naval forces to the Pacific and Indian Oceans, thus weakening its blockade capabilities in the Atlantic.[6]

Most of all, German leaders saw neutralizing Japan as a way to politically demoralize their enemies by dividing the Entente and thereby achieving an early separate peace with Russia. As the German chancellor, Theobald von Bethmann, reasoned in June 1915, Berlin had to do "everything to split the Entente" because "only through breaking the coalition can peace be obtained."[7] In 1917, Foreign Ministry official Richard von Kühlmann reprised the policy logic to the kaiser: "The splitting of the Entente . . . is the most important diplomatic war aim. Russia seemed the weakest link in the enemy chain; the task was therefore to loosen and detach her if possible."[8] And that is where Japan came in. As the Japanese ambassador in Stockholm, who was the channel for secret negotiations, suggested to German officials, Japan "possessed the key to a separate Russo-German peace."[9] Thus, "Berlin turned toward Tokyo as the bridge to a separate peace with Russia and, ultimately, triumph in the war."[10] Admiral von Capelle, secretary of the navy, described the unvarnished calculus: if concessions to Japan could secure its neutrality, and through it an "advantageous separate peace with Russia," then "the disadvantages of these cessions pale in comparison with such significant prospect for ending the war in a victorious manner."[11] Likewise, the chief of staff of the German Admiralty (Henning von Holtzendorff) presented a bold vision of the potential strategic weight of a separate peace with Japan: by delivering a "breakthrough in the enemies' intention to only conclude peace in common," it could foster an eventual alliance that "would prove decisive for the war's termination."[12] German leaders thus "ascribed to Japan a pivotal role in the psychological shattering of the Triple Entente."[13] They envisioned a war-tipping chain reaction that ran from neutralizing Japan to securing a separate peace with Russia, which would "paralyze France and force France to an understanding with Berlin," which would isolate Britain and allow Germany to compel a war-ending settlement.[14]

In concrete, material terms, Japan's alignment was seen to have an important effect on the eastern front, because it stiffened Russia's ability and determination to resist. Japan was a strategically critical supplier of material to the Russian war machine, one that helped Russia recover from early battlefield defeats and stay in the fight.[15] As the kaiser complained in February 1917, "Russia received gigantic quantities of weapons and munitions from Japan."[16] In addition to providing direct support to Russia, Japan was positioned as a key pass-through for support from other Entente powers, and from the U.S. Neutralizing Japan could, they hoped, cut this pipeline of support and thereby weaken Russia's resistance: as the Foreign Ministry's East Asian specialist, Arthur Kemnitz, put it, "By withholding supplies," Japan could "influence a separate peace in St. Petersburg."[17]

German officials also believed that Japanese adhesion to the Entente created a political barrier to Russia's willingness to accept a separate peace, because Tokyo's loyalty applied pressure on Russia to remain loyal to the Entente as well.[18] So, inducing Japan into a benevolent neutrality was not just a way to cut down Russia's material powers of resistance. It was the necessary first step in a "double diplomatic gambit" aimed at splitting not just Japan but Russia from the Entente.[19] For these reasons, German leaders perceived Japan to have high strategic weight and war-tipping potential.

PERCEPTIONS OF RELATIVE REWARD POWER

Germany did not have significant reward power relative to Japan, and officials in Berlin recognized their limited leverage. Their sense of Japan's war-tipping potential helps to explain why they persisted in attempts to neutralize Japan, despite these constraints. Still, German leaders did think they possessed some concessions that might induce Japan's shift, if developments in the war, and politics in Tokyo, were conducive.[20] Above all, they calculated that the promise to concede Japanese conquests over German holdings in Kiaochow and in the Pacific was something Japan would value. As Jagow put it to his deputy, Arthur Zimmermann, in January 1915, "The possibility of reaching an understanding with Japan is . . . not to be dismissed if we accept the loss of Kiaochow."[21] They also hoped that signaling a willingness to support Japan's larger ambitions in China, beyond what its allies would countenance, and the prospect of burgeoning postwar German-Japanese economic collaboration, would pull on Tokyo's loyalties.[22]

In the near term, however, Germany had little control over those values at stake. It lacked the hard power to recover territories it lost to Japan. As

Japan's negotiator in Stockholm put it to the German ambassador there (Hellmuth Lucius von Stoedten), "After the war no one in the world would be able to deprive Japan of the occupied territories."[23] And Germany hardly had more ability to sway wartime developments elsewhere in China and the Far East. More practically, in the near term, Berlin tried to curry Tokyo's favor by offering not to interdict Swedish iron ore exports to Japan (provided Japan did not reexport it to its allies).[24] And it sought a path to rapprochement through generous coverage of Japan's POW costs.[25] But such immediately convertible concessions were small change. Germany's selective accommodation efforts thus relied on long-range and ambiguous, low-credibility promises. Berlin extended them because it had high estimates of Japan's strategic weight and lacked other means for exerting influence on Japan.

Contingent Conditions

ATTEMPTED ALIGNMENT CHANGE

Germany tried to dealign Japan—a high degree of alignment change. The primary goal was to detach Japan from the well-established Anglo-Japanese Alliance of 1911 and its broader "no-separate-peace" commitment to the Entente forged in October 1915.[26] Given Japan's fixed alliance position, this was an ambitious undertaking. German leaders appreciated the difficulty of the task. In May 1915—*before* Japan had joined the Entente's "no-separate-peace" pact—Jagow and Zimmermann admitted that Japan could "decline negotiations on a separate peace at any time on formal grounds," just "on the basis of . . . the Anglo-Japanese Alliance."[27] In June 1915, Jagow's instructions to Paul von Hintze (the German ambassador in China, who was negotiating with his Japanese counterpart) admitted that "an official separate peace is difficult to attain."[28] In November 1916, as Zimmermann (who had replaced Jagow as secretary of state) prepared an offer meant to "loosen Japan from the Entente," he too noted, "Whether that will occur is doubtful."[29]

Nevertheless, some things about Japan's relationship with Germany fed hopes in Berlin. In Japan, there was no "great animus against Germany." Japan's alliance with Britain did not create any formal obligation to intervene, and "it could not be said [to have] predisposed Japan to make war against Germany."[30] Indeed, when the British foreign secretary, Edward Grey, realized in early August 1914 that Japan was entering the war with expansion in mind, his first reaction was to withdraw an initial request for Japanese naval assistance, and to advise Japan to stay out.[31] (Under pressure from First Lord of the Admiralty Winston Churchill and others, Grey soon backtracked from this politically unwise reversal.) In any case, Japan was not pushed into the war by its allies, or by domestic political pressures.[32] Moreover, the fact that Japanese and British interests in China conflicted, and the sense that Britain worked to curtail Japan's ambitions there (which seemed validated by the crisis surrounding Japan's "twenty-one demands" on China in early 1915), suggested a cleavage that Germany could exploit through selective accommodation. Thus, Bethmann counseled an approach timed for "whenever Japan should acquire serious differences with England."[33]

There was also reason for German leaders to surmise that the Japanese government could be responsive to a diplomatic, businesslike approach to changing its alignment.[34] Japan's decision to attack Germany was a cabinet-level initiative—it came, in particular, from Foreign Minister Katō Takaaki, "who promoted Japan's immediate entry."[35] The cabinet's calculus for war was based on pure expediency, not moral fervor or national antagonism: it focused on Japan's concrete opportunities to "profit from the power vacuum in East Asia" by consolidating and advancing its positions in China.[36] Moreover, Japan sent signals indicating an intent to moderate damage to its relations with Germany. Berlin noticed that after Tokyo declared war, it continued to pay interest on prewar loans taken on the German money market. And it conveyed regret that the Anglo-Japanese Alliance compelled it to act against Germany in Tsingtao.[37] Obviously, this was disingenuous: Japan decided to strike against Tsingtao and occupy the Pacific islands for its own reasons. But it was still a signal that Tokyo wanted to limit enmity with Germany.[38]

Berlin's near-term alignment goal was consistent—to neutralize Japan through a separate peace.[39] At different times, the views of civilian and military officials shifted over whether that could be linked to a formal wartime or postwar German-Japan pact. The policy embraced by Wilhelm, Bethmann, and the Foreign Ministry, nevertheless, viewed an alliance as a secondary, long-range option, one that could be fostered after the war had been won. Such aspirational concepts did not alter their practical policy focus on a separate peace.[40] "The immediate aim of the separate peace was to prise Japan and, through Japanese mediation, Russia away from the enemy coalition."[41] As Engram notes, "A separate peace promised the first small fracture in the links of the enemy coalition yet avoided the necessity of a political commitment to Japan." For Bethmann and his subordinates, the priority was to gain Japan's wartime diplomatic cooperation without taking on commitments for postwar alliances.[42] To make it a cat's-paw for separate peace with Russia, neutralizing Japan would suffice. But given Japan's fixed commitments to the Entente, doing that would still entail a high degree of alignment change.

ALLIANCE CONSTRAINTS

In its attempts to selectively accommodate Japan, Germany had low alliance constraints. Neither Austria-Hungary nor the Ottoman Empire had any colonial positions in East Asia and the Pacific. The brunt of concession making would naturally fall on Berlin, which did have interests and claims at stake in the conflict with Japan. Germany also was the dominant ally in the

Triplice and thus set the agenda in shaping the Central powers' diplomatic approach to peripheral powers like the U.S. and Japan. For the most part, Vienna and Constantinople were passive, partial observers of German attempts to induce separate peace with Japan. Nevertheless, as we would expect given the asymmetries in their alliance with Germany, their moments of involvement leaned in support of Berlin's initiative. Thus, in 1915, when Berlin was trying to keep its contacts with Japan disguised and deniable, it worked through the Austrian and Ottoman ambassadors in Stockholm for its primary communications with the Japanese ambassador.[43] After Germany's bids fizzled out, and Berlin relaxed its efforts in 1917, the Austro-Hungarian Foreign Ministry weighed in to encourage Berlin to restart negotiations with Japan, calculating that it would be useful and advantageous if, as seemed likely, war with the U.S. followed.[44] There is no evidence that Germany's main allies ever put cross-pressure against its initiatives with Japan.

Diplomacy of Selective Accommodation

GERMANY'S 1915 ATTEMPT

Berlin's first serious attempt to accommodate Tokyo was elicited by a public statement by the Japanese envoy in Stockholm (Sadatsuchi Uchida) that "Japan considered the war against Germany ended," and "wished to reach an understanding."[45] This prompted the Wilhelmstrasse to conceive an approach that sought to accommodate Japan's ambitions, while preserving Germany's economic interests in China. Thus, as Bethmann noted to Zimmermann in May, "We should arrange peace with Japan as soon as possible and secure the required influence in China in exchange for the renunciation of Kiaochow."[46] At the same time, however, it became evident in Berlin that the war in the west had settled into a military stalemate; so, the initially narrow formula for approaching Japan was grafted onto a grander concept for achieving wider war aims through diplomacy. A separate peace with Japan came to be seen as a tool for weakening Russia, and for bringing it to a separate peace through Tokyo's influence.

The development of this strategic concept coincided with a broader thrust in Germany's war diplomacy in 1915, seeking to capitalize on the massive losses inflicted on Russian forces in the Gorlice-Tarnów offensive, which had resulted in Russia's "great retreat" on the eastern front.[47] Berlin conjoined these battlefield results with an "extensive diplomatic campaign for a separate peace with the Russians," efforts that "reached their zenith in late June and July."[48] That was the context in June 1915, when Erich von Falkenhayn, chief of the German General Staff, urged Bethmann to seek "a secret understanding with Japan" to cut off its supplies to Russia, for "in general, supplies coming from that source make possible the Russian armed force's contin-ued resistance to our victorious army."[49]

Bethmann embraced this view, but oversaw a slower and more oblique approach to Japan that summer. An approach that was too forthcoming, he feared, would signal weakness. He also recognized the risk posed by Katō's pro-British bias: "As long as the Ōkuma cabinet governs with Baron Katō as foreign minister," he noted, "the danger exists that he would betray imme-diately any invitation to separate negotiations because of his outspoken, personal inclination toward England."[50] Thus, as Bethmann's concept of selective accommodation gelled in July, he instructed that the next steps toward an understanding with Japan should await "a change of ministry in Tokyo."[51] In August, that change came when Ishii Kikujirō replaced Katō.

Thus, in autumn 1915, the German approach gained momentum. The Ger-man Admiralty—which had until then been averse to the idea of giving up claim to the bases in Kiaochow and the Pacific islands—moved in favor of a trade with Japan. Tirpitz wrote to Bethmann in August 1915 that he would "sacrifice" Kiaochow for security cooperation with Japan.[52] Tensions be-tween Japan and Britain and the U.S. had been exposed earlier in the crisis surrounding Tokyo's "twenty-one" demands on China, suggesting that Ja-pan might look favorably on other alignment options. And Katō's departure from the Ōkuma cabinet seemed to Bethmann to portend an opening for rap-prochement. This latter premise was undermined in September when Ishii, on taking over as foreign minister, led Japan into the Entente's no-separate-peace agreement.[53] Grey had been pressing for this since July 1915, and its "decision [to embrace the no-separate-peace pact] reaffirmed Japan's com-mitment to the Anglo-Japanese Alliance."[54]

That development did not stall Berlin's initiative. In November, it formu-lated a set of terms for a bargain that were communicated to Tokyo through Uchida in Stockholm. In exchange for Japan's immediate cutting back of aid to Russia and the other Entente powers, Germany offered several postwar concessions. It would recognize Japan's claim to an exclusive sphere of in-fluence in Fukien Province, provided Japan allowed Germany's prewar eco-nomic interest there to resume. Such recognition would cover some of the more ambitious of the "twenty-one demands" that Japan leveled at China in April 1915. These demands had stirred tensions with Britain and provoked objections from the U.S., which was interested in establishing a naval base in Fukien.[55] Germany would also thus promise benevolent neutrality to Japan, should it get into a conflict with Britain or the U.S. over China. And most importantly, it would cede the Kiaochow Bay concession and Tsing-tao naval base to Japan. Germany would even cover the cost of refortifying Tsingtao after the war.[56]

But to close the deal, Berlin required an immediate "interim protocol" that would include a secret treaty covering Germany's commitment to refortify Tsingtao for Japan. This, then, was to be the backdoor maneuver to split the

Entente—by compromising Japan's formal embrace of the Entente's no-separate-peace commitment. If it were to take up the interim-protocol arrangement, Japan would in fact make a peace agreement with Germany. Soon after these terms were floated, Uchida rejected Germany's invitation to negotiate such a deal, on the predictable grounds that to do so would violate Japan's recent commitment to the Entente powers' no-separate-peace pact.[57]

The inducements Germany offered were underwhelming. The most tangible one was to cede—after the war—formal claim to territory in China that Japan had already pocketed through force. "Doubtless Japan took a calculating look at the German offer and found it wanting," remarks Nish; "Germany was offering something which was not within her power to give or withhold, for she would not be in a position to deprive Japan of her acquisitions after the war whether she was victorious or not."[58]

On the other hand, Japan had already made progress in securing assurances from allies to protect its wartime gains. In August 1914, the British government, speaking on behalf of itself and the other Entente allies, assured Japan that they would not object if it demanded permanent control over Kiaochow Bay in return for its war sacrifices. "It would be most unfair," wrote Grey, "for any of the Allied Powers to put claims in China which would in any way prejudice the terms of peace to be made by Japan."[59] In March 1915, Grey communicated to Kato that he recognized that Japan's interests and influence in China, and expansion in Manchuria, would "naturally" increase.[60] And once German-Japanese negotiations began in April 1915, Katō informed London of Germany's soundings. Over the following months—as Germany's secret feelers toward Japan developed—Tokyo extracted new assurances from the Entente powers that would reinforce its claims to formerly German possessions in China.[61] Thus, the additional assurance that Japan might get for its gains from Germany were also securable without the costs of severing its existing alliance ties. Indeed, Japan could hope to extract them from its current allies, by using the German probe as leverage. In January 1916, when the Japanese ambassador to Britain disclosed to Grey Germany's pitch in a secret meeting between its ambassador to China and a Japanese diplomat there, Grey responded: "When Germany is defeated and the terms of peace are dictated, the British government have no intention of acquiring any of the German concessions in China and will interpose no objection to Japan's negotiating with China the disposition of German concessions."[62] The intent of these assurances was to thwart potential understanding between Japan and Germany, as Grey explained to the British ambassador to China the next month: "If we had not made it clear that we should not bar Japan's expansion of interests in the Far East it would clearly have been to Japan's advantage to throw in her lot with Germany."[63]

As for the longer-range and more nebulous inducements, German endorsement of Japanese expansion in Fukien or Manchuria would hardly help if they were not backed by real assistance, and a Germany able to project power in the Far East was a distant if not dubious prospect. The lure of *future* German-Japanese trade relations, meanwhile, paled in comparison to the present value of its role as conduit for trade and aid flowing from Britain, France (and the U.S.), and Russia. As Jagow and Zimmermann confessed in a May 1915 memorandum: "We are not in the position to offer anything concrete to the Japanese with the exception of Tsingtao."[64] The lack of Japanese responsiveness to the German bid in November also testified to this basic truth.

Germany's selective accommodation approach in 1915 was not just unsuccessful, it was likely counterproductive. Aware of German soundings of Japan—both through intelligence intercepts and Tokyo's disclosures—the Entente allies were spurred to shore up ties with Japan.[65] Thus, in July 1915, London began to encourage Japan's adhesion to the Entente's no-separate-peace pact, because it feared a Japanese reversal. And when Japan did this in October, "the major benefit for the Entente," writes Nish, "was to minimize the danger of Japan making a separate peace with Germany."[66] St. Petersburg, at the same time, began stepping up efforts to secure a deeper Russo-Japanese alliance, for which adhesion to the Entente pact was seen as merely a first step.

GERMANY'S 1916 ATTEMPT

Despite the collapse of its 1915 initiative, Berlin renewed its attempts to neutralize Japan in March 1916. Feelers were resumed among the German and Japanese envoys in Stockholm.[67] As before, the overarching German concept was to detach Japan and use its influence to produce a separate peace with Russia.[68] While recognizing Japan's public position blocking separate peace negotiations, they hoped that the prospect of specific concessions in Asia would induce it to abandon the Entente. In late April 1916, Japan articulated its demands explicitly: an immediate German pledge to cede Tsingtao, and transfer to Tokyo of Germany's rights in the 1895 Sino-German agreement on Shantung. If Germany did this publicly, Japan could then "take up the question of peace" and use its influence to push Russia toward peace.[69] Jagow, in response, formulated Berlin's position thusly: "If Japan succeeds in prodding Russia toward peace, we would be prepared to promise abdication of our rights."[70]

Secret German-Japanese negotiations ensued between 28 April and 17 May. The apparent sticking point was sequencing. Japan wanted Germany to cede its rights first. As Uchida put it, either way, "Japan would retain Shantung after the war," but "an immediate waiver of [German] rights would win Germany a good friend." Then Japan would endeavor to "dispose Russia toward peace negotiations."[71] Germany wanted Japan to show results with Russia before it would commit to territorial cessions. Wilhelm was now ready to grant all Japan's claims in China and the Pacific Islands, if Japan would immediately "go into action with Russia."[72] As Bethmann put it: "If Japan promptly induces Russia to seek peace negotiations it shall retain all German territories under its control. However, Japan must see to it that the negotiations are not a hoax, but rather lead to an agreement."[73] To Stoedten in Stockholm, Jagow put it bluntly: "To issue a pledge immediately without any quid pro quo and with only the vague hope that Japan will work for peace in Russia can not be expected of us."[74] His instructions were thus that "actual cession of the territories could be discussed *only after* positive results" and the positive results sought were (1) the procurement of peace with Russia "without delay" and (2) the termination of Japan's military support for the Entente belligerents.[75]

When Germany followed up with a formal and lengthy specification of its quid pro quos, the initiative capsized.[76] As the Germans were hammering out their terms for a deal, Japan had again revealed the feelers first to the British, and then to the French and Russians. The Entente allies, in turn, jointly requested that Japan tell Germany to direct all peace bids to the Entente powers collectively.[77] The Japanese negotiator thus declared on 17 May that Japan "could not enter into peace negotiations without simultaneously informing the Entente powers of Germany's willingness to negotiate," which was tantamount to saying that Japan would only cooperate to facilitate a general peace negotiation. German leaders were outraged.[78] The kaiser fumed: "As soon as it becomes obvious that no separate peace can be concluded, the whole swindle is of no importance."[79] On 27 May, after the embarrassing turn of events, Berlin put the negotiations with Japan on ice.

Once again, Japan had "led Germany up the garden path."[80] As Jagow noted on 15 June, "The Jap[anese] [used] the negotiations with us in order to pressure Russia."[81] Two months later, the fruits of Japan's double game were displayed in a new treaty with Russia, containing further concessions to Japan. In August 1915, St. Petersburg had first hinted at its willingness to improve Japan's position in Manchuria, in return for greater arms supplies from Japan.[82] In December 1915 and January 1916, Russia sent the grand duke on a mission to Japan with the purpose of cultivating support for an expansion of Japanese arms supplies to Russia. Animating this Russian initiative was not just the need for weapons—although this was large—but also the desire to ward off a possible German-Japanese understanding.[83] In this context, Russia offered to cede ownership of a segment of the Chinese Eastern Railway located in Japan's sphere of interest in Manchuria. (Russia's foreign minister, Sergei Sazanov explicitly justified this costly concession as a means "to prevent Japanese-German rapprochement.")[84] The Russians' approach was strongly encouraged by the genro, and they then pressured Ōkuma and Ishii to reciprocate.[85] Formal negotiations toward a new Russo-Japanese alliance commenced in February.[86] From Tokyo's perspective, the "most immediate aim [was] an expansion of Japan's sphere of influence in Northeast

Asia."[87] In its negotiations with St. Petersburg—which coincided with Germany's talks with Japan in spring 1916—Tokyo proposed a Russo-Japanese offensive-defensive alliance with a pointedly anti-German character, which had the prime objective of eliminating all German economic interests in China.[88] Russia was forthcoming in the negotiations with Japan then, at least in part, because it knew that Japan was concurrently exploring a bargain with Germany. The key Russian side payments that won Japan's agreement were in Manchuria: navigation rights for Japanese shipping on the Sungari River that divided the Japanese and Russian spheres of influence (as defined in the 1907 Russo-Japanese secret treaty), and the segment of the Chinese Eastern Railway that ran south of the Sungari.[89]

On 7 July 1916, the new Russo-Japanese pact was announced.[90] The first article of the public convention expressed each party's commitment not to join any arrangement or political combination directed against the other. The second was a commitment to mutual aid against any outside threat to their territorial rights or special interests in the Far East.[91] Taken as a whole, the agreement erected yet another barrier against German efforts to flip Japan into a separate peace. Thus, to the Japanese ambassador, King George V praised it as a blow to Germany, which "had gone out of her way to adopt towards Japan a different attitude from that taken towards other members of the Entente."[92]

Summary and Alternative

Germany's attempt to detach Japan offers a stark example of basic conditions and dynamics of selective accommodation failure. Germany had a weak hand to play, and its leaders recognized their limited leverage. They played the hand nonetheless, because they perceived Japan to have war-tipping potential that warranted the effort. As it turned out, Germany simply could not offer Japan inducements in the immediate context that could beat Tokyo's opportunities for gain *inside* its alliance. The weakness was magnified by Berlin's alignment goal, which tried to induce Japan to defect in a dramatic (and therefore costly) way—ditching newly minted formal alliance ties for neutrality.

There was also another important dynamic at work that offers a complementary explanation. That is the determination of Japan's allies to "bind" it to the Entente through concessions that offset the rewards Germany could mobilize.[93] What stood out in particular was this prospect: that Britain and Russia would pay well for Japan's allegiance in the coin of acquiescence to its advances in China. A focus on these kinds of gains, as much as those that could be picked from Germany's holdings in Asia, led Japan to fight with and stay committed to the Entente during the war. Any German policy to detach Japan from its allies, therefore, would need to cater to its larger ambitions in China—and on that score, Berlin was in a weaker position than London and St. Petersburg. By baiting and using German attempts at selective accommodation, Japan had managed to obtain nearly all that Germany had tried to offer, without paying the price of a destructive break from its alliance commitments.

Germany Keeps the United States Neutral, 1914–16

> The open partisanship of the United States against us at this time must be prevented at all costs, if it is possible to prevent it. If the limitation of the submarine war is necessary to avoid such a break, then it has to be done. If a stopping of the submarine war is necessary, then this also cannot be avoided.
>
> Erich von Falkenhayn, chief of German General Staff,
> September 1915

> Once and for all, an *end* to negotiations with America. If Wilson wants war, let him make it, and let him then have it.
>
> Wilhelm II, emperor of Germany,
> March 1917

From the onset of war in August 1914 until the end of 1916, Germany successfully kept the U.S. from entering the ranks of its enemies. The risks of such a shift were made acute in crises sparked by German U-boat attacks on two large passenger ships: the *Lusitania* in May 1915, and the *Sussex* in March 1916. Both times, a break in U.S.-German diplomatic relations—which would have likely led to war—was averted by German concessions. In these years, German leaders believed the U.S. had war-tipping strategic weight. They expected its intervention would bring on certain defeat. They recognized that while it would be suicidal to try to neutralize the U.S. through threats, they could offer concessions that, though costly, would keep the U.S. sidelined. Berlin's attempts to do that relied principally on compromises concerning U-boat warfare, and provisional support for Washington's attempts to promote peace negotiations.

The contingent conditions favored success. First, Germany sought a low degree of alignment change—to reinforce U.S. neutrality, an alignment policy that President Woodrow Wilson adopted when the war started and which he championed in his campaign for reelection in 1916. Second, Germany had low alliance constraints. Its power dominated that of its principal allies, Austria-Hungary and the Ottoman Empire, and they were highly dependent on it. Naturally, they enthusiastically backed Berlin's policy of accommodating the U.S.[1]

Germany's policy of keeping the U.S. neutral through concessions worked—until its leaders decided to flagrantly violate them. Why did they do that? They came to believe they had a military strategy that could negate the U.S.'s war-tipping strategic weight. Thus, while this case displays the dynamics of successful selective accommodation under highly favorable contingent conditions, it also spotlights the critical role that beliefs about the target's strategic weight play in driving such efforts. As long as they perceived the U.S. to be a dangerous war-tipper, Germany's leaders maintained the strategy of accommodation and used concessions successfully. Once they were convinced, in January 1917, that they could nullify U.S. strategic weight through unlimited U-boat warfare, they dropped the policy of concessions and in February launched the U-boat campaign that they knew would sink U.S. ships and make the U.S. an enemy. The U.S. entered the war two months later. In short, German leaders made "a cold military calculation that the advantages of destroying all commerce flowing to Great Britain outweighed the disadvantages of a war with the United States."[2]

Initiation Conditions

PERCEPTIONS OF TARGET'S STRATEGIC WEIGHT

Berlin's approach to the U.S. reflected a larger strategy for dealing with the alliance contours of the war. While trying to shore up its own coalition, Berlin "sought to avoid fortifying and ideally to weaken the enemy alliance."[3] This emerged in the July Crisis and became, as shown in the previous chapter, a defining aspect of German efforts to weld diplomacy to war strategy. With regard to the U.S., that wish to avoid fortifying the enemy alliance was conjoined with a healthy fear of the U.S.'s strategic weight. Germany's civilian leaders and foreign policy makers saw the U.S. as a decisive war-tipper. To risk U.S. intervention was, as German chancellor Theobald von Bethmann described it, to play "a game of dice whose ante is nothing less than Germany's existence."[4]

Up until late 1916, such beliefs about the war-tipping risk of U.S. intervention largely prevailed. Thus, in the *Lusitania* crisis of May 1915, Bethmann concluded that "concessions would have to be made, even if this meant a serious restriction of U-boat operations."[5] In arguing that summer for the need to conciliate the U.S., he declared: "We *must* make concessions; otherwise we will have war with America. . . . Apart from questions of right lies the power question."[6]

In 1915, Kaiser Wilhelm and the chief of the Supreme High Command of the Army, Erich von Falkenhayn, embraced Bethmann's calculus. After the *Lusitania* sinking, Falkenhayn remarked, "The question of power is decisive, and we could not bear to have America intervene on the side of our enemies"; "Everything must be done which will forestall a conflict with the United States." The kaiser put it to the navy secretary, Admiral Alfred von Tirpitz, this way: "America had to be prevented from participating the war against us as an active enemy. . . . The war must first be won, and that requires that we do not make new enemies."[7]

These judgments of the U.S.'s war-tipping potential focused not only on the material power it could bring to bear but also on the political impact its intervention would have on the resilience of the enemy coalition, and on other key neutrals' alignments. "The break with the United States would have a notable effect," Bethmann warned in March 1916; "It would increase the moral strength of the Entente. . . . Points of disagreement between the Allies would vanish in a moment."[8] "The attitude of the United States toward us," he wrote, "causes every other possible state to stiffen against us; it is . . . an unmistakable barometer for the attitude of the Balkan states." Those Balkan states, he observed in June 1915, were "willing to follow America's lead" into the war, and then "the route to Constantinople would be cut and Turkey almost certainly overpowered. Austria would have to withdraw troops from the Russian front, and the Austrian Emperor might even lose his nerve and sue for peace." Bethmann also expected the Dutch to enter the war against the Central powers if the U.S. turned against Germany. This would give the Allies "Holland's small but well-trained army [and] even more important, access by sea to the rear of German lines."[9] For these reasons, then, it was imperative to avoid a situation in which, "through the adoption of unrestricted U-boat warfare, we drive the United States, and with the United States still other neutral powers, into making war upon us."[10]

Falkenhayn was, in 1915, likewise sensitive to the wider alignment context. Determined to wrest a separate peace from Russia, he perceived that the chances of doing so would "be blasted" if the U.S. joined the Entente.[11] He also worried about the smaller neutral powers. In June 1915, he wrote to the chief of the naval staff, Gustav Bachmann, that the U.S. should "not be brought into the ranks of our enemies" through U-boat warfare. "Not the armed might of the United States but rather the moral weight which it as an enemy power would have on the neutrals against us, above all on Rumania, Bulgaria, and Holland, would be fatal for us."[12]

In the same apocalyptic terms, the German treasury and interior secretary, Karl Helfferich, warned in August and September 1915 that "Germany could not survive if the United States joined her enemies."[13] At an August 1916 Imperial Conference addressing the option of unlimited U-boat warfare, he argued: "The assumption that the hostile attitude of the United States cannot reach a higher pitch . . . is erroneous. . . . In the case of war, the United

States will stand ready with all of its reserves available for the cause of the Allies, which will then become the cause of the United States. America will desire to win the war as quickly as possible and will summon all its energies for putting this wish into execution. Acting in cooperation with England, the very strongest kind of pressure can be exerted upon the neutral powers to join the Entente."[14] Likewise, Bethmann stressed the material implications of U.S. intervention: "America would turn over all her resources for the purposes of the war. The measures of her financial assistance [to the Allies] would be increased. The armies of our enemies would be increased . . . our import[s] from neutral countries would stop."[15] Civilian foreign policy officials continued to believe that making the U.S. an enemy would lead to a dangerous chain reaction among other neutrals, even after they made the decision that would provoke it. Thus, in January 1917, Secretary of State Arthur Zimmermann warned that once neutral ships were sunk again, "a [U.S.] declaration of war will be bound to follow immediately [and] would in all probability result in the remaining neutral Powers joining together against us."[16]

In sum, the view that dominated German foreign policymaking until late 1916 was that the U.S. was a war-tipper of high order. Consequently, throughout the crises between Washington and Berlin over U-boat attacks on civilian shipping, German policy was strongly shaped by measures intended to keep the U.S. out of the ranks of Germany's enemies.

PERCEPTIONS OF RELATIVE REWARD POWER

Germany's methods were essentially conciliatory: Berlin tried to adjust its war policy in ways that avoided or minimized points of friction with the U.S. In August 1915, the German ambassador to Washington, Johann Heinrich Bernstorff, put it directly to Wilson's advisor, Edward House: "My Government was ready to make concessions in order to meet the President's wishes."[17] Germany's policy relied on two kinds of concessions to U.S. demands and priorities—both of which addressed concrete and immediate rewards to U.S. interests. The first and most important was accepting restrictions on the use of U-boats against shipping to the Allies. The second was supporting Wilson's efforts to promote a settlement of the war.

For German leaders, exercising restraint in the use of the submarine was a very significant concession. Doing so handicapped Germany's only real weapon to counter the blockade, which was the greatest threat to its war strategy in the long run. For example, in February 1915, when Bethmann proposed to guarantee that U.S.-flagged ships would not be torpedoed—so as to accommodate Wilson's threat to hold Germany "strictly accountable" for attacks on neutral shipping—the German Admiralty chief, Bachmann, objected that such "concessions" to the U.S. would render "submarine action . . . completely without effect." Hugo von Pohl, the commander of the High Seas Fleet, agreed: "With this order any possibility of successfully prosecuting the submarine war is excluded."[18] In September 1916, to James W. Gerard, the U.S. ambassador to Germany, Jagow underscored those "sacrifices" Germany had made only "out of regard for the United States": by renouncing unrestricted U-boat war, Germany had given up "a powerful weapon, with which we could strike very effective blows against our principal enemy, England. . . . Every day, transports filled with troops and munitions of war were crossing the Channel [and] we were not in a position to blow these ships up."[19]

Accommodating the U.S. by embracing restraints on U-boat warfare was also costly to Berlin because it entailed significant domestic political costs to the government. The German note to the U.S. on 16 April 1916, responding to the *Sussex* crisis, thus emphasized, "We have modified submarine war to maintain friendly relations with America, sacrificing important military advantages and in contradiction to excited public opinion here."[20] As Jagow explained to Bernstorff in June 1916, those "concessions in the submarine question" were "regarded as impracticable in many broad and influential circles in Germany."[21]

Nevertheless, German leaders recognized that restraining the use of U-boats was a powerful lever for influencing U.S. policy. As Bethmann put it in April 1916, "In all probability, we shall be able to avoid the break with the United States if we carry on the U-boat war" within the limits Berlin had promised Washington it would observe.[22] That was true both because it politically rewarded Wilson and other forces in U.S. politics that favored neutrality in an election year, and because it conferred substantial immediate economic benefits on the U.S. Because Germany's U-boat war strategy—if it were fully unleashed—would impose high costs on U.S. trade with its enemies, any restraint exercised as a concession to the U.S. amounted to an economic bonus for it—for such restraint allowed the U.S. to continue to profit handsomely from the war trade.[23] U.S. Treasury Secretary William McAdoo reported to Wilson in August 1915 that exports to Britain, France, Russia, and Italy "have enormously increased. . . . The high prices for food products have brought great prosperity to our farmers, while the purchases of war munitions have stimulated industry and have set factories going to full capacity throughout the great manufacturing districts. . . . Great prosperity is coming. It is, in large measure, here already."[24] As German officials painfully recognized, the war trade their concessions enabled not only boosted the military power of their enemies, it also greatly benefited the U.S. economy.[25]

The consequences of unrestricted submarine warfare—in terms of damage to U.S. commerce and popular outrage—would make it almost impossible for the U.S. *not* to intervene. German leaders clearly understood this contingency in U.S. policy.[26] The same logic advised German support for Wilson's various plans to foster negotiations to stop the war.[27] Thus, in December 1915, Bethmann explained that by conveying an openness to U.S.

mediation, Germany would "reduce the danger of America's . . . actively going over to our enemies."[28] And in 1916, Bernstorff wrote to Bethmann that "we shall gain ground here daily as long as it is made clear that we are ready to meet the American peace move half way."[29]

It was also recognized that U-boat concessions, and support for U.S. peace moves, would encourage the U.S. to focus on conflicts with Britain over freedom of the seas, thus aggravating tensions between Washington and London.[30] Thus, in July 1915, Bernstorff advised Bethmann that making concessions demanded in Washington's third *Lusitania* note would enable Wilson to launch a diplomatic initiative to force Britain to back away from illegal blockade actions.[31]

Bernstorff hammered on these themes in his reporting to Berlin on the interaction between U.S. domestic politics and Wilson's policy toward Germany. Thus, in June 1915, he explained to Jagow that "neither the President nor the American people want a war with Germany. . . . Mr. Wilson has the best chance to gain public approval for himself if he averts conflict with us honorably."[32] Likewise, in April 1916, he reminded Berlin that cooperating with Wilson on U-boat restraints would engender "strong support" for Wilson's antiwar platform in the 1916 election.[33] Two days after Wilson's November 1916 election victory, one German embassy official reported to Berlin that "our chances from the standpoint of German-American relations are not unfavorable . . . if we are able to avoid a conflict with the United States" over U-boat warfare.[34] On 12 November, Bernstorff underscored this point to Jagow: if Germany could "refrain from the so-called ruthless U-boat war," then Wilson "will desire to dwell in peace with us."[35]

Contingent Conditions

ATTEMPTED ALIGNMENT CHANGE

Germany's policy of accommodating the U.S. aimed for a low degree of alignment change. The U.S. was neutral and Germany tried to keep it that way. On 4 August, as the war started, Wilson declared that the U.S. would conform to the laws of neutrality.[36] Two weeks later, in a speech to the Senate, he urged the American people to try to be neutral in both thought and speech. His strategic vision was to make the U.S. the primary defender of neutral rights—the "guardian of neutrality," as State Department counselor Robert Lansing put it—and the peace broker to which the belligerents would turn when it came time to settle.[37]

U.S. neutrality in the war was expressed, in part, by the fact that it developed sharp conflicts with both sides, not just Germany. With Britain, its escalating policy of economic warfare and blockade of the Central Powers increasingly damaged U.S. commercial rights and strained American goodwill.[38]

With Germany, of course, the primary problem was submarine attacks that killed U.S. citizens and if escalated, would hamper U.S. commerce, but there was also a German campaign of espionage and sabotage in the U.S. that added poison to the relationship.[39] As events progressed into 1916, Wilson took an increasingly tough line against German U-boat warfare and was encouraged by his closest foreign policy advisors to see that the U.S. should intervene to prevent a German victory, if that became imminent. Wilson, however, continued to hold to the formula of neutrality and peacemaking as long as possible. If the Entente could not win on its own, then Wilson would use the U.S. stance to broker a negotiated settlement that averted an Entente defeat.

In 1915 to 1916, Wilson's balanced policy was rewarded by direct German concessions to its expressed demands. For instance, after Bethmann issued the 4 May 1916 *Sussex* note calling off surprise U-boat attacks on merchant ships "even inside the restricted war-zone," he wrote to Bernstorff that he hoped "our note and great concession" would "finally put an end to the state of distrust" and engender "relations of mutual confidence" between Germany and the U.S.[40] That this concession effectively kept the U.S. neutral was made clear in the diplomatic language of the U.S. reply on 8 May to the German *Sussex* note: the U.S., it stated, would assume that Germany's "present altered policy . . . will, from this time on, be carried out in a conscientious manner, which will avoid the chief danger of a break in the friendly relations which exist between the United States and Germany."[41] Bernstorff reiterated the warning back to Berlin: a "withdrawal or deviation from the concessions made by us" in the 4 May *Sussex* note would "lead to a break and the entrance of the United States into the war."[42]

ALLIANCE CONSTRAINTS

In seeking to accommodate the U.S., Germany had low alliance constraints. The asymmetry in Germany's alliance relationships gave it considerable pull over allied policy. Austria-Hungary was Germany's most powerful ally and it was, as Schroeder notes, "one-sidedly dependent" on Germany.[43] Moreover, neither Austria-Hungary nor Turkey had particular interests at stake in the concessions Germany would have to make to the U.S. to keep it neutral. It is not surprising then that Vienna and Constantinople both strongly favored Germany's policy of conciliating the U.S.[44] Thus, there was no complicated bargaining between Germany and its principal allies on this front.

Indeed, what pressure Germany felt from its allies pushed in the direction of greater conciliation. In February 1916, when Berlin was contemplating escalating against unarmed merchant ships, "the Austrian Foreign Minister . . . virtually begged the German government to take no steps that might lead to a break with the United States," and "the Turkish government, through its representative at German Supreme Headquarters, made it known that it looked with extreme disfavor on an eventual break with America."[45] In April 1916, during the *Sussex* crisis, the Austro-Hungarian foreign minister, Baron Stephan von Burian, encouraged Bethmann "to admit liability in the *Sussex* attack and do everything possible to maintain peace" with the U.S.[46] Later, in August, when German officials considered (and decided against) initiating unrestricted submarine warfare, Burian stipulated that he could support a resumption of the U-boat war "provided it would not bring about a break with the United States, which is to avoided at all costs."[47] And in late 1916, when the question returned to the fore, Vienna and Turkey again strongly encouraged Berlin not to reescalate. At the same time, when Berlin was trying to cultivate U.S. favor by offering a peace proposal ahead of Wilson's impending peace moves in late 1916, its allies were extremely supportive of the German initiative.[48]

After the January 1917 decision to launch unrestricted submarine warfare, Berlin shifted to convincing its Austro-Hungarian allies to support the escalation. This was a "hard sell" in Vienna, where its leaders were "'negative' about its possible political ramifications." But here the asymmetry in the alliance relationship also came into play. As Herwig explains, "given its dependence on German financial, material, and military aid," Vienna "bowed to the inevitable and endorsed the U-boat campaign."[49] In sum, Germany's efforts to keep the U.S. neutral by accommodating its demands were not encumbered by alliance constraints. Germany's main allies had neither the strength nor the interests at stake to exert a contrary pull on Bethmann's policy of accommodating the U.S. And there is much evidence that whatever influence they could muster was directed toward encouraging it.

Diplomacy of Selective Accommodation

On 4 February 1915, Germany retaliated against Britain's total blockade of commerce running to Germany through the North Sea by declaring the start of a U-boat campaign against Allied merchant shipping in a war zone around the British Isles.[50] Germany warned that merchant ships could be sunk without warning, and without regard for the safety of crew or passengers. Because British merchant ships sometimes flew neutral flags for cover, Berlin also warned neutral ships to stay away from the war zone. In response to this declaration, Wilson sent a note warning that if U.S. ships or lives were lost due to U-boat action, Washington would hold Berlin to "strict accountability."[51] The U.S. would not be deterred by the U-boat threat from lucrative wartime trade with Britain.

The sharp U.S. protest prompted Germany's first steps to avert conflict with the U.S. through accommodation. As the U-boat campaign began later that month, the kaiser, at the urging of Bethmann and the Foreign Office, gave an order "compelling U-boat commanders to spare neutral ships."[52] The

U-boat campaign, thus hamstrung, produced unimpressive results over the next two months. So, in April, the kaiser secretly loosened the constraints. That led to an uptick in the sinking of neutral merchantmen without warning, including U.S. vessels, starting in May.[53] Nevertheless, the pattern of Germany making U-boat concessions to avert U.S. intervention was set and would recur in the two major U.S.-Germany disputes over U-boats that spanned the years 1915 to 1916. During this period, notes Birnbaum, "the political authorities in Berlin" never assumed "that the United States would on no account enter the war, and were therefore determined to make certain concessions to America with regard to the U-boat campaign."[54]

THE *LUSITANIA* AND THE *ARABIC* PLEDGE

After the sinking of the British passenger liner *Lusitania* on 7 May 1915, which killed hundreds of Americans, "the risk of the United States joining Germany's enemies became acute."[55] Wilson sent a series of escalating protest notes in May, June, and July, the last of which conveyed a sharp warning that the U.S. would regard any subsequent sinking of civilian liners as a "deliberately unfriendly" act.[56] The implied threats of war in these notes led Wilson's secretary of state, William Jennings Bryan, to resign.[57] The bellicose nature of the warning was clear. As Bernstorff recounted, Lansing, who replaced Bryan, warned that "if Americans again lost their lives through torpedoing of a merchant ship, war could not be avoided."[58]

In response, German leaders "decreed concessions [were] necessary to prevent an open conflict."[59] On 6 July, Bethmann convinced the kaiser to issue *secret* orders to U-boat commanders, forbidding attacks on large passenger liners until further notice.[60] This addressed Wilson's most direct demand for protection of American and other civilians on passenger steamers. On 8 July, a note from Berlin followed, promising safety to U.S. citizens passing through the war zone on ships with neutral flags.[61] On 30 July (in a response to U.S. protests over the sinking of the U.S. merchant ship *Frye*), Germany agreed to pay full damages for destruction of U.S. ships and cargos, even if such destruction were lawful because they carried contraband to Germany's enemies.[62]

In early August, while the U.S. waited for a satisfactory formal resolution to its protests concerning the illegality of the *Lusitania* attack, another British passenger ship, the *Arabic*, was struck without warning by a German submarine, and three American lives were lost. Wilson tipped the press with a warning to Germany that he would cut diplomatic ties if it became clear that the attack had official sanction.[63] With Washington thus preparing to break off relations, there began a "massive German effort to avert rupture."[64]

On 24 August, Jagow met with the U.S. ambassador and explained that if the attack on the *Arabic* had happened without warning, then it violated imperial orders.[65] The next day, Jagow elaborated the message to be formally conveyed to Lansing: "if *Arabic* [was] torpedoed as reported" then "it was contrary to instructions" and "would be disavowed and reparation made."[66] Jagow followed up with a cable to Bernstorff, to reinforce the message that German submarines were operating under official instructions not to torpedo passenger liners without notice and allowing passengers and crew to escape. Concurrently, Bethmann stated to the U.S. press that Germany would provide "complete satisfaction" if it turned out that the *Arabic* attack had been a "wanton" violation of such rules.[67]

Bethmann then escalated the issue of submarine warfare to a meeting of the Imperial Council, for a confrontation with the navy's most strident advocates of submarine warfare—Tirpitz and Bachmann—and a clear-cut decision from the kaiser to accommodate Washington.[68] A cable from Bernstorff warning that "it will not be possible to prevent rupture this time if our answer about the *Arabic* is not conciliatory" added to the urgency.[69] The chancellor could "now see no other solution" but that more restrictive rules against sinking passenger ships be adopted and strictly adhered to.[70] Falkenhayn fully supported that position: "Everything," he said, "must be done to forestall a conflict with the United States."[71] The kaiser agreed, issuing on 30 August a new directive to the fleet: "Henceforward any passenger vessel whatever, not only the large ones, shall only be sunk after warning and safeguarding of passengers."[72] In response to Lansing's request, Bethmann also wanted the kaiser's secret order prohibiting attacks on passenger liners to be communicated to the U.S. as formal assurance.[73] The kaiser agreed and thus "consented, in effect, to render the U-boat virtually impotent."[74] To Admiral Tirpitz, whose resulting offer of resignation he rebuffed, Wilhelm explained, "America must be prevented from taking part against us as an active enemy. . . . The *war must be won* and that end necessitates absolute protection against a new enemy."[75]

After this decision, on 8 September, Bernstorff informed Lansing confidentially that "*for several months* the commanders of our submarines had orders not to attack large ocean lines without warning. . . . If the *Arabic* was attacked without warning, this would have been done contrary to the instructions. . . . Those orders have now been modified, so as to comprise all liners."[76] When Lansing requested a declaration for the press, Bernstorff followed up with a statement that appeared the next day in the *New York Times*: "Liners will not be sunk by our submarines without warning and without safety of the lives of noncombatants, provided that the liners do not try to escape or offer resistance."[77]

Throughout September, relations between Washington and Berlin remained tense, as the Germans' first formal reply on the *Arabic* attack, which exculpated the submarine for acting to defend itself against ramming, was perceived by Wilson as both backtracking and unsupported by facts. Berlin, nevertheless, persisted in efforts to conciliate Washington and reaffirm the previous pledges. On 18 September, Jagow gave a statement to the press confirming Berlin's commitments:

> The attitude of Germany is perfectly clear. Enemy passenger steamers will not be subjected to attack without warning . . . and will be sunk only after opportunity for safety of passengers and crew is given. Instructions to German submarine commanders on this point are very precise and definite. . . . Neutral merchantmen, including Americans, are exempt from interference . . . except when carrying contraband and will then be destroyed only . . . when provision is made for the safety of those aboard. . . . Every precaution has been taken, so far as in the power of the Imperial Government, to safeguard the interests of neutrals.[78]

On 5 October, Bernstorff relayed to Lansing further assurance that "the orders issued by His Majesty the Emperor to commanders of the German submarines . . . have been made so stringent that the recurrence of incidents similar to the *Arabic* case is considered out of the question." Coupled with that assurance was a formal apology and disavowal of the *Arabic* attack, and an offer of indemnity.[79] At the same time, to lower the risk of another crisis, U-boat operations around the coasts of Britain were secretly put on hold, while those in the North Sea were confined to visit and search.[80] Although the U-boat war was not completely restrained—it continued to menace military shipping—it was dramatically scaled back. As Stevenson noted: "American protests did more than Allied countermeasures to contain Germany's first unrestricted submarine campaign" in 1915.[81]

SHARPENED U-BOAT WARFARE AND *SUSSEX* PLEDGE

With civilian liners largely protected by the German concessions, the issue of surprise attacks on armed merchant ships—which conveyed to the Allies vast quantities of American-made civilian and war material—came to the fore. After Falkenhayn shifted, in December 1915, to backing the unlimited U-boat warfare, Bethmann's policy of strict limits became unsustainable in the Imperial Council. German policy then became to treat all armed merchant ships as a threat to surfaced submarines which could—like enemy warships—be sunk without warning and without provisions for the safety of civilian passengers.[82] Thus, according to the kaiser's new orders, "enemy merchantmen carrying guns should be regarded as warships and destroyed by all means" and any armed merchant ship—even if it were neutral—would be presumed to be hostile, because surfaced submarines could not identify them as such without exposure to gunfire.[83] On this ground, German leaders moved into a campaign of "sharpened" U-boat warfare, which they announced would begin on 29 February 1916.

With this incremental escalation of the U-boat campaign, Bethmann sought to hold a line that ceded some ground to the champions of submarine warfare while keeping the violence below the level that would trigger U.S. intervention.[84] The latter part of the calculation was warranted, for Washington had signaled in various ways that it saw armed merchant ships as fair game.[85] The essential U.S. redline, as Lansing put it to Bernstorff on 16 February, was that German submarines must not sink unarmed passenger ships.[86] Bernstorff relayed this message to Berlin with his own warning: "If a catastrophe similar to the *Lusitania* case occurs again, war with the United States can not be prevented by any art known to diplomacy."[87] The kaiser agreed and, with an added dose of caution, cinched his orders even tighter: "Until further orders, *liners*, whether armed or not, will *not* be attacked."[88]

Bethmann's balanced approach was, nevertheless, further challenged in early March 1916 by naval officers seeking to open up an unrestricted U-boat offensive against all merchant shipping. As Bethmann put it to the press that month: "If this unrestricted U-boat war is announced, we shall be at war with America tomorrow. There is not the slightest doubt of this."[89] Through official channels, he beat back the challenge with an extensive and detailed critique of the advocates' premises, sent to the kaiser: "The question comes down to this, whether our position is so desperate that we are bound to play a win-all lose-all game in which our existence as a world power and our whole future as a nation would be at stake, whereas the chances of winning . . . are uncertain. The question is to be answered unqualifiedly in the negative. . . . Therefore there devolves upon us the task of carrying on the U-boat war in such a way as to make it possible to avoid the break with the United States."[90] Wilhelm "fully agreed with the stand taken" in Bethmann's report and assured the chancellor that "he would not permit the 'folly' of provoking America into war."[91]

Bethmann's hard-won policy of partial U-boat warfare was compromised later that month when a U-boat torpedoed the unarmed French steamer *Sussex*, killing eighty passengers including U.S. citizens, and thus sparked another crisis with Washington.[92] While Berlin maintained, at least initially, that it was not responsible for the attack, the U.S. had ironclad evidence that the ship was struck, without warning, by a German torpedo.[93] Wilson on 18 April delivered an ultimatum demanding a firm German promise not to sink *any* "passenger or freight carrying vessels" without warning and taking measures to ensure the safety of crew and passengers, or else the U.S. would "have no choice but to sever diplomatic relations with the German Empire altogether."[94] On 28 April, the U.S. followed up with the demand for a prompt declaration of Germany's abandonment of illegal submarine warfare.[95] The door was left open for Germany to accommodate the U.S. by adopting a limited form of "legal" submarine warfare against merchant shipping that conformed to traditional "visit and search" rules of cruiser warfare.[96]

On receiving the formal U.S. demands, Bethmann moved swiftly to avoid a rupture. Once again, his policy was nearly overturned by Falkenhayn's calls for unlimited use, which were bolstered by a personal plea from Tirpitz "imploring" the kaiser to hold nothing back.[97] But in a surprising turn, Admiral Holtzendorff, chief of the Admiralty Staff, offered an assessment that argued the timing was not yet right for taking steps certain to turn U.S. strategic weight against Germany. It agreed that unlimited submarine warfare could defeat Britain militarily, but only if it did not gain the U.S. as a new ally:

> This rich and inaccessible country can carry on a war for ten years: it will bring to our staggering enemies considerable moral and material aid and will strengthen them and prolong their resistance—*and in particular England*. Our goal, which is to obtain an end of the war within a short time, will be frustrated and Germany will be exposed to exhaustion. . . . It is necessary to protect our military advantage and to act *diplomatically* to prevent new enemies from assailing us, to look for and use new means of breaking the alliance of our enemies, and thus to open for us the possibility of a separate peace.[98]

Holtzendorff's qualified view, which was supported by the new navy minister (Eduard von Capelle, who had replaced Tirpitz) and the chief of the naval cabinet (Georg von Müller), was pressed into service by Bethmann and Jagow. That persuaded the kaiser, on 1 May, to accept new strict rules conforming to U.S. demands. As Müller recorded, he "immediately swung around . . . for the thought of having America, too, on our neck was for him quite frightful."[99]

On 4 May, Bethmann delivered a response that complied with Washington's ultimatum—the *Sussex* pledge. In this, Berlin assured Washington that "the German naval forces have received the following orders: In accordance with the general principles of visit and search and destruction of merchant vessels recognized by international law, such vessels, both within and without the area declared as naval war zone, shall not be sunk without warning and without saving human lives, unless these ships attempt to escape or offer resistance."[100] Immediately after this came a German note apologizing for the "deplorable" sinking of the *Sussex*, which was an accident that contravened official orders.[101] Thus the sharpened U-boat campaign of 1916 was halted.[102]

THE END OF ACCOMMODATION AND THE CHOICE FOR WAR

Soon after the May 1916 decision, the German navy's position diverged from Bethmann's. As early as January 1916, they were convinced that the record of success against British commerce that had been accomplished despite the limits conceded to the U.S. indicated that an all-out submarine war would force Britain to capitulate in six months.[103] Starting in June 1916, they argued that the time for launching the campaign had come. But they were not able to alter policy in the Imperial Council until late 1916, when German civil-military relations shifted heavily against the civilians. In autumn 1916, Bethmann's influence was increasingly sidelined, as Falkenhayn was replaced by Field Marshall Paul von Hindenburg and Quartermaster General Erich Ludendorff, and the kaiser handed over more power of decision to those military leaders. After October 1916, Bethmann's ability to defend the policy of accommodating the U.S. declined fast.[104] Washington was receiving alarming reports of the German navy's continuing preparations to resume unlimited submarine warfare in defiance of the *Sussex* pledge.[105] Still, in late October, Bethmann once more got enough backing from the kaiser, Hindenburg, and Helfferich to convince the opposition in the Reichstag to stop pressing for resumption of submarine warfare. But the pressure from the Admiralty continued to build.[106]

For the most part, navy and military views did not deny that the shift to unlimited submarine warfare would trigger U.S. intervention.[107] Instead, its advocates advanced several arguments to negate the war-tipping implications of U.S. intervention.

First, there was the notion that U.S. intervention would amount to little more than a formal recognition of an existing reality. As Ludendorff put it in December 1916, "America sooner or later would go against us."[108] To the Austrian chief of staff, Ludendorff stated that the U.S. was already supplying the maximum it could to the Entente powers and that its financial aid to them would not be decisive.[109] The military chiefs' December 1916 estimate of the impact "if America did join our enemy" stated, "As far as shipping capacity is concerned, this effect could only be small. . . . One should attribute just as little effect to American troops, which could not be transferred in large numbers anyhow for lack of shipping, and to American money, which cannot replace missing capacity."[110] On 8 January, Hindenburg remarked to Ludendorff and Holtzendorff: "We are counting on the possibility of war with the United States. . . . Things can not be worse than they are now."[111]

Second, there was the argument that whatever it might ultimately amount to, the material weight of U.S. power could not come into play soon enough "to intervene decisively in the European war."[112] The admirals saw Britain as the primary enemy and center of gravity in the war. The submarine used without restrictions could force Britain to capitulate before U.S. intervention would matter, in five or six months.[113] Contrary to his May 1916 view, Admiralty Chief Holtzendorff was now "prepared to accept the risk of a break with America." He informed Bethmann that U.S. intervention would not be "fatal, as Germany would be able to cope with both England and America if the U-boats were given freedom of action."[114] Similarly, Tirpitz argued in 1916 that "the disadvantages of a break with America were negligible since it could be assumed with a considerable degree of certainty that the entry of the United States into the war would not appreciably affect the military situation."[115] At the decisive 9 January 1917 Imperial Council meeting on

U-boat escalation, the chief of the High Seas Fleet's representative "assured those present that war with America was 'of no importance to the Fleet.'"[116]

The military leadership had similar views.[117] As Falkenhayn had put it in his May 1916 push for unrestricted submarine warfare: "America's step from the secret war in which it has long been engaged against us, to an openly declared hostility can effect no real change."[118] In the 9 January meeting, Ludendorff declared that he didn't "give a damn about America" and was ready to "accept the risk" of war with it. Hindenburg estimated that the effect of U.S. intervention would be "minimal, in any case not decisive."[119] Military officials also now dismissed the knock-on alignment effects of U.S. intervention. Now that Romania was defeated, Ludendorff and Hindenburg downplayed the danger that the Netherlands and Denmark would follow behind the U.S. German ground forces could now be deployed to deter them, and reports indicated that the Dutch and Danish would not intervene over the U-boat issue.[120]

In sum, the Supreme Command refuted the war-tipping implications of U.S. intervention with arguments against both the immediate and the longer-term impacts. Presented with these arguments, the kaiser agreed that he "fully expected" the U.S. to intervene, but that it would be "irrelevant."[121] After this point, then, it is clear that the German policy of accommodating the U.S. did not fail but rather was abandoned in favor of one that, at the price of provoking U.S. intervention, would promise a speedy victory.[122]

Summary and Alternatives

Germany was in a good position to neutralize the U.S. through selective accommodation. It was not hamstrung by alliance counterpressures, and the concessions it could make were important to Washington and of a sort that it could not easily secure by dispensing with the relationship. Moreover, its alignment goal—continued U.S. neutrality—was modest. In sum, the context was conducive to success. And success was had. Selective accommodation did not fail in 1917; Germany abandoned it. What changed the dynamics of the situation were Germany's altered estimates of U.S. war-tipping potential. As long as the U.S. was perceived to be a dangerous war-tipper, the strategy of accommodation was maintained, and concessions were successfully used. Once German leaders convinced themselves that U.S. strategic weight could be nullified, they embraced a war-fighting strategy they expected would provoke U.S. intervention—and it did.

Two alternative explanations need to be addressed. The first holds that the U.S. could not have entered the war sooner than 1917: German concessions therefore were not critical in keeping it out before then. The second holds that U.S. intervention was bound to occur in 1917, regardless of German U-boat action, and that Berlin's decision to escalate—based on the belief that U.S. strategic weight could be nullified—was therefore not the critical precipitant.

The first, and more important, alternative does not stem from a theoretical position but instead from the fact that there were considerable domestic political forces, separate from Berlin's accommodative efforts, restraining U.S. action. Did these, then, rule out any decision by Wilson to risk war in confronting Germany in the years 1915 to 1916? The answer is no. Here, we must consider two things: first, Wilson's attitudes, and those of his key advisors, about taking hardline steps vis-à-vis Germany at critical points in crises, and second, the extent to which the connection between a rupture in U.S.-German relations and likely war was understood by them.

Despite Wilson's general desire to avoid entering the war if possible, and his preference for patient diplomacy, he clearly indicated at key points, not only to the Germans but also internally, to his closest advisors, that he would break off relations with Germany if it did not limit U-boat warfare. Thus, on 14 July 1915, in the midst of the *Lusitania* crisis, Wilson instructed House to inform Bernstorff that insofar as "the Germans *are* modifying their methods[,] they must be made to feel that they must continue in their new way unless they deliberately wish to prove to us that they are unfriendly and wish war."[123] On 21 July 1915, as he prepared to deliver the third *Lusitania* note, which defined any further sinking of passenger ships by Germany as "deliberately unfriendly" acts, Wilson explained in a private letter to his fiancée, Edith Gault, that the note was "so direct and emphatic and uncompromising . . . that it brings us to the final parting of the ways, unless Germany yields—which I fear is most unlikely."[124] Wilson, at this point, was committed to breaking relations with Germany if it did not yield, and anticipated (incorrectly) that it probably would not. The note went out to Germany under the name of Lansing, who had, in an earlier draft, proposed an even sharper ultimatum.[125]

Wilson's willingness to follow through on a rupture with Germany was even more clearly revealed in April and May 1916, after he sent the *Sussex* ultimatum. Then, writes Link, "Wilson, Lansing, and House were . . . grimly determined to force the submarine issue even at the risk of war."[126] Wilson's note had unambiguously warned that if Germany "should not immediately declare its purpose to abandon its present methods of submarine warfare . . . the United States can have no choice but to sever diplomatic relations."[127] On 8 April, House warned Bernstorff that "a break was inevitable" unless Germany "renounced their submarine policy."[128] Lansing, likewise, advised Bernstoff on 21 April that there was "no other way" to avoid rupture except by a German announcement that it would abandon the submarine campaign.[129] Wilson went to Congress to publicly explain the note and the gravity of its ultimatum, and the reaction on the Hill—from both Democrats and Republicans—and in the press indicated support for the administration's position.[130] While they awaited Berlin's response, House noted in his diary on 3 May: "I find the President is set in his determination to make

Germany recede from her position regarding submarines. . . . I now find him unyielding and belligerent, and not caring as much as he ought to avert war."[131] Shortly before the German concession note came through, on 4 May, Bernstorff's passports and other arrangements were prepared for his departure. Gerard in Berlin was likewise poised to return. In sum, at key points in the *Lusitania* and *Sussex* crises, there is evidence that Wilson was prepared to break off relations with Germany if it did not accommodate U.S. demands.

Although Wilson hoped that a formal break in U.S.-German diplomatic relations would not automatically trigger war, he saw the risks that it would, and his advisors emphasized that such linkage was inevitable. As Wilson wrote to Gault on 22 August 1915, "The withdrawal of Gerard and the dismissal of Bernstorff will not necessarily lead to *war. We* will not declare it . . . but Germany may . . . and if she does . . . I must call Congress together and we are in for the whole terrible business." On the same day, House emphasized to Wilson that rupture *would* lead to war: "To send Bernstorff home and to recall Gerard would be the first act of war, for we would be without means of communication with one another and it would not be long before some act was committed that would force the issue." In a similar vein, Lansing wrote Wilson on 24 August 1915, outlining ways to proceed in view of "the danger of being involved in war with Germany in case we should sever diplomatic relations, *which appears probable*." For these, he stipulated "the assumption that we sever diplomatic intercourse with the German Government, which responds by a declaration of war."[132] Likewise, when Lansing advised Wilson during the 1916 *Sussex* crisis to take the "drastic" step of an ultimatum threatening to cut relations, he explained, "Doubtless the German Government would view the breaking off of diplomatic relations as an unfriendly act and might possibly go so far as to declare war." At the end of March, Wilson instructed House to communicate directly to Bernstorff that "we were at the breaking point and that we would surely go into the war unless some decisive change was made in their submarine policy." On 3 April, House wrote back to Wilson in terms that assumed a necessary linkage between diplomatic rupture and war: "Unless the Germans discontinue their present policy a break seems inevitable. . . . Would it not be wise to intervene now rather than to permit the break to come? Our becoming a belligerent would not be without its advantages." On 6 April, Wilson sent a note to British Foreign Secretary Edward Grey, stating "It now seems probable that this country must break with Germany on the submarine question unless the unexpected happens," which meant the U.S. would likely "become a belligerent" and the war would be prolonged.[133] In sum, Wilson's threats in 1915 and 1916 to cut off relations with Germany if it did not comply with U.S. demands to limit U-boat warfare were serious, and were made with the understanding that this would likely lead to war. The White House, despite the prevalence of antiwar domestic sentiment, was clearly prepared to go down this path before 1917.

The other competing explanation holds that the U.S. was bound to intervene in 1917, regardless of whether Germany resumed unrestricted submarine warfare or not. That is, with Germany appearing on the brink of victory in early 1917, fundamental balance of power pressures impelled the U.S. to step in, to save the Allies and stop Germany from establishing hegemony in Europe.[134] This argument need not imply that German accommodation of the U.S. was irrelevant before 1917, but it could, insofar as it asserts that the immediate prospect of German victory was the only thing that could activate U.S. intervention. This thesis, which reflects the general realist logic of offshore balancing, is in any case not well supported by evidence. That is, it conflicts with Wilson's actual perceptions of the situation in Europe at the time.

The most detailed and convincing rebuttal to the offshore balancing motivation is given by Jackson, who demonstrates, through meticulous process tracing, that "Wilson neither believed the Germans were on the cusp of defeating the Entente powers in the spring of 1917, nor was he especially worried about what the consequences of such an outcome would be."[135] Rather than reproduce Jackson's exhaustive review of the primary documents, it will suffice here to state his main findings. These show that, on balance, fear that Germany would soon militarily dominate Europe was not salient for Wilson in early 1917, nor were expectations of imminent military collapse of Russia, France, and Britain. Indeed, Wilson saw Germany's move as an act of desperation, driven by a recognition of the fragility of its own position, and the likely collapse of *its* allies.[136]

These claims are not controversial: they are reflected in the judgments of leading historians of Wilson's policy of neutrality and decision to intervene. On this point, Link is worth quoting at length:

[Wilson] did not accept belligerency because he thought that the Allies were in danger of losing the war and a German victory would imperil American national interests. We now know that the Allies were in desperate straits if not in danger of defeat. The French had begun to draw upon their last manpower. . . . The submarine campaign was succeeding, actually beyond expectations of the German Admiralty. . . . The British and French faced an exchange problem that seemed insoluble. But Wilson and his advisors knew virtually none of these facts. . . . Few persons in America . . . thought that the Russian Revolution would soon lead to Russian withdrawal from the war. On the contrary, virtually everyone assumed that the new Russian government would wage war more efficiently and enthusiastically than the old.[137]

Similarly, Cooper argues that "geopolitical forces" were "neither widely nor urgently recognized enough. . . . No one in America at the beginning of 1917 had any inkling of what dire straits [the Allies] were in."[138] Likewise, Thompson states: "Whereas there were certainly some Americans who had expressed anxiety about the consequences for national security of a German victory, there is no evidence that any saw such a victory as imminent in the spring of 1917, or thought that only U.S. intervention could prevent it. . . . Certainly, there was no indication of any concern with the fate of the Allies in the way the U.S. government responded to the submarine campaign [in early 1917]."[139] "As for the threat of a German victory to American security," writes Osgood, "this was not a consideration in [Wilson's] mind."[140]

As Cooper put it, Germany's escalation to unlimited submarine warfare was the deciding factor: "American intervention on the side of the Allies could not have happened if the Germans had not initiated submarine warfare. Without those attacks, there would have been no remotely plausible grounds for the United States to enter the war." Berlin's February 1917 U-boat campaign was "the indispensable precipitant to American intervention."[141] In the same spirit, Thompson emphasizes "the improbability of American intervention had it not been for the German campaign of unrestricted submarine warfare launched on 1 February."[142]

In Wilson's decision to intervene, the foremost concerns were the inability to protect U.S. shipping from Germany attack except by war, and the damage to U.S. prestige and ability to influence a peace settlement if it failed to defend its rights as a belligerent.[143] Thus, Link writes: "It is almost abundantly clear that Wilson simply concluded that there was no alternative to full-fledged belligerency. The United States was a great power. It could not submit to Germany's flagrant—so it seemed to Wilson and his contemporaries—assault on American sovereignty without yielding its honor and destroying its influence."[144] In his meeting with the cabinet on 20 March 1917, when Wilson presented to his advisors the question of whether to call on Congress to declare war, Wilson himself presented a rationale for war that was narrowly focused on the submarine issue and made no reference to a grander offshore balancing motivation. As Lansing's record of the meeting put it, "He did not see from a practical point of view what else could be done to safeguard American vessels more than had already been done unless we declared war."[145] Neither did any of the cabinet secretaries—who all spoke in support—invoke that larger strategic logic.

In sum, the case that the prospect of imminent German victory made it inevitable that the U.S. would intervene in early 1917 is weak. We thus return to the final claim of the theoretical account: it was Germany's shift from accommodating the U.S. to doing what was certain to provoke it that caused the U.S. to intervene. And Germany's decision to shift in that way reflected a recalculation of the U.S.'s strategic weight. Specifically, German leaders became convinced that the U.S.'s war-tipping potential could be negated by a decisive escalation to unrestricted submarine warfare, which would lay Britain low before U.S. power could be brought to bear in a significant way. As Gerard summed it up on 7 February 1917, "Even if there is war [the] German military calculate they can starve England before America can do anything."[146]

The Entente Fails to Keep Turkey Neutral, 1914

> It is so important for us to detach Turkey from Germany, that we must strive to as long as there remains the least hope of success.
>
> Mikhail von Giers, Russian ambassador to Turkey, August 1914
>
> We are daily trying to buy Turkish neutrality by promises and concessions.
>
> Winston Churchill, first lord of the British Admiralty, September 1914

In August 1914, Russia led its Entente allies, Britain and France, in a concerted attempt to accommodate the Ottoman Empire, which was then wavering between joining the Central powers or staying out of the war. The Entente partners did not, however, agree about Turkey's strategic weight. The bid they coordinated was thus weakened and bested by the Central powers, who then coaxed Turkey into the war.

This case highlights key elements and relationships in the theoretical framework. The Entente's goal was to keep a hedging Turkey neutral—it thus sought a low degree of alignment change, an easier thing to achieve. But the Entente powers' high alliance constraints proved detrimental. For while the allies (roughly equal in power and dependence) did agree about the basic goal and method of selective accommodation, they did not agree about Turkey's strategic weight. That lack of consensus impaired their ability to mobilize sufficient reward power. They did not combine the concessions to Turkey and each other that were both possible and, as it turned out, necessary to cement its neutrality. The case thus reveals the impediments to success that arise when highly constrained allies differ about the target's war-tipping potential.[1]

Initiation Conditions

PERCEPTIONS OF TARGET'S STRATEGIC WEIGHT

In August to September 1914, the Entente powers had several reinforcing reasons to keep Turkey neutral. The Russians, who initiated the joint effort, felt most keenly the dangers posed by Turkey's intervention and thus "placed a high value on [its] neutrality."[2] "For Russia," writes Howard, "Turkey was of vital importance as holding the Straits [was] the key to economic and strategic security."[3] If the Germans, by allying with Turkey, gained control of the Black Sea, they would close off a primary avenue of Russian communication with the Western Allies. And that could also trigger a domino effect, for the "weakening [of the Entente] would be obvious to neutral observers, who might then follow Turkey into the enemy camp."[4] For St. Petersburg, then, these prospects carried war-tipping potential, and for that reason, it both pushed the Entente's efforts to accommodate Turkey and was most willing to countenance far-reaching Allied concessions.[5] Thus, in response to the initial Turkish feelers in August 1914, the Russian ambassador to the Porte, Mikhail Giers, wrote to Russian foreign minister Sergei Sazonov, "It is so important for us to detach Turkey from Germany that we must strive to as long as there remains the least hope of success. . . . They must not be repulsed, for we should throw them into the arms of our enemies."[6] Sazonov agreed, advising the British government that "in order to secure [Turkey's] neutrality, we must go as far as we possibly could."[7]

Britain and France shared Russia's concern about closure of the Straits. But for them it did not carry the same immediate salience or long-term danger. Because the Suez Canal enabled easier access to their holdings in Asia, the geopolitical importance of the Straits had declined since the days of Disraeli, when blocking Russian control over them had been a supreme interest. On top of this, "both London and Paris underestimated the military strength of Turkey."[8] So, in 1914, British and French perceptions of Turkey's strategic weight centered on different and shorter-term concerns about imperial communications and control. At the start of war, when they desperately needed to move troop reinforcements from India and East Asia to stop the German offensive on the western front, they worried that Turkey might act in Egypt to block passage through Suez. The imperative, as British Foreign Minister Edward Grey later put it, was that "Turkey must be kept neutral, or, at any rate, Britain must not be involved in war with Turkey till after the Indian troops had got through the Suez Canal. We were, therefore, to delay the entry of Turkey into the war, irrespective of whether we could ultimately prevent it or not."[9] The Western Allies also feared that Ottoman enmity would stoke the danger of Muslim rebellion and jihad in their empires.[10] To extend the Porte's declared posture of neutrality and nonintervention was, then, a common goal of the Entente powers' alliance diplomacy, even if the motivations and time horizons underlying it were not congruent.

PERCEPTIONS OF RELATIVE REWARD POWER

"It ought not to be difficult to keep Turkey neutral," said Grey to the French and Russian ambassadors in London. "The proper course was to make Turkey feel that, should she remain neutral, and should Germany and Austria be defeated, we would take care that the integrity of Turkish possessions as they now were would be preserved."[11] The next month, Admiralty Lord Winston Churchill summed up the Entente's approach in blunter terms: "We are daily trying to buy Turkish neutrality by promises and concessions."[12] In that enterprise, the Entente powers operated according to a shared general concept of influence through rewards.

A catalytic mechanism was central to their policy concept: concessions could influence Turkey's alignment by tipping a decision in favor of the pro-neutrality faction within the Turkish leadership. Thus, in early August 1914, when Turkish officials first floated a possible deal with Russia, Sazonov's rationale for responding generously was that "we should not rebuff the moderate element."[13] The catalytic logic was most explicitly described by Andrew Ryan, a British diplomat in Constantinople: "We are working on the theory that two conflicting forces are at work in the highest places, one moderate, working for neutrality with, if anything, a tinge of sympathy with our side; the other, militantly pro-German. Our policy is to keep Turkey out of the war by backing up the moderates . . . by exhortation, promises, and advice."[14] As Louis Mallet, the British ambassador to Turkey, wrote, if London wanted to "preserv[e] the neutrality of Turkey during the war[,] we cannot do anything here unless we have something to offer which will help the moderates."[15]

In dealing with a Turkey that had been recently shorn of much territory in Europe and that still teetered toward disintegration, the Entente leaders believed that they had a strong inducement to offer—a guarantee of Turkey's integrity during the war and at a peace settlement. They well recognized the deep fears of Turkey's leaders about the survival of their state in an environment of great instability.[16] And the Porte, on its part, encouraged them to believe that such guarantees would influence its attitude.[17] Thus, the British chargé d'affaires in Constantinople cabled to Grey in mid-August that Turkey's "prevalent anxiety as to Russia's intentions" could be "allayed by positive assurance from France and Great Britain that they will guarantee the integrity of Turkey."[18] The Entente leaders, accordingly, placed special emphasis on such assurances in their approach to Turkey. Grey instructed representatives in Constantinople to declare that "if Turkey will observe scrupulous neutrality during the war England, France, and Russia will uphold her independence and integrity."[19] Likewise, he told the Turkish ambassador two days later that "Turkey would have nothing to fear of us and her integrity would be preserved in any conditions of peace" if Turkey "preserved a real neutrality."[20] In the same vein, Churchill sent a personal note to the Ottoman Minister of War, Ismail Enver Pasha, assuring that "if Turkey remains neutral," then once Germany and Austria were beaten, "a solemn agreement to respect the integrity of the Turkish empire must be a condition of any terms of peace that affect the near east."[21] And the Entente's most well developed concerted inducement—extended later August—offered a joint, formal guarantee "that the inviolability and independence of Turkey will be respected by the three Powers, and that the [postwar] treaty of peace shall contain no conditions conflicting with those principles."[22]

The Entente allies also controlled other rewards to influence Ottoman policy. Each was a principal backer of the regime of capitulations to external interference imposed on the Porte, and their power to delegitimize and roll back the capitulations represented an enormous potential benefit to the Porte. Again, the Porte encouraged the Allies to believe that their willingness to suspend the capitulations would foster Turkish restraint.[23] Thus, another inducement the Entente tried to manipulate was the prospect of negotiations with Turkey over substitute measures for regulating economic and juridical relations more consistent with norms of international law and sovereignty.[24] The fiscal strictures of the capitulations held particular value, for, as Mallet put it to Grey, "Economic freedom is one of the ideals most cherished by modern Turkish statesmen. A good deal might be offered with reasonable safety. . . . Give them economic freedom, which is what they want more than anything."[25] In that spirit, Grey instructed Mallet to tell the Turkish leaders that "so long as they maintain neutrality . . . we shall be prepared to consider reasonable concessions about Capitulations."[26]

The Entente powers also could trade promises of territory—that is, the return of recently lost adjacent lands and islands—and economic assets. Territorial compensation was an option they clearly recognized, for Turkish leaders proposed it. Thus, for example, Turkey's navy minister, Djemal Bey, proposed to the Entente a deal including "restoration of the Greek islands" and giving "western Thrace . . . back to Turkey" if Bulgaria intervened against the Entente.[27] Similarly, they recognized that they could also leverage promises to give the Porte German railroad and other economic assets in Turkish territory. As Sazonov urged his allies in August 1914, they "should lose no opportunity of dangling this bait before" the Turkish government.[28]

Finally, there was discernible a broader scenario of security cooperation that they could present to Constantinople, one that provided assurances not only of Turkey's territorial integrity after the war, but also of aid for its efforts to economically modernize and reconstitute internal sovereign control. The Young Turks had tried in recent years to elicit from the Entente powers such a comprehensive commitment to the internal reform and consolidation of Turkey. The powers had instead adopted piecemeal approaches that limited their commitments and preserved their control over their respective spheres of influence in the Ottoman Empire.[29] Nevertheless, the Allied leaders understood that the offer of a wholesale security commitment could influence Constantinople's alignment. When the Porte had approached London about an alliance with the Entente in 1911, even Churchill had urged a positive response: "If she wants to turn to England and to Russia and if Russia is herself anxious for association, we should carry Turkey in some sort of way into the system of the Triple Entente."[30]

The Entente, in sum, could dispose of the external and internal security that the Ottoman Empire craved. Although Austria-Hungary and Germany might try too, the scope of their control over such matters could not match that of the Russians, French, and British combined, whose naval power allowed them much greater access to the region than that possessed by their enemies. As Grey noted to the Russian ambassador, the Porte's judgement of the value of Entente inducements would be conditioned "by her opinion which side . . . is in a position to make offers good."[31] The Entente was certainly in such a position, and were they willing to deploy the full weight of their reward power, they stood a good chance of succeeding.

Contingent Conditions

ATTEMPTED ALIGNMENT CHANGE

With Turkey, the Entente tried to induce a low degree of alignment change. The Porte was in a hedged position, a defected neutral. The Entente powers sought, at a minimum, to reinforce this and if possible, to induce the Porte to formally embrace neutrality for the duration of the war.[32] "Sazonov's goal," writes Bobroff, "was 'playing for time,' which meant delaying Turkish entry into the war against the Entente for a long as possible."[33] Likewise, for Britain, the policy was, as Grey put it, "to delay the entry of Turkey into the war as long as we could."[34] "Our main object," wrote Ambassador Mallet, "[is] to postpone hostilities with this country in the hope of averting them altogether."[35] If the Entente's minimum goal was to extend the Porte's nonintervention, it also sought to entrench Turkey's position through a larger bargain that, as Eyre Crowe put it, would "secure Turkish neutrality."[36]

Although overt and covert Ottoman-German ties were by then established, considerable forces were at work in Turkey's high politics that still favored an Entente bargain and nonintervention. The recent trajectory of Turkey's alignment made this evident. After Turkey-in-Europe was dismantled by Greece, Serbia, Montenegro, and Bulgaria in the Balkan wars of 1912 to 1913, the Porte scrambled to find security in great power protection and had sought alliance with each of the Entente principals. Moreover, the European powers were at this time ensconced in its internal affairs. The "capitulations" regime granted them significant influence over the Porte's fiscal affairs, and their citizens living in the Ottoman Empire extraordinary juridical and economic privileges.[37] Germany and France claimed extensive railroad concessions. Russia oversaw a reform program in the Armenian provinces. German military advisors were brought in after 1913 to modernize the Ottoman army. British naval officers were hired to supervise the development of an Ottoman fleet. Despite, or, rather, because of all of this, the Porte retained foreign policy freedom of action: its exposure to pressure was diversified and the powers could be played off.[38] When the July Crisis began none of the powers were counting on or expecting it to intervene.[39] "The Turks," as Stevenson summed it, "were not firmly anchored to either camp."[40] Once the war started, in early August, Turkey made a secret alliance with Germany and Austria, but it then backtracked, declared neutrality, and "played a waiting game . . . making demands on the Entente for the preservation of her neutral attitude."[41] This was the context in which Russia initiated the Entente's efforts "actively to maintain Ottoman neutrality."[42]

ALLIANCE CONSTRAINTS

Among themselves, Russia, Britain, and France faced high alliance constraints in terms of both relative power and strategic dependence. Theirs was "an alliance of relatively equal partners."[43] This meant that when their respective parochial interests conflicted, they could not be just ignored or overridden by the others. Each had some degree of veto power. None could afford, in the midst of war, to risk a serious rupture to the alliance's overall solidarity by pursuing a unilateral policy toward Turkey. In addition, each had major specific interests at stake in the fate of Turkey: Russia and Britain had a long history of competition over control of the Straits, and for Russia its disposition was seen as vital. Russia, Britain, and France also had their own visions for establishing control in other parts of the empire and protecting ethnic or economic priorities in its region. Thus, any arrangements struck with Turkey had to reflect bargained compromises among the Allies.

ALLIED STRATEGIC CONSENSUS

Disagreements about Turkey's strategic weight impaired such bargains. To Russia, Turkey's alignment was critically important. As noted above, there was a real threat that the German ships in the straits would overmatch and neutralize the Russian Black Sea Fleet.[44] As Sazonov later expressed it: "Turkey's attitude to the war was a matter of first-rate importance. . . . The possibility of [it] siding with the Central Powers was particularly dangerous to Russia, for in that case the Black Sea would be open to the enemy's fleet, and a considerable part of our army needed on the Western front would have to be retained on the Turkish frontier, and, the Black Sea being closed, we should be cut off from the direct communication with our allies and paralyzed economically."[45] The last point was no exaggeration: Russia was highly dependent on the free passage of commerce through the Straits: 90 percent of its grain trade and 50 percent of its exports overall went through the Bosporus.[46]

British and French officials, however, rated Turkey's strategic weight lower. The British Foreign Office "considered a Turkish involvement to be simply a potential nuisance . . . and Grey seems to have been chiefly willing to accommodate the Porte in an effort simply to avoid adding a further factor to the already confused situation."[47] To them, the Ottoman army appeared decrepit and incompetent. Likewise, its navy—which the British were helping to reorganize—was judged, in the words of the Foreign Office permanent undersecretary, not "an important or efficient factor."[48] In February 1914, Colonel G. M. Harper of the War Office Staff dismissed Turkey's army in similar terms: "It would be hard to contend that Turkey, at the present moment, has much power of offensive action. . . . [Such action] demands most careful preparation, organization, and the highest training. It is open to doubt whether these qualities can ever be found in the Turkish Army."[49] Indeed, perceptions of Turkey's military weakness fed the assumption of Grey and others that it was so blatantly in the Porte's interest to remain neutral that the Entente need not sacrifice much to induce that outcome. Thus, on 17 August 1914, a Turkey expert in the Foreign Office argued that Britain should concede little because "if those concessions do not go far enough to please the Turks, [we] face, not the danger, but the inconvenience of war with Turkey."[50]

Finally, unlike Russia, the Western Allies considered the Near East a strategic sideshow. Turkish intervention would create complications for both sides, but would not crucially affect the ultimate decision. As the British military attaché in Constantinople put it, it was "quite a subsidiary theatre of war."[51]

Diplomacy of Selective Accommodation

On 22 July, when Enver first approached Germany about an alliance, he was rebuffed.[52] The German envoy, Baron Hans von Wangenheim, familiar with the state of the Ottoman army, expected that an alliance with Turkey would be a burden to Germany and Austria.[53] But the next day, Austria gave Serbia the ultimatum, and Kaiser Wilhelm reversed Wangenheim's response, insisting that Germany should exploit the opening.[54] "She makes a direct offer of herself," he wrote. "A refusal or a snub would amount to her going over to Russia-Gallia. . . . Under no circumstances at all can we afford to turn them away."[55] On 28 July, Enver presented a concrete proposal to Germany, which called for an alliance directed only against Russia. Berlin instructed Wangenheim to sign off if he was confident that Turkey had the intent and capability to fight Russia.[56]

At that moment, London made a decision that would seriously embitter Turkey.[57] The Admiralty impounded two nearly completed warships ordered and paid for by Constantinople.[58] Compounding the insult, Britain would refuse to refund the money until after the war.[59] The day London announced the embargo—2 August—Germany and Turkey signed a secret treaty, and Austria-Hungary concurred. The treaty, which was to remain in force until December 1918, stipulated that: (1) Turkey would enter the war against Russia if Germany and Russia fought over the Austrian-Serb dispute; (2) the German military advisors mission would remain in Turkey, under Ottoman control, but with "effective influence on the general direction" of the Turkish army; and (3) Germany would guarantee the territorial integrity of the Ottoman empire.[60]

With war breaking out, Turkey mobilized. That elevated Enver to the position of acting commander in chief of the army and navy, which enhanced his power over security policy in the Ottoman cabinet. Germany immediately requested Turkish intervention against Russia, and assistance against Britain and France.[61] But to Berlin's chagrin, the Porte declared a policy of "strict" neutrality on 3 August; it therewith mined the Straits, but left open a lane for free passage of merchant ships under escort.[62] To Berlin, it signaled that it would not declare war or take any overt action until its military was fully ready, and until the alignment of other states in the region—Bulgaria in particular—had taken a form conducive to Ottoman action.[63] Thus, within days of joining the alliance with Germany, Turkey hedged and became a defected neutral.[64]

Nevertheless, Ottoman-German ties were growing. The day after the 2 August treaty was signed, Berlin ordered its two cruisers in the Mediterranean (the *Goeben* and *Breslau*) to sail to Constantinople for refuge.[65] The Porte offered to allow the German cruisers to enter the Straits in return for new and stronger German commitments to support the abolition of the capitulations; foster diplomatic efforts to bring Bulgaria and Rumania into alliance with Turkey; guarantee that Germany and Austria would not make peace until enemy forces were removed from Turkish territories; guarantee that Turkey would recover Aegean islands if it defeated Greece; support an expansion of Turkey's eastern border with Russia; and a war indemnity.[66] German officials agreed immediately.[67] When the German cruisers put into the Straits a few days later, they were diverted away from Constantinople. The Porte then insisted that, in order to protect Turkey's neutrality, the ships would have to be converted to Ottoman property through a sham sale agreement.[68] It also informed Berlin that the ships could not operate in the Black Sea until Turkey and Bulgaria were tied into an offensive alliance against Russia, and the Turkish military had achieved full readiness for war. The latter were conditions that Constantinople would repeatedly invoke in order to temporize.[69]

On 5 August, the Ottoman cabinet opened up a channel of negotiations with Russia to explore a strategic accommodation.[70] Enver signaled to

St. Petersburg that Turkey retained its freedom of action and would "follow a course dictated solely by its own interests."[71] On 9 August he came forward with a proposal: if the Entente would ensure the return to Turkey of western Thrace and the Aegean islands and give it a five- to ten-year defensive alliance, Turkey would shift its forces from the border with Russia in the Caucasus to the west, abutting Bulgaria, and it would offer military assistance to Russia and send home the German military advisors.[72]

By this point, the Entente governments had some knowledge of the 2 August Ottoman-German pact.[73] So the Porte's hedging was discernible: while tilted toward the Central powers, it had retreated from full commitment; its current neutrality was conditional, subject to the influence of options and events. That would characterize Turkey's position for at least the next month. Until mid-September, the Porte tried to extract as much aid from Germany as possible without actually committing to war, and it negotiated with the Entente powers seeking a more profitable, less risky arrangement.[74] As Giers advised Sazonov, "The Turks are playing a double role . . . endeavoring to derive as much benefit as possible for themselves from the European war."[75]

Giers saw Enver's bid as offering an "historic moment" to gain advantage.[76] Sazonov was initially more hesitant to pursue the opening, but once the German warships arrived in the Dardanelles, he acted with alacrity. Indeed, at his prompting, the Entente soon developed a concerted approach to accommodating Turkey. But it reflected the kind of coordination that emerges when allies agree to accommodate a target but disagree about its strategic weight (see Figure 2). Russia "took the greatest initiative" in efforts to neutralize Turkey because it "saw most clearly what loss of the Straits to German control implied," while London and Paris avoided any concessions against their own priorities.[77] As Howard put it, although "neither France nor Britain . . . desired war with Turkey . . . they were unwilling to make the necessary sacrifices to conciliate [it]."[78]

On 15 August, Sazonov proposed to London and Paris a joint program for neutralizing Turkey. It contained three major elements. First, the Entente powers would guarantee Turkey's territorial integrity. Second, they would guarantee that Turkey would gain all German railroad concessions in Asia Minor and that transfer would be enshrined in the postwar peace treaty.[79] Third, in return, Turkey would begin military demobilization to signal its commitment to neutrality. Sazonov made it clear that Turkey needed a tripartite guarantee, because it was nervous about the Russia threat. As Howard observed, he "desired such a guarantee on the part of England and France, as he could scarcely hope to advance his Turkish negotiations without their complete support."[80] The next day, Sazonov proposed to the Allies two additional inducements: giving Turkey more territory in western Thrace and the Aegean island of Lemnos, which would augment Turkish control over the mouth of the Straits.[81]

Britain and France gutted Sazonov's proposals. France vetoed transferring Germany's concessions in Asia Minor—in particular the Baghdad Railway—fearing a precedent against French concessions.[82] French policymakers also opposed giving Turkey additional territory in Thrace. Paris wanted to reconstitute the Balkan League and turn it against Germany and Austria. That would require giving Bulgaria more territory in Thrace (from Greece) and Greece more territory in Epirus (from Serbia). The French calculated that this reformed Balkan bloc would also help to deter Turkey.[83] Grey, likewise, in his words, "strongly deprecated offering to Turkey any territorial concessions," such as giving it back the strategic island of Lemnos, which Greece had captured in 1912. Britain wanted Greece as an ally versus Germany, and promising Lemnos to Turkey would "alienate" it. Grey insisted that Britain "would not offer to Turkey any promises that meant injury to Greece."[84] Thus, by 18 August, the Entente could only agree to a "lackluster" inducement for Turkey's formal commitment to neutrality—a guarantee of territorial integrity for the duration of the war.[85]

On 19 August, Ottoman minister of finance, Mehmed Cavid Bey, met with Giers to emphasize that the Entente could strike an advantageous deal with Turkey but that it needed to offer "benefits . . . to give the conservative members of the Cabinet an effective weapon with which to combat the war-like colleagues who are under German influence." The deal that he proposed included "the grant to Turkey of complete economic independence and the suppression of the capitulations regime," which could be made contingent on the ejection of the German military advisors.[86] Sazonov was willing to support Cavid's proposals for immediate abolition on the condition that the Porte would ensure the subsequent protection of foreign nationals and interests.[87] To his British and French counterparts, Sazonov then proposed a tripartite declaration in Constantinople abolishing the capitulations, but "Russia's allies rejected" that option."[88] Sazonov was also willing to grant Turkey a "free hand with regard to commercial treaties." Yet, on this score too, his allies refused to give Turkey "entire liberty . . . in the matter of customs duties."[89] In sum, as Bobroff notes, "Sazonov was far more willing to agree with Turkish demands than his western allies."[90]

In addition, through meetings between Djemal and the British and French ambassadors, the Porte demanded robust territorial integrity guarantees from the Entente that would endure ten to fifteen years after the war. Fearing an Entente victory that left Russia dominant and unconstrained in the region, the Porte wanted Britain and France to each commit individually to upholding the integrity of the Ottoman Empire, in case Russia reneged.[91] On 21 August, the grand vizier relayed his need for "all the support that the Entente could give him. . . . The sooner they could give a written declaration respecting the independence and integrity of Turkey the better."[92] Sazonov encouraged the separate guarantees approach. The British, however, were just not willing to assume such far-reaching obligations or devise credible postwar promises. Consequently, the Entente declaration to uphold Ottoman territorial integrity that was eventually conveyed did not comprise bilateral guarantees and was not improved to address Turkey's long-term territorial integrity.

On 20 August, Djemal had also expressed several other desiderata. The Entente should promise to return the two warships embargoed by Britain, to transfer the Aegean islands taken by Greece and some land lost to Bulgaria, and to ensure that the Central powers also relinquished capitulations.[93] It is crucial to note that—with the exception of returning the battleships—these were all concessions Germany had approved. The Porte was asking as a price for remaining neutral what Germany would give it for intervening.[94]

The British poured cold water on the whole package: "The demands of the Turkish Government," wrote Grey, "are excessive."[95] Grey insisted on upfront commitments from Turkey to immediately send home the German crews on the warships *Goeben* and *Breslau* and to give written assurance of free passage of merchant shipping through the Straits and full compliance with obligations of neutrality. Only then would Britain agree to a partial modification of the capitulations' extraterritorial courts—to be implemented *after* Turkey had set up a modern "scheme of judicial administration"—and to give a "*joint* guarantee in writing [to] respect the independence and integrity of Turkey" during the war and in any end-of-war settlement.[96] Britain would not return the Turkish warships until after the war, and then only if it maintained "strict neutrality . . . without favour to the King's enemies."[97] On the capitulations, British officials calculated that an agreement to immediate abolition would have no influence on Turkey's alignment. London and Paris offered instead to consider some limited postwar adjustments to the economic elements of the regime, in return for a neutrality guarantee.[98] Contrary to the British thesis that Entente acceptance of the end of capitulations would not influence the Porte's alignment, historians surmise that it would have had a positive effect on both public opinion and the power of the proneutrality moderates in the Ottoman cabinet.[99]

In sum, "St. Petersburg was willing to concede more to the Porte than either Paris or London."[100] But consistent with the expected pattern of reciprocity in coordination, once Anglo-Franco shirking became evident, Russia matched it by refusing to make concessions on its special interest—support for Armenian minorities in Turkey.[101] On 28 August, the Allies presented their best bid to the Porte. This, Sazonov informed Giers, reflected a British proposal that he had accepted, and he expected "all three [Entente ambassadors] acting in concert [to] be guided by them in negotiations with the Porte."[102] The Entente thus offered to guarantee Turkey's territorial integrity for the duration of the war and not to impair it in a peace settlement, and to waive jurisdiction via the capitulations once a plan for guaranteeing justice that met modern conditions had been "perfected." In exchange, the Entente wanted Turkey to do three things immediately: to give a written commitment to remain neutral throughout the war's duration, to maintain free passage through the Straits of merchant shipping, and to send home the German naval and military personnel.[103]

"The Turks," writes Smith, "were unquestionably disappointed by the meagre Entente offer."[104] Meanwhile, Germany—with Austrian support—outbid the Entente on every dimension, and built up its political and military strength in Constantinople. Berlin and Vienna promised to support Turkish recovery of Aegean islands and territory in Thrace. They had begun to provide significant economic aid to energize Turkey's mobilization. The Porte removed British naval advisors from executive positions and assigned them to desks in the naval ministry, and London subsequently called them home.[105] German advisors filled their places on ships, and other specialists were sent to help bolster Turkish fortifications on the Straits.[106] And another piece supporting Ottoman intervention had fallen into place when Turkey and Bulgaria agreed on 19 August to form a defensive—but not offensive—alliance against Russia,.

The Entente had little opportunity, and diminishing hope, of keeping Turkey neutral after early September.[107] On 9 September, the Porte announced that it would soon abolish the capitulations.[108] Britain's response—that they could not be revoked unilaterally—fell on deaf ears.[109] After making a token gesture of joining the powers in an identical protest, Berlin and Vienna—having already secretly signaled "complete concurrence" with the Porte's move—let the matter drop.[110] The Entente powers were left scrambling on their own to negotiate provisional arrangements in view of an impending fait accompli.[111] When the capitulations were abolished on 1 October, the Entente had nothing to show for it.

Starting in early September, the Porte also multiplied its requests to Germany for men, material, and money to support military preparations. Berlin, on 10 September, began to ratchet up the pressure for prompt intervention, signaling that it would hold back further aid until Turkey took concrete action to enter the war. Constantinople shifted more overtly toward such action. This was not a moment when victory for the Central powers seemed imminent, but rather when "German armies [were] bogged down on the Western front and the news of heavy Habsburg losses [was] arriving from Galicia."[112] Berlin and Vienna ratcheted up pressure on the Porte for prompt intervention in order to divert Allied power.[113] The Entente powers were well informed of these communications and adopted a more menacing tone.[114] On 16 September, Grey delivered a cold warning: "So long as they maintain neutrality . . . we shall be prepared to consider reasonable concessions about the Capitulations; but they must not expect concessions from us while their present irregular conduct in the matter of German officers and crews continues [and] if they break peace we cannot be responsible for the consequences; we hope they will keep peace, but whether they do so or not is their own affair."[115] Ten days later, after a British patrol turned back a Turkish warship just outside the mouth of the Dardanelles, the Porte closed the Straits to all foreign shipping.[116]

On 20 September, under orders from Enver, several Turkish warships entered the Black Sea. The advocates for nonintervention in the Ottoman cabinet had clearly lost out. They had not started in a weak position. Enver and his prowar allies had worn down resistance from several powerful cabinet ministers with "anti-interventionist sentiments," which were also prevalent in the Committee of Union and Progress (CUP) and its larger party of Union and Progress.[117] Indeed, many of the contacts between the Turkish cabinet and the Entente were made by ministers in the anti-intervention camp: the grand vizier and foreign minister, Said Halim; the finance minister, Cavid; and the navy minister, Djemal.[118] Describing the internal politics of this period, Turkish historian Emin states that the anti-intervention moderates had "struggle[d] . . . to make the Entente pay a good price for Turkish neutrality, in order to be able to completely checkmate the partisans of war." When the Entente failed to offer serious concessions, those leaders were then left exposed to "an overwhelming pressure from the Germans."[119] In the end, the Central powers had offered Turkey "gains which far outdistanced anything [Britain] was willing to concede."[120]

On 9 October, Enver signaled to Berlin that there was now critical mass in the Ottoman cabinet in support of intervention; all that was wanting was German gold to finance the war effort. Berlin immediately agreed to send two million Turkish liras worth of bullion. On 12 October, the Porte sent Berlin a formal statement of war aims and strategic priorities, which the German political and military authorities endorsed.[121] On 16 October, Mallet reported that the cabinet ministers that favored neutrality were now "more or less powerless."[122] On 20 October, half of the German gold had arrived in Constantinople; the other half was on rails heading south. Russian intelligence followed these developments and anticipated that war with Turkey would soon begin.[123] On 28 October the Turkish fleet—including the German warships—steamed into the Black Sea, and the next day, the rupture came, with its naval raids against Odessa and Sebastopol and Russian and French ships.[124]

Summary and Alternatives

The Russian-led efforts to keep Turkey neutral failed because the Entente did not assemble inducements to Constantinople that could compete with the commitments Germany and Austria embraced. Even as Britain and France joined Russia in seeking accommodation, and considered Turkish neutrality to be a strategic interest, they coordinated to avoid sacrificing their particular interests and priorities. This approach, which also inhibited the kind of side compensations that could have facilitated a more generous joint offer, was reciprocated by Russia, once it became clear that its allies were holding out. Thus, the combined inducements they tendered amounted to little beyond the offer to respect Turkish territorial integrity during the war, and an over-the-horizon promise to consider reforms to the economic capitulations once it was over.

WAS OTTOMAN INTERVENTION INEVITABLE?

Three important historical propositions imply that this account is wrong, because Ottoman intervention was inevitable. The first holds that in autumn 1914 Germany captured Ottoman security policy decision making—through the position of the Liman von Sanders mission in the Ottoman army and its special ties to Enver—and dictated its preferred outcome.[125] Thus, a stronger offer would not have mattered because the Porte did not have the independence to take it. This line of argument has not held up in the face of serious historical research showing that Ottoman leaders—especially Enver—were not the pawns of Berlin, that they were assertive about protecting their military decision-making autonomy, that they doggedly deflected and blunted German pressure tactics, and that they remained sharply focused on advancing Ottoman security interests and not subordinating them to the ambitions of their allies.[126] On at least four major occasions in August to September, the Ottoman leadership rebuffed Germany's attempts to embroil them in war before they were ready to commit, on their own terms, to such a course.[127]

The second claim recognizes the Porte's freedom to decide, but holds that the Ottoman leaders were committed from the outset to the German alliance. Turkey's position was fixed on 2 August—it was "effectively a belligerent by virtue of its secret treaty with Germany," and the Porte's efforts to negotiate with the Entente were an elaborate ruse to cover preparations for an inevitable intervention.[128] If true, then a stronger Entente bid could not have deflected Constantinople from the Central alliance because the Ottoman leaders were simply unwilling to choose otherwise. There are several major problems with this line of argument. First, it suffers heavily from retrospective determinism. The facts used to support the unconditional commitment argument would also be consistent with the opposite assessment of Ottoman intentions if, in fact, Constantinople had refused to intervene.[129] Second, the argument for unconditional commitment, and the claim that feelers to the Entente were a charade, boil down to claims about *Enver's* attitudes and intentions. But the historians who make such claims *also* insist that Enver did not unilaterally decide Turkey's fate. Enver (as noted above) had to contend with and coopt prominent "anti-interventionist" cabinet ministers and their supporters in the larger Union Party.[130] If the Entente negotiations were, for Enver, a ruse, he did not initiate or control them all. Many of the contacts were made by anti-interventionist ministers who, seeking to sustain relations with the Entente, would not have shared Enver's tactical calculus. All of which points back to the conclusion that Ottoman commitment to enter the war with the Central powers was not inevitable in August and September 1914. A better Entente bid would have strengthened the ministers favoring nonintervention and undercut Enver and others who used German commitments and material largesse to bolster the case for their preferred policy.

The third proposition holds that Ottoman intervention was inevitable because strategic interests overdetermined Turkey's alignment against Russia. In particular, the legacy of Russo-Turkish rivalry and conflict over control of the Straits stacked the deck in favor of the Dual Alliance. Even if Britain and France had been more forthcoming, the Entente's approach would not have been able to overcome this constellation of geopolitical imperatives.

Against this high-altitude perspective are many historical facts that are inconsistent with it. To begin, in the years immediately preceding the war, the Ottoman government did not operate as though it was destined to align with Germany and against Russia. Instead, the Porte was "hesitant and divided" over how to align Turkey's international relationships.[131] In 1911, the Porte approached London about an alliance with the Entente for which, as noted before, Churchill had argued.[132] In June 1913, the Turks followed up their approach to Britain with new feelers for an alliance.[133] In May 1914, they sounded out Russia.[134] And in early July 1914, they made similar inquiries in Paris.[135] A powerful geopolitical interest disposing Turkey toward alliance with Germany and against Russia and the Entente should have prevented these overtures from ever happening.

Moreover, the construct of combined bilateral guarantees that the Porte floated to the Entente powers in August 1914 was meant to address precisely the concern about restraining Russia, and St. Petersburg supported that formula, but London and Paris did not. This again suggests that the active hostility between Turkey and Russia was not driven by unalterable strategic interests. Finally, it must be noted that—as chapter 9 shows—in World War II, the same enduring pattern of geopolitical interests and legacy of Russo-Turkish conflict did *not* drive Turkey to abandon its alignment with Britain and go to war with Russia in 1941, despite Germany's attempts to induce it to do so. In other words, against the strategic interest argument there stands a compelling nonevent: if geopolitical imperatives did not, in the best-case conditions of 1941, drive Turkey into the arms of Germany and war with Russia, there is good reason to believe that it was not inevitable that they would have in 1914. In sum, in August and September 1914, the Entente did have a chance to push the hedging Porte into permanent neutrality, *if* the Allies had offered an attractive bargain. But the Entente's bids came up paltry at best, and that favored the specific incentives extended by Germany, which induced Turkey to enter the war.[136]

The Entente Realigns Italy, 1915

If [Italy] can be induced to join us the Austrian Fleet would be powerless and the Mediterranean as safe as an English lake.

Winston Churchill, first lord of the Admiralty, 1915

Morally and materially, entrance of Italy would shorten the war.

Théophile Delcassé, French foreign minister, 1915

Italy's cooperation . . . ha[s] not the same value for us . . . and it would therefore be a mistake . . . to pay too high a price for it.

Sergei Sazonov, Russian foreign minister, 1915

In March 1915, Britain led its Entente allies, France and Russia, in an attempt to realign Italy. When the war began, Italy had defected from the Triple Alliance into hedged neutrality. The Entente wanted it to do one better and intervene on their side. While Italy's foreign policy leaders favored intervening—if the Entente promised big enough territorial gains—they faced strong proneutrality opposition in the legislature and public at large. The sweeping inducements amassed by the Entente helped the Italian government to weaken and marginalize that opposition, and in that way, the Entente successfully brought Italy into the war in May 1915.

The case highlights several important conditions and relationships in the theoretical framework. First, the Entente sought to achieve a high degree of alignment change: to convert Italy from a hedged neutral into a cobelligerent against its former allies. The theory expects that this would be a difficult alignment goal to achieve, because Italy would face high costs both for reneging on its alliance and for entering the war. To achieve this goal, then, the Entente needed to provide strong rewards to offset those costs and outbid Italy's erstwhile allies. Yet, the Entente allies faced high alliance constraints, which, if they disagreed about Italy's strategic weight, would make it hard for them to concert such rewards. Despite initial differences, the Entente allies did come to agree that Italy had war-tipping potential, and as the theory expects, they struck side bargains with each other in order to coordinate a powerful bid that well exceeded the bribes offered by Italy's erstwhile allies. This enabled the Italian government to defend a decision to intervene despite significant neutralist opposition, thus giving the Entente what it sought.[1]

Initiation Conditions

PERCEPTIONS OF TARGET'S STRATEGIC WEIGHT

The Entente began seriously to court Italy in early 1915. Britain initiated and drove that effort because its leaders started to see Italy as a war-tipper. As the British moved to force Turkish submission at the Straits, they became convinced that Italian intervention could decide the outcome, by weakening Austria-Hungary and setting loose a landslide of Balkan states joining the Entente.[2] Admiralty Lord Winston Churchill, for example, rated Italy's strategic weight thusly: "If she can be induced to join us the Austrian Fleet would be powerless and the Mediterranean as safe as an English lake."[3] This general view of Italy's strategic weight was seconded by France, but not, then, by Russia. Indeed, to Sergei Sazonov, Russia's foreign minister, the prospect of Italian intervention was "pretty well a matter of indifference to us." With the British ambassador in St. Petersburg, Sazonov did not mince words: because Italian "naval and military cooperation had lost much of its value," the Allies should "evade giving a definite answer" to Italian offers of "help."[4] St. Petersburg thus would drag down the negotiations through March with its resistance to making large concessions to Italy in the Adriatic. In April, though, escalating Russian defeats on the eastern front elevated St. Petersburg's estimate of Italy's value against Austria, and Russia's views of Italy's strategic weight shifted to match those of its allies.

PERCEPTIONS OF RELATIVE REWARD POWER

The Allies' effort to lure Italy into the war was guided by the understanding that strong inducements were needed to catalyze Rome's decision to take the fateful step. While key Italian foreign policy leaders might be inclined to intervene in return for advantageous terms, they faced formidable domestic opposition to doing so. Were it fully mobilized, that opposition could cashier the government and install one committed to neutralism. Moreover, Italy's current allies were themselves motivated to offer concessions that could foster these developments and thus lock Italy into a neutrality benevolent toward the Central powers.[5] The Entente's project, then, could succeed only if the Allies' approach both shored up the prestige and strength of the government in Rome and offered strong incentives for it to stay on the path to intervention. This, then, set the context and parameters of the

Entente's reward power potential: while a tightfisted or heavy-handed approach would weaken the Italian government that favored compliance, a more forthcoming one would bolster it domestically and catalyze compliance despite inside and outside countervailing pressures.

From the start of the war, the Entente leaders recognized that the Italian government, headed by Prime Minister Antonio Salandra, might intervene on their side if given a boost. As early as 9 August, the British ambassador to Italy, Rennell Rodd, described to British Foreign Minister Edward Grey a "growing tendency" in Italy suggesting "that she should join us is not inconceivable."[6] In the months that followed, Italy's leaders fed such hopes with repeated hints that favorable conditions could facilitate Italy's realignment. Thus, in late August 1914, the Italian foreign minister, the Marchese di San Giuliano, explained to the Russian ambassador that while "Italy intends to remain neutral to the end . . . circumstances might arise which might induce Italy" to join the war. Similarly, in early September 1914, Salandra admitted to Rodd that he thought Italy might "eventually be induced by circumstances" to intervene on the Allies' side.[7] The implication—that the Entente might furnish such inducing circumstances—was obvious.

More concretely, the Entente had in its actual or foreseeable grasp a potent mix of concessions and rewards with which to bargain. It was common knowledge that Italy sought territorial gains in the Tyrol, the Balkans, the Adriatic and Aegean Seas, and Turkey. Promises of territories torn from the Entente's enemies, as well other territorial gains, were thus prime currency. The logic of accommodating Italy's expansionist impulse was expressed, on a small scale, in the Allies' decision (detailed later) to acquiesce to its occupation of Valona, Albania, in October 1914.

Much larger stakes were on the horizon. The Italian foreign minister had, for example, signaled that any "decisive" military action by the Entente in the Adriatic—which might raise the prospect of the area falling under Slav control—would inspire Italy to join the Entente in order to "peg out claims for the future."[8] The Allies recognized also that once they began to attack the Dardanelles, the lure of gains in Turkey would become potent in Rome. San Giuliano admitted to Rodd that in such circumstances, the "prospect of Italy joining [the Entente] is not very remote."[9] Churchill would later describe the Turkish bait as "the real 'motor muscles' of Italian resolve" to intervene.[10] "The attraction of Italy as a co-belligerent" thus became one of the major goals of the "allies' attempt to force the Dardanelles."[11] In February 1915, when Allied attacks began, Rodd advised Grey that it was time to formulate "some definite offer," as there was now growing in Rome "general anxiety that Italy may lose title to have any voice in settlement in Asia Minor [and] that if a decision is not taken now it may be too late."[12] Knowing that Italy sought a piece of partitioned Turkey, they were ready to offer it an "appropriate share of the Mediterranean region adjacent to the province of Adalia [Antalya]."[13]

Beyond exploiting the lure of Turkey (an option obviously unavailable to Germany and Austria), the Entente powers also had the potential, if not the desire, to transfer concessions to Italy from their own positions in the Mediterranean and Middle East. For example, in March 1915, Rome dropped hints that in return for undertaking the "arduous task" of fighting Austria, it sought a "commensurate reward" that included a "rectification of frontier between Tripoli and Tunis, or some equivalent concession from France."[14] The Allies also were apprised of Italy's interest in "corresponding and equitable compensation" further afield—in Somalia and Eritrea—when the Allies took over German colonies elsewhere in Africa.[15]

Italy's economic woes opened up another channel for Entente inducements. As early as 16 September 1914, San Giuliano had hinted to Rodd that because of Italy's "unsatisfactory economical and financial conditions" and the likelihood of a war "of long duration," Italy would need to "raise a loan which would defer immediate pressure on the people of financial strain." Britain and France, then, would need to "see their way to helping to raise [a] loan" if Italy were to decide to join the fight.[16] In the succeed months, Grey would leverage this point, promising that "if Italy did join us we would facilitate the raising of a loan."[17] When Italy and the Allies sealed the deal in May 1915, Britain delivered with a loan of £60 million.[18]

Developments internal to the Salandra government added to Entente beliefs about the potential to induce Italian allegiance. San Giuliano, who died in October, had been the architect of Italy's hedged position, and Entente leaders perceived him to be, at heart, in favor of reaping the benefits of a long game of neutrality. His passing portended new possibilities. With it came a broader shake-up in Salandra's government in November 1914, which brought in a new foreign minister, Sidney Sonnino, and new finance, war, and colonial ministers, all with hawkish leanings.[19] This, Rodd advised Grey, improved "the prospect of Italy's finally ranging herself on the side of the allies." Rodd reported that Sonnino, in particular, "believes that Italy must eventually be drawn into the struggle, and that he even anticipates that circumstances may precipitate such an eventuality."[20] In January 1915, Rodd informed Grey that the "most conspicuous members" of Salandra's government were then "individually in favor of seeing Italy seize the opportunity of realizing her destiny . . . and convinced she must earn her right to have voice in the [war's] settlement."[21] Thus, the situation was ripe for an Entente initiative. If the Entente allies were willing to be generous, they had a strong hand relative to an Italy looking to profit from war, and to its abandoned allies still hoping to keep it sidelined. Willingness, then, was the critical question—would the Entente allies reach enough consensus about Italy's strategic weight to support a handsome and credible offer?

Contingent Conditions

ATTEMPTED ALIGNMENT CHANGE

What the Entente sought was a high degree of alignment change. Italy was hedged between neutrality and its commitment to the Triple Alliance; the Entente wanted to flip it into a formal ally and active belligerent. That was ambitious. To put it in context, one needs to consider Italy's position on the eve of war.

In August 1914, it was still a formal ally of Germany and Austria-Hungary. It had joined the Triple Alliance in 1882 and had even recommitted twice, most recently in December 1912 (when it extracted the promise of compensation if Austria made gains in the Balkans).[22] Its military strategy in 1914 reflected its formal alliance commitments. When the July Crisis started, the Italian General Staff expected and prepared to send troops to support German operations on the Rhine. German military leaders, also, more or less expected Italy's support against France.[23]

But Italy's alliance commitments and military plans were, even then, hedged by a secret diplomatic track with France. The rapprochement with France began with an 1898 agreement to end the Franco-Italian tariff war, a 1900 concord on imperial claims in North Africa, and a secret agreement in 1902 that Italy would remain neutral in a war between France and the Central powers.[24] And Italy had, as well, important conflicts of interest with Austria-Hungary. Those conflicts reached into the Balkans but were most intense over the irredenta, Trentino and Trieste, territories of intrinsic value to Vienna, which Italians claimed as unredeemed national territories.

Italy's prompt declaration of neutrality on 3 August 1914 was surprising in some ways, and had important and immediate strategic consequences.[25] But given the background, it was not a shock in Vienna, where suspicion of Italian treachery ran deep.[26] Italy, however, did not brazenly disavow its alliance commitment. Instead, it invoked loopholes—because Austria's action could provoke a general war, which ran counter to the defensive purpose of the alliance, and it had not consulted with Italy beforehand, Italy was not legally obligated to fight. Rome signaled that if Vienna wanted to preserve the alliance it would need to promptly compensate Italy for Austrian expansion in Serbia, as had been agreed in 1912. As the Austrian ambassador in Rome put it, Italy wanted "her attitude [to] be purchased on the principle of cash payment before delivery."[27] Italy thus began the war as a defected neutral. If there was little chance Italy would enter the war on the side of the Central powers, the question remained, would it stay out or switch allegiances and fight?

Thus, over the first nine months of the war, there was intense bargaining between Italy and the opposing alliances. Berlin—and with less enthusiasm, Vienna—tried to keep Italy at least benevolently neutral.[28] By early 1915,

Britain, France, and with less enthusiasm, Russia, were searching for a price sufficient to buy Italy into the fight. Ultimately, Italy would either be bribed by its putative allies to stay friendly or bought by the Entente to betray them.

ALLIANCE CONSTRAINTS

The Entente's high alliance constraints made that difficult to do. As explained in chapter 4, Britain, France, and Russia were relative equals in the alliance, and they were strategically dependent on each other. Britain and France counted on Russian fighting in the east to divert Germany's war effort on the western front; Russia counted on the Western Allies to do likewise, and to transfer desperately needed war material and aid. The prospect of Italy's intervention raised big questions about the parceling out of war gains among them. Italy, just as the others, had eyes on Turkish territory, and its Adriatic ambitions conflicted with Russia's Balkan interests and aspirations for Serbia.[29] Above these parochial tensions stood the general strategic value of alliance cohesion, which could be sacrificed only at the risk of a crushing German victory. The Entente allies could neither afford to ignore each other's priorities in respect to Italy's role nor take a detached attitude about the terms of its entry. Britain, as leader of the Entente's efforts to induce Italian intervention, had no choice but to bargain with allies with direct stakes and equal weight in determining the alliance's relations with Italy. As Grey assured Sazonov in March 1915, "No conditions for co-operation of any Power would be agreed to except by France, Great Britain, and Russia, in consultation and agreement with each other."[30]

ALLIED STRATEGIC CONSENSUS

When Britain began to push seriously for a deal with Italy, the Allies did not agree about Italy's strategic weight. British leaders perceived Italy to be a war-tipper because of its potential to weaken Austria militarily, and because it seemed to be the linchpin that would swing other Balkan neutrals to the Entente's side. Thus, in March 1915, Grey explained to the French and Russian foreign ministers, "The participation on our side of Italy and the Balkan states would enormously facilitate th[e] object [of winning the war]; it probably would, in a comparatively short time, effect the collapse of German and Austro-Hungarian resistance."[31] France shared this perspective: "Morally and materially," wrote the French foreign minister, Théophile Delcassé, "entrance of Italy would shorten the war."[32]

But Sazonov did not buy it.[33] As Britain approached Italy in March, Sazonov conveyed his "misgivings" about Italy and advised his allies to "evade" its offers of help.[34] To Grey's and Delcassé's protestations of Italy's strategic weight, Sazonov replied: "Italy's cooperation . . . had not the same value for us . . . and it would therefore be a mistake . . . to pay too high a price for it."[35] Consequently, throughout March and into early April 1915, Russian recalcitrance bogged down the Anglo-Franco initiative to realign Italy.[36] But later in April (as detailed below), Russian perceptions of Italy's war-tipping potential shifted into accord with those of British and French leaders. That prompted a fairly rapid conclusion of the negotiations over terms of Italian intervention. In this process of coordination, the Entente allies struck important bargains with each other that enabled them to make a compelling offer that won Italy over.

Diplomacy of Selective Accommodation

The Entente first sifted the possibility of Italian intervention in August and September 1914. This was triggered by a comment made by the Italian ambassador to Russia on 4 August, suggesting that Italy would intervene if it were guaranteed Trentino, the port of Valona in Albania, and a "preponderant position in the Adriatic."[37] Sazonov seized on this opportunity and was apparently willing to meet Italy's requests, given "the vital importance of getting Italian cooperation" at that moment.[38] Britain agreed. As Grey wrote George Buchanan, the British ambassador to Russia, the Entente "would derive the utmost advantage from Italy's cooperation at the present time," and he was prepared to see Valona, Trentino, and Trieste "being allotted to Italy" in exchange. Paris, meanwhile, also approved of this arrangement.[39] But timing was a stumbling block: the Entente needed Italy to intervene immediately; Italy, unprepared for war, needed time. Once Italy proved unable to act quickly, Sazonov declared that its help had "become less valuable to us."[40] British and French officials agreed, and the Entente pulled back.

Going forward, Britain was the ringleader of Entente efforts to accommodate Italy.[41] This became clear in late September when Italy decided to occupy Valona. Internal disturbances in the area had opened up the possibility that Greece would intervene to establish order and thus frustrate Italy's aim to control the Albanian coast. As Italy made ready to step in preemptively, the Entente faced a choice—protest the move or welcome it. For Russia, protest was called for.[42] St. Petersburg was not then ready to see Italian gains in the Balkans, and it envisioned Albania partitioned by Serbia and Greece. Moreover, Italy now intended to assert its Valona claim unilaterally, even though it had previously floated it as one prize for entering the war. Russia wanted to block Italy unless it committed to intervene. Salandra, however, convinced Grey that Italy's occupation of Valona should be considered "the preface to other engagements which we hoped to conclude [which] would be more difficult of accomplishment if the nation gained the impression that we had been thwarted . . . by the Entente. If the government is to act in another sense (as we hope) it will need a kind of prestige which could only result from the occupation of Valona."[43] Hence, it was clear, as Grey explained to Francis Bertie, his ambassador in Paris, "If we oppose this step we shall impair . . . the chances of Italy joining us." Britain thus met Russia's wish to protest with the argument that it would be better to endorse the fait accompli and thereby cultivate Italy's favor. After Grey's lobbying, the Entente agreed to "raise no objection" to Italy's move.[44]

But the stakes in Albania were small. When it came to Italy's wider desiderata in the Adriatic and Mediterranean, Grey would not push for concessions that stirred up controversy in the Entente, to curry a merely "hypothetical attitude" on Italy's part.[45] Once Italy was ready to fight, then they would talk. When Italy in October probed again for a deal that would give it (in addition to Trentino and Trieste) the whole of Dalmatia, Britain thus declined to engage, knowing that this request would incite strong Russian protests. As Grey later put it to Bertie, "We cannot promise definite concessions to Italy while she is not co-operating with us. On the other hand, we must be careful not to drive her into the opposite camp."[46]

Meanwhile, Italy negotiated with the Central powers.[47] German diplomacy first aimed to persuade Italy to declare war against the Entente, but soon shifted to the more realistic goal of "confirming her present attitude" of neutrality.[48] Austria balked at German pressure to make concessions for that purpose. With German backing, Italy demanded that Austria give up the Trentino as compensation for its gains in the Balkans.[49] After first rejecting this concession out of hand, Austria-Hungary's foreign minister, Leopold Berchtold, had second thoughts, and with backing from Berlin, tried to win agreement for it within his own government.[50] Having failed, he replied to Italy in January 1915 that its takeover of Valona should be sufficient compensation.[51] That was Berchtold's swan song. For his efforts to convince his colleagues to give up Trentino, he was rewarded with retirement. His replacement, Baron von Burian, meant to take a hard line against any Italian demands for compensation "consisting in a slice of our own flesh."[52]

By February, then, Italo-Austrian negotiations had reached an apparent dead end, and Italy withdrew the formula for the cession of Trentino.[53] Sonnino, working in secret, was putting the final touches on a program of demands to present to the Entente.[54] As Rodd had reported from Rome in late January, Salandra and Sonnino were "realizing that that the time is not far distant when this country may enter the valley of decision."[55] The Entente's operations in Salonika and against Turkey increased Rome's sense of urgency. Still, the Entente held back: they understood that Italy's ambitions were large.[56]

The conclusive round of Entente-Italy negotiations did not start until early March. That was when the Italian ambassador to Britain floated Sonnino's extensive list of conditions—sixteen in all. These included a number of important territorial compensations and adjustments infringing not only on Austria-Hungary and Turkey, but also on the positions of the Entente powers and their protégés. In particular, the Entente was asked to guarantee Italian gains in the Trentino and South Tyrol, Gradisca and Gorizia, Trieste and the Istrian peninsula, and islands in the Gulf of Quarnero; Dalmatia and its offshore islands; Saseno and Valona in Albania (with the rest of the Albanian coastline to be neutralized, whether taken by Serbia, Montenegro, or Greece); and territory around Antalya if the Ottoman Empire collapsed. Finally, if the other powers gained empire at Germany's expense, they were to compensate Italy by enlarging its holdings in Somalia, Eritrea, and Libya "with adjacent French possessions."[57]

On 8 March, Burian and the Vienna cabinet relented and agreed to cede the Trentino in exchange for Italian neutrality and a German promise to ensure Austria a free hand in the Balkans. Behind the reversal was the Dual Monarchy's deteriorating military position and its fear that Italian intervention would bring Romanian intervention.[58] But the mere cession of the Trentino would not now satisfy Italy. Vienna still refused to give up Trieste and a border on the Isonzo, and any other positions in the Adriatic and Dalmatia. Further diluting the credibility of its concession, Vienna insisted that it would not transfer the Trentino until after the war. That uncertain, distant payoff was a deal breaker for Sonnino.[59]

Britain, meanwhile, became eager to close the deal with Italy. It had expected the start of naval operations against the Turkish Straits in mid-February to propel a wave of Balkan bystanders—Greece, Bulgaria, and Romania—into the Entente. When that did not happen, "Italian adhesion" came to be seen as something that could "turn the scale . . . in deciding the Balkan waverers," with decisive effects on the outcome of war.[60] Russia, however, remained opposed to big rewards for Italy. To soften this position, London made a significant side bargain with St. Petersburg on control of the Straits if Constantinople fell. On 4 March, Russia, aware that Italy was maneuvering for a hand in Turkey, had sent a note to Britain and France staking its claim. Britain decided to recognize Russia's demands—thus discarding its hallowed policy of opposing Russia at the Straits. That decision, too, reflected London's perception of the strategic value of Italian intervention and the need to win Russian backing of concessions to Italy in the Adriatic.[61] France initially wanted to block Russia's Straits claim. The French president, Raymond Poincaré, sent St. Petersburg a protest. Once Britain agreed, however, France fell into line, but only after gaining Russian agreement to a temporary Anglo-Franco wartime government in Constantinople, if the Allies succeeded in taking the city. Such would enable the Allies to oversee their Ottoman interests during the transition to Russian control.[62]

With Entente naval operations in the Straits thwarted in mid-March, British and French leaders latched onto Italian intervention as the key to saving the situation. On 23 March, Grey instructed his ambassador in Russia to explain to Sazonov that "Italian cooperation will decide that of Roumania and probably some other neutral states. It will be the turning point in the war and very greatly hasten a successful conclusion of the conflict."[63] On

25 March, Prime Minister Asquith explained to the king that the "importance of bringing in Italy without delay appeared to be so great that it was agreed to give general consent to what she asks and to press Russia to do the same." Delcassé shared this assessment of Italy's war-tipping importance, stating to the British ambassador that "he would be ready to pay almost any price for Italian cooperation as he thinks it would bring to us Roumania and Greece and Bulgaria."[64]

Russia decided to defer to its allies: it would support any bargain that Britain and France could agree to that would bring Italy into the war—with one major exception.[65] Russia would not allow Italy to gain any of the Dalmatian coastline south of Split.[66] Italy, however, was arguing that its national security required control of both sides of the Adriatic down to Montenegro. British and French leaders, feeling the imperative to bring Italy into the war quickly, embraced the Italian arguments.[67] In late March they jointly presented Italy's full proposal to Russia, urging prompt approval because Italy's immediate intervention could turn the course of the war.[68] But Russia remained unwilling to sign off.

Because Russia's hope that they would fulfill the agreement on the Straits gave them leverage, Britain and France pressed Russia to sacrifice more Serb interests in the Adriatic. In late March, Russia agreed to concede a northern portion of the Dalmatian coast from Zara to Cape Planka, with the rest of the coastline down to Albania to fall to Serbia. Britain then proposed to Italy that it relinquish its claim to Split and the coastline around it, in exchange for the guarantee that the territory be neutralized. Italy came back with the proposal to give Serbia the coastline from just north of Split, and five adjacent islands, with guarantees that this would all be neutralized territory, and in exchange for all of the other coastal islands and the peninsula of Sabbioncello.

Russia rejected that Italian proposal, but offered a little bit more. It would allow the entire coastline from Zara in the north to Cattaro in the south (at the northern border of Montenegro), and the adjacent islands, to be neutralized. Italy could have four of the islands, but the rest of them, and the peninsula of Sabbioncello, would go to Serbia, and nothing south of the Narenta would be neutralized. St. Petersburg indicated that it would not budge further. Britain turned Russia's latest bid into a formal Entente offer and passed it to Italy. Rome rejected it and hinted that it would end negotiations. After Italy's reply, Russia did budge: Italy's portion of the Dalmatian coastline and its four coastline islands would not have to be neutralized.

France weighed in next. The French proposed that if Italy agreed to a neutralized, Serbian Sabbioncello, Russia should allow neighboring islands (Curzolari) to go to Italy, without requiring them to be neutralized. French pressure coincided with a turn for the worse for Russia on the battlefield. Although the Russian military had advocated Italian intervention, Sazonov and the tsar remained doubters. But the Russian position in the Carpathians deteriorated sharply in April, and the Grand Duke Nicholas, commander in chief of Russian armies, impressed on Sazonov that "at this very moment, Italy's intervention would be of particular importance."[69] It would force the Austrians to weaken their eastern front, which might allow the Russian offensive to regain momentum and knock Vienna out of the war. In view of that, "Serbia could accept a few sacrifices," argued the grand duke. "It would be quite sorrowful" if for Serbia's sake "we deprived ourselves of Italy's military help, needed by us and our allies."[70] That convinced Sazonov to give more to get Italy into the war. As Stevenson sums it, "The stalling of the Russian's progress on the Eastern Front in April . . . persuaded [St. Petersburg] to value Italian entry more highly at Serbia's expense, making possible a compromise."[71] Russia's estimates of Italy's strategic weight now approximated those of its allies. In a plea to the tsar for more flexibility to sacrifice Serbia's prospective gains, Sazonov argued, "We are not fighting alone. The Allies' mutual obligations as members of a coalition must take precedence over solely Russian interests."[72] Russia then accepted the French proposal and passed responsibility to Britain to hammer out the details. That breakthrough consummated the bargain. Italy raised a few subsequent amendments that Russia did not oppose.

There were, nevertheless, two more obstacles to surmount. The first was Italy's surprising request on 9 April for a month's delay before entering the war. Russia, which had caved to so many demands on the premise of immediate Italian action, came close to ditching the whole arrangement. Personal letters to the tsar from Poincaré and King George V averted the Russian veto. In return for its cooperation, Russia extracted another promise on the Straits. Sazonov wanted to require Italy to formally endorse all of the Allies' prior understandings, but that risked further delay. Britain and France agreed instead to secretly exchange notes with Russia redoubling their commitments to the prior Straits agreement.[73]

The more serious complication was Italian domestic politics. As Hamilton and Herwig note, when Italian leaders secretly signed the Pact of London on 26 April, they "were, in effect, giving a promissory note. Fulfilling that promise, actually taking the nation into the war, brought a major political crisis . . . since most Italians still approved the current policy, that is, neutrality."[74] Indeed, the leader of the Italian chamber's left-wing liberals, Giovanni Giolitti, had come out strongly in favor of staying neutral in exchange for a "good deal" from Austria.[75] In February he had published a letter in the *Tribuna* of Rome asserting that Italy's goals for territorial expansion could be largely satisfied through a bargain with Vienna.[76] To stave off the coalescing political forces against intervention, Salandra recessed the chamber from 22 March to 12 May. After the king signed the Pact of London, Salandra received reports on public opinion from all of Italy's prefects. Those "conclusively demonstrated that Italy was solidly neutralist in sentiment."[77] Most parties and voting blocs in the chamber were against intervention. Going into May, "the majority of the Chamber favored continued neutrality."[78]

On 13 May, after having surveyed the party leaders in the chamber and found "that only one . . . was in favor of war," Salandra and his cabinet decided to submit their resignations. King Victor Emmanuel—whose signature was about to be disowned—chose to delay rather than immediately accept Salandra's resignation. There followed four days of great uncertainty over whether Italy would follow through. Giolitti rallied the opposition and spread word that the chamber could nullify any secret agreement between Salandra and the Entente with a four-fifths vote for a new government that opposed intervention. The mobilization of Italian armed forces was put on hold during the interregnum.[79]

News that Salandra's government had tendered its resignation triggered large prointervention protests in Italy's major cities. The upsurge in support for war among the middle class and intellectuals, who joined nationalist factions in calling for intervention, was fueled by general knowledge of the gains promised to Italy in the London agreement.[80] Indications of the scope of territorial concessions quickly leaked from French papers into the uncensored Italian press. By the political crisis of 13 to 17 May, "rumors of the Pact of London were already commonplace," and it was understood that Italy had been promised major portions of the Adriatic littoral.[81] It was also then known that the king had exchanged personal letters with Entente heads of state concerning Italy's intent to intervene. The popular outpouring of support for the king and expansion into the Balkans demoralized the chamber's proneutrality champions. Giolitti did not step forward to form the antiintervention government that he could have given his base of support. As Renzi summarizes his predicament, "If he assumed office and annulled the King's pledge of intervention while reaching an accord with [Austria]" he "would have given Italy less than the Entente could promise."[82] On 17 May, King Victor Emmanuel refused Salandra's resignation offer and asked his government to resume. Within days, the chamber, "forsaken by their leader, Giolitti, and knowing now the extent of the King's involvement . . . gave the government full powers 'in case of war' by 407 votes to 74."[83] The Senate followed with unanimous approval.[84] On 22 May Italian forces resumed mobilization, and two days later, Italy officially entered the war.

Summary and Alternatives

The Entente allies' attempt to induce Italy's realignment was a clear success despite their high alliance constraints. The process that brought that about conforms to the patterns of coordination and influence expected to operate when there is a strong allied strategic consensus. Once the Allies' assessments of Italy's strategic weight converged at a high level, they offered Italy a generous and credible package of inducements. And they made side bargains with each other in order to make the scheme work. Britain and France assented to Russia's claim on the Straits and Russia sacrificed the strategic and territorial interests of its Slav protégés, Serbia in particular. The strength of the resulting bid was key to Italy's final movement into the war. It bested what the Central powers could offer to keep Italy neutral, and that helped the interventionists in Rome overcome domestic opposition and carry the decision through the governing crisis in May.

Two arguments suggest, however, that the quality of the Entente's bargain mattered little. The first points to Italy's exposed geographical position—in particular, its long Mediterranean and Adriatic coastlines—that rendered it vulnerable to British naval power and influence.[85] Given such exposure, one might surmise that in a major European war Italy would have little choice but to follow the dictates of the situation, and thus join with Britain and the Entente. As an explanation for why Italy entered the war on the side of the Entente, this line of argument suffers from two significant flaws.[86] The first is logical: it conflates the ability to deter with something that is much harder to achieve—the ability to compel.[87] If the implicit threat of British naval punishment was sufficient to ensure Italy's neutrality when the war broke out, it could not compel Italy to realign.[88] Indeed, because Italy remained formally allied to the Central powers, any overt attempt by the Britain to coerce Italy into joining the war on the Entente side would be likely to provoke the opposite response. The second flaw is that (as shown in chapter 6) the premise is contradicted by the facts of 1939 to 1940. Then, under similar geopolitical constraints and exposure to British naval power, Italy first adopted a de facto neutral position (as it did in 1914) but then jumped into the war against Britain when the Allies seemed beaten in France, but the British navy still dominated the Mediterranean. Italy's exposure to British naval power can explain its tendency to defect from alliance commitments and adopt a wait-and-see neutrality, but cannot explain why Italy would depart from neutrality to attack its erstwhile allies.

The second argument emphasizes the intensity of the Italian-Austrian conflict latent in the Triple Alliance. It is true that a major purpose of the Triple Alliance was to manage the friction between Rome and Vienna by "tethering" the two countries together.[89] And that, one could argue, meant that in a major war, it would take little effort by an outside power to ignite the conflict and realign Italy against Austria-Hungary. This argument has several weaknesses. It exaggerates the strength of the prointervention (i.e., anti-Austrian) forces in Italian politics at the time. Although there was a widely shared sense of grievance about the irredenta under Austrian control, in the run-up to war there was also broad and intense support for a policy of neutrality both at the level of the masses and in the Italian legislature.[90] There was also at work in Italian politics lingering public anger against France for its impositions on Italian national and imperial claims.[91] Italy also viewed

Savoy, Nice, and Corsica as unredeemed national territories and in 1911 to 1912, during the Libyan war, "Italo-Franco relations fell to a lower ebb than at any time in the previous decade."[92] That Italy would try to use the war to satisfy national aims may have been inevitable, but that it would choose to do so by warring against Austria-Hungary was not. The Entente powers grasped—correctly—that Italian intervention was not automatic: it would take strong inducements to bring Italy around.

Britain and France Fail to Neutralize Italy, 1936–40

Italian neutrality, if it could by any means be assured, would be decidedly preferable to her active hostility.

British cabinet, Committee of Imperial Defence,
July 1939

Italy was now in Germany's hands. . . . The worst thing France could do would be to yield.

Édouard Daladier, prime minister of France,
May 1939

Between 1936 and 1940 Britain tried to accommodate Italy, first to keep it from allying with Germany and then to keep it from entering the war on Germany's side. Throughout, British leaders believed that Italy had high strategic weight, and that they had reward power to influence its alignment. But they faced high alliance constraints. Britain could not decouple its relations with Italy from its relations with France, and not just British but also French concessions were needed to detach Italy. Together they controlled immediate rewards—material and symbolic—that Italy prized and could not obtain in other ways or without their assistance. Yet, London and Paris often disagreed about how to deal with Italy, due to divergent perceptions of Italy's strategic weight. Such frictions both hobbled their attempts to reach a bargain with Italy that would halt the trend of worsening relations that led to Italy's alliance with Germany in May 1939 and abetted Hitler's decisions to plunge into war later that summer.

That formation of the "Pact of Steel" splits this case into two parts. The first (A) runs from late 1936 to May 1939, when the British and French tried to keep Italy from making a formal alliance with Germany. The second (B) runs from May 1939 to June 1940, when they tried to promote Italy's defection from the alliance, and after August 1939, its nonbelligerence. Thus, the degree and difficulty of alignment change they sought changed over time.

This case highlights the challenges of concerting accommodation. Across both periods, the Allies were well positioned to influence Rome, *if* they coordinated well. They did not. Weak strategic consensus and Allied discord led to contradictory diplomacy, limited influence, and successive failures. This is particularly obvious *before* Italy formally allied with Germany, when the opportunity to neutralize Italy was large. Yet, process tracing also shows junctures in which the mechanisms that promote success took effect. British and French views of Italy's strategic value, and how to deal with it, sometimes converged; they brought their approaches to Italy into accord and achieved some observable (albeit fleeting) success. Notably, this occurred even *after* Italy had formally allied with Germany and became harder to neutralize.[1]

Initiation Conditions

PERCEPTIONS OF TARGET'S STRATEGIC WEIGHT

Starting in 1936, Britain initiated and led Anglo-Franco efforts to accommodate Italy. To British leaders, Italy had high strategic weight.[2] They believed that an Italian-German alliance would hasten war and that keeping Italy neutral would prevent or delay it. Thus, after the Anglo-Italian Gentleman's Agreement of January 1937—the product of Britain's first major push to accommodate Italy—Robert Vansittart, the permanent undersecretary for foreign affairs, wrote that by so "loosen[ing] the Italo-German tie," Britain would "have a more reasonable, or anyhow tamer, Germany to deal with."[3] If war with Germany did come, the British also believed that Italy could tip the war for or against them, depending on whether it intervened. An expected alignment ripple effect was part of their calculus. If Italy intervened, Japan would be more likely to as well. And Britain did not have the strength to fight that constellation of enemies. To fight Germany and Italy at the same time, Britain would have to sacrifice its defense in Asia.[4] But if war with Germany could not be avoided, fighting Italy too *could* be. British leaders "refused to accept that Italy posed an irreversible threat."[5] Indeed, they believed both that it was possible to keep Italy nonbelligerent and that doing so would help them to defeat Germany. They hewed to the advice of their military commanders in the Mediterranean: "In [a] war with Germany, it is of the highest importance that Italy should be kept out. . . . Our primary object should be to influence Italy to remain neutral."[6]

British leaders believed they had high relative reward power because Mussolini craved good relations with Britain and prized the freedom of action and prestige of a foreign policy not mortgaged to German priorities or clout.[7] They also recognized that they, working with France, uniquely controlled resources that were quite important to Italy. Their dominant position in the League gave them the ability to withhold (or grant) League recognition of Italian conquests and offer their own unilateral recognition (which would influence the choices of many others). Another point of leverage lay in their ability to strengthen or weaken support for the Republican government in Spain, which was resisting the Fascist forces backed by Mussolini. Finally, both London and Paris had positions in the Mediterranean and Middle East that were prized by Italy and subject to some compromise. For example, Rome wanted a seat on the Suez Canal board (which the British and French could grant or deny) and concessions from France over control of Tunisia and French Somalia. Of course, not all of these interests were to be thrown to Italy willy-nilly. But if they worked together, Britain and France were well positioned to influence Italy's alignment.

Contingent Conditions

ATTEMPTED ALIGNMENT CHANGE

Over time, their attempts to neutralize Italy sought different degrees of alignment change. Before the Pact of Steel, the Allies sought a low degree of change—they tried to reinforce Italy's formal neutrality and strategic independence from Germany. The goal, as put by Anthony Eden, the British foreign secretary in 1937, was to lessen "the probability of the formation of a firm German-Italian bloc."[8] This was an easier alignment goal to achieve through inducements. After the Pact of Steel, Britain and France had to do more: they had to detach Italy from its fixed alliance with Germany. At a minimum, their goal was to restore to Italy the freedom of action that it had sacrificed by entering the pact. As Lord Halifax, the British foreign minister in 1939, put it, the aim was to induce "Italy to sit more loosely to her Axis commitments."[9]

ALLIANCE CONSTRAINTS

Britain and France faced high alliance constraints: they were peer allies, highly dependent on each other in respect to security in Europe and the Mediterranean. Inevitably, French interests, actions, and postures in the region impinged on relations between Britain and Italy, and vice versa. So it was with all the major issues gripping Anglo-Italian relations: League recognition of Italy's Ethiopian empire; intervention in the Spanish Civil War; subversion in the Levant mandates; colonial claims in the Mediterranean and North Africa; the Anschluss and the Munich crisis. Britain also depended on France to help balance the German threat and maintain security in the Mediterranean, so it needed to cultivate France as a reliable ally. France faced the same constraints in reverse, but even more so.[10] If their strategic interdependence was inevitable, harmony was not. With respect to the goal of neutralizing Italy, the situation demanded tightly concerted accommodation. Britain and France, however, would struggle to "harmoniz[e] their policies" toward Italy.[11]

ALLIED STRATEGIC CONSENSUS

Between them, the quality of strategic consensus vis-à-vis Italy varied considerably. While several times it came together, it did not last, and often it was absent. Thus, it is coded as "mixed" in this case. They mostly agreed on the goal of separating Italy from Germany but they did not always agree about how to do it. For Britain, that goal necessarily implied accommodating Italy. French leaders, however, often favored intimidation and recoiled from concessions.[12]

Between 1936 and 1940, British and French perceptions of Italy's strategic weight swung between disarray and convergence. British leaders believed that keeping Italy neutral would help to prevent or delay war, because Hitler would be deterred from starting one without firm Italian allegiance. In April 1938, for example, Chamberlain responded to French warnings of Italy's increasing alignment with Germany by urging them "not to forget the great improvement which had taken place in relations between Great Britain and Italy"; by so playing their cards "carefully and wisely," the Allies could do much to "exercise the deterrent influence on Germany."[13] British leaders also believed that Mussolini had incentives—which could be capitalized on—to act as a brake on Hitler.[14] Mussolini, as Chamberlain put it, "dislikes or fears the Germans and will welcome anything which will make him less dependent on them."[15] To activate such possibilities, the Allies would need to continue to promote accommodation with Italy even as it drifted into Germany's orbit.[16] That thesis drove Chamberlain and Halifax's decision to negotiate directly with Mussolini in Rome in late 1938. For Chamberlain, "the definite purpose" was to persuade Mussolini "to prevent Herr Hitler from carrying out some 'mad dog act.'"[17] British officials also expected that successful Anglo-Italian deals would foster subsequent Franco-Italian ones, which would reinforce the tendencies described above.[18]

French leaders were often less sanguine about such possibilities, though there were always some that agreed with London's approach. French army leaders in particular "viewed Italy as strategically crucial to the future war against Nazi Germany. A friendly or neutral Italy would enhance the development of an eventual eastern front and allow France to . . . strengthe[n] the western front."[19] In the Chautemps government (June 1937–March 1938), the premier himself and his finance minister, Georges Bonnet, favored accommodating Italy.[20] In the Daladier government that came next, Bonnet became foreign minister, and his view was championed by André François-Poncet, the newly appointed ambassador to Italy. But the countertendency—to confront Italy—remained persistent and prevalent in French policy. After Léon Blum's Popular Front government came to power in June 1936, he declared that "any real rapprochement between Italy and France was no longer possible." His foreign minister, Yvon Delbos, refused to take "Mussolini and his overtures seriously."[21] In December 1938, the British ambassador in Paris described Daladier's government (which followed Blum's) as "not optimistic": "Much as she would like to detach Rome from Berlin, she does not feel that there is any single initiative or action on her part by which she can hope to do so."[22]

The French perceived strategic gaps between Italy and Germany to be superficial and destined to close. Concessions to promote such divergence, therefore, would be wasted. Moreover, because Mussolini meant to exploit German challenges to the status quo to advance his own, it was illusory to expect he would try to restrain Hitler. The Duce would both stoke tensions and try to profit from Allied hopes he would dampen them.[23] As the British ambassador in Paris reported, "in French eyes" the best way to constrain Italy was "to make [it] feel that France and England, with their authority, resources and friends," would in the long run overpower Germany.[24]

The French also harbored less fear of the strategic consequences of having to fight Italy and Germany in tandem.[25] In Anglo-Franco strategy talks in November 1938, Daladier described Italy as the "weak point of the Rome-Berlin Axis"; France "could always launch an attack against Italy by land."[26] Thus, in the French military view, if the Italian threat in the Mediterranean was growing, it could be effectively dismantled by Anglo-French strategic cooperation—without sacrifices elsewhere. After January 1937, the French navy advocated a hard-line political approach to Italy and a strategy of preemptive military action in the Mediterranean to cut down the Italian threat.[27]

By late 1938, Daladier had taken the view that a neutral Italy would be a disadvantage in war with Germany. Because the Allies could not assume it would remain neutral, no gain for concentrating force against Germany would accrue: they would have to maintain strength in the Mediterranean to protect against Italian treachery. Moreover, a neutral Italy would remain a source and conduit of economic exchange for Germany, which would undermine the Allies' blockade weapon. A Daladier-approved statement of the French military's "general strategic concept for war" put it this way: "In a Franco-British conflict against Germany and Italy, it is *against Italy* that the first Franco-British offensive efforts must be made."[28] Here, then, the strategic weight and war-tipping premises were inverted: war against both Germany and Italy should not be avoided—the best way to beat Germany was to fight Italy too. The British rejected that concept.[29]

In sum, underlying the Allies' convoluted efforts to neutralize Italy were divergent perceptions and premises about Italy's strategic weight. While Britain remained committed to the policy of neutralizing Italy if at all possible, the French, before August 1939, were more inclined to focus on fighting Germany and Italy combined. This only deepened their dependence on British support. Such dependence led Paris to contour its position to minimize conflict with London.[30] Consequently, even when its preferences ran contrary, France's declarative policy often conformed with Britain's diplomatic approach. Thus, coordination tracked two mechanisms in the model that describe how high alliance constraints can negatively impact concerted accommodation (see Figure 2). In the first, the divider's ally supports accommodation but disagrees about the target's strategic weight. In the second, the divider's ally opposes accommodation, but for the sake of maintaining cohesion, defers to the divider's policy at the declarative level. But sometimes, even the façade of unity was cracked by open discord that damaged the force of accommodative moves.

Diplomacy of Selective Accommodation

Between 1936 and 1940, both Britain and France identified German expansionism in Europe as the main threat. Italy and its African and Mediterranean ambitions were secondary. Intermittently, they also agreed that it would be advantageous to isolate Germany from Italy.[31] In 1935 there had even been a short-lived Anglo-Franco-Italian bloc against Germany. The impetus came from Hitler's clumsy putsch in Austria in July 1934. That provoked the January 1935 Laval-Mussolini Pact, in which France and Italy committed to uphold Austria's territorial integrity and independence and to oppose German rearmament. Then, in April, French, Italian, and British leaders met in Stresa, Italy, and forged agreements that signaled a common front against Germany.

The Stresa front soon evaporated. The Anglo-German naval accord of June 1935 acquiesced to German naval rearmament, and undermined French and Italian military positions.[32] Italy's ambitions in Ethiopia, and British and French disagreement over them, added to the fractures. The Laval-Mussolini Pact gave a French nod to Italy's goals, but the British were not (yet) prepared to go along.[33] France eventually reverted to the British policy, but until late 1935, remained determined to conciliate Italy to keep it away from Germany.[34] The Stresa front could not survive the contradictions.

By the end of 1935, Italy began to retreat from the Stresa front. With this, the rationale for selective accommodation snapped into focus. If Italy were not an ally it needed to be kept neutral. As Vansittart remarked, Italy had to be "bought off . . . in some form or another" or it would "volte-face into the arms of Germany."[35] In June 1936 the Popular Front won power in France and, in a jolt, took a hard line against Italy. Thenceforth, Britain would lead the efforts to accommodate Italy.

(A) TRYING TO KEEP ITALY NEUTRAL: FROM THE GENTLEMAN'S AGREEMENT TO THE PACT OF STEEL, 1937–39

The first step was the Anglo-Italian Gentleman's Agreement of January 1937. In early October 1936, the government of Prime Minister Stanley Baldwin signaled to Rome interest in a deal.[36] That interest was elevated by Mussolini's 1 November speech declaring the existence of the Italian-German "Axis." Mussolini responded to Britain's feeler a month later, calling for a "rapid and complete" accord based on "recognition of reciprocal interests" in the Mediterranean.[37] The British thus began negotiations seeking, in the narrow sense, to preserve the Mediterranean status quo and halt Italian efforts to subvert British rule in Palestine.[38] Their larger goal was to disrupt the nascent Axis.

French concerns complicated the initiative. In late November 1936, France requested joint naval talks to coordinate a strategy to confront Italian forces on the Spanish Balearics supporting Franco. Paris feared that permanent Italian military presence would follow, threatening Allied control in the western Mediterranean. The British refused naval talks. They thought the French were exaggerating the threat, and they wanted to avoid the backlash naval talks would have on Anglo-Italian negotiations.[39] When Italy insisted that Anglo-Italian negotiations stay bilateral (i.e., France could not weigh in), the British agreed.[40] To Paris, Eden explained that "an improvement in Anglo-Italian relations is as much in the French interests as our own, both because a potentially dangerous situation in the Mediterranean would thereby be eased and because the probability of the formation of a firm German-Italian bloc would thereby be lessened."[41] The French Foreign Ministry, however, tried "to throw a spanner into the works of Anglo-Italian diplomacy."[42] Paris wanted London to insist on French participation in the talks.[43] Britain refused but assured France that its interested would be protected, and it would be consulted and informed of progress in the talks. The French foreign minister, Yvon Delbos, relented and "approved of [the Gentleman's Agreement] in advance."[44]

On 4 January 1937, the elements of the Anglo-Italian Gentleman's Agreement became public. The parties declared that their vital interests in the Mediterranean were "in no way incompatible" and that they did not want to alter the territorial status quo in the region. In a separate note to Italy, the British addressed France's Balearics concerns, stating their assumption that Italy would not seek to acquire or control Spanish territory. Italy's reply confirmed that assumption.[45] There was a sliver of progress here. Vansittart explained, "If we never *talk* of detaching them from Germany, but merely exploit this success . . . we shall automatically loosen the Italo-German tie."[46] But just as the Gentleman's Agreement was announced, politics in France further hardened in attitude toward Italy. Premier Blum and (then) Defense Minister Daladier replaced the chief of the Naval Staff who favored accommodating Italy with François Darlan, who did not.[47]

Each party to the Gentleman's Agreement soon found reason to accuse the other of bad faith.[48] Yet Prime Minister Neville Chamberlain, who replaced Baldwin in May 1937, was determined to keep trying for a larger accord to protect British interests in the eastern Mediterranean. The bait was something Mussolini craved—de jure recognition of Italy's conquest of Ethiopia, baptized by the League of Nations. The Spanish Civil War—in the *western* Mediterranean—was a lower British priority; there, they were willing to accept some Italian involvement and deception. The French were not. Consequently, between July and September 1937, the Allies became mired in discord over demands for withdrawal of Italian forces in Spain. France tightened its resistance to de jure recognition of Italy's Ethiopian conquests, insisting that recognition be linked to a *completed* withdrawal of all Italian troops in Spain. Chamberlain's government, by contrast, wanted to expedite recognition and push for a broader Mediterranean agreement to accelerate Anglo-Italian cooperation.

Chamberlain decided not to allow this dispute with France to stall the process of conciliating Italy.[49] In late summer 1937 he launched a new effort, willing to "go it alone" if France dragged its heels.[50] Mussolini was receptive. Concerns about Hitler's intentions toward Austria seemed to encourage Mussolini's interest. Italy's tone toward France *also* improved. Those signals seemed to confirm the thesis that improved Anglo-Italian relations would translate into improved Franco-Italian relations. In September 1937, Paris endorsed London's renewed initiative toward Italy.

That month, Mussolini authorized a covert submarine campaign against Soviet shipping to Republican Spain. Though Italy's hand was poorly hidden, the problem was framed as "piracy" to avoid a full-blown confrontation. Italian recklessness brought Britain and France together at the Nyon Conference, and into close collaboration to enforce shipping protection, which brought the "piracy" to an end.[51] Britain and France met again in November 1937 to seek a broader common approach to threats confronting them. Here, Britain continued to insist on pursuing a far-reaching Anglo-Italian Mediterranean accord. But in response to French concerns, it agreed to several conditions to promote solidarity. On matters impacting French interests, Britain would not strike bilateral deals with Italy. It would demand an end to Italian propaganda against both Britain and France. And it would keep France fully informed of the Anglo-Italian talks. However, contrary to the Chautemps government's demand, the British did *not* agree to insist that France had to be made an equal partner in whatever accord resulted. Nevertheless, when Eden extended to the Italian ambassador the formal invitation to begin talks, he touted the "complete solidarity" of Britain and France in the determination to move forward.[52]

Once again, as a matter of declarative policy, France went along with Britain's approach. Yet, it maintained a deep reluctance to make any concessions to Italy, and a practical "policy in the Mediterranean almost directly at odds with Britain's."[53] France thus held fast to its reservations—no early de jure recognition of Italy's Ethiopian gains; complete withdrawal of Italian troops in Spain had to come first. These delayed and handicapped the critical inducement in Britain's selective accommodation strategy. Mussolini refused to accept the linkage France demanded. The consequences soon became evident. In November, Italy joined Germany and Japan in the Anti-Comintern Pact.[54] In December, it quit the League over the continued refusal to grant de jure recognition in Ethiopia.

Mussolini's actions drove Eden to oppose Chamberlain's policy and lobby for the "French view," which was "entirely opposed to talks with Mussolini."[55] Chamberlain, and others in the cabinet, however, saw the setbacks as reason to try harder to distance Italy from Germany. In early 1938, German ambitions toward Austria returned to the forefront. With Hitler pressuring the Vienna government to share power with Nazis, whether to try to coordinate a multilateral effort—with Italy—to check Germany became another point of contention between London and Paris. Chamberlain—backed by Lord Perth, the British ambassador in Rome—saw in the Austria crisis a chance to distance Italy from Germany and was willing to trade concessions over Italian intervention in Spain to make it happen. Here, Eden drew the line and resigned on 2 February 1938.[56] His successor, Lord Halifax, favored conciliating Italy. That cemented a cabinet consensus to try to exploit the Austrian crisis to advance an Anglo-Italian agreement. Italy, meanwhile, signaled that it was willing to begin bilateral talks on a progressive withdrawal of Italian troops from Spain. These negotiations were set to commence in early March.[57]

France recoiled from any effort to work with Italy to preserve Austrian independence. It called instead for a joint Anglo-Franco move that shut out Italy. Chamberlain rejected the French plan and avoided taking common action with it to deter a German coup in Austria "for fear of complicating and thus delaying completion of an Anglo-Italian accord." France, meanwhile, would neither act resolutely on its own nor move to mend fences with Italy. Instead, between January and March 1938, it tried to convince the British to stall Anglo-Italian talks until there had been more progress in relations between France and Italy.[58] To keep up appearances, Chamberlain declared that Britain would proceed with the Anglo-Italian talks "in close consultation" with France. But Britain, at this point, was simply "disinclined to consider seriously French concerns" in its negotiation strategy.[59]

On 11 March 1938 Hitler forced a Nazi government into power in Vienna, then annexed Austria two days later. While this unfolded, there was in

France a gap in government. Chautemps's administration fell on 10 March and Blum's second cabinet was not composed until the 13th. Four days later, Blum escalated on Spain, opening the border to allow resupply of the struggling Republican forces. That undercut British policy to expedite a deal with Italy, to which they hoped the Austria crisis would add momentum. Though Mussolini had anticipated the Anschluss and "signaled clearly to Hitler Italy's disinterest," it still rattled him.[60] The Anschluss thus "created a favorable climate for Anglo-Italian negotiation," making Mussolini "more receptive to blandishments from London with regard to an Anglo-Italian accord."[61] Blum's government, however, remained confrontational—until it collapsed on 10 April. Short-lived though it was, its decision to open the Spanish border and escalate Franco-Italian conflict torpedoed Britain's attempt to exploit the post-Anschluss chill in Italo-German relations.

The next French government, formed by Daladier on 10 April 1938, became "more inclined to accommodation" and willing to try "another tack" with Italy.[62] Daladier made Georges Bonnet, a proponent of Franco-Italian détente, foreign minister. The elements for a more concerted approach thus came together. The follow-on to the Gentleman's Agreement—the Anglo-Italian "Easter Accords"—was struck 16 April 1938.[63] It reaffirmed several commitments from the prior agreement while extending new concessions to Italy over influence and boundaries in the Middle East and northeast Africa. At the heart of the Accords was an agreement to link implementation to two reciprocal developments—a settlement of the Spanish conflict, and British recognition of Italy's African empire. The day the Accords were announced, Bonnet signaled to Italian foreign minister Galeazzo Ciano that France was ready to begin bilateral negotiations along similar lines.[64] Ciano replied that an agreement was within reach if France would appoint a new ambassador to Rome, which would involve protocol that conveyed a form of recognition of Italy's African empire. France signaled that it would soon do so, and it set forth four major demands: withdrawal of Italian volunteers from Spain; no Italian territorial gains in Spain; French admittance to the Anglo-Italian Red Sea agreement (embedded in the Easter Accords); and extension of the 1935 Laval-Mussolini agreement concerning Italian nationals in Tunisia.[65]

What came together in April 1938, then, was a constellation of conditions conducive to successful accommodation. As Chamberlain summed it, "The results of the Anglo-Italian agreement, followed up by the Franco-Italian conversations, should . . . weaken the Axis."[66] Indeed, there resulted a concrete success. In early May 1938, Hitler visited Italy pressing for an immediate and formal military alliance.[67] Italy rebuffed the overture. The incentives of cooperation with Britain and France were the reason.[68] According to Toscano, Mussolini and Ciano did not want to "endanger the results obtained from the Easter Pacts nor risk compromising Britain's recognition of the Italian empire."[69] According to Watt, "Mussolini still hoped for an agreement with Paris," and he was "sufficiently strengthened [by the Easter Accords] to feel free to reject" the German overtures.[70]

On 12 May, the League of Nations Council, prompted by *both* Britain and France, agreed that states could unilaterally recognize the Italian empire. The first concerted step toward Italy's payoff from the Easter Accords was thus taken. But difficulties in the Franco-Italian talks soon overshadowed it.[71] France would not agree to *any* accords with Italy until there was a satisfactory settlement of the Spanish Civil War. Mussolini, committed to Franco's complete victory, refused to compromise. When Italy and Britain had negotiated the Easter Accords, Nationalist victory seemed imminent. Blum's opening of the Spanish border, however, revived Republican resistance. Franco's forces did not win quickly that spring. Consequently, despite the Easter Accords assurances, Mussolini decided to surge more forces to help Franco to finish off the Republicans. When Mussolini began deriding Franco-Italian relations in a 14 May speech, he emphasized that France and Italy were still backing opposite sides in Spain. This was true: Daladier did not close the border with Spain until June.

France urged Britain not to ratify the Easter Accords until a Franco-Italian agreement was in place. Italy, in June, began to press for quick ratification. Mussolini asserted that Britain must do so *before* the Franco-Italian track could improve. He thus tried "to undermine Franco-British solidarity and to isolate France."[72] The French and British both diagnosed the Italian gambit.[73] In response to Rome's mid-July call for immediate implementation, London balked; implementation could not start because the Spanish conflict remained unsettled and Italy had not yet executed a major troop withdrawal. Italy should help Britain and France push for an armistice. Italy should understand that Daladier's decision in June to close the border with Spain was a goodwill gesture and reciprocate. And it should know that for Britain, a Franco-Italian understanding was the "logical complement" to implementation of the Easter Accords. Britain thus recommended that Italy propose a restart to talks with France, but also signaled that it did not, ultimately, consider their resumption to be a sine qua non for implementation. Mussolini replied that the Italo-French talks could "eventually" resume, "but never before" implementation.[74]

Still, Italy conditioned its alignment with Germany on the viability of the project with Britain. In mid-July, as the prospects for implementation of the Easter Accords improved, German pressure on Italy to form an alliance increased. Mussolini, again, rebuffed the German bid, because, as Ciano put it, "We want to see how relations with London develop."[75] By late summer 1938 the Munich crisis was brewing, and British leaders became acutely sensitive to Italy's position. Their military commanders in the Mediterranean warned that "in the initial stages of war with Germany, it is of the highest importance that Italy should be kept out." When the crisis escalated in September, raising the immediate prospect of war with Germany, Halifax then argued that Britain needed to quickly ratify the Easter Accords and extend economic incentives to Italy: the Italians wanted to extricate themselves from "a German mesh" but could not "without substantial help from Britain."[76]

Mussolini played an equivocal role in the Munich crisis. As tensions developed in spring and summer 1938, he encouraged Hitler to dismantle Czechoslovakia. In July/August he decided that if France, in defense of Czechoslovakia, attacked Germany, then Italy would aid Germany by attacking France.[77] But at the height of the crisis in late September, he thought twice and retreated. As Hitler's ultimatum ticked down on 28 September, Mussolini, at Chamberlain's request, pressed Hitler for a twenty-four-hour extension and forwarded Chamberlain's proposal for a conference of Britain, France, Germany, and Italy, to decide Czechoslovakia's fate. The conference agenda was then set by an Italian plan that was suggested by the German Foreign Ministry. Some historians attribute Italy's quasi-mediation in the crisis to its military unpreparedness.[78] But in Ciano's diary there is also evidence that Mussolini mediated in order to foster implementation of his deals struck with Britain.[79] After the Munich crisis, Ribbentrop again pressed his "project for a tripartite alliance." In his diary, Ciano remarked: "No doubt we will study it quite calmly and, perhaps, put it aside for some time."[80]

After Munich, Britain decided to quickly implement the Easter Accords.[81] Mussolini's mediation seemed to validate its strategy to induce Italy's detachment from Germany. The Spanish Civil War also appeared finally to have reached a point of low risk of international escalation; British positions on that issue could be relaxed. As for France, the "shock of Munich," writes Shorrock, "catalyze[d] a final effort in Paris to resuscitate an understanding with Rome."[82] In October 1938, Paris signaled to Rome that it would soon dispatch a fully accredited ambassador. Ambassador François-Poncet arrived in November. He brought French recognition of Italy's conquest of Ethiopia. On 16 November, the British had done likewise. Here, then, they moved back into tandem to accommodate Italy.

Hitler accelerated efforts to secure an alliance with Italy. Italy had *not* been willing to commit during the Munich crisis, and he needed to dispel the resulting aura of German isolation. His approach to Italy was further fueled by knowledge that "the British Cabinet was determined to implement the [Easter Accords]."[83] In late October, Ribbentrop pitched a plan to convert the Anti-Comintern Pact into a full-blown triple military alliance (including Japan).[84] Rome, for a third time, disowned Germany. As Ciano noted, "[Hitler] wants war in the course of the next three or four years. I was extremely reserved."[85] With Ribbentrop "taken aback," Mussolini assured him that he accepted the offer "in principle, though the date is postponed."[86] This postponement—quite indefinite—was meant to preserve the potential for rapprochement with Britain.[87] As Ciano noted, Italy would put the German bid "in cold storage . . . particularly since Perth has secretly informed me of the British decision to implement the Easter Accords [in] the middle of November. We must keep both doors open. An alliance would now close, perhaps forever, one of the two, and that not the less important. The Duce also seems to think so."[88] Indeed, Mussolini shrugged off Germany's overture, saying to Ribbentrop, "The Italian people have reached the stage of the Axis; but not yet that of the military alliance."[89] Britain's decision to start implementing the Easter Accords, announced in late October, and France's step forward on recognition, had their intended effects.[90] Concerted accommodation met again with temporary success.

However, in deciding to implement the Easter Accords quickly, the British discarded their position that Italy had to fully withdraw troops from Spain first. That undermined "French efforts to repair the lengthy breach in Franco-Italian relations," which hinged on the full-withdrawal position.[91] Almost immediately after implementation began on 16 November, Mussolini stiffened his tone toward France. At the end of the month, Ciano gave a foreign policy speech that referred to Italy's natural aspirations to expand, which evoked chants from the chamber of "Tunisia, Djibouti, Corsica, Nice."[92] France then demanded that Italy clarify its stand on the 1935 Laval-Mussolini accords. Chamberlain swiftly joined the protest, noting that to do otherwise would "giv[e] the impression that we were very willing to see a wedge inserted between ourselves and France." Ciano downplayed the incident as an unauthorized outburst and reiterated Italy's adherence to the Laval-Mussolini accords.[93]

But Britain's next steps exacerbated the problem. It announced in early December that Chamberlain and Halifax would pay a state visit to Italy the next month. The purpose, wrote Chamberlain, was to make Mussolini "feel that our friendship would give him a greater freedom of manoeuvre . . . to escape from German toils."[94] Chamberlain then made an overly technical statement in the Commons raising doubts that Britain would back France in a Mediterranean conflict. France reacted by reverting to inflexibility. On 13 December Daladier declared to the Chamber that France would not make any concessions of colonial holdings to Italy, even if it meant war.[95] He simultaneously announced visits to Corsica, Tunisia, and Algeria, timed to precede the Chamberlain-Halifax mission. Then, on 17 December, Ciano denounced the 1935 Laval-Mussolini agreement as historically outdated. France was now "mired in an intense . . . dispute with that power the British most wanted to befriend."[96]

The Chamberlain-Halifax mission to Italy in January 1939 accented Anglo-Franco disunity.[97] In Rome, they "did not intervene in support of the French position," but they did try "to persuade [Daladier] to make concessions, in order to tear Italy away from the German influence."[98] Meanwhile, Mussolini and Ciano had become more interested in stepping toward a formal alliance with Germany.[99] This might tighten the pressure on France, and perhaps corner it, without alienating Britain. The British cabinet saw the hazards and for that reason, authorized joint military staff planning for a war against both Germany and Italy in the Mediterranean. In February 1939, Chamberlain publicly committed Britain to the defense of France, while Mussolini pressed Germany to start and publicize military staff talks ahead of an alliance deal.[100] The polarization of alignments intensified.

But when the Nazis rolled up Czechoslovakia in mid-March, Italy slowed its slide toward Germany. Hitler's gambit caused "consternation, resentment, and uncertainty" in Rome. Given no warning, Italian leaders were "stunned and indignant."[101] The coup demolished the Munich agreements on which Mussolini had staked personal prestige. On 19 March, Ciano wrote: "The[se] events . . . have reversed my opinion of the Fuhrer and Germany; he, too, is unfaithful and treacherous and we cannot carry on any policy with him." Mussolini, wrote Ciano, "agrees that it is now impossible to present to the Italian people . . . an alliance with Germany. Even the stones would cry out against it."[102] Italy's ambassador in Berlin, Bernardo Attolico, wrote a scathing memorandum detailing Germany's failure to abide by "the most elementary reciprocal obligations" and protested to Berlin about the lack of warning. Mussolini focused on the fact that the Prague coup foreshadowed a German move into Croatia, which would intrude on Italy's sphere in the Adriatic and Mediterranean.[103]

British officials then, and many historians since, saw here another chance to reverse Italy's movement toward Germany.[104] Mussolini, heedful of Attolico's warnings, wanted to pause; Ciano, more thoroughly alienated, wanted to revive rapprochement with Britain and France.[105] But once again, discordant British and French policies quashed the opportunity. Two things needed to happen to turn Italy's pause into stasis: France needed to be conciliatory enough to strengthen Ciano's case, and Germany needed to continue its diplomatic incompetence with Italy.[106] Neither condition was met. While France stuck to its hard line, Hitler acted fast to reassure Mussolini that he would respect—even promote—Italy's interests. On 20 March, Ciano received from Ribbentrop Hitler's promise "that in all Mediterranean questions the policy of the Axis is to be determined by Rome. . . . This decision will always be an immutable law of our foreign policy."[107]

British leaders decided then to address the German threat in two ways. They would deepen the continental commitment to France.[108] At the same time, they would extend "accommodation to Italy."[109] But Britain's ability to advance both lines was pinched by the preeminent need to bolster France. Joint Anglo-Franco defense negotiations were announced on 21 March. Mussolini took that as a threat and denounced the Western powers for trying to encircle the Axis. Ciano sent a back-channel envoy to Paris, urging the French not to exaggerate the significance of Mussolini's complaints. The envoy encouraged Daladier to give Ciano some prospect for progress in negotiations. François-Poncet, likewise, urged Paris to keep looking for a means to conciliate Italy. But Daladier dug in. In a speech on 29 March, he declared that the French would "cede neither an acre of our territory nor a single one of our rights." To drive the point home, he ordered military mobilization.[110]

Meanwhile, after Ribbentrop's 20 March assurances, Mussolini decided to conquer Albania. The operation began on 7 April and was over in a week. As Salerno argues, the "stark contrast" between the British and French reactions formed another gap between them over Italy. The British treated the Albanian coup as a marginal problem, to be dealt with in quiet diplomacy. The French reacted with serious alarm and prepared for a war in the Mediterranean.[111] Nevertheless, Italy's Albania grab did spur Britain and France to extend defense guarantees to Greece and Romania in April (and to Turkey the next month; see chapter 9). These deterrence commitments were targeted at Italy as well as Germany.

The British tried also to midwife progress in Franco-Italian relations. After encouraging signals from Rome on 19 April, they pressed France to make a move. To prime the initiative, Ciano verbally conveyed Italian demands to François-Poncet on 25 April. Italy sought: (1) a free port in Djibouti, (2) a share in the Djibouti railway, (3) two Italian directorships on the Suez Canal board, and (4) maintenance of the 1896 agreement on Tunis.[112] The British pressed Daladier to respond favorably.[113] The cabinet reminded Paris that Britain's decision to mobilize an army for continental defense should make France feel more able to negotiate from a position of strength. But Daladier was determined not to give, for fear that a forthcoming gesture would incite further Italian demands and demoralize French domestic support.[114] If Italy was seeking concessions, Daladier insisted that Mussolini come forward first, offering reciprocity. When Bonnet proposed to the Council of Ministers that France reopen negotiations with Italy, they refused: the prevailing view was "the two dictators were acting in concert. . . . It would be folly to seek to divide them."[115] In short, on the basic premise of wedge strategy, the British and French governments did not agree.

When briefed on the Ciano–François-Poncet exchange of 25 April, Mussolini stated that he had "no intention of starting negotiations with France until after the signing of the treaty with Germany."[116] But he did not stop the feelers. In early May, just before Ribbentrop came to Italy to talk alliance, Mussolini signaled to Britain that France should offer some inducements not to sign an alliance with Germany.[117]

British officials scrambled to jumpstart Franco-Italian negotiations. Joint military consultations made clear to Paris the Eastern Allies' vulnerability if Italy and Germany aggressed simultaneously. Their fate would hinge entirely on Soviet support—which was hardly certain. The British hoped that this reality would instill a French mindset more open to compromise. The British ambassador to France took up the theme in Paris, while the British ambassador to Italy informed Ciano that London was pressuring France for concessions.[118] That pressure elicited a symbolic gesture from Daladier. On 3 May, Ciano was invited to spell out Italian wishes in writing. On 11 May, François-Poncet reported back Italy's demands—identical to the April list—and a reassurance that Italy did not seek French territory. Daladier did not follow up.

Instead, on 12 May, he gave a speech reiterating that France would give no ground. As Shorrock sums it, French leaders "believed that Italy was already committed to Germany [and] saw little point in making even modest concessions to Italy as the price of normalization."[119] Mussolini ordered Ciano to stop any further discussions. Then, matching Daladier's tone, he gave speeches on 14 and 20 May that "mov[ed] from moderation to veiled menaces."[120] The Germans, meanwhile, were crafting an alliance proposal with Ciano, ahead of Hitler's trip to Rome later that month.[121]

On 20 May, Halifax met Daladier and implored him to take "some risk in the hope of stimulating signor Mussolini to restrain Herr Hitler from mad adventure."[122] He warned Daladier not to "lose opportunities" to weaken Italy's ties to Germany, by making concessions on colonial issues. And he hinted that France owed Britain such an effort in return for its guarantee of Romania (for which France had lobbied hard) and its decision to begin conscripting an army for the continent.[123] Daladier replied, "Italy was now in Germany's hands"; "The worst thing France could do would be to yield."[124]

Such was the state of discord between Britain and France when, on 22 May, Italy and Germany signed the Pact of Steel, the formal political and military alliance that Britain had consistently, and France half-heartedly, tried to prevent.[125] Italy's calculus expressed the desire to use the German alliance to pry concessions from France and Britain. It would nevertheless be harder now to neutralize Italy, for its costs of backing away from a formal alliance would be higher.[126] Although the Allies' attempts to keep Italy neutral through negotiations had fleeting successes in 1938—when they concerted effectively—recurrent discord took its toll. Their failure to stop Italy from allying with Germany in May 1939 had grave wider consequences. This was when Hitler made key decisions that led directly to war three months later—the decisions to target Poland and to seek accommodation with the USSR (see chapter 7). Both decisions were abetted by Italy's commitment. Had Italy held back in May 1939, as it had the year before, Hitler's calculations and timetable for war might have been disrupted.

(B) TRYING TO DETACH ITALY: THE POLISH CRISIS
TO ITALIAN INTERVENTION, 1939–40

At the end of May 1939, a new British ambassador, Percy Loraine, met with Mussolini to try rekindle Anglo-Italian rapprochement. He was poorly received. Disparaging Britain for prosecuting a policy of encirclement that was leading Europe into war, Mussolini questioned whether there was any value left in the Easter Accords.[127] In June, Loraine returned bearing Britain's assurances that it remained committed to the Easter Accords and considered them "the keystone of Anglo-Italian relations for many years to come."[128] Britain also prepared to persuade Daladier to "see reason." Chamberlain wrote Daladier on 13 July urging him to resume Franco-Italian negotiations, which might encourage Mussolini to "exercise a restraining influence" on Hitler, and "at least [gain] time which is of great value to us."[129] Presenting the letter to Daladier, the British Ambassador, Eric Phipps, underscored Chamberlain's view that on Franco-Italian relations "probably hung the question of war or peace."[130] But Daladier was still in no mood to conciliate Italy.

Italian officials, nevertheless, soon began to harbor doubts about the Pact of Steel. Ciano suspected that Hitler meant to force the issue on Poland, despite assurances when the pact was negotiated that Germany, like Italy, wanted to avoid war for at least three years.[131] When the Polish crisis escalated in July, so did Italian fears that Hitler would ditch those limits.[132] Ciano again began denouncing the Germans as treacherous allies and warning Mussolini that Italy should not be entrapped. Just as the crisis activated Italy's fear of entrapment, it also reinforced Britain's sense of the importance of detaching Italy. In a July 1939 assessment of the prospects for war with Germany over Poland, the cabinet's Committee of Imperial Defence emphasized: "Italian neutrality, if it could by any means be assured, would be decidedly preferable to her active hostility."[133]

On 12 August, Ribbentrop and Hitler finally disclosed to Ciano the intention to attack Poland immediately.[134] After that, Ciano lobbied hard against Italian intervention in what he expected would be a general conflict. The Italian military and the king of Italy joined Ciano in advising Mussolini not to be pulled into the war Germany was about to start.[135] So, as the Polish crisis peaked in late August, Italy hedged in earnest. Mussolini and Ciano first offered to mediate in the crisis.[136] Once it became clear that Hitler would not, as he had at Munich, play along, Italy began to backpedal. To establish a pretext for defecting, Mussolini wrote Hitler on 25 August that "in view of the *present* state of Italian war preparations" it would be "opportune for me not to take the *initiative* in military operations" unless Germany immediately delivered to Italy the military supplies and raw materials it would need to resist British and French attacks.[137] When Hitler requested a detailed statement of Italy's requirements, Mussolini demanded an impossible level of support.[138]

Hitler declined to commit to the transfers and requested that Italy show loyalty by mobilizing its forces on the French border so as to complicate Anglo-Franco military preparations.[139] Mussolini agreed, but encouraged Hitler to not miss the still available "opportunity for a political solution" to the Polish crisis—advice he would repeatedly give in the days ahead.[140] When Hitler then asked Mussolini to disguise his intentions so that "at least until the outbreak of the struggle the world should have no idea of the attitude Italy intends to adopt," the Duce replied with assurances that proved to be hollow.[141]

By then, the French approach to Italy had begun to conform with the British. The stimulus was the Nazi-Soviet pact and the concomitant failure of the Anglo-Franco-Soviet alliance talks (see chapter 7). Stalin's reversal overturned French calculations of the value of Italian neutrality.[142] So long as the USSR remained a plausible supporter of France's eastern allies, Italian belligerency did not pose a decisive threat to France's overall, two-front war strategy.[143] But with the Soviets neutralized, Italy's enmity became much more dangerous—it would make it impossible to hold together an Eastern bloc and, simultaneously, force France to divert forces from the German front to defend the southern frontiers. Italy's alignment could make or break France's war plan. French leaders upped their estimates of Italy's strategic weight. On 22 August, Bonnet declared "categorically" that "the French Government . . . were of the definite opinion that it would be preferable for us that Italy should maintain a durable neutrality." Daladier confirmed the next day that "nothing should be done to force Italy into hostilities." To Rome, Paris signaled willingness to compromise on Djibouti and the Suez Canal board (two of Italy's key demands from April).[144] On 25 August, Halifax conveyed to Mussolini that if Italy, by detaching itself, incurred German hostility, Britain promised "collaboration and support."[145] At this late stage, then, the Western Allies recovered the consensus needed to deeply coordinate concerted accommodation.

Though Mussolini promised Hitler to not reveal his intent to go nonbelligerent and to pressure the French border, he did the opposite. On 31 August, with Mussolini's approval, Ciano assured Loraine, "under seal of secrecy," that Italy would not "fight against either England or France" unless they attacked first.[146] Thus, before Britain and France declared war on Germany on 3 September, Italy had shifted toward defected neutrality. Mussolini's decision was driven by more than just the prospect of Anglo-Franco concessions—neither Italy's economy nor its military was ready for major war. Nevertheless, there is reason to believe that the changed circumstances, which were now more favorable to extracting concessions from the Allies, also contributed to its posture. Those new conditions were (1) the sharp, unavoidable danger of war with Germany, which clarified the Allies' need to isolate that threat and thereby enhanced Italy's leverage as an uncommitted power; and (2) manifest Anglo-Franco unity on the need to accommodate Italy.[147] To exploit those circumstances was a major purpose of Italian foreign policy in the months ahead.

Throughout the period of "phony war" that followed (September 1939–May 1940), the main lines of interaction among Italy and the Anglo-Franco allies fit the theory's expectations. First, in the months after Britain and France united behind concerted accommodation, Italy's relations with them improved while its relations with Germany—its formal ally—foundered.

Second, Italy's relations with the Allies deteriorated in early 1940, as Britain pulled into a more confrontational approach to Italy, which had the effect—recognized at the time—of increasing Italy's strategic dependence on Germany. As prospects for negotiating with the Allies to extract concessions dimmed, Mussolini made decisions that put Italy back on the path of cohesion with Germany and intervention.

In September 1939, the Allies began a campaign of concerted accommodation that Ciano dubbed their "serenade under the balcony."[148] Besides the obvious step of not directly threatening Italy and thus forcing it to fight, it was also necessary not to isolate it and thus force it into dependence on Germany. France, "with British encouragement," moved quickly to adopt a "deliberately nonprovocative posture with regard to Italy" while extending assurances and openings for cooperation. Tellingly, "Paris offered to discuss with Italy all issues except Corsica, Nice, and Savoy."[149] The Allies' policy of accommodating Italy was also manifest in aspects of war planning. For example, in October 1939 negotiations with Turkey over the military convention of the Tripartite Alliance, the British and French refused to agree to facilitate Turkey's early intervention against Italy in the Dodecanese (see chapter 9). Similarly, the Allies decided against a joint operation to take control of Thessaloniki because they did not want to challenge Italy's Balkan interests.[150]

The Allies also adopted commercial policies favorable to Italy. In early September, France initiated negotiations for a secret Franco-Italian commercial accord that would be advantageous to the Italians. Under the agreement, France bought Italian arms, including contracts for aircraft engines, munitions components, and petroleum; in return, Italy received raw materials from France and French colonies. The military transactions were hidden from Germany, run covertly through a Portuguese third party.[151] Britain, likewise, calibrated its commercial and economic warfare policies to reward Italian nonintervention.[152] It gave Italy a break in the blockade, allowing it to import goods freely. When Britain could not get Italy to formally commit not to reexport to Germany, it set up the Anglo-Italian Joint Standing Committee to continue negotiating the issue, while allowing trade to continue largely uncontrolled. Through November 1939, the British did not enforce contraband control over Italy, precisely to avoid forcing it into Germany's corner. Italy received a great deal of coal from Germany via sea transport from Rotterdam—Britain let this trade flow. Like France, it launched efforts to negotiate a broad trade agreement with Italy.[153]

Between Italy and Germany, frictions built up. There was lingering anger and distrust over Hitler's precipitous plunge into war. There was the German population in South Tyrol/Alto Adige militating for secession along the lines of the Sudeten Germans. Though Hitler had promised to solve the problem in 1938, he stalled, and Mussolini had accordingly "reinforced [Italy's] frontier security in the North."[154] There was sharp divergence over the

Soviet-Finnish war. Mussolini openly denounced the Soviet action, and when he tried to ship arms to Finland through Germany, Hitler blocked the way.[155] Geopolitical tensions also loomed: Germany and the Soviet Union were liable to carve up the Balkans and become Mediterranean powers—encroaching on Italy's principal spheres of interest.[156] In mid-December, the tensions were exposed in speeches by Ciano criticizing Germany's failures as an ally and justifying Italy's nonbelligerence in response to those lapses.[157] In early January, Mussolini wrote to Hitler underlining Ciano's points and warning him against trying to defeat Britain and France, because the U.S. was certain to step in. Mussolini tried in this fashion to push Germany toward a negotiated settlement that Italy would mediate.[158] "By the end of 1939," writes Umbreit, "the German-Italian alliance had reached a low point."[159]

But in December, Britain began tightening its economic warfare policies in ways that undermined the goal of neutralizing Italy. It announced that it would begin blocking German coal exports shipped to Italy from Rotterdam. French policymakers had argued against such a move, to no avail. Now, once more, London and Paris began to follow policies toward Italy "which placed them at cross purposes with one another, and with Rome."[160] Britain increasingly pushed a policy that began treating Italy as an adversary unless it agreed to become a dependent protégé. Though France kept trying, through friendly trade, to reinforce Italy's neutrality, it retreated from offering territorial and colonial compensations.[161] Thus, as Italian nonbelligerence wore on, the British and French approaches became less coordinated and accommodative.

Throughout December and January, London limited the embargo enough to give Italy time to negotiate a deal for more British coal to substitute for the impending loss of the German seaborne supply. Then, in February, London attached a condition: in order to gain currency to pay for British coal, Italy had to sell Britain weapons. Otherwise, it would lose access to the British coal that already accounted for 20 percent of its supply, which would rise once German seaborne deliveries were cut off. Mussolini refused and ordered an end to economic negotiations with the Allies. Then he restarted negotiations with Germany, which led to an extensive trade agreement that included Germany's commitment to fully meet Italy's coal needs.[162] On 1 March, the British decisively blocked Germany's seaborne deliveries. Unless Mussolini made a dramatic move toward Britain, Italy would only get what Germany could deliver overland by rail.[163]

Thus began a new phase of Italy's nonbelligerence. Mussolini's "eagerness to join the struggle on the German side returned."[164] He met with Hitler at the Brenner Pass on 18 March and promised that Italy would intervene (although when still remained undetermined).[165] Reinforcing Rome's shift toward belligerency, the friendly French government fell to a vote of no confidence on 21 March. Paul Reynaud, who championed a more confrontational policy, became the new premier, minister of defense, and foreign minister.[166] Yet Mussolini still hedged.[167] On 31 March, he signed a secret memorandum that "envisaged an offensive on the alpine front only in the event that France was already defeated by Germany. Otherwise the Italian forces were to adopt a defensive stance, both there and with regard to Corsica[,]the Aegean and North Africa." In any scenario short of decisive French defeat, therefore, Italy would conduct a "parallel war"—limited to offensives in East Africa and perhaps the Balkans.[168] When the German High Command, on 10 April, proposed a joint war plan against France (with Italian forces fighting on the Upper Rhine), Rome declined.[169]

Italy's nonbelligerence, then, hinged principally on whether or not the Allies could continue to deter Germany or quickly blunt a German attack. As long as the Allies remained strong, and Italy's military readiness continued to lag, Italy was likely to stay a bystander to the central contest in Europe. Despite his stated intent to intervene eventually, throughout April 1940 Mussolini kept pushing back the date of entry: on one day it was not until after "the second week of August [1940]," on the next it was "spring of 1941."[170] But Germany's quick and decisive military success in France in May 1940 compelled Mussolini's decision.[171]

One of the attractions of Italy's nonbelligerency was that it left open the possibility of negotiating French concessions bilaterally. But once France collapsed, Mussolini could no longer extract concessions that way.[172] Hitler's diktat would become a deciding factor. Italy now had to enter the war fast to secure any of the objectives it had otherwise meant to reap through blackmail.[173] As the magnitude of the Allies' defeat became undeniable, British and French leaders both reached out to Italy with generous offers to negotiate all relevant problems between them in order to satisfy Italian concerns.[174] Britain was willing to substantially loosen the blockade regime; France to compromise on the nettlesome colonial issues in North and East Africa.[175] This newfound flexibility, however, came too late to matter. On 13 May, Mussolini declared to Ciano, the Allies "have lost the war. . . . We have no time to lose. Within a month, I shall declare war." Ciano noted afterward, "Only a new turn of events can induce him to revise his decision, but . . . things are going so badly for the allies that there is no hope."[176] Italy declared war on France on 10 June 1940.

Summary and Alternatives

The military defeat of May to June 1940 was a forcing event—a sufficient condition for Italian intervention—that makes it hard to gauge the importance of the shifts toward confrontation in Anglo-Franco policy in the last months before Italy intervened. Even if the Allies had sustained a well-coordinated policy of accommodation toward Italy until May 1940, the loss of the Battle of France might have brought Italy into the war. But running through the actual train of events, from 1936 to 1940, is considerable evidence that the depth of coordination behind British and French efforts to accommodate Italy influenced its inclination to align with or diverge from Germany.

In the first period (A), when it was easier to neutralize Italy because it had not formally joined Germany, poor Allied coordination (rooted in divergent beliefs about Italy's strategic weight) abetted Italy's drift toward Germany. At certain junctures, however, more tightly coordinated accommodation coincided with clear-cut Italian decisions to keep distance from Germany. Likewise, in period (B), both sides of the dynamic played out—especially during the phony war, when Italy was a nonbelligerent. After the British and French leaders agreed about Italy's strategic weight in autumn 1939, they came together solidly behind a policy of accommodation and extended immediate and credible rewards. Italy's relations with them improved, while its relations with Germany tanked. By the same token, Italy's relations with the Allies deteriorated, and Mussolini became more inclined to intervene, as Britain's approach hardened in early 1940.

WAS ITALIAN BELLIGERENCE INEVITABLE?

My argument is challenged by a more deterministic perspective on Italy's path to war. In this view, Italy was decisively alienated from the Western democracies by 1937 or 1938 and entrenched on the path to alliance with Germany and eventual war against them.[177] This vision of an irreversible hardening of conflict between Italy and the Western powers by 1937 implies there were no missed opportunities for concerted accommodation.[178] Even a more credible, skillfully coordinated approach would not have deflected Italy from its march into Germany's arms and war.

But there are good reasons to doubt that after 1937 Italy was irrevocably committed to Germany and the march into war with it. The first is a compelling piece of negative evidence—the fact that Italy did *not* go to war in August 1939, just four months after it joined the alliance with Germany. Indeed, its defection into hedged neutrality even involved some covert collusion with the Allies to Germany's detriment. This posture, and Mussolini's intent to use it to glean gains through "practical political action" instead of force, continued well into March 1940, when Mussolini proposed to U.S. Undersecretary of State Sumner Welles that Italy and the U.S. work together to broker a negotiated settlement that included some territorial compensations for Italy.[179] As late as 1 April 1940, according to Ciano, Mussolini harbored the idea of leading mediation to end the war before Germany attacked in the west.[180]

The second is positive evidence: when Italy *did* go to war against the Western Allies, it was only once the Battle of France had turned decisively in Germany's favor in June 1940. This too weighs against the thesis that Italy's attachment to Germany and its path to war against the Western powers was entrenched in prior years. A counterfactual question makes this clear: What would Italy have done if in May 1940 France and Britain had stopped the German offensive, while continuing the efforts to accommodate Italy they began at that time? Most likely, Italy would have remained nonbelligerent.[181] In that case, our understanding of Italy's "fundamental" alignment in the late 1930s would be much more complex. It would appear to have never been irrevocably bound to Germany, but instead to have been using it for leverage to negotiate concessions from the Western powers—the actual pattern of Italian diplomacy from 1937 to March 1940.[182] An inevitable trajectory to war, in lockstep with Germany, only emerges when one looks back from June 1940.

The most important reason to reject the inevitability argument is rooted in the empirical record of high-level statements and private correspondence issued by Mussolini and Ciano in December 1939 and January 1940. These indicated an intent to dispel expectations of ironclad commitment to Germany and rule out intervention *except* in the most propitious circumstances. This evidence shows that intervention on Germany's side was far from inevitable, and that Mussolini did not consider Italy irrevocably committed to it. It confirms what Mussolini had written directly to Hitler on the eve of war in August—that he preferred "a solution in the political field" and would adopt a "practical attitude" if Germany started the war.[183]

Ciano's 16 December 1939 speech to the Fascist Grand Council (noted before), which disassociated Italy from Hitler's deal with the Soviet Union and aggression against Poland, was clearly intended by Ciano *and* Mussolini as a distancing signal, and perceived as such by both German and Western leaders.[184] Mussolini's letter to Hitler on 3 January did little to dispel the message. He had approved Ciano's speech in advance and, as he explained to Hitler, "It represents my thoughts from the first to the last word." Though Mussolini did assure Hitler that Italy would not switch sides against Germany (the "phenomenon of 1914–15 [would not be] repeated in 1940 or 1941"), he left little doubt that Italy might wait out events and would go to war only if it saw an opening for certain and quick victory. On top of that, there was a warning not to "delude oneself" that the democracies could be totally defeated, because "the United States would not permit [it]," and the astonishing recommendation that Hitler "reaffirm that you do not have any war aims in the west [and] refrain from taking the initiative on the western front."[185] That he wanted to stop such a move is made clear by the fact that when "the Italian military attaché in Berlin heard in late December of German intentions to invade the low Countries, Mussolini ordered Ciano to warn their ambassadors."[186] In sum, Mussolini's final decision in late May 1940 to enter the war was not the inevitable expression of an unconditional determination to join his ally's fight against Britain and France, but instead a response to an unexpected and narrow window of opportunity that resulted from a German escalation of the war that *he had repeatedly tried to stop.*[187] The fact that Italy remained a bystander until June 1940, then, supports the idea that Mussolini's calculus was essentially opportunist and—and even into 1940—uncommitted and conditional.[188] If the Duce was not dead set on upholding his alliance with Hitler and following Germany into war against the Allies, then Anglo-Franco accommodation of Italy was possible. That means their discord over dealing with Italy would have hurt their ability to influence it in favorable ways.

THE ROLE OF IDEOLOGICAL FACTORS

Patterns of ideological distance—the degree of affinity between some governments and antipathy between others—influenced these events in ways that reinforced the outcomes.[189] Clearly, Fascist affinity with National Socialism was a key force driving Italy toward Germany in the 1930s.[190] It was a taproot of that strategic convergence that created the Allies' need to divide Italy from Germany in the first place. Conservatives of Baldwin's and Chamberlain's governments were undoubtedly more willing to countenance an arrangement with Mussolini's regime than were the British Left; that they championed the policy to accommodate Italy is thus consistent with ideological expectations. Likewise, intense ideological hostility between the French Popular Front governments and Italian Fascism also magnified the difficulties London faced in trying to get Paris to steer a course that supported conciliation of Italy.[191] Under Blum, for example, French determination to revitalize the Left's collapsing position in Spain stoked Franco-Italian conflict and undermined Britain's plans to sequence deals between London, Paris, and Rome that would halt Italy's drift toward Germany.

Nevertheless, such ideological constraints did not doom accommodation of Italy. Shared ideological stripes did not ensure that Italy would leap into war when Germany did, or that the two countries would achieve effective strategic collaboration during *any* part of the war.[192] As Watt once warned, "One has to avoid the very simple equation; like government, like aim, therefore alliance. While there are clear likenesses and parallels between the two dictators and their systems of government, only an acceptance of Axis propaganda at its face value can make them into an explanation for the existence of the Axis."[193] Close ideological affinity did not prevent Mussolini from intensely fearing German aggression in the Alto Adige in April 1938.[194] Nor did it prevent Ciano from concluding in August 1939 that Germany was a most untrustworthy and dangerous ally that Italy should drop.[195] Fascist affinity also did not stop Italy from seeking—in open and covert ways—to cooperate with the Allies while remaining a nonbelligerent. In December 1939, Mussolini and his circle nearly nullified the alliance that, in their eyes, they had been conned into. Ideological affinity, in other words, did not make for a close bond between Germany and Italy, and it did not stop Italy's practical defection from it. Comparisons with cases that follow help to underscore this point. As shown in in chapter 7, massive ideological antipathies did nothing to inhibit the Nazi-Soviet bargain of August 1939. And, as shown in chapter 8, strong ideological ties between Fascist Spain, Germany, and Italy were not strong enough to stop Britain and the U.S. from successfully inducing Spanish nonbelligerence in 1940 to 1941.

Germany Divides the USSR from Britain and France, 1939

> The Führer believes he's in the position of scrounging for favors and beggars can't be choosers.
>
> Joseph Goebbels, Reich minister of propaganda,
> August 1939
>
> The Anglo-French policy of encirclement against Germany [had] been so greatly intensified . . . [that] Germany had been forced to take desperate measures. . . . We had no choice but to neutralize the Soviet Union quickly.
>
> Joachim von Ribbentrop, German foreign minister,
> October 1939

About World War II, no belief is more ingrained than that Western appeasement of Hitler caused it. But if one looks to immediate causes, what stands out is another campaign of appeasement, surprising because of who authored it (Hitler), and remarkable in its devastating success. Hitler's policy to conciliate the Soviet Union in the summer of 1939 resulted in the 23 August Nazi-Soviet "nonaggression" pact. In pursuit of it, Hitler proved willing to make major concessions.[1] As Ernst von Weizsäcker, who was then state secretary of the German Foreign Office, recalled, Hitler "changed from abusing Stalin to attempting to seize his hand[, and] Stalin grasped his hand, after Hitler had thrown into his lap a large share of the Baltic area as his sphere of influence."[2] In return, "Stalin relieved Hitler of the fear of a two-front war," and that, says Kissinger, made "a general war inevitable."[3]

Hitler accommodated the Soviet Union for one reason—to prevent it from joining Britain, France, and other East European states in an encircling alliance.[4] That alliance was a pure expression of the balancing impulse. Forming in reaction to Germany's takeover of Czechoslovakia, it was meant to deter Hitler from attacking Poland and pursuing wider ambitions in Europe. To break that ring, Hitler was willing to make large political, economic, and strategic concessions to buy Soviet neutrality. The theoretical framework describes and explains conditions that propelled that enterprise and enabled it to succeed.

Hitler's policy was informed by two beliefs about Soviet strategic weight. The first was that Soviet neutrality was necessary for victory in a war against Poland that included British and French intervention. Soviet neutrality would diminish the effects of the Allied strategy of economic blockade and punishment. The second was that the shock of Moscow's neutralization would likely compel Britain and France to abandon their commitments to Poland and thus allow Germany to attack it isolated. In Soviet neutrality, then, lay two kinds of war-tipping potential: it could make possible a certain victory over an isolated Poland, and if Britain and France did intervene, it would make it possible to beat them in a general war.

Throughout the spring and summer of 1939, German leaders worried that the Soviet Union might close ranks with their enemies, and indeed, they were nearly certain it would unless they convinced it not to.[5] On that score, German leaders believed they had relative reward power to work with. The Soviet economy's breakneck industrialization craved capital goods that Germany could offer, and Moscow had for years sought (to no avail) a large expansion of German-Soviet trade. Stalin's intense fears of German expansion eastward—from Finland and the Baltics to Poland, Ukraine, and Romania—offered another handle. German commitments to restraint in these areas, and even acquiescence to Soviet expansion into them, could be dangled as rewards for Soviet neutrality. Threats to the Soviet Union in the Far East—from Japan—presented another way for Berlin to reward Moscow as no other power could. Germany could use its influence to restrain Japan; and, in a larger sense, any German rapprochement with the Soviets would isolate and weaken Moscow's eastern enemy. As German leaders foresaw, despite the apparent long odds, their policy to accommodate the Soviet Union might work because they could extend strategic benefits to Moscow that the Allies' alliance plans could not.

Other conditions, captured in the theory, strongly favored success. First, Germany's policy tried to induce a low degree of alignment change. The Soviet Union was uncommitted; the German goal was to solidify this in a formal arrangement. Second, Germany faced low alliance constraints at the time. Its closest (and only formal) military ally, Italy, was weak relative to Germany and had little direct influence or interests at stake in the elements of the bargain, and it favored compromise with USSR for the same general reasons Germany did. If the essential driver of the policy's impact was its far-reaching inducements, these conditions made it easier for the inducements to work.[6]

Initiation Conditions

After Hitler broke the Munich agreements and conquered Czechoslovakia in March 1939, Britain tried to surround Germany with a deterrent bloc of powers. It was, as the British foreign minister, Lord Halifax, put it, a "question of encirclement": "What we want to secure is the certainty for Germany of a war on two fronts—East and West."[7] German leaders anticipated this reaction. As early as October 1938, Joachim von Ribbentrop, the German foreign minister, warned of the coming need to "counterbalance this Britain-France-Russia combination of power and the ties prevailing between [them]."[8] In late May 1939, Ribbentrop reported to Hitler that Moscow was now deeply "engaged in negotiations with England, which indicate that Moscow is more or less determined to enter actively into the English policy of encirclement."[9] By then, according to Weizsäcker, "Hitler was thinking of coming to terms with Soviet Russia."[10] To counter the encirclement, German leaders believed that they needed to both form a Rome-Berlin alliance (see chapter 6) and neutralize Russia.

PERCEPTIONS OF TARGET'S STRATEGIC WEIGHT

German leaders perceived the USSR to be a strategic heavyweight.[11] They held two views of Soviet strategic weight, both of which framed it as a war-tipper. At the broad level, Hitler wanted to avoid the two-front war that had doomed his predecessors. As war approached in August 1939, he explained to German military leaders that if the deal with Russia came to fruition, he would risk war with Britain and France over Poland, because Poland would in any case be "hopelessly isolated and any British blockade broken by the opening to the [USSR]. . . . The pact with the Soviet Union would be helpful to Germany whether the war with the Western Powers took place simultaneously with the one against Poland or subsequent to it."[12] In this sense, neutralizing the Soviets was seen as a necessary condition for a successful war against Poland if Britain and France intervened: if Moscow were neutral, victory would be possible; if it were not, Germany could not win and would not therefore fight. As Hitler put it to his generals on 22 August, "With this [pact with Russia] I have knocked the weapons out the hands of these gentry. Poland has been maneuvered into the position that we need for military success."[13] Conversely, Hitler "contemplated backing down if the Western powers' negotiations in Moscow were successful. In that case, he would have apparently called off the operation against Poland."[14] Thus, as Weizsäcker then noted, Germany's "decision between peace and war" depended on whether the "negotiations in Moscow bring Russia into the orbit of the Western powers."[15]

But German perceptions of the Soviets' strategic weight went deeper, extending to a concept of coercive isolation.[16] Hitler thought it likely that the "Pact with Russia would deter the West from intervention."[17] Thus Soviet neutrality was valued highly because of its expected knock-on political effects, which would completely isolate Poland.[18] As Hitler declared to the military staff on 23 May, "Our task is to isolate Poland. Success in isolating her will be decisive."[19] In May 1939, when Britain and France began scrambling to ally with the USSR, it seemed evident that they believed they needed a Soviet alliance to uphold their commitments to Poland, and reasonable to surmise that they would abandon Poland if Moscow did not join them.[20] As Hermann Göering, the supreme commander of the Luftwaffe, once put it to Mussolini, "Any declaration of neutrality on the part of Russia would . . . make a deep impression on Poland and the Western Powers."[21] Weizsäcker recorded Hitler's belief in late July that if the alliance talks between the Soviet Union and the Western Powers failed, "the depression in that quarter will be such that we can do what we like with Poland."[22] To German military elites on 22 August, Hitler explained why he "was hopeful that Britain and France would stay out. . . . The forthcoming treaty with the Soviet Union, just publicly announced, would be of great assistance."[23] According to Weizsäcker, Hitler figured that the shock of the of the "Moscow coup" would throw British prime minister Neville Chamberlain "from his saddle. . . . His Cabinet will fall," and the British would then drop the Polish guarantee.[24] Hitler also expected the ripple effects of Soviet neutrality to reach Britain's allies Turkey and Romania: the prospect of German agreement with Russia, he said to the Italian foreign minister, Galeazzo Ciano, would have "the effect of neutralizing these countries."[25]

In sum, German calculations of Soviet strategic weight were twofold. In the worst case of a general war over Poland, it was a necessary condition for victory—the only way to avert a two-front war. But it was also a lever of coercive diplomacy that could produce a much more favorable scenario, deterring the Western powers from intervening, and thus averting a general war in the first place. Neutralizing Moscow, in short, could make it possible to wage a cheap and quick war against Poland alone.

PERCEPTIONS OF RELATIVE REWARD POWER

After the British guaranteed Poland in March 1939, Hitler decided that only "a very far-reaching offer to the Soviet Union" would "forestall" an Anglo-Franco-Soviet alliance.[26] German leaders and diplomats believed that though it would "certainly not be easy to prevent" the alliance, they held reward power relative to Moscow that just might work.[27] The main lines were well known, and gradually put into service: expansion of commercial relations on terms favorable to Moscow; acquiescence to Soviet expansion and influence over territories in the Baltics, Poland, and Balkans; and the application of German pressure to restrain Japanese hostility toward the Soviet Union.

Trade concessions were the first and most obvious lever.[28] Thus, when Göering met Mussolini in Rome in April, they agreed that "possibilities for rapprochement existed" due to Moscow's "desire to expand the scope of the [1935] Russo-German economic treaty."[29] Surveying the situation in late May, Weizsäcker concluded: "There still remains fairly wide scope for action in Russo-German relations," and, for this, Germany should stress the theme of "intensifying Russo-German trade," while hinting that "*all* possibilities remained open between Germany and Russia."[30] Indeed, throughout May and June, German diplomats were left in doubt about the opportunity offered by the Soviets' appetite for expanded trade. The Soviet ambassador, Alexei Merekalov, and chargé d'affaires, Georgi Astakhov, repeatedly expressed to them that the Soviet Union and Germany could have normal and closer economic relations, just as the Soviet Union and Italy did, notwithstanding the ideological obstacles.[31]

The key point of leverage for Germany arose from the Soviets' intense industrialization and rearmament programs: the USSR "desperately needed weapons and industrial equipment. Germany could supply both."[32] As the Germans began their effort to shape Soviet alignment, they recognized that a commercial arrangement based on Soviet proposals—which advantaged Moscow more than Berlin—would be needed to cut through the haggling and close a deal quickly.[33] Thus, on 22 July, with Soviet trade negotiators in Berlin ready to parley, Weizsäcker summed up the approach: "At all events" the German government would "act in a markedly forthcoming manner, since a conclusion, and this at the earliest possible date, is desired for general reasons."[34] The deal that was ultimately worked out in early August, which cleared the way for negotiating the nonaggression pact, was an "economic settlement with the Soviets [that was] largely on their terms."[35] As Molotov explained on 31 August, "This agreement differs favorably . . . from all previous [German] agreements, [and] we have never had any equally advantageous economic agreement with Great Britain, France, or any other country."[36]

The second facet of German reward power lay in its ability to cede to the Soviet Union an exclusive sphere of influence on its western glacis, in the Baltics and part of Poland. German officials knew that Moscow was intensely interested in securing those areas. By early June, they knew that Soviet insistence on strong guarantees over the Baltic states had become a sticking point in the negotiations over the political terms of an Anglo-Franco-Soviet alliance.[37] Addressing his military staff on 14 August, Hitler declared that "Stalin has no intention of pulling England's chestnuts out of the fire. . . . His interests at most extend to the Baltic states." Thus, Hitler explained, he might "promise a delimitation of spheres of interest [concerning the] Baltic states." The "Russians want[ed] to discuss [the] subject more closely." To overcome their distrust, Hitler was "inclined to meet [them] half way."[38] As it turned out, "half way" meant a division of spheres resting on Lithuania that turned over Latvia, Estonia, and Finland to Moscow's tender mercies, and, as Molotov's gentle hint to Astakhov in early August suggested, "an understanding" with Russia on Poland's fate.

The third element of German reward power lay in its unique potential to restrain Japan—which was then escalating a military crisis in the Soviet Far East—and, by extension, foster a Russo-Japan détente. As Weizsäcker wrote to Friedrich-Werner von Schulenburg, the German ambassador to Moscow, on 27 May, "one link in the whole chain" of inducements to the USSR was Germany's potential to promote "a gradual conciliation of relations between Moscow and Tokyo."[39] Thus did Weizsäcker suggest to Astakhov on 24 July "that a modus vivendi might very well be possible between [Japan and Russia] for a good many years to come."[40] Ribbentrop repeated this point to Astakhov on 3 August, noting that he had "special ideas" about Russian-Japanese relations, "by which I meant a long-term modus vivendi between the two countries."[41] German officials recognized that Moscow believed Berlin could influence Japan's aggressiveness; such was conveyed by Molotov's complaints that Germany "had supported and encouraged the aggressive attitude of Japan," and demands that Germany "cease to support Japanese 'aggression.'"[42] On 16 August, Molotov put the matter directly to Schulenburg: Was Berlin "prepared to influence Japan for the purpose of improving Soviet-Japanese relations and eliminating border conflicts"?[43] The next day he returned to the theme, emphasizing that it was one of the questions that "above all else" needed to be answered: Did "Germany see any real possibility of influencing Japan in the direction of a better relationship with the Soviet Union"? Ribbentrop's reply was unambiguous: "Germany is prepared to exercise influence for an improvement and consolidation of Russo-Japanese relations"; he was "prepared to interest himself in this matter, since his influence upon the Japanese government was certainly not slight."[44] When Hitler spoke to the military staff on 22 August, he identified "intervention in Russo-Japanese conflict" as one of the key points in "our Russian initiative," along with progress toward a nonaggression pact and a deal on the Baltic states.[45]

Contingent Conditions

ATTEMPTED ALIGNMENT CHANGE

Germany's policy tried to induce a low degree of alignment change. It tried to neutralize Moscow by reinforcing its hedged position.[46] In April 1939, Göering posed to Mussolini the possibility that Germany would "put out feelers cautiously to Russia . . . with a view to a rapprochement." Mussolini agreed that "the object of such an approach would be to induce Russia to react coolly and unfavorably to Britain's efforts at encirclement . . . and to take up a neutral position."[47] Berlin, in fact, was already working in this direction.[48] In May, Ribbentrop informed Ciano that he was taking steps "to prevent Russia's joining the anti-totalitarian bloc."[49] Later that month, as the alliance talks accelerated, Weizsäcker, noted: "It should be our aim to prevent Anglo-Franco-Soviet relations from . . . becoming intensified any further."[50] According to Gustav Hilger, the German embassy councilor in Moscow, Hitler was by August "convinced of the need to secure Soviet Russia's neutrality."[51] To do this, he would not have to move the USSR far. Although Moscow paid lip service to "collective security" well into the summer, it had stayed free of formal alliance commitments and demonstrably hedged in such a way that, as Weinberg notes, a "swing away from the West was certainly indicated, but toward a neutral—bargaining—position, rather than a pro-German one."[52]

ALLIANCE CONSTRAINTS

Germany faced low alliance constraints, and those that arose Hitler avoided through a combination of guile and disciplined policy choices. When he began trying, in mid-1939, to build military alliances on the foundations of the Anti-Comintern Pact, accommodating the USSR could conflict with his agenda in two ways. It could subvert immediate efforts to tie Italy into military agreement, and it could have a similar effect on Japan.

Italy was the more immediate concern. Its prompt adhesion to a formal alliance was needed in May 1939 if Germany were to reduce the risk of fighting in Europe alone. In this sense only was Germany then dependent on Italian support. But several factors went in Germany's favor. Most importantly, Italy did not have direct stakes in the major values—in the Baltics and Poland, and Russo-German trade—that would be exchanged in a bargain with Moscow. Italy's material weaknesses, moreover, ensured that even if it had wanted to obstruct or degrade such a bargain, it had little means or leverage to do so. But this was never a concern, for Italian leaders did not intend to be spoilers; from the outset, they bought into the goal of accommodating Stalin in order to divide the USSR from an Anglo-Franco alliance.

ALLIED STRATEGIC CONSENSUS

In an unofficial conversation on 16 April, even before the Pact of Steel was signed, Göering and Mussolini converged on the concept. When Göering floated it, Mussolini "welcomed th[e] idea most warmly." He had "had similar ideas for some time" and "had already adopted a more friendly tone toward the Russians." Indeed, he wanted Germany to reach out to Stalin because "Britain was also making advances to the Russians at the moment." Summing up, Göering and Mussolini agreed: "Germany and Italy ought to endeavor to play the so-called petit jeu with [Russia]. Possibilities for rapprochement existed."[53] When Ribbentrop and Ciano met in early May to negotiate the alliance, the consensus held firm. As Ciano recorded in his meeting notes, Ribbentrop wanted to seize "any favorable occasion . . . to prevent the adhesion of Russia to the anti-totalitarian bloc"; he insisted on the need to achieve "détente" with Moscow.[54] Mussolini, for his part, had already instructed Ciano to say "yes to a policy that would prevent Russia from joining the anti-Axis bloc."[55] In mid-June, Mussolini assured the German ambassador that he "welcomed" Germany's steps toward Moscow, which might "still be in time to prevent the Soviets from concluding an agreement with Britain and France."[56] Later that month, Rome messaged Berlin that "the moment had arrived for thwarting the Anglo-Franco-Soviet negotiations."[57]

In the weeks leading up to the Nazi-Soviet Pact, Berlin did not disclose to Rome the progress in negotiations, but Mussolini and Ciano were kept apprised by well-placed informants in the Moscow embassies.[58] At several points, the Duce quietly warned Berlin against a deal with the Soviet Union that went "too far," but otherwise "neither Mussolini nor Ciano attempted to restrain the Germans."[59] During this period, both Mussolini and Ciano "still saw the main benefit of détente between Berlin and Moscow in the detrimental effect it could have on the alliance plans of Great Britain, France, and the Soviet Union." Their instructions to the Italian ambassador in Moscow in late June, and the ambassador's actions there in early July, both supported this view and foresaw the possibility of a German-Soviet nonaggression pact, a broad trade agreement, and a deal over the Baltics.[60] When the pact was announced publicly, the Italian leaders feigned surprise, but they had advance warning of the main agreement and its secret protocols.[61] If they did not then welcome the war that immediately followed, they had given early approval and then largely acquiesced to Germany's initiative. Italy did not contribute in any material way to the inducements Germany extended to the Soviet Union, but consensus and coordination at that level was unnecessary. The bargain Germany extended to the USSR did not depend on Italian generosity.

With Japan it would not be so easy. Germany therefore deceived and avoided allying with it. Japan in 1939 was intent on confronting the Soviet Union, not the other powers in Europe; in fact, it was then fighting Soviet forces in the Far East. Germany, by contrast, meant to confront Poland, and it wanted an alliance with Japan to help deter the Western powers' intervention.[62] With Poland its immediate target, Berlin was wary of making an alliance that served Japan's aims—to encircle the USSR—as long as it might be possible to prevent the encirclement of Germany by stabilizing relations with Moscow. In April and May 1939, Berlin tried first to persuade Tokyo to support a policy of working with Russia; Japan's refusal to cooperate along these lines brought the effort to a standstill.[63] As Schulenburg wrote to Berlin in early June, Japan did not want to see "even the smallest agreement between [Germany] and Soviet Russia."[64] Hitler solved the looming alliance contradictions by downgrading efforts to ally with Japan. Over the summer of 1939, he left Tokyo in the dark about the impending reversal of Germany's relations with the Soviet Union. When the pact was announced in late August, Japan was surprised and made suddenly more vulnerable.[65]

In sum, when it set out to accommodate Moscow, Germany had low alliance constraints. With Italy, a basic level of coordination was all that was needed and it came naturally—Italy was a junior partner, it had no strings to pull in the crux of a German-Soviet bargain, and Mussolini fully bought into the strategic concept. With Japan, it quickly became clear that coordination of any kind would be impossible, so Hitler dodged the dilemma by deciding not to ally with Japan at that time.

Diplomacy of Selective Accommodation

In August 1939 Hitler proved willing to make, as Weinberg put it, "the most extensive concessions to the Soviet Union."[66] Goebbels described Hitler's mindset this way: "The Führer believes he's in the position of scrounging for favors and beggars can't be choosers."[67] The diplomatic bases for this dramatic bargain were laid down over a fairly compressed five-month timeline. What made the resulting success so surprising was the pattern, over prior years, of intensifying conflict between Germany and the Soviet Union. From that pattern arose expectations that the USSR and Western democracies would find a way to join together, as they tried to do in the summer of 1939.

THE PRELUDE

In 1935, the Comintern, under Moscow's diktat, adopted a resolution identifying Japan and Germany as its worst enemies.[68] In the November 1936 Anti-Comintern Pact, Germany and Japan declared themselves enemies of the Communist International and, in a secret annex, of the USSR. Thus, at the end of 1936, Germany and Japan had fingered the USSR as their number one common enemy, and the Soviet Union reciprocated the enmity. A stream of escalating tensions between the USSR and Germany and Japan followed. When Japan invaded China in 1937, the USSR was "the first power to begin supplying substantial material assistance and solid political backing for China's war of resistance against Japan."[69] At the same time, Japanese-Soviet fighting around the Far Eastern borders escalated into a "quasi-war."[70] In Europe, the Germans were moving against the Soviet ally Czechoslovakia and working to construct a pointedly anti-Soviet alliance with Italy. As Ribbentrop prepared for Hitler's trip to Italy in April 1938, his memo of talking points listed at the top, "Bolshevism as the common enemy."[71] At the Munich conference in August 1938 Hitler had insisted, with success, that the USSR be excluded from the negotiations. Thus, Germany had politically isolated the USSR at the onset of its threatening moves to the east. Hitler declared to the Reichstag in January 1939 that the Soviet Union was as a "satanic apparition," and that he would make the Anti-Comintern Pact a "group of powers whose ultimate aim is none other than to eliminate the menace to the peace and culture of the world."[72] In the same month, Soviet fears of a Nazi move into Ukraine spiked.[73] In March, Germany reneged on the Munich agreements and rolled up Czechoslovakia. Then Berlin began to seek an anti-Soviet alliance with Poland.[74]

As the post-Munich maneuvers ensued, Moscow began to hedge; it would not let itself be isolated again like it had been during the Munich conference. Stalin's 10 March speech to the Eighteenth Party Congress was the harbinger of this new orientation. Moscow, he signaled, would not plead for Western commitments to collective security and would not be made the tool of a Western policy to redirect Nazi aggression eastward. It would stand with those opposed to aggression, and the victims of it, but it would not foreclose regular, peaceful economic relations with any power—including Germany.[75]

That stance made sense. Until March 1939, Britain's search for security against the German threat had avoided firm commitments and especially closer ties to Moscow.[76] British prime minister Neville Chamberlain's Conservative cabinet had not yet set aside its ideological antipathy to Soviet Communism enough to seek partnership against Germany.[77] Military misgivings reinforced this: between 1937 and mid-1939, the British chiefs of staff judged Soviet military strength unfavorably, and an alliance with Moscow to be a military and political liability.[78] But after the Munich agreements failed, and the immediacy of the German menace increased, Britain and France sought alliances to bolster deterrence. Thus, in April 1939, they extended guarantees to Poland, Romania, and Greece.[79] Concomitantly, they began to sound Soviet intentions if Romania became Hitler's next target.[80]

In reply, the Soviet foreign minister at the time, Maxim Litvinov, proposed a conference for "joint consultation" of Soviet, British, French, Polish, and Romanian officials to work out practical plans.[81] That would be too time-consuming for Halifax, who wanted a faster signal to deter Germany. He countered with a proposal for a prompt Four Power Declaration (by Britain, France, Poland, and the USSR) to "consult" on "joint resistance" to any aggressive action by Germany. Once that had been declared, Britain would rope in support from Romania, Turkey, Greece, Bulgaria, and Yugoslavia. Litvinov accepted this formula on the conditions that both France and Poland agreed, and that the Baltics and Finland also be made to give secondary endorsements, which would tie the whole arrangement together.[82] Before it could be tested, Halifax's plan collapsed: Poland and Romania refused to join any kind of bloc with the USSR, and indeed with each other.[83]

Britain then turned to a different two-step strategy: first it would extend direct guarantees to Poland, then it would try to work out an arrangement with the Soviet Union. This sequencing was encouraged by the bizarre belief that Poland's military power was more valuable for containing Hitler than the Soviet Union's.[84] At the same time, France tried to garner Soviet commitment under the aegis of the 1935 Franco-Soviet pact. After signing that pact, France had backed away from making the military convention that was supposed to follow. The Soviets thus considered it "to be merely a paper delusion."[85] Nevertheless, France now invoked the moribund pact, and asked Moscow to discuss joint responses to a German attack on Poland or Romania. Moscow responded coolly: it would consider any concrete proposals for military cooperation.[86] But Britain and France were not yet reconciled to the need for a formal alliance with the Soviet Union. In mid-April, Britain tried the indirect approach again. It had decided to extend commitments to Greece and Turkey, and it was seeking a trilateral guarantee of Romania backed by Britain, France, and Poland. On 11 April, Halifax tried to pin down Ivan Maisky, the Soviet ambassador to Britain, on how the Soviets might help Romania if it were attacked by Germany. Maisky's reply made it clear that Moscow was against the Allies' piecemeal approaches to balancing against Germany, and it put the onus on Britain to put forward a concrete proposal for a more general mechanism that included the USSR.[87]

On the same day (11 April), Hitler authorized "Case White" directing his military to be ready to attack Poland by September.[88] Soviet intelligence learned of this almost immediately and by mid-May, had given Stalin indications that Hitler had firmly decided to conquer Poland.[89] For Moscow, the German threat became concrete in terms of location and timing—Hitler would soon move east. Soviet alliance diplomacy shifted into a higher gear. It notified Halifax that it was now ready to "take part in giving assistance to Roumania" and Britain should recommend the "best methods" for doing so.[90] But Britain still wanted to avoid direct commitments with Moscow; what it wanted was a unilateral Soviet declaration that it would defend Romania. The Kremlin refused to give it. Moscow's counteroffer came on 18 April. It reflected Stalin's direct instructions—he had even edited Litvinov's wording of the proposal. It called for a sweeping trilateral pact: formal reciprocal commitments all around; guarantees for all European states bordering the USSR; and a real military convention. This formula had to be the basis for further negotiations.[91] In taking this approach, Stalin also ruled out a statement proposed by Litvinov that would have precluded the USSR from pursuing negotiations with Germany.[92] Stalin was now bargaining hard—while cultivating the alliance, he kept his German option open.[93]

Stalin's ambitious alliance proposal "went farther" than Chamberlain and Halifax had wanted to go and triggered more than four weeks of intense cabinet deliberations, consultations with France and other allies, crossed signals with Moscow, and a failed last effort to persuade it to agree to the more limited proposal for unilateral Soviet declarations.[94] Despite much reluctance and backtracking throughout April, all this culminated, in late May, in a firm decision to seek an Anglo-Franco-Soviet alliance along the lines Stalin proposed.[95] Critical to that final decision was a big change in the military viewpoint: Soviet support was now identified by the chiefs of staff as key to defending Poland and Romania and effecting an economic blockade against Germany.[96] Along with this changed outlook, two other things catalyzed the British decision: Germany and Italy inked the Pact of Steel on 22 May, and Poland and Romania rescinded their opposition to a tripartite pact the next day. So, at the decisive cabinet meeting on 24 May, Halifax, with Chamberlain's assent, argued that Britain must pursue a "direct mutual guarantee agreement" with the Soviets and could not allow those negotiations to collapse.[97] The cabinet unanimously backed a triple alliance counterproposal envisioning mutual, reciprocal commitment. It was sent to the Soviets the next day.[98]

The reticence suggested by Britain's slow, clumsy reply had already undone Litvinov. On 4 May, Stalin replaced him with Vyacheslav Molotov. Over the next three months, Soviet diplomacy continued to pursue a comprehensive alliance, consistent with Litvinov's 18 April proposal, and the British 25 May counterproposal—but it also protected the option for rapprochement with Germany.[99] Stalin's knowledge of Hitler's plans to attack Poland in late August shaped his approach to the ensuing alliance negotiations. He insisted on getting to the specifics of military cooperation and focusing on the tricky problem of getting Allied commitments to securing the Baltics, where Leningrad was exposed to creeping German expansion.[100]

On 27 May, Molotov got Britain's counterproposal, which framed the three-way commitment as a promise to consult if one of them were attacked, couched in terms referring to the League's mechanisms of collective security. This was unacceptable: it fudged the demand for direct three-way commitments and, moreover, lacked guarantees to protect the Baltics from German aggression.[101] In a way that would be repeated over the next three months, London then moved deliberately to address Moscow's various demands for stronger political commitments and a simultaneously arranged, detailed military convention.[102] When the process culminated in a dramatic failure for Britain and France in August, it was not because they, or the Soviets, were engaged half-heartedly. It was because the Germans—sensing the seriousness of their moves toward alliance—launched an extraordinary diplomatic effort to subvert the process, offering strong economic inducements, as well as concessions with respect to Poland and the Baltics that the Allies could not match.

GERMANY'S CAMPAIGN TO ACCOMMODATE THE SOVIET UNION

Oblique feelers between Berlin and Moscow began in April 1939.[103] The most concrete signals occurred in Berlin on 17 April, between Weizsäcker and Merekalov.[104] Their nominal reason for meeting was to discuss improving German-Soviet economic relations, but the larger political possibilities were surfaced. While Weizsäcker voiced concerns about a new Triple Entente, Merekalov hinted that the USSR might wish to stay out of a general war in Europe and pointedly noted that ideological differences need not hinder "normal" and "improved" relations.[105] After that meeting, Germany promptly met Merekalov's request for fulfilment of a Soviet order for arms from the Skoda works in Czechoslovakia.[106]

Berlin also decided to press forward in seeking a general commercial agreement. Hitler and Ribbentrop conferred in mid-May with Schulenburg and returned him to Moscow with instructions to seek an opening for trade talks.[107] When Schulenburg approached Molotov about this on 20 May, Molotov's reply—that progress in commercial matters depended on a change in the political bases of the relationship—came across as a rebuff.[108] Ribbentrop then pivoted to present the Pact of Steel proposal to Italy, which Mussolini accepted on 22 May. That decision to quickly cement a German-Italian alliance was also a decision to ignore Japan's beckoning for a tripartite alliance against the USSR.[109]

There followed two months of unrequited German efforts to coax Moscow away from "the enticements of London."[110] In late May, German officials deliberated "whether and how . . . to put a spoke in the wheel of Anglo-Russian negotiations."[111] Weizsäcker warned Ribbentrop that the "Anglo-Russian negotiations appear to be coming to a conclusion," and that German policy "must [aim] to prevent the Russian-English-French relations from acquiring a yet more binding character."[112] Ribbentrop, with Hitler's blessing, instructed Schulenburg to tell Molotov that Berlin welcomed a "frank examination" of the political bases of the relationship, and if "hostilities with Poland occur . . . this would not necessarily lead to a conflict of interests with Soviet Russia." Indeed, Germany wished to pay "the greatest possible regard" to Russian interests in any solution of the "German-Polish problem."[113] On 29 May, Ribbentrop instructed Hilger in Moscow to lean forward on the economic negotiations.[114] On 30 May, Weizsäcker explained to Astakhov that Berlin wanted to revive economic talks, but it had to consider "a political orientation in Moscow" that seemed to encourage "Britain's efforts . . . to draw Russia into her orbit." Was there "any room at all for a possible gradual normalization of relations between Soviet Russia and Germany," he asked, "now that Moscow had perhaps already listened to the enticements of London?"[115]

Molotov's 31 May speech answered the query and set Moscow's bargaining posture: the USSR's main object was to "strengthe[n] political relations between U.S.S.R., England, and France" and "sto[p] further aggression" by creating "a reliable and effective front of non-aggressive powers." At the same time, Moscow would not "refus[e] commercial relations with such countries as Germany and Italy."[116] But from then until mid-July, there was no forward movement in German-Russian relations. Moscow waited for the Germans to be more forthcoming on the political "fundamentals" of an accord and for the negotiations with Britain and France to mature. To kindle commercial talks as a path to political breakthrough, Hitler ordered foreign ministry negotiator Karl Schnurre to "act in a markedly forthcoming manner, since a conclusion, and this at the earliest possible date, is desired for general reasons."[117] Schnurre made little headway; the Anglo-Franco-Soviet alliance talks ground on.

On 27 July, Schnurre changed the approach: with Astakhov, he now spoke explicitly about politics rather than trade, trying to reassure him that German intentions did not threaten Soviet interests. Its ties to Japan were "that of a well-founded friendship" but "not aimed against Russia." It "would respect the integrity of the Baltic countries and Finland." It was indeed possible for Germany and the USSR to strike "a far-reaching compromise of mutual interests with due consideration of the problems which were vital to Russia," as long as Moscow did not "sid[e] with England against Germany."[118] One of Astakhov's response stood out—"Besides economic penetration," did Germany have "more far reaching political aims" in the Baltics? Schnurre reported to Ribbentrop that Ashtakov's question suggested that "Moscow, after months of negotiation with England, still remains uncertain as to what she ought to do eventually."[119] To Weizsäcker, whether Germany would ever "get as far as negotiating with Moscow in the economic field is not yet quite clear. The Russians are very slow and cautious in this question."[120]

The German Foreign Office came under intense pressure to bring Moscow into a fuller dialogue. At the beginning of August, according to Weizsäcker, Hitler "started to knock ever louder on Moscow's door, and his eagerness increased in direct proportion as the Polish crisis seemed to grow more acute."[121] His diplomats leaned on the Baltic issue in particular. On 2 August, Ribbentrop confirmed to Astakhov that Germany was "favorably disposed toward Moscow" and "that there was no problem from the Baltic to the Black Sea that could not be solved between us." "On all problems, it is possible to reach agreement . . . in more concrete terms."[122] On 4 August, Schulenburg delivered instructed lines to Molotov: Germany was ready "to orient [its] behavior with regard to the Baltic States . . . so as to safeguard vital Soviet interests."[123]

As German diplomacy went into overdrive, the Anglo-Franco-Soviet alliance talks also took a critical step forward. Although the Allies still disagreed about *how* to define (in a secret protocol) the "indirect aggression" against the Baltic states that they had agreed to oppose, sufficient consensus had been reached on all other political questions to advance negotiations to the specifics of military cooperation. At Stalin's request, the talks would be in Moscow, and the British and French were prepping delegations to begin them. Molotov then inched open the door to Berlin. In response to the Schnurre-Ashtakov talks of late July, he replied that Moscow was not against better political relations, but since Germany had embittered the relationship, Germany should propose how to fix it. At that, the Germans increased the "tempo of their bidding."[124] Moscow did not reply in any substantial way until 11 August, when it finally agreed to hold formal *trade* talks. And, Fleischhauer observes, it was only on 15 August that "Soviet negotiators made a real attempt to agree to the German offers. The talks [until then] had been characterized by a one-sidedness which frustrated the Germans."[125] On the other hand, writes Uldricks, "the Soviet diplomats negotiated seriously and energetically for an alliance with Britain and France well into August 1939."[126]

That was when the Anglo-Franco-Soviet alliance talks were overtaken by German diplomacy. The negotiations for a military convention started on 14 August, and on that day the Soviet delegation made it clear that they were focused on joint war planning in the event of a German attack on Poland or Romania. The Soviets demanded overland access to Polish and Romanian territory, in order to deploy forces against German invaders.[127] Poland simply refused to agree to grant such access. The talks stalled on this issue by 15 August. Over the next five days, the British and French governments pressured Poland to acquiesce, but there was no give.[128] On 17 August, the military talks adjourned—the Allies expected to resume them four days later.

But by then, the Western Allies had been outbid by the Germans, who were ready to make large concessions to Soviet security demands in the Baltic and Balkans in a way that the Allies were not. Stalin knew that time was short—Germany was about to attack Poland—and he reached for the better option given that expectation. On 15 August, Schulenburg delivered instructed comments: "There is no question between the Baltic and the Black Seas which cannot be settled to the complete satisfaction of both countries. Among these are such questions as: The Baltic Sea, the Baltic area, Poland, Southeastern countries [i.e., Roumania], etc."[129] Then Schulenburg proposed that Ribbentrop go immediately to Moscow for talks. Molotov welcomed Germany's intention to improve relations, but did not want Ribbentrop to come before Germany put forward a concrete plan. He asked Berlin to clarify an earlier reported idea for a breakthrough (floated by Ciano) that included a nonaggression treaty, a joint guarantee of the Baltics, and German intercession with Japan.[130]

Schulenburg returned on 17 August with a well-articulated German offer—a proposal for a nonaggression pact, with a secret protocol that would contain the critical pieces of the accommodative bargain.[131] Molotov took the proposal under consideration, but indicated that the special protocol's specifics had to be set before Ribbentrop's trip, which should come one week after the trade agreement was finalized. On that day—19 August—the

German-Soviet trade agreement was sealed. Publicly announced on 21 August, it was the first open signal of the volte face.[132] The timeline for negotiations was dramatically compressed on 21 August, when Hitler wrote Stalin requesting a Ribbentrop visit in the next two days. Stalin quickly accepted. That day, Berlin announced that Ribbentrop would fly to Moscow on 23 August to ink a deal.[133] Even before the Nazi-Soviet Pact was signed that night, its political shockwaves were being felt.[134] "Within twenty-four hours," writes Weizsäcker, "Ribbentrop had disposed in Moscow of the destinies of Finland, Estonia, Latvia, Poland, and Bessarabia."[135] On 3 September, when Germany invaded Poland, the Soviet Union stood by while Britain and France declared war. On 17 September, Moscow formally announced neutrality, while its forces moved in to occupy the eastern side of Poland, in keeping with the plan in the pact's secret protocol. In November 1939, when the Soviet Union invaded Finland, Germany stood by. And in June 1940, as German forces neared victory in the Battle of France, Soviet forces took over Latvia, Estonia, Lithuania, and the Bessarabian portion of Romania.

If Hitler had not become willing in August to make, as Weinberg put it, "the most extensive concessions to the Soviet Union," but had instead continued to confront the Soviets with hostility, Stalin would have continued the Anglo-Franco-Soviet alliance talks, probably to completion.[136] In deciding to avert encirclement by accommodating the USSR, Germany opted to forgo a formal alliance with Japan against the common Soviet enemy. Hitler's deal violated the secret terms of the November 1936 Anti-Comintern Pact, which stipulated that "without mutual consent" neither party would conclude "political treaties with the Soviet Socialist Republics contrary to the spirit of this agreement."[137] The Nazi-Soviet Pact thus not only divided Germany's likely adversaries, it also undercut the anti-Soviet thesis central to the German-Japanese alignment. The strategic advantages of this for Soviet security in the Far East were enormous.[138] In the late 1930s Soviet leaders obsessed over the problem of fighting Germany and Japan simultaneously, and in the summer of 1939, they were engaged in high-intensity conflict with the Japanese around Nomonhan.[139] In short, the Nazi-Soviet Pact served both Germany and the USSR as a device to divide adversaries.

The Nazi-Soviet Pact was a critical proximate cause of World War II because it sunk the only great power–balancing coalition that could have derailed Hitler in 1939. If the Nazi-Soviet Pact had not happened, the Anglo-Franco-Soviet alliance talks would have continued, and might have produced an extended deterrence success story.[140] The plausibility of this hypothetical is supported by contemporaneous private statements of German officials indicating that in late July and early August, Hitler saw neutralizing Russia as a necessary condition for moving against Poland.[141]

Summary and Alternatives

The theoretical framework offers three big reasons why Hitler successfully stopped the incipient Anglo-Franco-Soviet alliance. First, and most importantly, Germany employed heavy, immediately credible inducements to influence Moscow—and eschewed threats. Given the strong geopolitical and ideological forces driving the Soviet Union to balance against Germany, a coercive approach would have only reinforced Moscow's incentives to side with the Western Allies. Berlin's willingness to go so far to accommodate Moscow was driven by high estimates of Soviet strategic weight. Hitler believed that neutralizing it would make the Western Allies unlikely to intervene to protect Poland; and if they did intervene, would make German victory possible. Second, Germany's low alignment objective—to neutralize the Soviet Union—was also conducive to success. Third, Germany faced low alliance constraints at the time. Its closest and only formal military ally—Italy—was weaker than Germany, had little direct influence or interests at stake in the territories offered up in the bargain, and conveniently favored an accommodation with the USSR. Although the Nazi-Soviet Pact was a shocking geopolitical and ideological reversal, those conditions made Hitler's attempt to neutralize Moscow more likely to succeed than it otherwise seemed.

The thrust of the argument is that Germany's policy of selective accommodation was a necessary condition and the "propelling" cause of Moscow's decision to divert from the Western alliance and acquiesce to Germany's attack on Poland.[142] The critical issue posed by competing explanations, then, is whether other factors were sufficient to destroy the incipient Anglo-Franco-Soviet alliance in the autumn of 1939. While there is an extensive debate about these issues—which are to some extent unresolvable, because they hinge on assumptions about Stalin's own calculus, which is not disclosed in contemporaneous documents—the main challenges can be lumped into two categories.[143] The first locates the sufficient cause of failure in the behavior of Britain and France. The second locates the sufficient cause of failure in the behavior of the Soviet Union. They are addressed next.

THE WESTERN ALLIES WERE NOT SERIOUS

Many observers argue that the Anglo-Franco-Soviet alliance project failed (and the Nazi-Soviet Pact then resulted) because the British and French alliance bids were not, for one reason or another, good or serious enough to meet Moscow's terms. One line of argument suggests that the British and French left Stalin "no choice" but to turn to Hitler, because they did not—due to ideological antipathy, or other inhibitions—pursue the negotiations expeditiously and offer adequate terms that would allow Moscow to risk

Soviet security on the Western alliance.[144] Thus, in their lukewarm approach to Moscow, the Allies' complacency and disregard for the nature and urgency of the Soviet Union's security concerns discredited the alliance negotiations, leaving Stalin no choice but to take his "second-best alternative"—the deal with Hitler.[145] Hence, "Stalin's acceptance of the Nazi-Soviet Pact was the result of the failure of the Russo-Franco-British talks, not the cause of that failure."[146] Empirically, the problem with this argument is the record of British and French steps, throughout May, June, and July, to meet most of Moscow's demands and objections concerning the political and military terms of the alliance. Logically, there is a flawed assumption at the root of the argument—that Moscow's demands for security from a Western alliance were independently fixed and unconditional, *and not a function of how generous (or menacing) was Germany's approach.*[147]

In the negotiations over the alliance's political terms, the most important sticking point was Stalin's demand for explicit trilateral guarantees to oppose indirect aggression against the Baltics. From Moscow's perspective, any move on Latvia's or Estonia's part to slip under Nazi control had to be prevented—even if seemed to be made willingly by the governments. From the Allies' perspective, what had to be stopped were such moves taken under German threat; they could not publicly commit themselves to intervene against the Baltics' legitimate, independent foreign policy choices, or give Moscow a green light to do so. That, they feared, would contradict a main point of the alliance—to protect the independence and integrity of the small powers—and embolden Moscow to preempt any sign that a Baltic state might choose to become a German satellite. But the Western Allies *did* agree, in response to Molotov's demands, to include an explicit mutual commitment to oppose both "direct" and "indirect aggression" in the treaty's Article 1 defining the casus foederis, and they proposed in a *secret* protocol a definition of indirect aggression that addressed the Soviet fears that German subversion (like that which occurred in Czechoslovakia) would suborn the Baltics.[148] Moreover, Molotov's initial response to this proposal, on 24 July, was that he did not think the question "would raise insuperable difficulties and he was convinced that the three Governments could find a formula that would satisfy them."[149] The disagreement over how to wordsmith that piece of the secret protocol did not stop him from then pressing the Allies to begin simultaneous negotiations for a military convention. Molotov's strident inflexibility on the issue arose (on 2 August) only after Hitler had strongly signaled that he was willing to solve the Baltics issue on terms highly favorable to Stalin's interests—ceding the states north of Lithuania to the Soviet sphere.[150] The Allies' concessions to Stalin on the issue of indirect aggression against the Baltics were, ultimately, inferior to the carte blanche Hitler offered.[151] But that does not mean they would have remained unacceptable to Stalin *in the absence of the German bid.*

This general line is manifest in two different depictions of Stalin's mind-set, both of which imply that his aversion to a Western alliance was a sufficient condition for the failure of the talks. The first suggests that the British and French could never have addressed Moscow's security concerns because, ultimately, Stalin's decisions were controlled by his deep "pre-existing doubts about the intentions of the Western powers *ever* to align with the Soviets, or stand up to Hitler."[152] In particular, he was convinced that the Allies meant to double-cross Russia, ensnaring it in a war with Germany while standing aside and coming to terms with Hitler.[153] Stalin meant to turn the tables: to have the capitalist powers fight among themselves, while the Soviet Union stood back and profited.[154] In this view, then, Stalin never wanted an alliance with Britain and France and would have dismissed even one that expeditiously met all of Moscow's demands, because he could never be convinced of the Allies' good faith or that they would live up to their commitments. The second take is a reverse image of the first. It posits that Stalin was basically an aggressive expansionist and therefore had no desire to join a real status-quo alliance like the Western powers offered. His expansionist aims were unconditional and went well beyond what the Western Allies ever could endorse or deliver, given the basic purpose of the alliance.[155] His alliance talks with Britain and France were merely a device to lever generous concessions from Hitler.[156]

In either the first or second variant, Stalin's basic motivations made any alliance deal with the West infeasible and were sufficient to ensure that the Western approach failed. The problem with them is noted by Kotkin: those "who deny that Stalin ever wanted a military alliance with the West have to explain why he offered one, in written form," in April 1939.[157] Indeed, it was Stalin, recall, who dictated Litvinov's April 18 proposal for a full-scale, formalized, tripartite defensive military alliance to preserve the status quo. And on 16 June, Molotov communicated to London and Paris that Moscow was ready to table the issue of guarantees to "nonsignatory" secondary states and make a more streamlined tripartite alliance, confined to commitments among the three powers of mutual assistance in the event of direct aggression against them.[158] These facts are inconsistent with both the notion that Stalin fundamentally did not trust the Allies to keep an agreement, and the notion that he was unconditionally revisionist.

The strongest challenge to our claim that Hitler's policy was necessary to stop the alliance from consolidating is a synthesis of two perspectives outlined above. Here, the Anglo-Franco-Soviet alliance was killed by the conjunction of two things (each necessary, together sufficient): the Allies' slow and stinting approach to alliance negotiations, and Stalin's preexisting doubts about their good faith, which the Allies' approach reinforced.[159] If the Allies had moved faster, done more to meet Stalin's political demands sooner, and come to Moscow ready to quickly hammer out military commitments, Stalin's suspicions would have been allayed, and he would have stuck with the alliance track. Likewise, if Stalin had been less paranoid, he would have seen that the Allies—despite their laggardly and parsimonious approach—were politically committed to going to war with Germany if it attacked Poland, and he would have stuck with the process in order to keep the threat of a two-front war hanging over Hitler. Instead, the Allies' go-slow approach to negotiations confirmed Stalin's suspicions, and he walked away once he concluded they were either insufficiently committed or not acting in good faith.

This account is compelling because it plausibly incorporates many of the apparent facts: Stalin's outwardly demonstrated interest in a comprehensive alliance with the Western powers, as well as his manifest distrust of them; and the Western powers' clear (if tardy) decision to make a tripartite political and military alliance with the USSR, despite their doubts and aversions to it, as well as their persistent if clumsy approach to the negotiations.

What infirms the synthetic account is what it leaves out, or rather assumes—that Stalin would have a good alternative to the Anglo-Franco-Soviet alliance. Only if that were a given, would the account provide a sufficient explanation. Stalin, in fact, pulled the plug on the alliance talks only after the main lines of the deal with Hitler were in hand; one cannot assume that he would have done so if there were not an attractive German option.[160] Indeed, with no such deal readily available, and an imminent German threat to Poland bearing down, it is unlikely that Stalin would have cast aside the three-power alliance option that, whatever its limitations, still might have deterred Hitler and, if not, helped stop him from going further.

Neither the availability, generosity, nor credibility of Germany's approach can be taken for granted. In the preceding years, writes Weizsäcker, "Hitler had done everything possible to create hostility between himself and Moscow; indeed, he had built up his whole political system on the foundation of anti-Moscow ideology."[161] Until late in the summer of 1939, the Soviet Union was powerfully constrained to seek an Anglo-Franco alliance. Given "the Hitler regime's overt hostility" writes Haslam, "Stalin had no alternative until Hitler reversed his line against Moscow."[162] And it was not until "late July/early August" that Hitler began "his definitive move" to accommodate Stalin.[163] Not just any German olive branch would have been enough to doom the Anglo-Franco-Soviet alliance. What was necessary had to come quickly, and it had to be far-reaching *and* credible enough to overcome Stalin's distrust. It was Hitler's willingness to offer up specific and immediate geopolitical concessions to Moscow—in Poland and the Baltics especially— that made the Anglo-Franco alliance pale by comparison. For Stalin, the deal that Hitler ultimately offered was the better, not second-best option.

Even after Hitler's line reversal began to appear, Moscow had to be cautious, given the ferocity of Nazi hostility that had preceded the overtures. If it is true, as Kissinger remarked, that the democracies had "no hope" of enlisting the USSR as an ally "if Hitler was prepared to make [Moscow] a serious offer," it was not obvious that Hitler could make a serious offer that would be credible to Stalin.[164] Indeed, his credibility problem with Stalin was at least as bad if not worse than the Western democracies'. As Roberts put it, "While Stalin did not trust the British and French, he trusted Hitler even less."[165] One cannot thus blame the Anglo-Franco-Soviet alliance's failure on Stalin's distrust of the Allies and, at the same time, assume that Stalin would drop his distrust of Hitler in order to embrace a less-than-blockbuster German bid for détente.[166] To overcome the heavy burden of suspicion, Hitler had to promise large and immediately tangible rewards. It took a persistent, forthcoming effort on Hitler's part to convince Stalin such an enormously rewarding arrangement was obtainable, and thus move him to drop the alliance with Britain and France.[167]

If Hitler had not been determined, then, to strike a deal with Moscow, neither the Western Allies' reluctance to grant Stalin a free hand in the Baltics, nor Stalin's appetite for one, would have stood in the way of an Anglo-Franco-Soviet alliance. Nor would Soviet doubts about the reliability of Western commitments. It was a question of alternatives. This point is critical. It means that Berlin's selective accommodation policy—coming at the time and in the generous and credible fashion that it did—was the necessary, propelling cause of the failure to form of the Anglo-Franco-Soviet alliance.

THE ROLE OF IDEOLOGICAL FACTORS

Stalin's approach to alignment considerations was unconstrained by ideological precepts: it was "essentially one of level-headed Realpolitik" and "cold-blooded" pragmatism.[168] Ideological divergences among the major powers had mixed but important effects in this context. At the most obvious level, it is clear that the sharp ideological antagonisms between Nazi Germany and the Soviet Union did not doom Germany's selective accommodation policy. Neither Hitler nor Stalin was rhetorically "entrapped" by their intense and prolonged ideological enmity.[169] If the antipathies were inconvenient, leaders in Berlin and Moscow blithely skipped over them. As Ribbentrop said in August 1939, "Differing philosophies [did] not prohibit a reasonable relationship" between Berlin and Moscow.[170] Or, as Weizsäcker put it: "The dogmas of internal politics were being completely ignored."[171] After the Nazi-Soviet Pact was announced, a British Foreign Office spokesman observed, "All the isms are now wasims."[172] By the same token, despite the misgivings of British and French Conservative leaders, they had decided by May 1939 to set them aside: the need to recruit Soviet power into the balancing coalition took priority over fears of Communist subversion and Soviet ambitions in Eastern Europe. Power political concerns "overrode" ideological inhibitions.[173]

But at another level, as Haas shows, ideological multipolarity in Europe did contribute in important ways to Germany's success.[174] The apparent convergence between British, French, and German hostility to Soviet Communism clouded threat perceptions in the Western democracies, which delayed the timing and attenuated the vigor of their engagement with Moscow. This created the opening for Berlin to take the initiative in accommodating Moscow, constrained the extent of the alliance bargain the Western Allies offered, and encouraged the Soviet leaders' doubts about the commitment of the Western democracies to an anti-Nazi alliance. All of these things increased the attractiveness to Moscow of Germany's bid and thus amounted to another force pulling in Hitler's favor. Along with Germany's strong inducements (which included isolation of Moscow's Japanese foe) and its low alignment change goal (which was generally supported by its Italian ally), ideological multipolarity, too, helped Berlin win the bidding war.

Britain and the United States Neutralize Spain, 1940–41

The Führer has now had his projected meeting with Franco. . . .
Everything went smoothly. . . . Spain is firmly ours.

> Joseph Goebbels, Reich minister of propaganda, October 1940

An offer by you to dole out food month by month so long as [the
Spaniards] keep out of the war might be decisive. . . . This is a time for
very plain talk to them. . . . We must gain as much time as possible.

> Winston Churchill to Franklin D. Roosevelt, November 1940

At our meeting we reached an agreement that Spain would proclaim
her willingness to sign the Tripartite Pact and enter the war. In setting
the date, we never contemplated, far less mentioned, periods in the
remote future. . . . It was never considered in our conversations that
Spain would not enter the war until perhaps next autumn or winter.

> Adolf Hitler to Francisco Franco, February 1941

Spain nearly entered World War II on the Axis side in late 1940. A conflu-
ence of impulses—ideological, revisionist, and economic—were propelling it in that direction, especially after Germany conquered France in
June 1940 and forced an isolated Britain on the defensive in Europe and
the Mediterranean. By the end of the year, Hitler—angling for control of the
Mediterranean Sea and Eastern Atlantic—was eager to recruit Spain, and
he had authorized military plans for a joint operation to conquer Gibraltar, a long-standing goal of Spanish nationalists. Yet, at the most crucial
decision point—in December 1940—Spain's dictator Francisco Franco rebuffed the Axis alliance offers. Thus, "against all historical likelihood,"
Spain remained nonbelligerent, and did so for the rest of the war.[1]

Franco's decision was due in large part to an Anglo-American effort—
initiated and led by Britain—to use inducements to keep Spain sidelined.
When Hitler and Franco were converging on an alliance, Spain desperately needed not just military support to fight, but also economic aid—to

recover from the civil war, survive severe shortages of food, and secure other basic economic necessities. The concerted Anglo-American policy convinced Franco that Spain's economic needs could best be met through British and U.S. largesse, which could only be obtained if Spain remained nonbelligerent.[2]

The Anglo-American effort was advantaged by conducive conditions. Their alignment change goal was limited—to reinforce Spain's formal position of nonbelligerence, and Franco's practical independence from German control. Nevertheless, in pushing forward concerted accommodation, the British faced high alliance constraints. After June 1940, their security was deeply dependent on a nascent alliance with the U.S., which would inevitably become the dominant military partner. Britain could not disregard the U.S.'s transatlantic priorities and Spain's place in them. Moreover, to conciliate Spain effectively required not just U.S. acquiescence but its support. Yet, these constraints did not doom the policy of accommodation; they were obviated by strong Anglo-American strategic consensus. The British and Americans agreed on the goal (to keep Spain nonbelligerent), on the way achieve it (inducements), and most of all, about Spain's high strategic weight. This produced a powerful wedge strategy, because the duo was in a good position to influence Spain through coordinated inducements. Together, they controlled and could credibly commit to deliver goods that Spain prized, which it could not very well obtain in other ways or without their assistance. The Allies' consensus about Spain's strategic weight thus abetted a strong and successful concerted bid.[3]

Initiation Conditions

Strong motivation and means came together in Britain's policy to accommodate Spain. British leaders believed that Spain had dangerous war-tipping potential and so had to be kept neutral. Spain was not just ideologically aligned with the Fascist powers, it was economically desperate, which made it ripe for German economic influence. To keep Spain neutral, Britain would have to outbid German bribes. Britain leaders considered it possible to do so because they had rewards to manipulate that Spain badly needed, and they had the potential to bring U.S. support into the equation in a big way.

PERCEPTIONS OF TARGET'S STRATEGIC WEIGHT

To British leaders fighting to hold on to their country and empire, Spain carried high strategic weight. Britain's virtual isolation in Europe after the defeat of France magnified this perception. Even before the war started, British officials attributed war-tipping potential to Spain. Thus, in May 1939, the Chiefs of Staff Subcommittee of the cabinet's Committee of Imperial

Defense issued an analysis that highlighted key dangers of Spanish enmity, including, among others, the loss of Gibraltar, which controlled western access to the Mediterranean; Axis bases in the Canary Islands, which would threaten sea-lanes in the Atlantic; and Spanish takeover of Portugal, which would eliminate access to Lisbon as a friendly base on the Atlantic seaboard. In summary, they wrote: "The active enmity of Spain, and the exploitation by Germany and Italy of the geographical position of Spain and her dependencies would weaken our position in the Western Mediterranean and threaten our Atlantic communications."[4] After France fell, it was obvious then that Spain's intervention could tip the war against the British in two big ways. It would enable Germany to control Gibraltar and Spanish Morocco and thus imperil British positions and communications in the Mediterranean.[5] As Churchill put it, "Spain held the key to all British enterprises" in the Mediterranean.[6] And it would endanger the Atlantic supply lines on which they now depended. The chiefs of staff expected that if Spain entered the war, Portugal would follow, and the Axis would then "acquire in Lisbon a naval base . . . from which they can directly threaten the Atlantic patrol" and make a "further breach in the blockade." Thus, it was "clear from a strategic point of view that everything should be done to prevent Spain entering the war against us."[7]

PERCEPTIONS OF RELATIVE REWARD POWER

From that premise, the need to accommodate Spain flowed. To bully it would backfire. As Samuel Hoare, Britain's ambassador to Spain, warned: "To treat [it] as an enemy is playing into the hands of the Germans."[8] Thus, to influence Franco's regime to stay neutral, one had to offer inducements. With Spain struggling to recover from the economic wreckage of civil war, that meant, above all else, economic rewards. The essential quid pro quo, as Hoare put it to the Spanish foreign minister, Juan Beigbeder, in June 1940, was simple: "As long as Franco maintained" nonbelligerence, Britain could provide "useful help" for Franco's "work of reconstruction."[9] Accordingly, Britain's policy, soon buttressed by the U.S., emphasized economic aid. Spain badly needed it, and Britain—with its fleet, its ability to loosen and tighten blockades, and its close ties to the Commonwealth and the U.S.—could mobilize and manipulate it with considerable force. That approach, as Hoare put it in July 1940, was "the most effective way of keeping Spain out of the war altogether if possible, and, if that is not possible, for as long a period as we can."[10] Churchill's embrace of this concept informed his plea to FDR for U.S. food aid to augment British inducements: "An offer by you to dole out food month by month so long as they keep out of the war might be decisive."[11]

British leaders also recognized Spain's revisionist interests, and so they also dangled prospects of territorial gain. In October 1940, London decided not only to "continue with the policy of economic agreements" but also to "take into sympathetic account the aspirations of Spain in North Africa."[12] In particular, territorial adjustments at the expense of Vichy France were on the table.[13] Churchill also agreed to let Hoare "give at least a tentative indication of Britain's sympathy with Spain's irredentist claim" to Gibraltar, and a willingness to address it in postwar talks.[14] All of this figured in a more general message, communicated by Hoare to Franco, of supporting the elevation of the "new Spain" to its "rightful part" in "the new world that will be reconstructed at the end of the war."[15]

Contingent Conditions

ATTEMPTED ALIGNMENT CHANGE

The British-led effort to accommodate Spain aimed for a low degree of alignment change. The point, as British foreign minister Lord Halifax put it, was "to secure the continued neutrality of Spain."[16] There was no intention, then, to try to recruit Spain as an ally. Given Britain's strategic plight, and Spain's ideological orientation and revisionist agenda, there was little chance of flipping Franco. Moreover, if Britain tried to do it, that would likely provoke a German invasion of Spain (from occupied France) that Britain could not stop. So, the definition of success was a negative one: to keep Spain, for all practical purposes, on the sidelines.

But even that limited goal would not be easy to achieve. There were strong pressures and incentives driving Spain and Germany toward alliance. Germany and Italy had clear claims to Nationalist Spain's allegiance—they had been its crucial supporters during the Spanish Civil War.[17] To Spain's leaders, their friends were Germany and Italy, and their enemies were the Soviet Union and the liberal democracies of Britain, France, and the United States. The magnetism of ideological affinity—shared "foundational principles of political legitimacy"—pulled Spain's regime toward the Axis powers.[18] Franco and the people in his regime shared Fascism's bitter antipathy for democracy.[19] His key political protégé, the Spanish interior minister (and later foreign minister) Ramón Serrano Suñer, was described at the time as a "fanatical enemy of democracies."[20]

The Nationalist government's revisionist agenda also put Spain in the ranks of Britain's opponents.[21] Indeed, Spain was as dissatisfied a revisionist state as any other on the Continent. Setting aside what had been done to its empire in the Americas, it had been exploited more recently and closer to home by Britain and France, in both Europe and North Africa.[22] As Suñer would put it in late 1940, British-controlled Gibraltar was "a part of the living and torn flesh" of the Spanish "motherland," and French Morocco was "Spain's Lebensraum and . . . her natural expansion objective."[23]

In the run-up to the war, Spanish diplomacy closely tracked that of the Axis powers.[24] In late March 1939, Spain joined the Anti-Comintern Pact and signed a bilateral "treaty of friendship" with Germany.[25] In early May, Spain exited the League of Nations, and after the Pact of Steel formed, Franco added to the menace by concentrating Spanish troops around Gibraltar.[26] In early August 1939, Franco began consulting with Italy on ways to close the Straits and reconquer Gibraltar.[27] The trend continued into the war. In April 1940, Beigbeder predicted to the German ambassador Eberhard von Stohrer, that "if Italy enters the war Spain will be automatically drawn in."[28] On 13 June 1940, with Germany's victory in France climaxing, Spain declared itself a "nonbelligerent"; its officials understood this stance, however, to be a prelude to joining the war, as Italy's had been.[29] Spanish troops next occupied the internationally administrated port of Tangier. This was purportedly to preserve Tangier's neutrality (Italy, France, and Britain were part of its administrative apparatus), but it signaled Spain's intentions to expand in North Africa. In sum, in the summer of 1940, when Germany appeared to be the strongest power in Europe, Spain was about to join the Axis powers in their war for a new order.

Indeed, on 16 June 1940, Franco's minister of war, General Juan Vigón, met with Hitler and German foreign minister Ribbentrop, carrying a letter from Franco offering Spanish belligerency in return for an ambitious list of territorial gains, and contingent on supply of food and material (a formula that would remain essentially unchanged for the rest of the year). Vigón's contact was followed up three days later with a formal approach from the Spanish ambassador to Berlin, offering to enter the war.[30] At the same time, Franco wrote to Mussolini that "the French defeat" had made Spain's political situation "brighter," and he assured the Duce of Spain's "unconditional support for [Italian] expansion" and its desire to "take [its] place in the struggle against the common enemies."[31]

At this juncture, Hitler snubbed the Spanish offer. Hitler did not think he needed Spain's assistance at all. He was still expecting Britain to go down gracefully after France was defeated.[32] Through the early summer, Franco's alliance offer met with "complete reserve" from Germany, as Hitler pondered cross-channel invasion versus other ways to force England's surrender and position Germany for future conflict versus the U.S.[33] In this context, it became clear that an indirect but potentially devastating way to beat Britain was to eliminate its position in the Mediterranean, which would also allow Germany to begin building strategic infrastructure in northwest Africa against the U.S. threat to come.[34] Gibraltar was an obvious linchpin in this scheme. For this, Madrid's cooperation was needed. In July, Hitler's attitude toward Spain thus "changed dramatically": he began "an all-out effort to convince Franco to enter the war" and he ordered his military to begin planning a Gibraltar attack on the assumption that Spain would cooperate.[35]

That remained a reasonable premise. On 18 July Franco "openly boasted that two million soldiers stood ready to create a new empire, recover Gibraltar and realize Spain's historic destiny in Africa."[36] Ten days later, a German military envoy informed Vigón that Berlin wanted to plan for a joint Gibraltar attack and was committed to a full defense of Spain should Britain counterattack.[37] On 29 July, Spain signed a nonaggression pact with Portugal, which in a secret addendum gave Spain a free hand to enter the war against Britain, Portugal's ancient ally. Ribbentrop instructed Stohrer in Madrid on 2 August: "What we want to achieve now is Spain's early entry into the war."[38] The political context was shaping up. Spain had military needs and imperial aspirations that still had to be addressed, but there were strong signals in Madrid pointing to Spanish entry.[39] Spain's deepening economic distress added to it. Throughout August, as the dimensions of the looming economic crisis forced themselves on Franco's government, Franco pressed for an Axis alliance as a means to gain both territory and economic relief.[40] On 6 September Hitler decided that conquering the Rock of Gibraltar should be prioritized as "one of the main blows against Britain," and he ordered his military chiefs to speed up preparations for an assault.[41] Three days later, Hitler's military envoy brought assurances to Franco that Germany would meet Spain's needs for food, fuel, and other material and also supply the forces and resources to take Gibraltar.[42]

In view of such worrisome developments, then, Britain's alignment goal was limited, if not modest: keep Spain from becoming a base for Nazi military power. Two requisites followed. First, Spain had to be kept nonbelligerent. Second, Franco's regime had to be shored up, not subverted. Subversion was liable to backfire—by elevating Falange figures even more pro-Nazi than Franco's entourage, or by triggering German intervention.

ALLIANCE CONSTRAINTS

Britain faced high alliance constraints, even though, in 1940, it was not yet formally allied to the U.S. (the Atlantic Conference and Charter of August 1941 were still many months away). Washington was a first-rank power and had important security interests at stake in Spain's alignment. For both Britain and the U.S., it was about more than just the fate of Gibraltar and the Mediterranean: it was about the transatlantic lines of communication, which ran through Spain's Canary Islands and Portugal's Azores (the fate of the latter was seen to be bound up in that of the former, just as Lisbon's alignment was perceived to be linked to Madrid's). Because U.S. security was at stake in Iberian alignments, it could not be ignored. But more than that, after France fell, Britain profoundly needed the U.S.'s support. By May 1940, the British chiefs of staff had adopted the premise that if France were knocked out, Britain could not "continue the war with any chance of success" without full U.S. economic assistance.[43] Britain was thus in a position of steep dependence: it badly needed aid from an ally that had an independent stake in the approach toward Spain. That dependence extended to its strategy of accommodating Spain. Thus, in November 1940, when London was preparing an aid package to induce Franco to remain neutral, a British diplomat wrote the State Department that "the British cause would greatly suffer" if the U.S. proved unwilling to help Spain economically.[44] Later that month, along the same lines, Churchill argued to FDR that the U.S. could provide "decisive" support for the British policy by offering to send food to Spain if it stayed out of the war.[45] So having the U.S. fully behind the strategy to appease Spain was seen as a key condition for success. The situation was primed for awkward missteps and poor coordination.

ALLIED STRATEGIC CONSENSUS

Two things helped to minimize inter-Allied friction. First, there was general agreement on the basic question of whether to induce Spanish nonbelligerence. Second, like Churchill's government, the Roosevelt administration saw major strategic value in keeping Spain out of the war. As Secretary of State Cordell Hull put it later, "Keeping her neutral . . . would be of great advantage to the Allied side."[46] For the U.S., Spain's alignment had war-tipping potential because it would affect Britain's ability to avoid defeat in 1940 and 1941. Such defeat would imperil U.S. security. Harry Hopkins, FDR's personal envoy to Churchill, described Roosevelt's thinking: "If England lost, America too would be encircled and beaten."[47] Driven by this perception, FDR in the fall of 1940 pushed the American public and strategic elites to embrace the goal of helping Britain in all ways "short of war."[48] In mid-December 1940, Hull's instructions to the U.S. ambassador to Spain (Alexander Weddell) stated explicitly that the U.S. had "a vital interest" in ensuring that Spain "remain[ed] outside the present war" and did not extend "aid to the Axis powers."[49] By then it was understood among U.S. leaders that U.S. security was at stake in Britain's survival and in preventing "the disruption" of its empire.[50] Because Britain's ability to hang on in the Mediterranean, and keep the Atlantic open to shipping, could hinge on Spain's choices, Spain's alignment had war-tipping potential.

One element supporting consensus about Spain's strategic weight was Roosevelt's and Churchill's shared background as makers of naval policy. To cultivate this affinity in their private correspondence, Churchill had early in the war adopted the moniker "Former Naval Person."[51] From such a mindset, it was obvious that Spain's value as a geostrategic asset lay in its potential to facilitate access to or control over Gibraltar and Atlantic outposts that were seen by U.S. (and British) officials as vital in a global war.[52] But the personalities were also of course a reflection of the overlapping geographic interests and priorities of the two Atlantic powers.

Spain's particular influence in Latin America also contributed to U.S. perceptions of its strategic weight. In 1939 the U.S. had adopted a national security strategy based on "hemispheric defense," stimulated in large part by fear of the Axis gaining bases and allies in Latin America that would permit them to apply airpower against the U.S. homeland. If Spain's (and Portugal's) alignment with the Axis triggered similar shifts in Latin America, that threat would have concrete vectors into the hemisphere. One particular scenario was especially troubling: Axis control of Spain and Gibraltar, leading to bases on the edge of West Africa, which could link by air directly to Natal in Brazil. From there, air attacks on the Panama Canal became possible.[53] Once the war started, FDR spoke explicitly about the likelihood that "if Germany won the war, Hitler would try to get his hands on the Azores or Cape Verde islands, as bases for operations against the Americas."[54] What Spanish intervention on the Axis side would make possible, however, was German access to these bases *without* having to win in Europe. In May 1940, with France going down to defeat, FDR expressly directed the chiefs to focus on South American vulnerabilities.[55]

After France collapsed, senior U.S. officials began to look squarely at the Axis threat to Britain's position, the Atlantic sea-lanes, and ultimately U.S. security in the Western Hemisphere.[56] In his 27 May 1941 fireside chat about the declaration of unlimited national emergency, FDR proclaimed it "unmistakably apparent . . . that, unless the advance of Hitlerism is forcibly checked now, the Western Hemisphere will be within range of the Nazi weapons of destruction."[57] In his 10 June speech, he explained that "it was necessary for Great Britain to maintain its defense, for if Britain were to fall [the U.S.] would have to face the Nazis alone"; thus the U.S. must "extend to the opponents of force the material resources of our nation."[58] When FDR completed the Destroyers-for-bases deal in September 1940, the general policy of giving Britain all aid possible short of war was entrenched.[59] It flowed naturally from this that the U.S. should support Britain's policy to keep Spain neutral.

The logic was evident in the "Strong Memorandum" composed in the late summer of 1940 by the War Plans Division of the General Staff, in the War Department. The document was reviewed by General George Marshall (chief of staff), Admiral Harold Stark (chief of Naval Operations), Secretary of War Henry Stimson, Secretary of the Navy Frank Knox, Secretary of the Treasury Henry Morgenthau, and Undersecretary of State Sumner Welles—one of FDR's closest foreign policy advisors and, after 1940, the de facto head of the State Department and its main conduit to the White House.[60] In the memorandum, potential German control over Spain, Gibraltar, and the Iberian islands in the Atlantic, was flagged as a plausible near-term scenario through which Germany could "inflict a major defeat on Great Britain." With the immediate threat of a German cross-channel invasion declining, the greatest vulnerability stemmed from Britain's uncertain hold on the Mediterranean.

"The loss of Gibraltar by Great Britain would not only react seriously on the possibility of continued British operations in the Mediterranean, but would also open the way to serious consequences to the United States, by opening the way for movement of Italian naval forces into the Atlantic, especially if based on Dakar." The estimate went on to consider the implications of Spain and Portugal being "drawn into the orbit of Axis control." Here, unless the U.S. or Britain acted preemptively, it was to be "expected that the Azores, Canary, and Cape Verde Islands will be occupied and defended by Axis forces [and used] to disturb British naval control of the Atlantic. Axis control of the Azores would offer a definite threat to the security of the Western Hemisphere."[61] The chiefs anticipated that over the next year, U.S. ground and air forces would not be up to the task of hemisphere defense—it would have to rest on the U.S. fleet, which needed then to remain flexible so that it could be fully committed effectively should a direct threat materialize. If the threat came from Europe, then U.S. and European positions in Asia would be left vulnerable to Japan. Thus, whether Spain remained neutral could determine whether Britain retained control of the Mediterranean and eastern Atlantic, which in turn bore on the prospect of war in the Pacific and the American hemisphere.

It is not clear whether FDR read the Strong Memorandum. But, as Langer and Gleason note, the estimate "in any case represented the best official opinion available to him," and, according to Watson, "its recommendations implicit or explicit evidently were communicated to him in one way or another. The influence of the reasoning is discernable long afterward in 1941 plans."[62] In October, Sumner Welles promised the chiefs that he would take it up with FDR directly.[63] In his speech to Boston on 30 October 1940, Roosevelt declared, "Our objective is to keep any potential attacker as far from our continental shores as we possibly can," and he pointed to the destroyers-for-bases deal that had allowed the U.S. to acquire "new naval and air bases in British territory in the Atantic Ocean; extending all the way from Newfoundland in the north to that part of South America where the Atlantic Ocean begins to get narrow, with Africa not far away." FDR was "deeply concerned" by the "dangers of [German moves to] North Africa by way of Spain" and "with the effect of these possible developments on the Portuguese and Spanish islands in the Atlantic."[64]

Letters between Churchill and Roosevelt in spring 1941 show that, at the apex of the U.S. and British governments, there prevailed a common view of the danger of loss of British control in the Mediterranean (a likely result of Spanish intervention). To FDR, Churchill wrote that the collapse of Britain's position there "would seriously increase the hazards of the Atlantic and Pacific and could hardly fail to prolong the war with all the suffering and military dangers that this would entail." In his reply, FDR assured Churchill that he recognized "the gravity of the situation" in the Mediterranean: "I am well aware of its great strategic importance and I share your anxiety."[65]

Consequently, though there were recurring tactical disagreements between the Allies over dealing with Franco's regime, at moments when coordination mattered most, U.S. policy moved into line with Britain's.[66]

Diplomacy of Concerted Accommodation

There was a narrow time frame in which selective accommodation, concerted by Britain and the U.S., was key to keeping Spain out of the war. The conjuncture of Hitler's intentions and Franco's interest defined it. According to Detwiler, "There was only one period when [attacking Gibraltar] fitted into [Hitler's] timetable, when he wanted to do it, and when he had the means at hand." That was between November 1940 and January 1941.[67] So, to demonstrate that Anglo-American policy mattered, one must focus on that critical juncture, when Hitler and Franco were actively seeking partnership. Nevertheless, it is impossible to grasp the central dynamics of that crucial period without a sense of the direction and momentum of relations in the months before and after it.

BUILDING THE INCENTIVE STRUCTURE: JUNE–OCTOBER 1940

Britain's policy—which "bordered on economic appeasement"—was launched in the summer of 1940.[68] The primary inducements were economic, but there were also prospects of territorial concessions. In July 1940, London authorized Hoare to tell Spain's leaders that if French rule in Morocco collapsed, Britain "would welcome Spanish intervention to restore law and order, and that the future of the territories could be defined by post-war negotiation."[69] Consequently, in September, Churchill's government dropped plans for a joint intervention (with the Free French) in Vichy-controlled Morocco, so as to avoid provoking Spain, which then viewed expansion in Morocco as "central" and "vital" to its strategic position. Hoare was then instructed to tell Franco and Suñer that Britain did not wish to impair Spain's interests in French African possessions, and that it wanted to find a "modus vivendi" on the Moroccan question.[70] On 15 October, Hoare privately informed one of Franco's generals that Britain "recognized Spanish claims in Morocco and welcomed a Spanish occupation of the entire area."[71]

On the commercial front, the inducement strategy was backstopped by a latent threat of economic strangulation. The economic aid to Spain was filtered through a tight blockade of the Continent, which required special certificates (navicerts) from London to permit entry of all regulated (i.e., important) imports. The goal was to keep Spain's economy and population buoyant, without allowing it to build up surpluses that could be exploited by the Nazi war machine. As Economic Warfare Minister Hugh Dalton liked to stress, the idea was to keep "Spain so short that she cannot re-export and is not worth pillaging."[72] This "game of just so much" was "like a loosened tourniquet [which] could be twisted tight on a moment's notice," allowing Britain "to choke off the arteries of the Spanish economy almost at will."[73]

That aspect emerged clearly in the summer of 1940, when Britain imposed a forty-three-day blockade on petroleum shipments to Spain after signs of dangerous accumulation.[74] Collaboration with the U.S. was central to the success of the policy. Early in June 1940, Britain brought to Washington's attention the fact that Spain was importing U.S. oil in large quantities, raising the danger that some would be diverted to Italy and Germany. Over the next two months, the U.S. constricted that supply, forcing Madrid to then deplete its own reserves of oil and gasoline. As Spanish requests for U.S. oil mounted in urgency, Washington took the position that Madrid had to work through arrangements made with Britain, which the U.S. would in various ways support. Thus, U.S. policy, "in almost complete harmony [with Britain] with respect to Spain," boosted Britain's strategy of using "controlled supply" of oil to promote Spain's neutrality.[75]

Throughout this period, Hoare reminded London not to lapse into a posture of isolating Spain: "to treat [it] as an enemy is playing into the hands of the Germans."[76] Hoare was always backed by Churchill, Halifax (until he was replaced by Anthony Eden in late December 1940), and the military chiefs. In September 1940, Britain extended to Spain a long-term oil import quota, thus lifting the July fuel embargo. In the new arrangement, Spanish oil stocks would be sustained by mostly U.S. exports at a level of 160,000 tons (down from 224,000 tons in July), roughly enough surplus for two and a half months. Coming when it did, as negotiations for an Hispano-German alliance were starting to build momentum, this agreement was a significant coup for Britain.[77] Just two weeks later, during Suñer's alliance talks in Berlin, the Germans balked at meeting Spain's projected wartime fuel requirement of 56,000 tons per month, with Ribbentrop quibbling that the figure was "perhaps set too high."[78] Hitler wanted Spain to believe that it had no choice but to ally with Germany, because Britain would try to strangle Spain regardless of what it did. The September oil agreement put the lie to that proposition.

Also in September, Britain intensified its efforts to increase Spain's dependency on Western supply of basic foodstuffs. In this context, Madrid sought a U.S. proposal to provide credits to Spain to purchase food and raw materials. Washington modulated its response in a way that reinforced the British policy, which focused on providing near-term relief to help Madrid avert impending famine, while working out larger and longer-range commitments conditional on Spain's remaining out of the war. Thus, Washington initially replied that it was ready to sign off on a prompt Red Cross food delivery (funded by a small State Department budget to give relief to countries affected by the war), if Spain would give assurances of its intent to remain out of the war. But it was more hesitant, and vague, about a larger deal on import credits—such would have to await stronger signs of goodwill from Madrid. When Britain soon thereafter, however, asked the U.S. to be more forthcoming (because a moment of political decisions in Madrid seemed near), "the President and the Secretary of State decided to act more boldly."[79] They then instructed Weddell to tell Franco that the Red Cross shipment was en route and that the U.S. was ready to start talks on a large credit deal, if Spain gave formal public assurances it would stay nonbelligerent. This shift was well timed to complicate Spanish feelers toward Germany.

Franco sent Suñer to Berlin in mid-September to clarify "the conditions under which Spain was ready to fight the war together with Germany." The first was clear-cut: "Whenever Spain's supply of foodstuffs and war material was secure she could immediately enter the war."[80] Suñer's lengthy list also included Gibraltar, French Morocco, Oran, and border changes in Africa and with France.[81] He also emphasized that Spain was going to be short 600,000 tons of grain that winter, and given what could be expected to come through the British cordon, Germany would need to provide 400,000 tons. That was just for Spain to be *ready to enter* the war: once it started fighting, of course, its needs would multiply. Hitler responded, "Germany would do everything in her power to help Spain." Likewise, Ribbentrop assured that Germany would "satisfy Spain completely" on this score.[82] But it never would.[83] At the end of his meeting, Suñer asked Hitler "to put down in writing" the substance and specifics of the German assurances.[84] Hitler did so two days later, yet his letter to Franco exposed further doubts that Germany could or would meet Spain's food needs before it entered the war. What Hitler stressed was that Germany would provide all the necessary firepower; Spain should enter the war quickly so that Gibraltar could be captured and the British run out of the Mediterranean. That "alone would allow a radical solution to Spain's supply problem."[85]

On 22 September, Franco replied, voicing doubts that beating the British in the Mediterranean would solve Spain's supply problems. For that reason, pressed Franco, the "economic aid which you offer me . . . is just as important as the military equipment."[86] Franco sent Berlin a draft protocol for alliance with Germany and Italy, which committed Spain to future belligerency in return for (1) immediate recognition of Spanish claims to French Morocco, Oran, Gibraltar; and (2) a period of economic and military preparation for war subsidized by the Axis powers. Moreover, *all three* powers had to agree that the period of preparation was complete before Spain would enter the fight actively. In other words, Spain would enter the war on *Franco's* timetable, not Hitler's.[87]

Suñer received the German counteroffer in Berlin. In return for liberating Gibraltar, Hitler wanted (1) commanding ownership of (formerly) British and French industries in Spain; (2) control of a Canary island, from which Germany could defend against an Anglo-American riposte; (3) economic concessions and two bases in Morocco; and (4) portions of Spain's central

African colonies (Spanish Guinea and Fernando Pó). Suñer expressed doubts that Spain could meet any of these conditions, but he would relay them back to Franco. Before leaving Berlin he signed a statement (dated 27 September 1940) declaring Spanish "solidarity with the policy of the Axis" and agreeing to a ten-year "tripartite pact [which gives] definite expression to Spain's desire to carry through the task, in cooperation with Germany and Italy, of establishing an order of maximum justice."[88] There was, however, a hitch—Spain's agreement was predicated on German and Italian recognition of Spanish claims to Gibraltar and Oran and "the whole of Morocco."

In early October, as the Battle of Britain fizzled out, and the prospects for a cross-channel invasion along with it, the führer and Il Duce met at Brenner Pass. The key question was how to finish off Britain quickly, and the answer, they agreed, was Gibraltar. The problem was that Spain kept asking for French Morocco as a price for entering the war. The difficulty was not so much that it would require sacrificing some German and Italian ambitions there, but that promising to meet Spain's aims ex ante would alienate French Africa, which might then go over to the side of Britain and Free French forces.[89] The dictators concocted a con: Franco would be told that they would give Spain Gibraltar, and had agreed "in principle" to alterations of French Moroccan territory in Spain's favor. But those could not be determined until after the war.[90] On 10 October Suñer wrote to Ribbentrop asking that the negotiations surrounding the tentative "ten-year military alliance" be conducted "with the utmost secrecy in order not to jeopardize the several shiploads of Argentine and Canadian wheat which we are endeavoring—with great difficulty—to acquire."[91]

Then Franco cashiered Beigbeder and made Suñer foreign minister. The British, aware of Suñer's travels to Berlin, were alarmed. London heeded Hoare's advice to delay aid negotiations with Spain until London received "satisfactory assurances" about "the future direction of Spanish foreign policy." Washington adopted this approach, too.[92]

There things stood when Franco met Hitler at Hendaye, on 23 October 1940, to talk terms.[93] The partial record of the meeting shows that Franco wanted to focus on concrete preparations needed in the "economic, military, and political spheres" before Spain could go to war, and on Spain's "growing provisioning difficulties," which "would be intensified by the bad harvests."[94] In an extraordinary non sequitur, Hitler reeled off excuses for the failed air offensive against Britain, then tried to assure Franco that the German military could be counted on to bolster Spanish capabilities, finish off Gibraltar, and defend Spain afterward. Hitler, in all of this, did not address how Germany could solve Spain's "provisioning difficulties."[95] As for the conflicting Spanish and French territorial goals in North Africa, they would be reconciled through the magic of German diplomacy and military victory.[96] Hitler's parting message to Franco was that, because of the dangers of French Africa going over to the British, some compromise had to be found—for the time being—between "Spanish claims and French hopes."[97] Germany could not commit in detail to the territories to be given to Spain prior to negotiations at war's end. Suñer and Ribbentrop then drafted (but did not sign) a secret protocol in which Spain promised to enter the war as an Axis ally, at a time to be agreed by all three powers, after a period of economic and military preparation in Spain.[98]

What Franco meant to do at this juncture remains unclear. A number of indications suggest that he was inclined to jump, even with the fuzzy territorial promises, and it is known that Hitler now sought, unequivocally, to impel Spain to join the Axis war effort. Italy's botched attack on Greece in late October "forced [Hitler] to recognize the vulnerability of the Axis in this area" and "convinced Hitler [that] he must now make every effort to bring Spain into the war" in order to quickly shut the Western Mediterranean to Britain.[99] At this time, the Spanish ambassador in London warned British leaders that they "must woo Spain since she was hesitating between [Britain] and Germany."[100] Goebbels wrote in his diary for 25 October: "The Führer has now had his projected meeting with Franco. I am informed . . . that everything went smoothly. . . . Spain is firmly ours."[101] Also, on 3 November, Hitler received from Franco a letter (sent on 30 October) that, though it continued to stress "the Spanish aspiration" (i.e., not demand) to the "part of Morocco which is in French hands," was positive enough that Hitler the next day gave orders to begin large-scale military movements and preparations for the Gibraltar attack.[102] Hendaye's vague territorial compromises were acceptable enough to Franco that he continued to push ahead for an alliance.[103] Something beyond a close tally of territorial gains drove him—famine.[104]

By early November, Britain was ready to resume the aid initiatives. Hoare met Suñer on 30 October and left cautiously optimistic that Spain still wanted to maintain good relations.[105] Hendaye had not produced any overt shifts in Spain's position, and Churchill wanted to keep it that way. The Roosevelt administration, however, on the brink of reelection, wanted to take a harder line. When Weddell met with Suñer on 31 October, Suñer touted Spain's "political solidarity" and "natural sympathy" for Germany and Italy. Secretary Hull decided that the U.S. should hold firm. He instructed Weddell not to push to meet Franco; but if he did, he should remind Franco that it was U.S. policy to "furnish all possible assistance to [Britain] in its present struggle against aggression." And if Spain's "political solidarity" with Germany and Italy meant that Spain would assist Germany and Italy against Britain, "it would be manifestly impossible for the [U.S.] to lend assistance to Spain." The previous proposals for U.S. aid to Spain had been "premised" on Spain's "absolutely neutral attitude." Now that Spain seemed to have "no intention of maintaining such an attitude," the U.S. could "no longer give favorable consideration" to such proposals.[106]

This position was out of step with Britain's. But the U.S. reinforced British policy at a deeper level. It "did not interfere with the purposeful expansion of Britain's aid. In fact, [it] quietly sustained British measures to help Spain obtain food from [Argentina] and Canada, and oil from the United States and the Caribbean."[107] Meanwhile, Weddell tried to soften Hull's intransigence. He argued that Suñer's rhetoric did not translate into a concrete shift in Spain's existing alignment position; the British government had reached the same conclusion and were resuming aid negotiations. Given that U.S. policy was "to furnish all possible assistance to Great Britain short of war," Weddell urged Hull to reconsider and reopen the talks with Madrid.[108]

A wave of direct British lobbying along similar lines followed. On 9 November, Nevile Butler, the British chargé d'affaires in Washington, warned that his government believed "there is a very serious risk that Spain will be driven into the arms of Germany" if the U.S. were to "withdraw their offer of economic help," and he emphasized that his government wanted the U.S. to "send a wheat ship to Spain and negotiate an American loan for wheat and possibly other commodities" and to "keep closely in touch" on "all questions of supply and credit to Spain."[109] On 11 November, Welles explained to Butler that U.S. policy, set forth in "final instructions" to Weddell, was that the U.S. would be willing to proceed with the aid plans only if the Spanish government gave "positive" and "public" assurances that it would not "facilitate" the Axis war against Britain or "acquiesce" in Axis troops moving through Spanish territory.[110] In a 19 November meeting with Welles, Butler underscored his government's "reiterated request" that the U.S. relent: the Spanish government could not give the explicit assurances Washington wanted, and it was being presented with counteroffers of wheat from Germany. Given the strategic interests at stake—"the possible control by Germany of the Iberian ports and of the Iberian islands in the Atlantic"—London urged the U.S. to drop its demand.[111] The next day, Halifax followed up: he "hoped [the U.S.] would not insist on General Franco's making a public declaration of non-belligerency as a condition for receiving food supplies from the United States." Politically, it was "quite impossible" for Franco to make the declaration, and the food shortages inside Spain were "so critical" that more pragmatism was needed.[112] That day, Weddell also reported back that Spanish officials saw "a public declaration of policy along the lines demanded by us" as liable to invite German intervention, but that "private assurances" from Franco might be obtainable.

Welles (then the acting secretary of state) took the question back to Roosevelt, who acquiesced. By FDR's "personal direction," Weddell was to "modify the position previously taken": Franco's assurances could be privately communicated.[113] This seemed to clear the way for the prompt shipment of Red Cross wheat to Spain and brought U.S. policy more closely into sync with Britain's. London nevertheless continued to press for additional immediate steps toward a common strategy of aiding Spain. On 23 November, Churchill wrote to FDR directly, calling for "very plain talk" with the Spanish about a longer-term credit and aid arrangement. Again, Churchill emphasized the strategic stakes: "The Rock of Gibraltar will stand a long siege, but what is the good of that if we cannot use the harbor or pass the Straits? Once in Morocco the Germans will work south, and U-boats and aircraft will soon be operating freely from Casablanca to Dakar. I need not, Mr. President, enlarge upon the trouble this will cause to us or the approach of trouble to the Western Hemisphere. We must gain as much time as possible."[114]

HOLDING SPAIN BACK: NOVEMBER–DECEMBER 1940

Meanwhile, Spanish negotiations with Germany continued. On 9 November, Suñer sent Berlin and Rome signed copies of the general protocol drafted at Hendaye.[115] Three days later, Hitler inked the "Führer Directive No. 18" for Operation Felix against Gibraltar. Ribbentrop then invited Suñer to Berchtesgaden to tie up the loose ends. Their Berchtesgaden meeting, on 18 November, was contentious. While Hitler harped on the need to act "as quickly as possible" to "attack the English vigorously" in the Mediterranean, Suñer tried to explain the enormity of the "shortages and hunger" in Spain and the need for Germany to act to allay them. Before Spain could join any war effort in the Mediterranean, the "economic" and "public morale" problems had to be remedied. Just then, Suñer noted, Spain was receiving the first installment of 400,000 tons of wheat from Canada. Closing the Western Mediterranean to the British would mean closing the Atlantic to the Spanish. And that 400,000 tons en route would "by no means be sufficient"—it was just the bare minimum "without which an entry of Spain into the war would be absolute folly." Spain's needs for the year, he repeated, amounted to 600,000 tons. Hitler snapped back: "There was no doubt that all these problems would have been settled if Spain had already entered the war"; "Germany used all available material for the conduct of the war. If Spain were a belligerent power, Germany would supply her with material in the same way as was done very amply during the Civil War."[116] So that, for Hitler, is what it came down to: if the Spanish wanted to eat on his dime, they had to start fighting first.

Suñer then reverted to the problem of "public morale," by which, it turned out, he meant the need for concrete promises to fulfill "Spanish aspirations in Africa." The Hendaye protocol was too vague. Hitler again explained the need to keep French North Africa quiescent, lest it "break away" and join the ranks of Britain and the U.S. He could "only declare emphatically that in no circumstances would Germany's friends emerge from this war dissatisfied and the enemies satisfied. . . . When Germany had reached her aim, Spain could be satisfied in Morocco. Germany would then only claim for herself a base there." The transcript notes that Hitler's responses "appeared to dispel" Suñer's objections on the Morocco matter. The accuracy of this observation is questionable, but it is suggestive of Spain's priorities that Suñer's parting words to Hitler were about not territory but food: he would use the period of military preparation prior to the start of the actual Gibraltar attack "to get as much Canadian, American, and Argentine wheat as possible."[117]

When Suñer spoke with him alone, Ribbentrop proffered a new formula for meeting Spain's food problem: as soon as Franco committed firmly to a date in January for the entry of German troops into Spain to ready the Gibraltar assault, Germany would start sending wheat. In that case, said Suñer, he would still want to use the time between Franco's agreement and the actual attack to "import from England and America the greatest possible amount of grain to cover the deficit in supply." Suñer then suggested Ribbentrop should see to the *immediate* delivery of 100,000 tons of wheat, "as an inducement to facilitate grain deliveries on [Britain's] part, too, since the neutrality of Spain was a matter of exceeding importance to her."[118] It was an extraordinary ploy to exploit the bidding war over Spain's alignment. Ribbentrop even seemed to buy it. But, again, Germany never delivered.

By now, as Preston notes, "a disastrous harvest meant that Spain needed considerably more grain than specified in her earlier requests to the Germans."[119] And yet, Germany's position was still essentially "no food until you go to war." On the other hand, Franco was informed by a source within the British embassy, on 20 November, that Hoare would soon be offering a "more complete" aid package reflecting a firm "desire of collaboration with Spain." Later that month, with Hoare's encouragement, Spain applied for a loan of £2.5 million to be used to purchase basic necessities. On 28 November, Suñer said bluntly to Hoare that the "situation in Spain is delicate and dangerous. Spain wished to live at peace and had not finally chosen her friends and enemies. She was, however, faced with famine. Spain must eat and Spain would not be isolated. In order to prevent isolation of Spain, he had made his personal contacts with Germany and Italy."[120]

It is hard to know whether Suñer's description of the situation at that time was part of a plan to bilk Britain before going to war. Two facts are suggestive. On 28 November he and Franco approved a cable from Stohrer to Berlin stating that Spain had agreed to speed up its own military preparations to support the Gibraltar plan.[121] On 29 November, Stohrer sent a fuller report to Ribbentrop stating that Franco had indicated his desire to establish an early date to enter the war and requested German military experts to help Spain prepare.[122] That last message, according to Burdick, gave the Germans "confidence that the diplomatic requirements would be met in time" for the Gibraltar plan to work. Indeed, the German chief of staff, at that point, even told his subordinates that Spain had agreed to a January start date for the operation.[123] Franco's end-of-November responses strongly suggest that Hitler's refusal to move beyond a fuzzy Morocco formula was not the deal breaker that some claim. Franco was perched on the edge of a decision to intervene, while the Anglo-American aid option matured.

In these precarious moments, the Anglo-American policy of concerted accommodation hit home. On 29 November, Franco gave Weddell the private assurances that Washington had insisted on.[124] On 2 December, Suñer also formally confirmed Spain's agreement to U.S. conditions for food aid. The way was cleared to immediately ship the Red Cross wheat. The next day, Britain presented Madrid with a fully fleshed-out offer of credits and navicerts for wheat imports on a major scale. Hoare stressed to Suñer that Britain intended "to make its policy with Spain harmonize with that of the United States even if it did not follow identical lines."[125] Britain's offer—a loan of £2 million immediately, with potential to go up to £4 million in six months "if the political situation developed favorably"—almost *doubled* Spain's November request.[126] Britain also offered facilities for up to one million tons of wheat imports over the next twelve months, and immediate delivery of surplus rice from Egypt. At the same time, Britain encouraged Madrid to seek improved relations with the U.S., clearly signaling that more could be done via that channel too. Suñer responded to the 3 December offer by requesting delivery of 100,000 tons of wheat "at once," and indicated that he wanted to start negotiations over implementation of the offer—"the sooner the better."[127] As it approached Franco in early December, then, both barrels of the Anglo-American inducement strategy were firing.

The timing was propitious. Franco must have weighed the concessions in the scales of his next decision—to delay intervention. This is when the Anglo-American policy of concerted accommodation very likely *caused* Spain to remain nonbelligerent. On 5 December Hitler and his military chiefs decided that 10 January would be the start date for deploying German forces into Spain to attack Gibraltar in early February.[128] Admiral Wilhelm Canaris, chief of German military intelligence, went to get Franco's assent. On 7 December, Hoare was instructed to inform Franco that Britain was ready to immediately ship 35,000 tons of wheat from its stocks in Argentina and Canada, plus 40,000 more tons from Argentina a week later, and to arrange in January for Spain to buy 200,000 more tons from Argentina.[129] All of this was offered with minimal political conditions beyond the obvious requirement that Spain remain nonbelligerent.

That same day (7 December), Canaris met with Franco to secure his approval of the 10 January launch date for Operation Felix. German economic aid, he assured Franco, would begin "as soon as [the] march of troops began."[130] Franco did not give the green light. "Spain's provisioning," he explained, "was absolutely inadequate." In addition to the "incipient exhaustion of all supplies," Spain's military was unready, the Canary Islands were poorly defended, and there was the British naval threat in the Mediterranean. Still, stressed Franco, "the difficulties in the way were not so much military as economic; food and all other necessities of life were lacking."[131] When Canaris asked him to propose an alternative start date for military operations, Franco demurred. The clear implication was that Germany would have to begin helping Spain to prepare to enter the war *before* Spain would commit to a date certain. Two days later, Stohrer reported to Ribbentrop that the famine had now "taken precedence over" all other Spanish concerns.[132] On 10 December, under orders from Hitler to press Franco harder, Canaris "repeatedly and urgently asked if [Franco] were prepared to accept a new deadline for entrance into the war or could suggest an exact time limit for [the] latter." Franco, again, refused, since "it depended on the further economic development of Spain."[133] With that, Hitler decided on 11 December to postpone Operation Felix.

And thus, a corner was turned. Spain would not again come as near to becoming belligerent, and Germany would never again be willing to do as much to plan for, pay for, and militarily support Spain's entry. In late December, Hitler committed the German military to preparing for the vast undertaking that was Operation Barbarossa; he would never again have the military resources available to offer Spain. Throughout the first half of 1941, German forces were thrown into occupation of Bulgaria and fighting in Yugoslavia and Greece, delaying Barbarossa by six weeks. After Barbarossa began in June 1941, the material basis for a real Hispano-German alliance—disposable German military power—evaporated.

AFTER FRANCO BALKED: CONCERTED ACCOMMODATION IN 1941

A few days after Hitler postponed Operation Felix, Britain applied the brakes to concerted accommodation. Spanish authorities had moved in November to abolish Tangier's international administration. The cabinet had insisted then that, as a condition for further aid, Spain should "consult" with London before taking any further unilateral steps in Tangier. Unfortunately, Spain took just such a step before the message could get across. On 1 December, Madrid passed a law setting up a new legal regime in Tangier. Churchill, Halifax, and Hoare were determined not to let the tiny drama of Tangier subvert the larger policy toward Spain, but they needed some compromise. So, in mid-December, they held up implementation of the loan agreement, pending Spanish assurances that British rights under the new Tangier regime would be protected.

Here again, U.S. policy backed up Britain's. Thus, on 14 December, U.S. policy shifted: the first Red Cross shipment would now not begin until Britain released the shipments of wheat from Argentina and Canada that it had arranged on Spain's behalf.[134] Hull's instructions were explicit: "As soon as public announcement is made by the British government . . . we are ready to go ahead." FDR also agreed to then go forward with negotiations with Spain for the extension of credits, conditional, of course, on Spain staying nonbelligerent and refraining from aiding the Axis powers.[135] In early January 1941, despite Madrid's sluggish moves to satisfy London's demands,

Churchill decided to end the holdup. U.S. policy reverted back to extending inducements. As Hull wrote to Weddell, after "agreement [had] been reached with the British Government," the U.S. was set to proceed with the Red Cross shipment of wheat and milk products to Spain.[136] Thus, despite the delays, by the middle of January, Britain had shipped 15,000 tons of Canadian wheat and signed off on transfers of 50,000 more tons from Argentina. At the end of the month, Argentina agreed to sell Spain 400,000 tons of wheat. And to facilitate rapid delivery, London agreed to increase Spain's wheat import quotas to 200,000 tons per month for February and March.[137]

Hitler had not yet given up on Spain entirely. Franco continued to talk like an enthusiastic ally (and would for the rest of the war). But, as Stohrer reported, Franco, for all of his bravado, was focused on Spain's famine and economic malaise.[138] Ribbentrop sent back bitter missives questioning Spain's gratitude and trying to get Franco to understand that Spain's "bad economic situation" should "be the *motive* for" Spain's "immediate entry into the war" because "England will not and cannot help Spain economically. . . . Only Germany can do this."[139] Franco did not agree.[140]

On 6 February Hitler wrote a "Dear Caudillo!" letter. It was an extended rebuttal of Franco's various reasons for balking.[141] There was nevertheless an obvious tone of resignation to Franco's "mistaken" choice. Hitler, at any rate, had by then "ordered the final cessation of all preparations" for Operation Felix: postponement became permanent.[142] Mussolini could do no better on 12 February, when he tried to get Franco to commit to entering the war. By mid-February, then, Germany and Italy gave up on Spain as a potential ally, and the feeling was mutual. Berlin came to view Franco's escalating resource demands "as an expression of the endeavor . . . to avoid an entry into the war." Conversely, Franco's regime "had to conclude that Germany would not provide Spain with most of the goods the country really needed. [German] arms could neither feed a starving population, nor could a decaying economy be run with them."[143]

At about the same time—February 1941—Spain was wrapping up the political requisites for securing major economic aid from Britain.[144] Yet, it was blocking progress with the U.S.: both the Red Cross shipment and the credit negotiations were stalled over secondary disagreements that Suñer seized on to freeze relations with Washington. Thus, while London forged ahead in February and March with decisions to help Spain import grain, Spain's relations with the U.S. remained cool. Behind the scenes, however, Britain began another campaign in March to enlist U.S. support in a grand scheme to provide Spain credit. Washington, despite its tense relations with Madrid, agreed to participate in the enterprise. So, after Spain had agreed to the major credit deal with Britain in April 1941 (a £2.5 million loan), the U.S. tried to follow up with another offer to initiate talks for a much broader and more open trade relationship.[145] Despite that effort to keep in step, the Allies' initiatives toward Spain diverged. This was not, however, due to Anglo-American discord. Instead, it was the result of Suñer's continuing refusal to meet with Weddell, which prevented him from laying U.S. proposals before Franco. Yet, even during this period, U.S. policy passively supported Britain's.[146]

Poor Spanish-American relations continued into the autumn of 1941. After Germany attacked the USSR, Spanish propaganda escalated in praise of the Axis and hostility toward the Allies, including the U.S. Spain also sent a division of volunteers to the eastern front.[147] By then, although London still believed it was important to keep Spain out of the war, the strategic imperative to do so had weakened: Lend-Lease (passed in March 1941) had deepened U.S. commitment almost irreversibly, and then Germany had committed massive forces in the East. In July, Churchill's cabinet decided to "not press the United States" to keep reaching out to Spain, and they themselves adopted the public position that "the unfriendly attitude of General Franco made it extremely difficult for us to go on sending economic assistance to Spain," even as they continued trying to do so.[148]

Finally, in October 1941, Franco and Suñer switched back to courting U.S. aid and trade and were met then with a wary American hand. Spain's greatest need then was for oil, the flow of which the U.S.—with an eye toward impending entry into the war—was tightly controlling. The U.S. presented Spain with a plan to provide oil and other essential goods on a very short leash; it was "given without warmth, given because the American government did not think it could afford disorder in Spain."[149] Spain's relevance as a strategic factor in the war was, then, in decline. Stimson, expressing the chiefs' and his own view, informed FDR that with Germany entangled in the "Russian mire" for at least several months(!), it "must give up or slack up on any invasion of the British Isles" as well as "her pressure on West Africa, Dakar, and Latin America" and "Libya and the Mediterranean."[150] After Pearl Harbor in December 1941, and the U.S. commitment to beat Nazi Germany first, Spain lost all war-tipping potential. U.S. policy toward Spain then "ceased to be only an extension of the British policy" of accommodation. Thenceforth, the U.S. would "bargain for reciprocal benefits" from Spain.[151]

In sum, after Franco's decision in December 1940 to dodge commitment to Hitler's war, the pattern of relations in the months that followed shows two important things. First, well into 1941, the U.S. continued to adjust its policy to support Britain's approach to Spain, which reflected continuing perceptions of it as a potential war-tipper. The gap that opened then between the Allies' approaches reflected Madrid's resistance more than Washington's hard line. Second, later in the year, when the U.S. position hardened and became more transactional, Spain's war-tipping potential had clearly waned, and even Britain saw less need to keep the U.S. in sync.

Summary and Alternatives

Spain's nonbelligerence in 1940 had enormous implications for the future course and duration of the conflict. Hugh Trevor Roper argued that if Spain had entered the war in 1940, it would have put Hitler "in a position to conquer the world" in 1941. "If General Franco . . . had effectively substituted one monosyllable for another—if instead of *No* he had said *Yes*—our world would be quite different."[152] Even a conservative estimate of the historical consequences leads to startling implications:

> Had Gibraltar fallen, Malta would hardly have been tenable, French North Africa would have been subject to perhaps irresistible German pressure, the British might well not have been able to save Suez, and the [Allied] invasion of North Africa, had it taken place, would have only been possible under far more difficult circumstances than actually did pertain. In short, if Gibraltar, the key to the Western Mediterranean, had fallen into Axis hands, the war would have run a different course. It would probably not have ended differently, but it would have been longer and more costly and, in the end, atomic bombs might have been used on Essen and Berlin as well as Hiroshima and Nagasaki.[153]

Given such possibilities, it is important to understand what caused Spain to say no. The account given here argues that the necessary condition for Franco's crucial December 1940 decision was the Allies' policy of concerted accommodation. Had Britain and the U.S. *not simultaneously* been promising and delivering on promises to meet Spain's food and energy demands if it remained nonbelligerent—when Spain's economic needs trumped all else—Franco would have taken Hitler's alliance bid and Spain into the war. What drove the concerted Anglo-American policy were shared perceptions that Spain was a potential war-tipper, and that the Allies—together—held a strong hand of inducements to influence it. The Allies' limited alignment goal added to their advantage: for their strategic purposes, it would be sufficient to keep Spain nonbelligerent. Three alternative explanations challenge this account. Each implies that the Allies' concerted accommodation policy was not necessary to keep Spain out of the war, because other factors existed sufficient to do so.

FRANCO NEVER INTENDED TO INTERVENE

After the war, when Spain had compelling reasons to mend fences with the liberal democratic victors, the Franco regime's official history (and apologists in the West) argued that its policy had *always* been to stay out. Madrid's well-documented diplomatic efforts to create the conditions for an advantageous entry were thus really a clever shell game designed to throw off Nazi pressures for intervention. Such would allow Spain to "hide" and profitably ride out the war as a neutral.[154] There is scant contemporary evidence to support these interpretations, and an avalanche of contemporary Spanish and non-Spanish archival evidence to support the opposite thesis.[155]

SPAIN WAS TOO POOR TO ENTER WAR

A variant of neoclassical realism suggests that a state may be too weak in terms of economy, government cohesion, and extractive power to "actualize" its revisionist impulses or take advantage of opportunities for expansion.[156] This view is consistent with important elements of the argument. It is true that in 1940 Spain was in bad economic shape and Franco's government was poorly consolidated. Material scarcity and technological backwardness were compounded by government inefficiency. There is no getting around it: Spain's internal crisis was a central factor in its war and peace calculations. Here is perhaps the strongest theoretically informed explanation of the outcome: Spain's economic disarray was so pervasive that it simply could not summon itself to enter the war and fight.[157]

Yet, in the specific situation presented to Franco in late 1940, the actual military performance required of Spain was quite modest and was to be fully underwritten by Germany, which, recall, was looking rather formidable. In fact, Hitler had promised (and acted to deliver) all of the elite military capabilities (to be operated formally "under Spanish command") needed to conquer Gibraltar. The Spanish government did not need to mobilize a massive new war machine to take back Gibraltar; all it had to do was agree that Spanish troops would show up, and logistically support the movement of German forces into Spanish territory. Given that Nazi "volunteers" had *already spent years* in Spain during the civil war, fighting on the Nationalists' behalf, this was not a controversial operational concept. Moreover, Hitler promised to provide Spain major economic aid as payoff for entering the war. If economic distress and political disarray can be seen as reasons why Spain would stay out of the war, they are also reasons why Spain would have been likely to join it. Nevertheless, Spain's internal woes *were* a necessary condition for its remaining nonbelligerent, for they were what made Spain vulnerable to the Allies' economic inducements.

Thus, economic hardship was not sufficient to make Spain sit out the war. That is because it was not inevitable that Britain and the U.S. would concert to engage Spain rather than isolate it. Given the searing recent failures of Western appeasement, the isolation approach was a likely one. In London there was serious deliberation over and support for an alternative policy— to treat Spain as if it were *already* an enemy, to blockade the country and try to subvert Franco's regime. The policy of accommodating Spain was opposed by pro–Spanish Republic liberals and even Conservative anti-appeasers within Churchill's unity government.[158] In the U.S., even after Churchill

155

convinced FDR personally to support it, decent liberal opinion reviled the idea of treating Franco's Spain like a potential friend.[159] So the Anglo-American approach—to aid rather than isolate Spain—was not a given. Because there was nothing automatic about their efforts to accommodate Spain, there was no ineluctable tie between Spain's economic plight and its remaining nonbelligerent. Had Britain and the U.S. chosen *not* to aid Spain, and instead to strangle it, Spain would have been too hungry and weak to turn down Hitler's bargain. Its economic desperation would have propelled it into the war rather than held it back.

GERMANY DID NOT OFFER ENOUGH TERRITORIAL PLUMS

Although it is true that Hitler did not agree to grant all of Spain's territorial demands for French possessions in North Africa, and indeed made a few of his own, the argument that Franco said no to war because Hitler did not promise enough territory is also unpersuasive.[160] It ignores the fact that this was a bargaining context in which Spanish leaders would demand from the Axis powers more than they expected to get. And the argument offers no explanation for why Spain's *Africanista* leaders, so desirous of expansion in French Morocco, would prefer to get "none" rather than "some" of it, along with, of course, Gibraltar.

Franco's 30 October letter to Hitler, though it continued to stress Spain's "aspiration" to the "part of Morocco . . . in French hands," was promising enough that Hitler, after receiving it, ordered the start of military movements and preparations for the Gibraltar attack.[161] If the vague territorial compromises Hitler outlined at Hendaye were unacceptable to Franco, he nevertheless pushed ahead on his *own initiative*. It is likely that Spain would be satisfied with Gibraltar and partial gains in French Morocco because there was something looming for Spain that dominated all strategic questions—famine. Franco and Suñer, on November 28, approved a cable to Berlin stating that they had agreed to speed up Spain's own military preparations to support the Gibraltar plan.[162] The next day, Stohrer sent a fuller report to Ribbentrop stating that Franco had indicated his desire to set an early date to enter the war and requested German military experts to help Spain do so.[163] Franco's late November responses strongly suggest that Hitler's refusal to move beyond a fuzzy Morocco formula was not the deal breaker. Instead, Franco was teetering between committing to war and remaining nonbelligerent, and what tipped him toward the latter was the major prospect of economic aid that Britain and the U.S. presented to him in early December.

Germany Fails to Realign Turkey, 1941

All of the conditions necessary for a really friendly cooperation
between Germany and Turkey will exist. . . . The new territorial
arrangements which will occur after this war can never put Germany
in opposition with the aims of Turkish policy; on the contrary, a
rapprochement of the two countries will be equally advantageous for
the interests of Turkey and those of the Axis.

Adolf Hitler to İsmet İnönü, president of Turkey,
March 1941

We certainly want more from the Turks than neutrality.

Ernst von Weizsäcker, German Foreign Ministry
state secretary, May 1941

We have no other intention than to bring Turkey back to neutrality.

Joachim von Ribbentrop, Reich foreign minister, June 1941

By spring 1941, Turkey had become a defected neutral. To Germany, opportunity beckoned. It tried to induce Turkey to break its alliance with Britain and become a German ally. That would entail a high degree of alignment
change. If Berlin were to convince Ankara to take that step, it had to deliver
a handsome and credible package of rewards that advanced Turkey's most
important revisionist aims in the region—namely, the (re)acquisition of territory in Bulgaria, the Dodecanese Islands, Syria, and Iraq. In seeking to di-
vorce Turkey from Britain—and to use it as a pass-through for moving men
and arms against British forces in the Middle East—Berlin intimated that
such rewards were obtainable and initiated secret negotiations to find a
bargain. But the negotiations ran into a wall. Ankara's price for realignment would require Germany to make promises that challenged important
interests of its key allies at that time—Italy, Vichy France, and Japan. About
to start a war against the Soviet Union, Berlin would not risk alienating
those partners, so it abandoned the attempt.

The theoretical framework helps explain the demise of Germany's attempt in three ways. First, Germany sought to create a high degree of alignment change—realignment. Inducing realignment is hard because a naked volte-face involves steep costs for the target, costs that must be covered in the bargain. Second, Germany had high alliance constraints. Its material strength relative to its allies was cancelled out by its dependence on them in the immediate context of the war. Third, Germany needed those allies' support or acquiescence to make accommodation work, but there was no allied consensus to support it. The anticipated and unexpected push-back from its allies ramped up the costs to Germany of the concessions needed to influence Turkey. In the face of these, Germany withdrew its bid to realign Turkey and settled for an agreement that reinforced its neutrality. The process leading to that decision evinces two of the mechanisms, depicted in Figure 2 (chapter 1), which connect high alliance constraints to failure. Those constraints impaired the quality of Germany's inducement, and Germany, anticipating Allied opposition, retreated from the effort. Its decision to retreat was made easier because German leaders did not then perceive Turkey to have high strategic weight.[1]

Initiation Conditions

PERCEPTIONS OF TARGET'S STRATEGIC WEIGHT

When the war started, neither the German Foreign Office nor the High Command saw the Fertile Crescent as having "strategic significance for the war in Europe."[2] But after Hitler's December 1940 decision to attack the USSR, Italy's military breakdown in North Africa, and the German conquests of Yugoslavia and Greece, Berlin began to elevate its estimate of the region's importance and to accept the need to take a more proactive role (even while continuing formally to give Italy the lead).[3] The German Foreign Office's political department director, Under State Secretary Ernst Woermann, argued in March 1941 that in the fight against Britain, the region had "great strategic significance."[4] That perspective was also championed by Berlin's most experienced Middle East hand, Fritz Grobba.[5] And it dovetailed with strategic arguments the German ambassador to Turkey, Franz von Papen, was making then too, touting Turkey's strategic value as an ally and landbridge to Mosul and Basra.[6]

The strategic motive for Germany's attempt to realign Turkey thus began as a spin-off of the German High Command's indirect (or peripheral) strategy against Britain—the plan to defeat it by breaking its hold in the Mediterranean.[7] The indirect strategy first emerged in mid- to late 1940 as an *alternative* to attacking Russia, but after Hitler committed to Barbarossa, it lived on as an adjunct to the main strategy. Thus, in April 1941, German foreign minister Joachim von Ribbentrop's view was that if Britain were not beaten that year, "the questions of the Middle East might become of decisive importance." In that spirit, he urged Hitler to support the Iraq government in its growing confrontation with Britain, in the hopes of preventing Britain from gaining control of Mosul oil and positions from which to attack Syria.[8] Hitler's late May Directive No. 30, however, while praising Arab rebellions and approving aid for them, made it clear that the Middle East strategy was second fiddle to defeating Russia: "Whether and how it may be possible . . . finally to break the British position between the Mediterranean and the Persian Gulf is a question that will be answered only after Barbarossa."[9]

Thus, for Hitler and his closest advisors, defeating Russia was primary, defeating Britain secondary. In that context, Turkey's realignment would have some strategic weight, because it could help support Barbarossa while weakening Britain's grip in the Middle East.[10] But not more than that. German leaders did not see Turkey as a potential war-tipper. Its military weakness and isolation meant that its alignment, one way or another, would not affect the disposition of other neighboring states, which were already under the control of Germany, Russia, Vichy France, or Britain. Nevertheless, for some months in 1941, the potential advantages of flipping Turkey, especially if it could be done at low cost, were tempting enough to Berlin to warrant a serious try.

PERCEPTIONS OF RELATIVE REWARD POWER

In spring 1941, Germany's reward power relative to Turkey seemed promising. It was enough, as Hitler put it to the Italian foreign minister, Galeazzo Ciano, to make it "possible to loosen somewhat the position of Turkey."[11] From that modest baseline, German perceptions of their leverage would increase over the next two months. As they would come to see it, the main sources fell into three categories.

First, in a general sense, German leaders sensed that Turkey's discomfort at facing a very dangerous situation around its borders, with only an impaired ally in Britain to lean on, would make it eager to respond to German overtures. As Ribbentrop put it in April, "Much closer cooperation was of advantage to Turkey, who had an interest in having a strong friend in Europe."[12] One particular manifestation of this inclination was connected to the Straits "question" and Turkey's desire to see Soviet ambitions there checked. As Mehmet Saracoğlu, Turkey's foreign minister, explained to Papen, "Since Stalin had resumed the tsarist policy toward the Balkans and the Straits, Turkey again had to regard Russia as her greatest enemy."[13] When soundings for a Germany-Turkey treaty began in April, the Turkish ambassador to Germany had thus stated directly that "assurances in the Straits question would perforce be of extremely great value for his government."[14] Berlin had reason to believe, then, that the wish to pit German influence against Russia would, as Papen put it, "make the Turkish government inclined to come to an agreement with us that will perhaps go much further." For this reason alone, Papen argued, there was a good chance of reaching an agreement "preparing the transition of Turkey to our camp."[15] Ribbentrop agreed that "our extensive promises in guaranteeing Turkey's security and her interests in the question of the Straits" should make it possible to shift Turkey into at least a covert ally.[16]

Second, arms transfers were another lever for Germany to pull. That this was something Ankara craved was left in no doubt in mid-May, when Saracoğlu queried Papen, "Would you be now really willing to supply us with war material?" Turkey's president, İsmet İnönü, doubled down on the request the following day: "The greatest proof of confidence which Germany could give Turkey . . . would be the resumption of deliveries of war material."[17]

Turkey's general dissatisfaction with the territorial losses it had suffered after the First World War—and its desire to recover at least some of them—provided the third and most important avenue of influence, for Germany could make revisionist promises that Britain could not. Thus, Hitler wanted the Turks to know that if they "found their way back to Germany," he would help "satisfy their revisionist aims."[18] From the start, German leaders envisioned doing so on two lines. First, they could offer to return some of the territory Turkey had ceded to Bulgaria (near Edirne) in 1915, which had then been taken by Greece after World War I. Now that Germany was conquering Greece, Turkey could have it back.[19] (With this would come another plum: Turkish control over the segment of the Sofia–Istanbul railroad line that ran through Greece.) Second, and also at Athens's expense, Berlin could use the lure of Turkey's obtaining islands in the Aegean Sea. With possibilities like these, Hitler and Ribbentrop hoped to grease the dealmaking in Ankara and, for a time at least, they were eager to see what diplomacy could produce.

Contingent Conditions

ATTEMPTED ALIGNMENT CHANGE

When it began seriously to court Turkey in May 1941, Germany tried for a high degree of alignment change—realignment. Turkey was then a defected neutral. It was still formally Britain's ally, and it declared as much. But after France's defeat, Ankara invoked treaty loopholes to justify inaction and remain "outside of the war." Hitler wanted to "switch [it] over" to the Axis camp: as the German Foreign Ministry state secretary, Ernst von Weizsäcker, put it, "We certainly want more from the Turks than neutrality."[20] This was an ambitious and difficult undertaking, as the theoretical framework posits. Yet, the movement in Turkey's alignment over the prior two years suggested that success was possible.

Until 1939, Turkey had maintained a policy of strategic isolation that began with the founding of the Turkish Republic in 1923.[21] All that changed in spring 1939. As shown in chapter 7, when Germany reneged on the Munich agreement in March 1939, that convinced Britain and France that appeasement had failed and war was coming unless Hitler could be deterred. Britain then extended the Polish guarantee and tried to augment deterrence with further guarantees to Romania, Greece, and Turkey. But it was the Italian threat, as much as the German, that moved Turkey to close ranks with Britain in the joint guarantee of 12 May 1939.[22] The month before, Italy had invaded Albania, and it still had well-known designs on Turkish territory around Antalya dating back to World War I.[23] At the same time, Britain was shifting toward more robust naval preparations in the Mediterranean to defend against and deter Italy. Thus, there was a very strong convergence in British and Turkish strategic interests and priorities that undergirded the initial Anglo-Turkish declaration.

The French would also join in, but first it was necessary to resolve an outstanding Turkish claim on Alexandretta/Hatay in the French mandate of Syria.[24] Turkey had given up claim to most parts of the former Ottoman Empire with Arab majorities, but Hatay's population was close to 40 percent Turkish, and Turkey's leaders wanted it back. Here there was a very pronounced *revisionist* determination. As one historian notes, in November 1936 "Kemal Ataturk and the Grand National Assembly enthusiastically committed themselves . . . to revising the postwar borders and claiming territory outside their own state that, they claimed, was inhabited by Turks."[25] Now, in the middle of 1939, Turkey had the leverage over France to convert its revisionist goals into reality, and in June 1939 they agreed to a process allowing Turkey to annex the territory; this cleared the way for a Franco-Turkish declaration.[26]

On 19 October 1939, the relationship was consummated in the Anglo-Franco-Turkish military alliance.[27] It stipulated that if the war came to the Mediterranean, Turkey would give "all the assistance in its power" to Britain and France; if Turkey became involved in war in the Mediterranean, Britain and France would do likewise; and Turkey would also militarily support the Anglo-Franco guarantees to Rumania and Greece. Protocol II of the treaty contained an important escape clause—Turkey would not be obligated to take any action that would bring it into conflict with the Soviet Union.[28] The military understandings behind the pact included, at Turkish insistence, an Anglo-Franco commitment to expel Italy from the Dodecanese Islands and give them to Turkey. This operation was supposed to be one of the alliance's first moves once war broke out, undertaken "as soon as local command of the Air and Sea could be achieved."[29] The treaty also promised major military aid and financial rewards for Turkey—£25 million credit and £15 million worth of gold bullion. It was understood that these resources were necessary to enable Turkey to improve its military capabilities and also to compensate it for the economic loses it incurred by alienating Germany, which had in previous years achieved a preeminent position as Turkey's export and import partner.[30] A secret protocol of the treaty released Turkey from obligations if the rewards and resources were not delivered.[31]

During the "Phony War" (September 1939–May 1940), the Anglo-Franco-Turkish alliance moved haltingly toward consolidation. Once Italy declared that it would remain "nonbelligerent" in August 1939, Britain and France sought to preserve this defection by continuing to accommodate Italy (see chapter 6). Accordingly, the Western Allies subordinated the tie to Turkey—which for Turkey was principally a device for balancing and making gains against Italy. Meanwhile, despite Allied requests, Turkey did not adopt military mobilization: it claimed that it could not do so until Britain and France completed deliveries of the promised military and financial aid.[32]

Once the war began in earnest in May 1940, the alliance lost more traction. The agreed trigger for Turkish intervention was Italian aggression in the Mediterranean, but Italy did not enter the war until June, when France was nearly defeated. Thus, a corner of the alliance triad was knocked out: the support of French power had been a key element in Turkey's strategic calculus. Britain was seriously weakened, and Germany, meanwhile, still had good relations with the Soviet Union. On 26 June 1940, therefore, Turkey defected into a form of quasi-neutrality: it announced that it would not declare war on Germany and Italy. It still claimed to remain loyal to the British alliance, but invoked two reasons why it would stay "outside the war" as a nonbelligerent ally.[33] First, French defeat rendered moot prior military plans for Turkish involvement. Second, Turkey invoked the alliance's second protocol, which absolved it from action that might put it into conflict with the Soviet Union.[34]

British policymakers were furious at the betrayal, but in order to minimize the significance of the breach, the cabinet declared that in the circumstances, it did not seek Turkish intervention.[35] Britain, in any case, had no alternative, given its precarious position at the time. That weakness was in fact behind one decision that contributed to Turkey's refusal to step in. In early June, the British ditched the plan to drive Italy from the Dodecanese: without French support, Britain could not spare the military resources to hand-deliver Turkish territorial gains in this way, especially in light of the need to bolster defense of Egypt and the Suez Canal. Ankara's demands in response, that Britain keep the focus in the Mediterranean on efforts to capture the Dodecanese and liberate Albania, were ignored.[36] At the same time, Germany stepped forward to cultivate Turkish neutrality through inducements. Berlin offered to begin negotiating an agreement to provide Turkey with 21 million Turkish lira worth of industrial and military goods in exchange for Turkish agricultural products, one-third of which was tobacco.[37]

In October 1940, two more Axis moves triggered Turkey's obligations under the Anglo-Turkish treaty of mutual assistance, which both parties—

London and Ankara—still claimed was in force. Germany intervened in Romania, and then Italy attacked Greece through Albania. In both cases, Ankara invoked loopholes and special circumstances to avoid taking action and Britain, for all intents and purposes, accepted Turkey's defection to neutrality.[38] Thus, by late October 1940, Turkey's alignment position was that of a defected neutral. British policymakers understood that the force of events, and the reshuffling of strategic positions, had created a situation in which the challenge was no longer to get Turkey to fulfill its alliance commitment but rather to keep it out of the German camp and benevolently neutral.[39]

That was with good reason, for both defensive and offensive interests were nudging Turkey to bandwagon with Germany. First, with France defeated and Britain barely able to hold its own, joining the weaker side to balance was not prudent. Second, there were also revisionist possibilities in play.[40] In late 1940, London had resisted Turkey's requests for territorial compensations in return for implementing its alliance agreements. Turkey sought these in the Dodecanese and Albania (to be extracted from Italy), in Bulgaria, and in Salonika (to be extracted from Greece).[41] If Turkey were to regain territories as a consequence of the war, it would need to explore other options—options that an alliance with Germany might afford.

From late 1940 to the summer of 1941, a phase of bargaining and decision over such matters opened up. Berlin, through Ambassador Papen, initiated a series of efforts to capitalize on the slippage in Turkey's alignment to bring about a complete reversal. A Turkish proposal to Germany in November 1940, which called for an expanded "Turkish zone of interest" in the Balkans, was rejected by Germany because it contradicted Italian strategic precedence in the region.[42] But it was nevertheless important as an indicator of Turkey's inclinations at the time. Like Spain, it was putting feelers out for an advantageous jump onto the revisionist bandwagon.[43]

Finally, in the first four months of 1941, several developments increased Turkey's defensive incentives to realign with Germany. Turkey's northern neighbor Bulgaria joined the Axis. German forces conquered Yugoslavia and Greece. Turkey was surrounded by Axis powers and protégés, with the exception of the Soviet Union, which was still at peace with Germany, and Iraq, a British client state that succumbed to an anti-British nationalist rebellion in April 1941. Britain's overall position was shaky: its power in the Mediterranean was isolated in Cyprus and separated from Turkey in the south by a Vichy-controlled Syria.

Germany then began trying in earnest to realign Turkey. Hitler began the charm offensive in March, when he wrote to assure İnönü that German forces moving through Bulgaria were not a threat and to convey his "deepest conviction" that "really friendly cooperation between Germany and Turkey" was possible.[44] Hitler, as Ribbentrop put it to the Turkish ambassador in April, wanted "Germany's old allies at our side again."[45] Hitler's timing was good. Ankara had already hedged by declaring itself nonbelligerent. Now, with German forces on its doorstep in Bulgaria and Greece, Ankara wanted to reinsure with a friendship treaty with Germany. As İnönü put it to Papen on 14 May, "Turkey had her treaty with England, to be sure, but she would do everything to avoid coming into conflict with Germany," including forging new agreements "to clarify . . . her good relationship with Germany." Hitler, with an eye to both the coming attack on the USSR and a next move against Britain in the Middle East, wanted quickly to exploit the opening. The idea, as Ribbentrop explained to Papen on 16 May, was to forge a "treaty with Turkey which would unloose the country from its present tie with Britain and more or less lead it into our camp."[46]

ALLIANCE CONSTRAINTS

High alliance constraints worked against Germany's realignment bid. Berlin juggled a bundle of contradictory alliance commitments and aspirations. The first and most important arose from its alliance ties to Italy. Although, strictly in material terms, Germany was the stronger ally, it related to Italy as a peer, not a patron, at that point in the war, in the context of the Mediterranean and Middle East theaters. Germany's inability to defeat Britain directly in 1940, and its resultant shift to the indirect strategy in the Mediterranean, elevated the importance of Italy's military cooperation; there, the balance of dependence in the alliance approached equality, and Italy had major stakes in play. This relationship was formalized in August 1940, when Berlin declared, via a document circulated to all its embassies, that it recognized the Eastern Mediterranean as Italy's sphere of interest and that Italy had the "unrestricted lead" in the "political reorganization" of the Arab world, which included Syria, Iraq, Transjordan, Lebanon, Palestine, Egypt, and the Arabian Peninsula. As Woermann had put it to Ribbentrop, "A German claim for leadership in the Arab world, or a shared leadership claim with Italy is out of the question."[47] The principle of Italian political paramountcy in the Arab world was recognized again, by Germany, in the negotiations surrounding the Tripartite Pact of 27 September 1940.

Hitler's policy to give Italy precedence in Mediterranean and Middle Eastern affairs hamstrung Germany's attempt to "switch over" Turkey, because Ankara sought concessions in places Italy either controlled or had ambitions to control—for example, in the Dodecanese, and in Iraq.[48] Rome would also have a large say on anything affecting relations between Turkey and Vichy Syria. Indeed, Italy was leading the International Armistice Commission in Syria and had its imperial sights set there as well.[49] In sum, Turkey's ambitions in the Aegean, and in Iraq and Syria, all impinged on Italian interests to which Germany needed to cater.

If Italy was Germany's most important ally, two others added to the complications. In the first half of 1941, Berlin was trying to negotiate an agreement with Vichy that would make it a more active supporter of the

Axis. In this enterprise it needed to protect French colonial positions in the region. Any deal to support Turkish moves in Syria would cut directly against such promises and might embolden Ankara to take precipitous military action there that undermined Vichy's already shaky hold.[50]

And then there was Japan, which had "Pan Asian" ambitions to pursue in the region. The Tripartite Pact had given Japan leadership in creating the new order in "Greater East Asia"—the limits of which were not defined. Japan's concept of "Greater" East Asia, it so happened, came to include territory otherwise known as West Asia or the Middle East.[51] Japan's earmarking of this region as part of its sphere of interest was made clear in February 1941, when the Japanese foreign minister warned Ribbentrop against any exclusive German-Turkish carve-up of the Middle East and stated Japan's intention to have a hand in any such postwar arrangement.[52] In addition to asserting this claim, Japan came forward as an enthusiastic arms patron and political champion of the Iraqi nationalist government revolting against Britain.[53] Japan's agenda too, then, conflicted with what would be a powerful inducement to Turkey—the prospect of recovering territory in Iraq, which Ankara clearly signaled it sought. In combination, these divergent priorities constricted Hitler's options, draining quality and credibility from his attempts to accommodate Turkey.

ALLIED STRATEGIC CONSENSUS

There was no allied strategic consensus to support Germany's bid. None of Germany's main allies saw a potential German-Turkish alliance to be a strategic advantage. For Italy, Turkey was, first and foremost, an object of revisionist aims. Turkey was also an obstacle to Italy's wider imperial aspirations in the Mediterranean and Middle East, regardless of which side it aligned with.[54] After the Germany-Turkey friendship treaty of June 1941 (which was a nonaggression pact, not a military alliance), Italy did probe for a similar arrangement with Turkey, to reduce the danger of a *Turkish* strike against Italy's collapsing positions in the Mediterranean.[55] But this was not a high-priority concern. To Japan, a Turkey allied to Germany also offered no advantage; indeed, it ran counter to Japanese ambitions to establish itself as a protector and patron of an independent Iraq. Inter-Axis bargaining over how to buy off Turkey never occurred; Germany's anticipated reaction to Italian and Vichy opposition, and uncoordinated, contradictory action by Japan, would instead condemn the enterprise to a rapid and unsuccessful end.

Diplomacy of Selective Accommodation

In March, Hitler declared to the Turkish ambassador that in seeking closer ties to Ankara, "he had no intention of seeking any aid from Turkey."[56] To

Ciano, he stated that his goal was merely "to bring about a certain rapprochement."[57] That minimalist conception of aims was short lived. By May, according to Weizsäcker, Germany "certainly want[ed] more from the Turks than neutrality."[58] It wanted two big things—and fast. First, Turkey should agree to a public treaty of friendship that nullified its alliance with Britain by including no reference to it—not even an oblique or ambiguous one. (The Turks, by contrast, insisted on a formal cross-reference to their existing obligations.) Second, Turkey should agree to covert cooperation with the German military: in Ribbentrop's words, "secret . . . unlimited transit of arms and war material through Turkey" to Iraqi forces fighting the British. This would also include admission and transit of "escorting personnel . . . a certain amount of troops in a camouflaged manner." This, he explained, was "the decisive point in the planned agreement" and it had to be "laid down in an additional secret agreement."[59] Germany, in short, did not want Turkey neutral—it wanted it to become a secret ally. Papen had a more nuanced conception of how to do it: the idea was to first get a neutrality agreement, which would create conditions enabling Turkey "gradually to shift her foreign policy toward cooperation with us."[60] The envisaged process was subtler, but the end result was the same—realignment.

That goal—to realign Turkey—was a hard one to reach. When Turkey committed to the British alliance, it had insisted on a "fully articulated and reciprocal alliance" rather than a unilateral British guarantee.[61] Naked realignment would therefore carry high costs to Turkey's general alliance reputation. If Turkey's realignment could be bought, it could only be with a far-reaching and credible offer.

Papen warned Berlin of Ankara's sensitivity to the reputational costs of a sharp realignment.[62] He advised Ribbentrop to grasp that "the prestige" of the Turkish government was heavily implicated in any request for Turkey's assistance that could be exposed and constitute treachery against its British ally. Inklings of Turkey's wish "to reorient its policy toward Germany" had already provoked a "massive reaction by England" that put Turkey's reputation on the line. For this reason, penny-ante bids and haggling—"promise[s] of this or that island"—were not going to cut it with a Turkish government that felt defensive about its "clean reputation."[63]

To Ribbentrop, "the fact that the Turks want to save face [was] understandable." In this spirit, he had suggested some arguments the Turks could deploy to "save face" and allay "any scruples" over betraying Britain. The Anglo-Franco-Turkish treaty had entailed mutual obligations: with France "beaten" and Britain "in no position at all to render any assistance to Turkey," Turkey was free to walk. Moreover, France was "now swinging toward our side."[64] So the old treaty was both legally and politically defunct. Given the extenuating circumstances, Turkey would not lose face from realignment. Furthermore, Turkey would be justified in aligning with Germany because by doing so it would obtain some things manifestly vital—security against the Soviet Union, and avowed German support for Turkish control over the Straits. In exchange, Turkey had to grant "merely the permission for transit of war material with escorting personnel for the support of Arab nations" against British attacks or treaty violations. That was the only place where Turks had to "give rather than receive"; it would be "Turkey's concession in return for our extensive promises in guaranteeing [her] security and her interests in the question of the Straits."[65]

But of course, Berlin understood that to realign, Turkey needed bigger incentives. It offered these in the currency of territorial gains. In early April, Ribbentrop approached the Turkish ambassador with a message that clearly hinted at territory payoffs. Hitler now "desired a closer relationship with Turkey. . . . All of [Germany's] old allies who had found the way back to Germany had been put in position to satisfy their revisionist claims." Ribbentrop urged Papen to propose a specific carrot: Germany, via its special relationship with Bulgaria, could see Turkey regaining "the glacis in front of Edirne" that it had ceded to Bulgaria in 1915.[66] This was but a teaser. Berlin's bid, encouraged by Ankara, would build.

Papen reported on 13 May to Berlin discussions with Saracoğlu that suggested that Germany could "definitely and also very quickly find a treaty instrument with Turkey preparing the transition of Turkey to our camp." Papen had again reassured Saracoğlu that Hitler and Ribbentrop "had always adhered to the idea of winning over the old ally of former times."[67] Saracoğlu, in reply, asked if Germany would supply Turkey with war material; Papen retorted, "as soon as you are on our side."[68] He also informed Saracoğlu that Germany intended to send arms to Turkey's neighbors—Iraq and Iran—and wanted to ship them through Turkey, under some scheme that would make it "outwardly possible for Turkey not to raise objections." To this, Saracoğlu agreed. The next day, Papen met with İnönü, who repeated the request for German arms and offered directly the assurance that if it came to a "German-Russian conflict," Turkey would be on Germany's side.[69] Papen, in response, called for a formal agreement and dangled the prospect of Turkish territorial gains: it was time "to establish each other's position" and important "for Germany's decisions regarding the future organization in the southeast to know whether Turkey was willing . . . to restore the old friendly relationship by means of a treaty." İnönü declared: "Tell the Fuhrer that I am entirely prepared to do so." If Germany would commit not to join any power in a conflict against Turkey, Turkey would likewise commit "never to enter a conflict against" Germany. But there was a hitch: "We must find formulations in this [treaty] which are compatible with our obligations toward the other side [Britain]—but where there is the will a formula will be found."[70] So the murky terrain of negotiating positions was laid out—Germany wanted Turkey on its side, and Turkish help with German intervention in Iraq; Turkey wanted German arms, assurances about the Straits and its interests in neighboring territory, and a treaty that somehow did not explicitly contravene its commitments to Britain. Whether such a formula would be found depended, ultimately, on Turkey's will, for only *it* could decide whether new commitments were compatible with older ones. And whether Turkey found that will depended, of course, on the incentives Germany gave it to do so.

On 17 May, Ribbentrop instructed Papen: "The moment for reaching an agreement with Turkey has now arrived." He appended some important additional objectives and guidelines. Papen was to "go a little further with the Turks than we have up to now anticipated." What did Ribbentrop mean by "a little further"? A lot: "a secret treaty which will permit us unlimited transit of arms and material through Turkey." Germany was not "merely" asking Turkey to allow "small shipments of material" such as those contracted for delivery to Iran. It wanted carte blanche for "more considerable shipments the extent of which left to our discretion," along with "escorting personnel," routed directly "through Turkey to Syria or Iraq" for use against British forces. In return, Berlin could offer the Bulgarian border adjustment and "one or the other island in the Aegean."[71] All such arrangements would be tucked into secret protocols that would accompany an official German-Turkish friendship treaty that "outwardly" meshed with Turkey's other obligations. Finally, Ribbentrop advised Papen not to generate a draft treaty in the preliminary negotiations or "put things in writing in any other way." The negotiating agenda was just too explosive.[72]

With that, Papen, Saracoğlu, and his principal aide, Numan Menemencioğlu, began to negotiate the potential elements of a treaty.[73] Papen—despite Ribbentrop's instructions—did create a paper trail which not only underscored that Berlin was pressing Turkey to do things that would shift it "into open opposition to England . . . in sharp contrast to the political course which Turkey had followed so far," but also revealed the quid pro quos Turkey sought in return for such a switch over. Early on, Turkey had notified the British of their intent to negotiate a neutrality agreement with Germany. Before Britain responded, they resumed talks with Papen, who laid out the main elements of a bargain, cleared by Berlin: (1) an "open treaty" defining the political relationship between Germany and Turkey; (2) a secret protocol detailing Germany's promises to comply at "the conclusion of the peace with Turkish wishes" concerning the Bulgarian border, Aegean islands, the Straits, and Turkey's south and east "neighboring areas"; and (3) another secret protocol with Turkey's agreement concerning transport of German arms.[74] In approving this approach, Ribbentrop reminded Papen to keep the first secret protocol vague, with such language as: "politically and diplomatically Germany will support the aspirations of Turkey to secure her possessions and achieve a revision of the Treaty of Lausanne in accordance with Turkey's vital necessities."[75]

Papen provided an update to Ribbentrop on 27 May that, in essence, relayed Turkey's hard bargaining position. Turkey would not agree to sign the second secret protocol, nor even to give oral assurances, committing to ship arms against the British (although it had already allowed several disguised shipments to go through, both to Iraq and Syria).[76] London had by then responded harshly to Turkey's notification that it would seek a neutrality deal with Germany—Ankara would not expose itself further to British charges of betrayal.[77] Yet, despite such concerns, Saracoğlu *did* (through Papen) put across more specific language detailing Turkey's revisionist agenda. This provisional draft of the treaty's "first" secret protocol, expressed Ankara's demands for payoff for realignment with the kind of precision Ribbentrop wanted to avoid.[78] The message was clear: before Turkey would make a radical change in its alignment, Germany had to commit to strong and concrete territorial rewards.

Beyond the Bulgarian border rectification, Ankara's payoff demands raised many conflicting interests with Germany's allies. Turkey's desire to regain control over the Dodecanese Islands—which were ceded to Italy in the Lausanne Treaty—was well established. Recall that Britain and France, as part of their 1939 alliance with Ankara, had made plans to liberate those islands for Turkey early in a war with Italy. In trying to keep Italy nonbelligerent before June 1940, they had then shelved those plans. But it was clear then that Turkey was let down and still wanted the islands back. Given that Hitler had recently reconfirmed his promise to Mussolini that he would defer to Italy's strategic interests in the Mediterranean area, this was an inducement that—transparently—had little prospect of materializing. This was especially true given the timing of the discussion: Germany was about to attack the Soviet Union, and there was accordingly a strong sense in Berlin that Italy needed to be kept and upheld as a loyal ally, to protect Germany's southern flank. This was no time to stab Italy in the back with promised giveaways to Turkey of Italian-held territory. Ribbentrop's 26 May guidance to Papen had conveyed the extreme sensitivity of the issue: "In regards to prospects for acquisition of one or the other island in the Aegean sea . . . it is recommended that the phrasing be chosen very carefully until the treaty project has become more concrete."[79] The 27 May draft that Papen sent to Ribbentrop, which Saracoğlu and Menemencioğlu had helped craft, was not vague enough: it described Turkey's claim to "the islands in the Mediterranean near the Turkish shore," which, Weizsäcker noted, meant "Dodec." And it called for German support for an "equitable solution" if, during the course of the war, "it should prove useful to introduce Turkish administration" in those islands.[80] In short, Ankara asked Berlin to endorse a Turkish takeover of the Dodecanese Islands held by Italy, and to uphold Turkey's claim to them at war's end.

Germany went no further down this road with Ankara, and not surprisingly, camoflauged the issue in its consultations with Italy. In the 2 June meeting at Brenner between Hitler, Mussolini, and their foreign ministers, Hitler briefed the Italians about the just-failed attempt to gain Turkey's consent to transit of "arms and ammunition" in exchange for concessions. Hitler and Ribbentrop's account of the latter included a stipulation of Turkey's territorial integrity, recognition of Turkey "as the guardian of the Dardanelles," and border rectifications around Edirne. It had also, said Hitler, "been intimated that at the conclusion of peace Turkish wishes concerning certain islands off the coast of Asia Minor might possibly be fulfilled." At that point, Ribbentrop interjected that "Mytilene [Lesbos] and Chios were meant."[81] Two things here are telling. First, there was a crucial distortion: Lesbos and Chios were two Greek islands occupied by German forces in April 1941. Germany trading these to Turkey would not have been harmful to Italy. But in the previous weeks' secret talks with Ankara, it had been made clear to Ribbentrop (recall Weizsäcker's "Dodec" note) that the Turks wanted to recover the Dodecanese with Berlin's support. German leaders dared not disclose that these had even been considered as coinage for Turkish realignment. Second, there was a rather large omission—the proposal to support Turkish aims and interests in its "southern and eastern zones." These areas were smack-dab in Italy's sphere of influence. German leaders suppressed this dimension of the negotiations, too. Italy would no doubt object vehemently to any such arrangements. Germany did not coordinate with Rome on these matters; expecting a toxic reaction from Italy, it dropped the issue with Turkey.[82]

Turkey's demand for a green light to expand into Syria (the "southern neighboring area") if fighting spread there was also problematic. The Turks were eyeing a particular scenario, which would unfold in the event of a British attack on Syria, which was then impending. If that happened, Turkey wanted to take adjacent Syrian territory that contained lengths of the Baghdad Railway, which Ankara considered Turkish property. To Papen, Menemencioğlu laid out the case for German support: if there was going to be a "new policy" between Germany and Turkey (i.e., one in which Turkey shipped German arms to Iraq), it would disadvantage Germany "if England laid hands on the Baghdad Railway."[83] It is worth noting that Turkey, five months earlier, had won British support for a Turkish move into the same Syrian territory, with the argument that full control over the railway would help it to fulfill its alliance *with Britain*.[84] In early June, the Turks and British were considering it again. Hirszowicz writes: "It is now clear that the Turks would have gladly occupied Northern Syria, but only by agreement of both belligerents."[85] Thus, Papen's warnings, discussed next, probably deterred a Turkish move.

In March, Woermann had observed that negotiations with Turkey on "Arab questions" would, in practical terms, be likely to involve giving Turkey "a portion of Syria under certain conditions." How that consideration should then fit into German calculations depended on a more basic question—"whether French influence in Syria is to continue at all."[86] By May 1941, Berlin had decided that it should, and was negotiating with Paris over Vichy military and naval cooperation in the Middle East and Africa, and indeed protocols for such cooperation were signed at the end of the month.[87] The German High Command described Vichy military cooperation as "vital for the German war effort."[88] With an invasion of the Soviet Union just weeks away, Berlin would not risk destabilizing its western and southern flanks by alienating Vichy, as any such deal with Turkey would certainly do by violating the June 1940 armistice agreement, which perpetuated Vichy authority in French colonies and mandates. Thus, in respect to Turkey's demand for expansion in its "southern neighboring areas," Ribbentrop instructed Papen to "avoid any reference to precise geographical definition of the direction which such Turkish aspirations may take. . . . Our relations with France today and our cooperation with [it] in Syria do not permit us to encourage any ambitions of Turkey in this direction."[89] Consequently, in early June, Papen put it to Saracoğlu and Menemencioğlu bluntly: "German-French cooperation in no case permitted a step by [Turkey] directed against the French interest." Ribbentrop reinforced the point: "Consideration for France makes it simply impossible for us now to give Turkey any written or even oral promises regarding Syria."[90]

Finally, there was Turkey's "eastern neighboring area." That meant Iraq, and more specifically Mosul, which the League of Nations had given to Iraq in 1926, over Turkish protest. Mosul had a significant Turkic community, and more importantly, the rich oilfields of Kirkuk. That was, in raw material terms, the most attractive territorial inducement Germany could find to realign Turkey. It would also have a self-enforcing kind of effect—for directing Turkish expansion toward Mosul would put Turkey into direct conflict with Britain, making the realignment decisive.

Yet, even though Germany, as Papen said to Saracoğlu, "had no interest" in Iraq, Berlin's ability to sway Turkey was thwarted by conflicting and uncoordinated allied agendas. These were entangled in the complicated context of the Iraqi nationalists' fight against the British, which challenged the basing of British forces in Iraq and their transit through the country to the Mediterranean theater. Rashid Ali al-Gaylani, the head of the Iraqi nationalist government, which came to power in a coup in April 1941, had ties to a broader Arab nationalist movement. That movement was seen as a useful tool for subverting Britain in the region, and it had received some encouragement and support from the Axis powers.[91] After the April coup, Germany gave a political assurance to Rashid Ali's government that it would aid it "in so far as was possible" in light of other obligations and transport difficulties. Still, Berlin refused even to grant official recognition to Rashid Ali's regime. Berlin was not optimistic about the new regime's prospects, but providing aid to it would promote German prestige and make trouble for the British.[92] It would allow German forces to get at least a small foothold in the country.

As Rashid Ali built bridges to the Axis, Britain moved to occupy Iraq with significant forces—an open challenge to the new regime's demands. In early May, Iraqi and British forces starting fighting around the British base at Habbaniya. Hitler agreed to send military support to the Iraq rebels immediately, mostly in the form of Luftwaffe aircraft and pilots.[93] The German Foreign Office and Military High Command then rushed to work out plans and arrangements for ground support. Indeed, the German-Turkish negotiations that produced the 27 May alliance proposal had been propelled, in part, by Berlin's immediate wish to use Turkish facilities to transport aid to Iraq's rebel government.

By the end of May, the Iraqi nationalist position was collapsing.[94] The British bolstered their bases in Iraq with troops from India and sent a column from Palestine, and it became clear that the Iraqis could not defeat them without immediate and significant outside help. That never came. The most important reason why Germany did little to strengthen the Iraqi nationalist government was the strategic priority placed on Barbarossa. The German military was loath to divert resources away from that enterprise. Along with this was the deference to Italy's imperial ambitions in the area—which were, inevitably, hostile to full Arab independence (and also to Turkish expansion).

The provisional alliance framework of 27 May died soon after Papen sent it to Berlin. The defeat of Iraqi resistance removed an important German incentive for such an extensive bargain.[95] But even before that, Berlin's willingness to support Turkish gains in Iraq was dampened by cross-pressures from yet another ally—Japan. While Papen was negotiating with Ankara, Japan signaled to Germany that it intended to bring Iraq within its sphere of influence and to make the rebel Iraqi government a protégé. Japan's foreign minister demanded that Tokyo be consulted by Berlin about strategic decisions in the region, and he indicated that the Japanese military was working on plans for Iraq's defense. The vague division of spheres of influence in the Tripartite Pact (signed between Germany, Italy, and Japan in September 1940) had left unresolved the question of how far west Japan's "Greater East Asia" sphere reached. Tokyo now asserted that it extended to Iraq.[96] Again, with Germany on the verge of war against the Soviet Union—and hoping for a supporting Japanese attack in the Far East—Berlin was not going to push for a breakup of Iraq that snubbed Japan.

By June 1941, Berlin had aborted its attempt to forge an offensive German-Turkish alliance. As far as Ribbentrop was concerned, it was Turkey's refusal to allow the large-scale transit of weapons and men through its territory that broke the deal. But Germany's offers to support Turkey's territorial desiderata were vague and could not be made specific or credible. Ribbentrop had instructed Papen to "limit yourself to phrases of very little concrete character" when it came to promises to support Turkish ambitions in "southern and eastern neighboring areas"; such things had to be conveyed with "special caution" because they implicated a dense thicket of conflicting Axis priorities.[97] Germany's alliance commitments and priorities meant that it could not convert such vague promises into actionable rewards; so Berlin, in the end, had little to offer Ankara for making a costly move from waiting neutrality to firm alliance.

Berlin then resigned itself to pursuing a "more modest program."[98] Ribbentrop instructed Papen to restart negotiations with Ankara for a purely political friendship treaty that did not explicitly reject Turkey's treaty with Britain and did not entail Turkey's secret military cooperation. Ribbentrop now conceded that Germany could still benefit if "Turkey detache[d] herself somewhat from her English ally."[99] And, on 13 June, he guided Papen to describe Germany's intent in markedly different terms. Far from wanting the treaty "to force Turkey out of the British camp into the German . . . we intend nothing else than to bring Turkey back to neutrality, which the Turkish Government itself at the beginning of the negotiations wanted expressly to proclaim of its own accord." Ribbentrop underscored the lowered objective (while denying that the goalposts had been moved). If the Turks had gotten the "impression" that Berlin had intended "to force Turkey to pass immediately from the English camp into that of Germany," the "impression [was] wrong." "We have no other intention," he insisted to Papen, "than to bring Turkey back to neutrality." By mid-June 1941, then, Berlin had backed off: it was now willing to endorse a "treaty without prejudice to [Turkey's] existing obligations."[100] It combined this concession with a denial campaign in the Turkish press, the gist of which was that "Germany [had] never made or even considered a demand addressed to Turkey for the passage of troops. Such a possibility belongs in the realm of fantasy."[101]

The verbal footwork could not disguise what had happened: the Germans had dropped their alignment goal. The conflicting claims and interests of Germany's allies meant that Berlin could not offer enough rewards to induce Turkey to realign. So, Germany lowered its sights. It asked Turkey to do what it was already doing: hold to a kind of paradoxical neutrality that allowed it to remain a British ally—something that Ribbentrop had before ruled out "as naturally unacceptable to us."[102]

On 18 June, Germany and Turkey announced their nonaggression treaty.[103] It essentially formalized Turkey's half-in, half-out neutrality, although Ankara continued to assert that there was no contradiction between the new treaty and its alliance with Britain.[104] Under the aegis of the former, German-Turkish relations would continue to develop, especially in commercial affairs, but Ankara would not again get so close to realignment. Indeed, as Germany's position declined later in the war, and the Soviet threat to Turkey increased, Ankara would again tack back toward Britain and its U.S. ally. But it did not denounce its nonaggression pact with Berlin, and break off relations with Germany, until August 1944, when German defeat had become inevitable. Although Turkey would provide the Allies with basing facilities, it never entered the war as an active belligerent. It formally declared war on Germany on 23 February 1945 in order to ensure an invitation to the United Nations conference in San Francisco.

Summary and Alternative

German leaders did not start trying to realign Turkey because it was a strategic heavyweight. But they did think that flipping Turkey could help them against the Soviet Union and degrade Britain's strength and position in the Mediterranean. And they figured they had reward power that would enable them to do it at relatively low cost. Once they started negotiating with Turkey, it became clear that latter belief was wrong. At that point, German leaders abandoned the effort: the game was not worth the candle. The theoretical framework identifies three reasons why the costs of their accommodation attempt proved too high. First, Germany tried to induce a high degree of alignment change—realignment. From the start, this was a costly and difficult endeavor. Second, Berlin faced high alliance constraints. At that point in the war, with its focus shifted to beating Britain in the Mediterranean and invading Russia, Germany needed cooperation from allies that had direct—and conflicting—interests at stake in the kind of bargains Turkey demanded. Third, those alliance constraints were magnified by the fact that none of Germany's main allies would view a potential German-Turkish alliance as a strategic advantage. The anticipated and unexpected opposition of its allies meant that any deal generous enough to swing Ankara risked serious damage to Germany's alliance network. This account implies that Germany's attempt to realign Turkey failed because Germany could not (or would not) bear the costs of making it work. There is another perspective on the failure of the attempt that challenges this line of argument in a fundamental way.

TURKEY WAS NOT REVISIONIST—IT WAS JUST STALLING
TO DEFLECT GERMAN PRESSURE

That view, which is the conventional one, asserts that İnönü never seriously contemplated betraying Britain in exchange for German support for expanding Turkey's borders. Turkey was instead just trying to tread a narrow path to survival—to manage the German threat without alienating Britain entirely. In this depiction, the negotiations over the secret protocols to a friendship treaty were a charade—a clever stalling device, and a way to get Berlin to drop its more ambitious demands.[105] Thus Turkey's position in respect to the proposed secret protocols—the refusal to formally commit to permit transport of German forces *coupled with* extensive requests for German support for Turkey's expansion—was designed to take the wind out of

Germany's sails without rejecting it in a manner that harmed the prospects for the more anodyne friendship treaty.

It is not possible to rule out this scenario because it involves a deception calculus that İnönü, Saracoğlu, and Menemencioğlu would have been very careful not to disclose at the time—if ever. The fact that the collapse of the Iraqi nationalists removed a source of urgency behind Berlin's courtship of Ankara would have vindicated the Turks' strategy of playing out negotiations to buy time. Needless to say, the fact that the Turks disclosed to London that they were negotiating a neutrality/friendship agreement with Germany does not prove that Ankara never meant to defect.[106] For we know that Saracoğlu and Menemencioğlu did *not* disclose to Britain in May 1941 their requests for German arms and support for territorial gains in the Aegean and areas to its "south and east." We also know that Turkey's demands for some of these gains were not limited to its secret talks with Berlin: it had, more or less discretely, conveyed the same aspirations to the British and French over the previous two years, and as recently as January 1941.[107] For this reason alone, the underlying premise—that Turkey's leaders were fundamentally against expansion—is implausible.

Nevertheless, there are two things central to the conventional interpretation that affirm the theory's logic. First, Turkey was very sensitive to the alliance reputation costs of a naked betrayal of the British pact it had cultivated.[108] Second, if Ankara *was* able to cleverly blunt Berlin's approach by lodging those demands for Turkish territorial gains, Ankara could only do so because it would be very hard for Germany to agree to them, given its conflicting alliance ties.

When Does Selective Accommodation Work?

Claims and Case Comparisons

The theory situates selective accommodation in a larger bidding war over a target's alignment and thus implies that "realized" relative reward power is what determines outcomes. Process tracing in the cases confirms that perceptions of potential reward power are (along with high estimates of the target's strategic weight) a key driver of selective accommodation attempts.[1] But it is also clear that dividers' perceptions of reward power potential are often not matched by outcomes. The theory helps to explain why, by specifying contingent conditions that promote success or failure by influencing the scope, viability, and relative competitiveness of reward power. This chapter reviews those propositions and evidence for them from the cases. Because each case study has already presented, and summarized, extensive "within-case" evidence concerning those conditions, an exhaustive synthesis of such process-level evidence is not attempted here. Instead, I use a comparative method, leveraging similarities and differences across cases, to support general inferences. (For a full summary of study variables, values, and observations across the cases, see Appendix, Table 14.)

Contingent Conditions and Paired Comparisons

The contingent condition propositions specify circumstances that make selective accommodation more or less likely to work. In order to spotlight the key relationships and claims captured in the cases, they are broken down into four paired comparisons.[2] Matching up pairs in this way holds certain variable constant and isolates differences in others that show the effects expected to result from the contingent conditions. The first pair (I), shown in Table 9, captures the expectation that big differences in alignment change goals contribute to different outcomes. Holding the other conditions constant, it shows a link between high alignment change goals and failure, on the one hand; and low alignment change goals and success, on the other. The next three pairs (II, III, IV) focus in different ways on the influence of alliance constraints (see Tables 10, 11, 12). Each pair holds constant attempted alignment change. Pair II flexes alliance constraints. Pairs III and IV hold alliance constraints constant at a high level, while flexing the level of allied strategic consensus. With each of those pairs, the key differences are associated with the expected divergence of outcomes (success or failure).

ATTEMPTED ALIGNMENT CHANGE

The theory posits that the influence of inducements—and thus the likelihood that selective accommodation will succeed or fail—is conditioned by how much change in the target's alignment the divider tries to achieve. The degree of alignment change attempted thus provides a first-cut gauge of how much difficulty is involved in a selective accommodation attempt. High change is harder to induce than lower change because, all else being equal, big changes are costlier to make than small ones. To induce targets to make big changes, dividers must pay them higher rewards. Because small changes cost targets less, they are easier and less costly to induce. That is why the theory posits that selective accommodation is more likely to succeed when the alignment change goal is low (e.g., to reinforce a target's hedged or neutral position) and more likely to fail with the alignment change goal is high (e.g., to dealign the target from a fixed alliance or, more ambitiously, to make it into an ally). The first two cases in the study form a paired comparison that shows variation consistent with the argument.

As one can see, Germany's attempts toward Japan and the U.S. in World War I are similar in important ways. In both instances, the divider had low alliance constraints. In both cases, Germany's main allies, Austria-Hungary and the Ottoman Empire, had no direct interests in the values at stake and were highly dependent on Germany. Moreover, as expected in such circumstances, those allies were strongly supportive of Germany's efforts to accommodate Japan and the U.S. That control allows one to focus on where the

Table 9 Pair I—high vs. low attempted alignment change

Cases	Attempted Alignment Change	Divider's Alliance Constraints	Allied Strategic Consensus	Outcome
1. Germany-Japan WWI	**High** (dealign-fixed)	Low	Yes	Failure
2. Germany-U.S. WWI	**Low** (reinforce-neutral)	Low	Yes	Success

two cases differ—the degree of alignment change attempted. In the first case, Germany tried to detach Japan from its recently forged formal commitments to the Entente and make it a neutral (a high goal). In the second, Germany tried to reinforce the neutral position that the U.S. already held (a low goal). In short, Germany tried to achieve a bigger and harder degree of alignment change with Japan than it did with the U.S. Germany failed in the first attempt and succeeded in the second.[3]

The theory holds that when a divider has high alliance constraints, the quality of allied strategic consensus is a key determinant of success or failure. There is strong support for this across the cases. The condition's baseline value is *low* alliance constraints, which holds when the divider does *not* depend on allies with direct interests or conflicts at stake in relations with the target. Here selective accommodation's prospects hinge on the quality of its reward power relative to the target and the level of alignment change attempted. The divider has high alliance constraints when it does depend on allies with direct interests or conflicts at stake in relations with the target. In those circumstances, high alliance constraints make failure likely—except when a favorable allied strategic consensus supports the attempt. Such obtains when the divider's allies agree that (a) the target should be accommodated and (b) that it has high strategic weight. The three paired comparisons below are consistent with these expectations, highlighting congruent patterns of expected variation between different conditions (highlighted in **bold)** and outcomes.

The first pair (see Table 10) captures the difference between an attempt with low alliance constraints and an attempt with high constraints (and weak allied strategic consensus). Both cases occurred in the run-up to World War II. In the first, Germany tried to accommodate the USSR. In the second, Britain (in tandem with France) tried to accommodate Italy. The first contingent condition is held constant—in both cases, the dividers tried to induce a low degree of alignment change. For Germany, in mid-1939, the goal was to neutralize the USSR after it had started moving toward an Anglo-Franco-Soviet military pact. For Britain and France, the goal was to neutralize Italy after it had started moving toward a military alliance with Germany.[4]

Thus, the big difference is alliance constraints. Germany had low alliance constraints: it could approach the Soviet Union and parlay inducements untrammeled by resistant allies. While it was formally tied to Italy after May 1939, the power asymmetry in the Pact of Steel favored Germany's prerogatives, and Rome did not have strong stakes in the details of the bargain Berlin pitched to Moscow. On top of that, Italy embraced the German initiative and the strategic weight rationale behind it. By contrast, Britain was burdened by high alliance constraints with France, and their sometimes

Table 10 Pair II—high vs. low alliance constraints

Cases	Attempted Alignment Change	Divider's Alliance Constraints	Allied Strategic Consensus	Outcome
6. Germany-USSR WWII	Low (reinforce-neutral)	**Low**	Yes	Success
5. Britain & France-Italy WWII (a)	Low (reinforce-neutral)	**High**	Mixed	Failure

common approaches to Italy were marred by recurring disagreements about whether to accommodate it, and its strategic weight. In sum, Germany approached the USSR unencumbered by the kind of allied discord that hobbled the British and French approach to Italy. The outcomes match the theory's expectations. Germany stopped the Soviet Union from making an alliance with the Western powers; Britain and France did not stop Italy from making the military alliance with Germany.

The next pair (see Table 11) isolates cases with high alliance constraints that differ in allied strategic consensus. It highlights the connections between the presence of allied strategic consensus and success and the absence of allied strategic consensus and failure. With the first two contingent conditions held constant, those relationships are accentuated.

Thus, in both cases, the dividers pursued a low degree of alignment change, which favored success. In 1914, the Entente tried to reinforce Constantinople's position of neutral nonbelligerence, which it had adopted shortly after signing a secret alliance with Germany. In 1940, Britain and the U.S. tried to reinforce Spain's position of neutral nonbelligerence, which it had declared shortly before beginning secret negotiations for a military alliance with Germany.

At the same time, in both cases the dividers had high alliance constraints. They acted in concert with partners that were relative equals in terms of strategic dependence and strength and had interests and conflicts at stake in the relationship with the target. Russia and its Entente allies in 1914 had to coordinate among themselves any bargain they offered Constantinople, if only because they had competing ambitions at stake in its fate, and Turkey demanded from them a combined commitment. The British in 1940 needed U.S. support for their enterprise with Spain, and they had to consider Washington's interests in Atlantic affairs if they were to forge the larger common front they desperately needed in the war. In both cases, the allies also came to the bargaining with a basic agreement on the goal of neutralizing the target through inducements and considerable—potentially combined—reward power.

Given these commonalities, the critical difference between the two cases appears in the quality of allied strategic consensus and the resulting strength

179

Table 11 Pair III—alliance constraints and strategic consensus

Cases	Attempted Alignment Change	Divider's Alliance Constraints	Allied Strategic Consensus	Outcome
3. Entente-Ottoman WWI	Low (reinforce-hedged neutral)	High	**No**	Failure
7. Britain & U.S.-Spain WWII	Low (reinforce-hedged neutral)	High	**Yes**	Success

of their accommodative bids. In the first case, the Entente did not effectively mobilize and coordinate their potential reward power vis-à-vis Constantinople to beat the pressures and incentives coming from Germany. Behind the lowball bid lay significant disagreement about Constantinople's strategic weight, with British and French leaders in particular doubtful about the dangers posed by Ottoman intervention. By contrast, in the Spain case, British and U.S. leaders presented strong combined inducements that effectively promoted Franco's decision to put off Hitler's entreaties for alliance, and their concerted effort was fueled by shared beliefs about Spain's war-tipping potential.

The last paired comparison (see Table 12) extends the focus on cases with high alliance constraints but differences in allied strategic consensus. But with this pair, the level of difficulty is increased, because the first two contingent conditions are both held constant at levels unfavorable to success.

Thus, in both cases, the dividers tried to achieve a *high* degree of alignment change, which stacked the deck against success.[5] In the first, Britain—along with its constraining allies, France and Russia—tried to realign Italy during World War I. Italy was a defected neutral still formally allied with the Central powers (Germany and Austria-Hungary). In the second case, Germany—without the support of its constraining allies Italy, Japan, and Vichy France—tried to realign Turkey during World War II. Turkey was a defected neutral still formally allied to Britain.

Alliance constraints were also high in both cases. With Britain and its Entente allies in World War I, the circumstances of strategic interdependence and constraint were mutually recognized and made explicit in the negotiations over how to deal with Italy. With Germany's approach to Turkey in World War II, the high alliance constraints were felt by Berlin but dealt with differently: it did not try to coordinate the conflicting allied agendas through bargaining. Instead, Germany tried to work around expected allied opposition, without success. Thus, again, the key difference between the two cases turns on allied strategic consensus, which helped to drive the different outcomes.[6] The Entente allies converged in their views of Italy's war-tipping potential and concerted a compelling realignment package for Italy in 1915

Table 12 Pair IV—alliance constraints and strategic consensus

Cases	Attempted Alignment Change	Divider's Alliance Constraints	Allied Strategic Consensus	Outcome
4. Entente-Italy WWI	High (realignment)	High	**Yes**	Success
5. Germany-Turkey WWII	High (realignment)	High	**No**	Failure

that successfully flipped it. Germany, by contrast, was thwarted in its bid to realign Turkey by the irreconcilable ambitions and priorities of its allies. When confronted with their conflicting agendas, and the costs of trying to manage them, Germany had to abandon the realignment attempt.

Summary

The paired comparisons lend support to the key claims contained in the contingent condition propositions. In the next chapter, those claims inform the analysis of contemporary policy scenarios. Before going there, it is useful to recap the main answers they give to the question posed at the start of this chapter: When is selective accommodation likely to succeed or fail? First, attempts to induce small alignment change are more likely to succeed than attempts to induce big alignment change. Second, if the divider has high alliance constraints, attempts are more likely to succeed when there is allied strategic consensus—that is, agreement that the target should be accommodated and that it has high strategic weight—and more likely to fail when there is not.

Selective Accommodation in Great Power Competition and U.S. Grand Strategy

This chapter has two parts. The first examines a pair of scenarios built around hinge points in current U.S. grand strategy. The second concludes with suggestions for policy thinking, arranged in six general answers to the question, what makes selective accommodation work?

The scenarios envision surprising departures from current alignment trends and prevailing precepts in U.S. foreign policy. One explores how China might undermine the deepening Indo-American partnership by accommodating India. The other explores how the U.S. might short-circuit the emerging Russia-China alliance by accommodating Russia. These scenarios show how the book's theoretical constructs may describe and explain future developments. They also illuminate potential changes in great power politics that today's orthodoxies in U.S. grand strategy make hard to imagine, let alone think about carefully.

To begin, it is useful to reprise several ideas that inform the scenarios' construction. First, in great power alliance competition, the main action revolves around big potential movers on the margins. Dividers thus tend to target states that are in (or leaning toward) an opposing alliance and have strategic weight, but are not primary adversaries. Second, dividers target states that they have (or expect to have) reward power over. Third, dividers may aim for small, incremental changes—those that either reinforce or push targets into hedged or neutral positions. Fourth, because a divider's alliance constraints may encumber its ability to induce divisions (especially if there is not a strong allied strategic consensus about the target's strategic weight and the value of accommodating it), the divider may do better if it accommodates in ways that credit the interests of key allies and uses side bargains to boost their support. With these general ideas as backbone, the scenarios use current trends in great power alignment to set the stage for selective accommodation attempts and then use my theory's key concepts to flesh out and assess the possibilities.

China and the U.S.-India Strategic Partnership

A network of U.S. alliances surrounds China today, from Northeast Asia to South Asia, and feeds Chinese perceptions of hostile encirclement.[1] Beijing's attempts to weaken that alliance system will increasingly strain the U.S.'s grand strategy of deep engagement and forward military presence in Asia.[2] In that enterprise, the Donald J. Trump administration emulated its predecessors: it made political and resource commitments to allies and partners across Asia that deepened and expanded the posture for such a strategy.[3] Indeed, the administration's December 2017 *National Security Strategy of the United States of America* singled out Chinese attempts to divide the U.S. and its allies as one of the principle threats to that strategy, warning that China "seeks to displace the United States in the Indo-Pacific region . . . and reorder the region in its favor."[4] Such efforts by China are likely to spark destabilizing crises in Southeast Asia and elsewhere, in which military confrontation with the U.S. is likely.[5]

Rather than attempt to define the specifics of such conflicts and what might happen *after* they begin, this scenario centers on the prelude: when China anticipates taking a more aggressive line in the region and, to offset U.S. counterpressure, tries to prepare the political ground to its advantage.[6] Here, Beijing would likely do what it has done before—try to isolate opponents by showing flexibility on secondary conflicts elsewhere.[7] Thus, it would likely target U.S. partners in the region that possess enough strategic weight and interests to matter in a China-U.S. conflict. That boils down to two countries: Japan, which is entrenched in an alliance with the U.S.; and India, which is not a formal U.S. ally but is, increasingly, a strategic partner in U.S. efforts to balance rising China.[8]

Japan would appear to be the bigger prize. It has the more potent navy and ability to use it in tandem with the U.S. Removing Japan from the scales would create the greater material and political strain on Washington's regional posture. Furthermore, China does have an attractive inducement that it could manipulate—its claim to the Senkaku Islands, also claimed and administered by Japan, which is a recent focal point of tension between China and Japan.[9] The islands themselves lack intrinsic strategic value to China. In reaction to Japan's moves (starting in 2010) to monopolize them, China escalated its claims, for bargaining purposes and to cater to nationalist sentiment at home. But Beijing has not showed pressing interest in them in the past and could probably decouple with relative ease.

Nevertheless, Japan would be a very hard target for Chinese selective accommodation. Achieving a meaningful result would require a degree of alignment change impossible to procure from such a limited concession. It would require detaching Japan from a robust formal alliance, which has recently been upgraded with new political and strategic commitments by both Tokyo and Washington, targeted against China.[10] Given the bitter history between Japan and China, and the depth of U.S. commitment to Japan, re-alignment would, as a practical matter, be unreachable: the best China could hope for would be to cultivate the prospect of Japanese hedging once a regional crisis breaks out. However, given the centrality of Japan's position in the U.S.'s alliance system, Washington would be certain to exert extraordinary efforts to blunt China's enterprise and outbid its inducements.[11] In short, Japan does not offer promising ground for a Chinese selective accommodation strategy.[12] A serious Chinese bid to neutralize Japan ahead of a confrontation with the U.S. would be very unlikely to succeed, and Beijing—anticipating this—would be unlikely to try.

Beijing will have stronger incentives to try to sideline India and better prospects for doing so. As Garver put it, "From the standpoint of China's struggle against U.S., Japanese, and Indian 'encirclement,' India might be deemed the weak link in the tightening ring."[13] Given the trend of U.S.-India strategic convergence against China, Beijing has a prima facie interest in disrupting it. Joining a great power effort to contain China is nothing new for India—it did so in the 1970s when it aligned with the USSR.[14] Today, its strategic elites once again generally view China as a competitor and major threat.[15] That nicely facilitates Washington's efforts to build a "progressively closer entente" with India that supports its efforts to balance against China's rise in the region.[16] As U.S. secretary of defense Leon Panetta enthused in 2012, India would be made into a "linchpin" in the U.S.'s strategy to "rebalance" toward Asia.[17] After the 2014 Indian elections, when Narendra Modi's National Democratic Alliance government took power, the tempo of U.S.-India strategic convergence increased.[18] This has been manifest in its military-to-military exchanges with India, trade of conventional military technology, cooperation in defense industry R&D, and many steps toward logistics collaboration and interoperability of forces. In May 2018, the Pentagon rebranded the Pacific Command as the "Indo-Pacific Command" so as to recognize, as Defense Secretary James Mattis put it, "the increasing connectivity between the Indian and Pacific Oceans," and the critical "relationships with our Pacific and Indian Ocean allies and partners."[19] Since then, the U.S. and Indian defense agencies have taken further significant steps toward devising the infrastructure of military cooperation, agreeing to work toward greater interoperability and "real-time" intelligence exchange. In 2019, the U.S. and India held their first "tri-service" (army, navy, air force) joint military exercise.[20] In February 2020, coinciding with President Trump's visit to India, the two countries declared a "comprehensive global strategic partnership" reflecting their "strategic convergence in the Indo-Pacific." With this would come deeper "defense and security cooperation, especially through greater maritime and space domain awareness and information sharing," encompassing "joint cooperation, exchange of military liaison personnel; advanced training and expanded exercises between all services and special forces; closer collaboration on co-development and co-production of advanced defense components, equipment, and platforms; and partnership between their defense industries." Along with this came the announcement of a $3 billion arms sale to India, including twenty-four MH-60R Seahawk naval helicopters.[21]

India, in line with its "Look East" and "Act East" foreign policy concepts, has enlarged its strategic and commercial ties in Southeast Asia and the Pacific, which have helped deepen the U.S.-India strategic partnership.[22] India has developed specific interests in Southeast Asia and the South China Sea—for example, with Vietnam—that conflict with China's.[23] India's navy is, to some extent, preparing to protect those interests.[24] These steps, and other signs of increased Indian naval activism in the region, thus make it more likely that India and the U.S. will range on the same side in a Southeast Asia–China crisis.[25] In short, many signs point to India's growing adhesion to the U.S.-led "loose anti-China balancing coalition" in the region.[26] Beijing can no longer assume that India will be a bystander to a U.S.-China conflict.

INDIA'S STRATEGIC WEIGHT

But China's motivation to defuse Indo-U.S. convergence will rest on more practical calculations of India's strategic weight. How much trouble for China could India, allied to the U.S., cause? How much advantage might China gain by distancing India from the U.S. and its anti-China coalition, ahead of a regional crisis?

To some observers, India's growth as a regional power already gives it obvious strategic weight.[27] For now, one can say that India—more than any other country in Southeast Asia—has some potential, on its own, to counterbalance China locally. At the same time, in the wider region, it is far from a match for China's naval and military power. But it is not necessary that India match Chinese military power in that sense for Beijing to take India's strategic weight seriously. Both the way in which Indian military capabilities could augment a U.S.-led coalition, and the political effects of its alignment on other states' willingness to contest Chinese expansion, would contribute to China's perception of India's strategic weight.

As for the force India could contribute to combined action against China in a regional crisis, the possibilities are easy to discern. In a maritime conflict, Indian naval and air power could become important. Especially in the Indian Ocean area, India has a geographic advantage that boosts its naval and air strength relative to Chinese maritime forces.[28] That advantage is extended by India's potential to establish "negative control" over the Malacca Strait, which is a "focal point" of its maritime strategy. India's naval and air facilities in the Andaman and Nicobar Islands—which are located near the top of the Malacca Strait—give India some capacity to disrupt Chinese access into the Indian Ocean, and they "form a natural base for [it] to project power into the South China Sea."[29]

Indian force in the maritime domain is thus where its strategic weight, in material terms, would matter most to Beijing. It is not surprising, then, that "Chinese attention has focused" on that Indian potential to hamper China's access to the Indian Ocean and sea-lanes running through it from the Malacca Strait to the Persian Gulf.[30] Indeed, "Chinese strategists are concerned that an adversary may use these vulnerabilities as a bargaining chip in the context of a wider dispute."[31] And "looming behind" that potential, Chinese strategists see the "shadow" of long-term U.S. efforts to encircle China by extending India's "maritime footprint into the Asia-Pacific region" and moving it into a "potential 'anti-China club.'"[32] For these reasons, then, China's leaders would have to reckon with the possibility of India's naval intervention against Chinese shipping through the Indian Ocean and Malacca Strait in a full-blown U.S.-China conflict in Southeast Asia, and have incentives to reduce its likelihood.[33]

Beyond that potential, India's strategic weight would stem from the possible knock-on political effects of its taking a *detached* position. How might these play out? The first would involve Japan—but not to China's advantage. Since 2008, Tokyo and Delhi have significantly increased their security cooperation.[34] For both, this is a way to hedge against China's growing power and the possibility of reduced U.S. commitment.[35] But if China were to neutralize India, Japan would *not* be likely to distance itself from the U.S. While India's detachment would be jarring, Japan is a great power and it would balance. Thus, by neutralizing India, China would reinforce the already strong likelihood—noted above—that Japan would cooperate in a U.S.-allied response.

More advantageous for China would be the knock-on effects involving the U.S.'s smaller Southeast Asian partners. For these parties, security cooperation with India (in tandem with the U.S.) is an important defense against China's growing power and assertiveness.[36] Since the early 2000s, India has developed defense cooperation ties to Singapore, Vietnam, the Philippines, and Indonesia. The impulse to balance against China propelled this convergence and the U.S. has worked assiduously to accelerate it.[37] Trends suggest that such security cooperation will deepen in the years ahead. If India is increasingly seen by Southeast Asian partners as an important element in the front against China, the critical issue is, how will they react to an accommodation between China and India? From the change in their expectations of Indian support against China, their resolve would be likely to weaken. As small powers, they would become more prone to bandwagon with China than to resist it.[38] That, at least, is what strategists in Beijing might reasonably figure. Of course, the small partners might instead stiffen their opposition to China, betting that the U.S. will defend them. But India, recall, would have been a hedge in their prior calculation to depend so heavily on U.S. assurances. The discounting of that India fallback would make coming to terms with China more attractive. In sum, insofar as those countries vulnerable to China pretensions *did in fact* see India as an important buttress against China's power and unpredictable U.S. commitment, Beijing would have a strong incentive to try to negate their hedge.

To recap, for China, the strategic benefits of neutralizing India ahead of a confrontation with the U.S. would fall into two categories. First, it would reduce the threat of combined Indo-U.S. naval action against its shipping across the Indian Ocean and through the Malacca Strait if a crisis escalated to open warfare. While a bystanding India could decide to intervene, despite Chinese accommodation, it would also have incentives to use its detached posture to pull more concessions from China for remaining so. Second, China could benefit from the political effects that neutralizing India would have on other local opponents of China's expansion, and the determination of the U.S. to defend them. Beijing's hope—and Washington's fear—would be that India's defection would preemptively demoralize and weaken the cohesion of the local balancing coalition. Finding regional partners hesitant could lead Washington itself to moderate its response. If neither India nor regional partners directly exposed to Chinese pretensions were resolved to stand firm, it would be harder.—and probably imprudent—for the U.S. to insist on a showdown.

CHINA'S ALIGNMENT GOAL

Chinese strategists undoubtedly see the trends of U.S.-Indian convergence—and the strategic ties between India and other regional players that it promotes—and Beijing clearly has an interest in blunting them.[39] A Chinese attempt to bully India away from the U.S. would almost certainly fail. Given India's increasing tilt toward the U.S., and the strong desire in Washington to bind India closer, any move by China to seriously threaten India will drive India into a tighter alliance.[40] Thus, if China were seeking to set the stage for confrontation with the U.S., it would more probably try to coax India into a neutral position. That low alignment change goal would be to China's advantage. Unless India were to drastically change the nature of its strategic relationship with the U.S.—as an "entente" that avoids formal political or military commitments—Indian compliance with China's overtures would be but a small step backward, into a hedging position consistent with its traditional posture of "nonalignment" and "strategic autonomy."[41]

CHINA'S ACCOMMODATION OPTIONS

Whether China tried seriously to do this would hinge on Chinese leaders' sense of their reward power relative to India. China does control some strategic values very important to India, over which it could compromise to influence India's alignment. Chinese leaders are no strangers to the logic of such strategy. Indeed, in China's dealings with territorial disputes over time, it has sometimes adopted a flexible approach to resolving certain disputes in order to reduce tensions with states that might come together in opposition.[42] In the 2000s, for example, Beijing switched between soft-line and hardline approaches to Japan and India, lest "simultaneous efforts to pressure [them] drive those countries further together."[43] There were also indications then that "China [was] engaging India with more intensity . . . precisely due to its fear that India may be dragged too close into America's orbit."[44]

Three sources of strain in the Sino-India relationship offer potential areas for accommodation. The first centers on China's border disputes with India on India's northeast frontier in Arunachal Pradesh. The second involves the expansion of Chinese influence around the Indian Ocean. The third is China's alliance with Pakistan. Of the three, China's best inducement options lie in the potential to settle outstanding border disputes with India.

Manipulation of Border Disputes. China's unresolved border disputes with India are among the most potent drivers of Indian perceptions of threat. China's inflexibility on these issues is not inevitable: they constitute a set of bargaining points that can be aggravated to apply pressure on India and relaxed to conciliate it. One recent border flare-up—at Doklam, in the northeast corner of Sikkim, in July and August 2017—evinces this pattern. In an area where tensions had been dormant for decades, China went from escalation to deescalation in a matter of weeks, drawing a defensive military response from India.[45] Adding to the bargaining utility for China of border issues like these is the asymmetry in threat perceptions that arise from them. While "India tends to be deeply apprehensive of threats stemming from the[m]," China "has not considered the boundary problem as a serious challenge to its security."[46] Setting aside India's desire to overcome the historical setback of the 1962 border war, and to establish its claims in general, an important strategic reason for India's heightened concern is that the unresolved disputes give China a ready "excuse to take military action" to deflect or dampen Indian concentrations of force against Pakistan, as it did in 1965. Thus, India has long been "more eager to solve the border problem than China."[47]

China's traditional approach to the border settlement issue has two major characteristics. First, it has stressed the importance of an overall "package deal" involving mutual compromise, in which Beijing's recognition of certain Indian claims is traded for Delhi's recognition of certain Chinese claims.[48] Second, China has shown much greater satisfaction with delaying steps toward final resolution, content to work out the minimal confidence-building measures and negotiation processes necessary to keep tensions down.

China's best avenue for accommodating India lies in the border dispute over Arunachal Pradesh, which for India is the most serious dispute. Historically, China demonstrated a relatively weak interest in defending its claims to this part of the "eastern sector."[49] Indeed, in the 1960s, Beijing repeatedly indicated willingness to recognize India's sovereignty and border claims there if India would recognize China's border in the Aksai Chin (in the "western sector"). The utility of a Chinese concession to India on Arunachal Pradesh is thus enhanced by the unequal strategic value the territory holds for the two parties. China's security interests at stake there are quite small: its claims are principally a linkage lever for promoting India's acquiescence to China's border claim in the western sector. By contrast, for India, the eastern sector is "of crucial importance" and security concerns are "acute" in Arunachal Pradesh, "which control[s] the high ground north of Assam and [gives] China direct access to the narrow Siliguri corridor . . . a strategic bottleneck in India's defence of the northeastern frontier."[50] Thus, China has the ability to reward India with something very important to Delhi, at relatively low cost to itself.[51]

China, however, has in recent years taken a harder line on the eastern sector.[52] In 2005, Chinese officials began to refer to Arunachal Pradesh as "southern Tibet."[53] More pointedly, in 2007 China laid down the new demand that any settlement must include, at minimum, the transfer to China of the Tawang district.[54] And in 2013, there was an incursion of Chinese troops in the Depsang Plains area of Arunachal Pradesh. India, in response, has poured resources into strengthening its political and military presence in the area.[55] China's escalating demands in Arunachal Pradesh thus touch on a position of great sensitivity to India.

China could ameliorate that tension—and thereby encourage India to hedge in a U.S.-China crisis—by initiating a process of Chinese concessions around that dispute. First, it could emphasize a desire to reach a settlement agreeable to India on the Arunanchal Pradesh border, *without* linkage to any progress toward Indian recognition of China's border in the Aksai Chin. It could revert to its earlier position that a border agreement in the eastern sector reflecting the McMahon Line boundaries would, as a practical matter, be acceptable.[56] And it could signal a willingness to retract the earlier demand for Tawang in the context of an overall border settlement in Arunanchal Pradesh. As an immediately credible signal of goodwill, it could reduce its military presence in the border area adjacent to Arunanchal Pradesh.

If this sounds far-fetched, consider this: China has in the recent past settled a border dispute in the eastern sector on terms favorable to India, without holding out for an overall package deal. Between 2002 and 2005, it completed a process of recognizing Indian sovereignty over Sikkim, which Delhi had annexed in 1975.[57] There was, of course, a de facto linkage—India's 2003 recognition of Tibet as part of the PRC.[58] But that is the point—China, in this scenario, would be looking for de facto linkage to India's dealignment from the U.S.

Chinese Restraint in the Indian Ocean. Another key driver of Indian perceptions of the China threat is China's attempts to develop dual-use, civilian port and naval access facilities, and an expanded naval presence in the Indian

Ocean region.[59] Elements of China's "Maritime Silk Road" strategy, these efforts seek to guard China's ability to ship oil from East Africa and the Persian Gulf to the home market.[60] China's most significant move in this domain is its development of a deepwater port at Gwadar, in the southwest corner of Pakistan near the mouth of the Strait of Hormuz. But China has also pushed to develop bases in Bangladesh and Burma (next to India, on the east coast of the Bay of Bengal) and in Sri Lanka and the Maldives (off the southeastern and southwestern tip of India). These, too, encroach on the core of India's sphere of maritime security. Between 2015 and 2016, Indian diplomatic and commercial pressures convinced Bangladesh, Sri Lanka, and the Maldives each to shut down some of China's base-building efforts and to offer India assurances that China would not be granted military use of the nascent ports. Such assurances from the local authorities have tempered but not eliminated Indian concerns. Here lies another area for potential Chinese accommodation of India.

Recognizing India's considerable political and strategic clout in the area, in any case, Beijing could offer Delhi an informal bargain to concede the Indian Ocean as a special sphere of Indian influence and curtail initiatives overtly aimed to support sustained Chinese naval operations in it. In addition, Beijing could invite India to join it in forging a kind of bilateral regime for protecting commercial shipping in Indian Ocean sea-lanes important to both, with the lure of reduced unilateral Chinese naval presence in exchange for Indian cooperation. Other areas for bilateral maritime security cooperation might include agreements to reduce risks of "incidents at sea" through transparency measures (e.g., information exchange, notification, observation, and inspection). The Sino-Indian "maritime affairs dialogue," first convened in February 2016, and then again in July 2018, could provide the institutional platform for this kind of exchange.[61]

Such efforts, however, would garner Beijing little influence over India's alignment. India has already, through its own political and economic resources, done much to blunt or roll back Chinese inroads in the Indian Ocean, and Delhi gains credibility by reinforcing its regional hegemony in this way. Moreover, if India wanted or needed additional clout to deflect its neighbors' basing deals with China, it can turn to another very powerful actor that shares its strategic priorities in the region—the U.S. Thus, because China has far from exclusive control over whether it erects a basing network in the Indian Ocean, its restraint in this area will do little to influence Indian alignment.

Sino-Pakistani Relations. China's alliance with Pakistan is another possible—but not promising—avenue for accommodating India. Indians' greatest antipathy is directed toward that historical enemy. Reducing Chinese support for Pakistan in overt ways could certainly help China's relations with India. In fact, China *has* modified its level of support of Pakistan over the years to serve other strategic interests. As Malik noted, "A desire for stability on its southwestern flank and fears of an Indian-U.S. alliance have already caused Beijing to take a more evenhanded approach, while still favoring Pakistan."[62] After the Cold War, China moved from its unequivocal support of Pakistan's position in the Kashmir conflict to a neutral position.[63] It "shifted from a focus on exploiting the India-Pakistan conflict to a policy designed to help stabilize" it.[64] This adjustment was manifest in several ways. China began to advance the view that the Kashmir conflict should be settled by direct negotiations between Pakistan and India, contrary to Pakistan's emphasis on an international settlement via the UN. During the 1999 crisis, which started when Pakistani forces crossed the Line of Control, China also called for restraint from both sides and urged them both to respect the Line of Control. In the crises of 2002 and 2008, China did the same again while also quietly encouraging negotiations. Nevertheless, China has also recently put some pressure on the India position by issuing unconventional visas for Indians from Kashmir wishing to travel to China, thus signaling that it views Indian-held Kashmir as still disputed territory rather than part of Indian sovereignty.[65]

There is thus some room for China to use its Pakistan ties instrumentally, and China could conciliate India by further manipulating its stance on the Kashmir issue. Beijing could, for example, modify its refusal to recognize India's move in 2019 to divide Indian-controlled Kashmir into two federally integrated territories, with Ladakh (which encompasses Chinese-claimed territory) under direct central rule. China could also agree to limit the presence of its own troops in Pakistan-controlled Kashmir, which has grown in recent years.[66] Finally, in addition to these things directly involving Kashmir, China could also alter its defense ties with Pakistan in ways that would benefit India, without necessarily tanking the Sino-Pakistani relationship. Although unlikely, one significant way it could do this would be to downgrade its arms transfers to Pakistan in some categories—for example, in the realm of missile guidance technology—that are especially sensitive to India's national security.

But there are sharp limits to how far China would go in alienating Pakistan, for the strategic relationship is rooted in strong geopolitical incentives. For China, strategic ties to Pakistan have long been a key means for checking Indian power in the subcontinent, and that interest will remain. Moreover, China's Pakistan ties presently advance two other strategic interests supremely important to China. First, they constitute its single best overland route for secure access to Middle East oil. This makes Pakistan "central to China's energy strategy and grand strategy for South Asia."[67] In 2016, Beijing and Islamabad launched plans to build a "mega" oil pipeline running from Pakistan's Gwadar port to Kashgar in Xinjiang, which could carry 17 percent of China's oil imports. That, according to one report, could "eliminate [China's] need to ship crude through Malacca Strait."[68] Given the geopolitical value of this means to alleviate China's energy vulnerability, Beijing will not trade against it for the sake of better relations with India. Second, close relations with Pakistan help Beijing to deal with a sensitive internal threat from Muslim Chinese rebels in Xinjiang. Beijing works quietly with Islamabad to suppress militant groups in Pakistan's tribal areas that tend to support those groups.[69] Because these advantages, too, are unique to the Sino-Pakistan relationship, and highly valued by China, they ensure that Beijing will protect the relationship in any approach to India.

In sum, Beijing's best options for inducing Indian neutrality in a U.S.-China crisis in Southeast Asia are found in the border disputes over Arunachal Pradesh. There the stakes are high for India and low for China, and China's flexibility on them is not constrained by allied cross-pressures. Moreover, the U.S. has virtually no avenue for influencing or offsetting the value to Delhi of the territorial nexus in Sino-Indian relations. Thus, in relation to the limited goal of distancing India from the U.S. in a crisis, a China policy of conciliation in Arunachal Pradesh could very well gain traction. The bottom line: China's chances for disrupting the U.S.-India strategic partnership are better than one might expect from a cursory tally of their conflicts of interest. Setting aside all the high-flown rhetoric of U.S.-India strategic affinity, serious thinking about the contours of future U.S.-China crises in Southeast Asia should not rule out the "surprise" of a bystanding India.

From this analysis, one can extract an important warning indicator. If China were to move seriously toward settling the Arunachal Pradesh sovereignty dispute on terms favorable to India, it may not be a harbinger of a broader Chinese shift toward conciliation around its periphery. Instead, it could be an indicator of trouble to come. What might the U.S. and its regional allies do to reduce their vulnerability to such a move? Delhi, for the foreseeable future, will remain allergic to a deeper and more formal alliance with the U.S. against China.[70] Thus, the remedy must lie in things the U.S. and its Southeast Asian partners can do *without* cementing India's allegiance. First, they could signal and demonstrate that they neither need nor expect Indian support of their plans to respond to Chinese coercion in the region. Second, they could signal that Indian support in such a context would be *unwanted*, because it would unnecessarily complicate the response of the U.S. and its directly implicated allies and partners. If Chinese leaders think the U.S. and its Southeast Asian partners neither depend on nor want Indian intervention in such a crisis, neutralizing India will lose its allure.

The U.S. and the Emerging Russia-China Alliance

For the U.S., the warrant to accommodate Russia arises from the prospect that it will ally with China and the dangers this would pose to the U.S.'s primary interest in checking and deterring China's expansion. In 2016, former

U.S. national security advisor Zbigniew Brzezinski warned that "the most dangerous" future threat to U.S. security would be "a grand coalition of China and Russia" conjoined "by complementary grievances."[71] Today, such an alliance is coalescing. The premise of what follows is that not just U.S. power but also the alliance network that projects it are central to the "complementary grievances" pulling Russia and China together. The U.S. erected that network seventy years ago, precisely to corral them. After the Cold War ended, those alliances enlarged and deepened. Adding more than a dozen new members in the East, NATO advanced deep into Russia's traditional security sphere. In 2010, Russia adopted a new military doctrine that identified NATO expansion as a primary threat.[72] Russia's predictably aggressive reactions to the prospect of further enlargement—in Georgia in 2008 and Ukraine in 2014—fed a swirl of fear of Russian revisionism, which generated new and further-forward U.S. military and naval commitments in the region, reaching from the Baltic to the Black Sea. On the other side of Eurasia, the U.S. has been coaxing India, Vietnam, and other Southeast Asian partners into a system of alliances centered on Japan, Australia, South Korea, Taiwan, and the Philippines, for the purposes of restraining China.

One of the fundament forces that propels states to form alliances is the growth of *other* alliances organized around and against them; indeed, that is the central idea of an alliance "spiral."[73] U.S. preponderance has not short-circuited that elementary mechanism of international politics. Its military alignments against Russia and China today are getting bigger and stronger on both sides—which makes an alliance between them likely to form. If the primary goal of U.S. grand strategy in the decades ahead is to tame and deter China's growing power and ambitions in Asia, then preventing a Russia-China alliance from consolidating is critical. For that, it will be necessary for the U.S. to accommodate Russia.

Skepticism about the likelihood and danger of a serious Russia-China alliance remains common among U.S. security policy elites.[74] It is not surprising that those accustomed to championing U.S. primacy—and the globe-spanning alliance system it entails—would doubt that such a manifestly negative consequence would result from the grand strategy to which they are professionally and ideologically committed.[75] But such skepticism is also suggested by certain theoretical understandings of how balancing in power politics works.[76] The first holds that Russia and China simply do not—and in the foreseeable future will not—face threats to their national security from the U.S. and its allies that are intense enough to impel a deeper alliance. Moscow and Beijing both have relatively secure nuclear deterrents, as well as competent and modern conventional forces. What more could either gain from a stronger alliance that could only come at a high cost to their autonomy? To that argument there are two answers. First, the threat they face from the U.S. and its alliance system is not of direct invasion, but of resistance to or further erosion of their respective spheres of influence, which are of primary interest to them. A stronger alliance between them would improve their ability to coordinate simultaneous actions that, as Mitchell and Grygiel put it, "test the United States on the outer rim of its influence, where [their] own interests are strongest while the U.S. is at its furthest commitments and therefore most vulnerable to defeat."[77] Second, with such an alliance could come greater certainty of stability in the areas in Central Asia and the Far East where their spheres overlap. This additional security where their "backyards" meet could help each to concentrate on advancing their priorities directly exposed to U.S. power and allies.

Another line of skepticism starts from the opposite direction: it holds that the large gap between U.S. military power, on the one hand, and the combination of Russian and Chinese military power, on the other, makes it futile for them to try, on a global level, to counterbalance the U.S. When even working closely together offers no escape from such relative weakness, the incentives to try are low. And when one plugs in the collective action problems that normally corrode external balancing, then, one might expect that Russia and China—even when surrounded by the U.S. alliance system—would not form a strong counteralliance.[78]

This argument underestimates the near-term prospects of a Russia-China alliance in three ways. The first is embedded in the logic of the argument itself, which implies that external balancing, by the U.S.'s great power competitors, will resume as its relative military edge erodes (even if it remains clearly on top). That trend is clearly evident today and is likely to endure.[79] Second, the incentive driving Russia and China to form an alliance against the U.S. need not be to create a "global equilibrium" versus U.S. power. To assume that some potential to do so is necessary to activate their movement toward a counterbalancing alliance sets the bar too high. Sufficient incentive exists if increased Russia-China security cooperation will help them to deal with the challenges posed, closer to home, by U.S. and allied forces. As Brooks and Wohlforth note, even if the gap between U.S. military capabilities and China's and Russia's does make "global" balancing "inoperative," it will not stop them from engaging in "so-called local balancing."[80] As the gap between U.S. and Chinese and Russian capabilities narrows in those domains, the U.S. moves back into the realm of "balance-able."[81] Such local balancing need not be limited to internal means and exclude alliance.[82] Third, there is something unusual about the strategic context of great power relations today that is especially conducive to Russia and China forming an alliance against the U.S. Neither Moscow nor Beijing has serious bilateral alliances with other countries—let alone big unruly alliance systems—that might stand in the way of them forming one with each other. In short, the U.S.'s two main great power competitors have considerable freedom of action to close ranks.[83]

Recent real-world developments provide the strongest rebuttal to the notion that a China-Russia alliance is improbable. As the U.S. national intelligence community's 2019 *Worldwide Threat Assessment* summed it: "China and

Russia are more aligned than at any point since the mid-1950s."[84] China and Russia have already gone far toward constructing what political scientists would consider an alliance. They have put into regular operation the kinds of security cooperation, across an array of issues, that are, according to objective alliance measurement criteria, consistent with a "moderately" institutionalized alliance.[85] What matters most of all is trajectory. Even if Russia and China do not yet have a fully articulated, formal military alliance, they have taken many steps that put them "on the verge" of one.[86] Russia's Vostok 2018 exercise provided one alarming indicator of that trend. In the past, Vostok exercises—held in Siberia and Russia's Eastern Military District—were run with China as the notional enemy, long seen as a threat liable to overrun the Russian Far East. In 2018, however, for the first time ever, China participated as a jointly operating partner, bringing along 3,500 People's Liberation Army (PLA) troops, 900 heavy weapons, and 30 planes.[87] July 2019 brought another first, with the inaugural joint Russia-China nuclear-capable bomber patrol over the Sea of Japan and East China Sea.[88] Russia's 2018 and 2019 Tsentr exercises also included contingents of PLA troops.[89]

RUSSIA'S STRATEGIC WEIGHT

Russia's military alignment with China increases the danger China poses to the U.S.'s grand strategic priorities and interests in Asia—this gives Russia high strategic weight. In general, its convergence with China will give Beijing more opportunity and ability to risk conflict with the U.S. in the South China Sea and Northeast Asia. Russian transfers of advanced weapons to China—including the Su-35 fighter jet and the S-400 surface-to-air missile system—strengthen Chinese capabilities against the U.S. by "augmenting China's air-defense, long-range sensor, and anti-ship capabilities [and increasing] the PLA's ability to threaten U.S. forces operating in the Pacific in line with China's goal to deny foreign navies access to waters and airspace Beijing considers strategically important."[90] Russia is also helping China to upgrade its strategic early warning missile system.[91] Russia's increasing combined military exercises with China also give Chinese forces unique opportunities to train with and learn from an advanced military power with recent, tangible experience in conducting major military operations.[92]

More than these aids to China's military strength, however, the strategic weight of Russia's alignment with China stems from the greater likelihood of Chinese adventurism it incites. Any confrontation between the U.S. and Russia in Eastern Europe will invite China to "exploit U.S. preoccupation . . . to achieve gains at U.S. expense" by taking risks and provoking crises in Asia, where the U.S.'s *most* important, long-range strategic interests are concentrated.[93] Furthermore, even in the absence of such a precipitating crisis in Europe, Russia's partnership with China could embolden Beijing. Any direct or indirect Russian involvement in a U.S.-China clash will increase the risks and complications of U.S. response.[94] If they expect direct support from Russia (or a diversionary reaction by it), China's leaders may be willing to run greater risks of conflict with the U.S. in Asia. By the same token, reducing or removing such expectations could make it easier for the U.S. to deter China. In other words, the success of U.S. grand strategy in Asia may hinge on how close Russia and China become.

If the U.S. does not yet face a fully formalized China-Russia military alliance, the trend toward one is now hard to miss. Thus, policy consensus in Washington is shifting from denial to recognition of the dangers of Russia-China military alignment. Kendall-Taylor and Shullman encapsulate it: "The depth of relations between Beijing and Moscow has exceeded what observers would have expected just a few years ago[;] the two countries acting in concert could inflict significant damage on U.S. interests even if they never form an alliance."[95] Such recognition, however, is rarely coupled with a serious look at possibilities of dividing them by accommodating Russia.[96] Indeed, the Trump administration's new strategy concept for great power competition doubled down on dual confrontation of China and Russia, with an intensified buildup of U.S.-led military alignments against both.[97] It is very likely that the administration that takes office in 2021—whatever its partisan hue—will follow the same grand strategic formula.[98]

If, however, the U.S. administration wanted to avoid that dead end and instead, as Mearsheimer put it, "go to great lengths to pull Russia out of China's orbit," what would such an effort entail?[99] Beyond a general willingness to conciliate Russia for strategic purposes, how might it be crafted to promote success?[100] Those questions are addressed next.

Four key scenario assumptions must be stipulated up front. First, U.S. leaders continue to identify China as the main adversary now and for the foreseeable future—it is, as Secretary of State Michael Pompeo put it, "the central threat of our times."[101] Second, and by implication, they perceive Russia to be a less serious great power competitor.[102] Its power trajectory—as they see it—will not return it to the position of a "near peer" global challenger, able to make a run at hegemony in Europe. Russia's ambitions are also seen as more limited: its desire to maintain a sphere of influence in Eastern Europe and the Caucasus does not extend to a larger appetite for preeminence in Europe. Third, U.S. leaders, in order to cope with the top-tier threat posed by China, will place high value on policy options with the potential to weaken China's relative power, ambitions, and appetite for risk in challenging the U.S. in pursuit of them. Fourth, U.S. leaders recognize the alliance spiral logic posited earlier—that a mainspring of Russia-China convergence is the expansion and deepening of American military alignments.[103]

In such circumstances, my theoretical framework suggests that a U.S. initiative to distance Russia from China through accommodation would be more likely to succeed if it conformed to the following principles. First, the alignment change goal is limited: not to flip Russia into an ally against

China, but to stop Russia's strategic relationship with China from growing deeper, and to weaken it.[104] Doing so would (1) help to deter China by reducing the moral hazard created by Russia's close alignment, and (2) reduce tensions with Russia that otherwise inhibit the concentration of U.S. political and military resources on balancing China in Asia. Second, accommodation is focused on the mainspring of Russia's convergence with China—the continued growth and tightening of U.S. military alignments against Russia on its western frontier. This is an arena in which the U.S. has a considerable menu of inducement options that are both very valuable to Russian security and largely under Washington's control. Third, the inducements utilized offer Russia some immediate or near-term (not distant) benefits that involve tangible security gains, not just symbolic or nebulous ones. Fourth, the promises to extend these benefits are credible—that is, they are not subject to others' vetoes, or predicated on the outcome of lengthy, indeterminate, and inevitably contentious, multilateral political negotiations in Europe. Fifth, the offered rewards do not mobilize strong backlash from the U.S.'s most important and capable, core NATO allies in Europe (i.e., Britain, France, and Germany). Thus, the inducements should (1) *not* contravene the U.S.'s existing formal NATO alliance commitments and (2) *improve* cohesion between the U.S. and its core NATO allies. This will help mitigate the alliance constraints activated by accommodating Russia, which will surely arouse opposition from other (weaker, newer, and more peripheral) allies on NATO's frontier with Russia, especially Poland and Romania, which have in recent years lobbied hard for the U.S. to permanently station heavy forces in their territories and thus override the 1997 NATO-Russia Founding Act.[105]

U.S. ACCOMMODATION OPTIONS

End of Formal NATO Enlargement. As Vladimir Putin warned NATO members in 2008, "We view the appearance of a powerful military bloc on our borders . . . as a direct threat to the security of our country."[106] A serious attempt to distance Russia from China would start with a public signal that Washington's drive for further NATO enlargement is over.[107] The U.S. has always been the prime mover behind enlargement.[108] As a practical matter, then, a U.S. administration could unilaterally end it by announcing that, going forward, it will oppose the extension by the North Atlantic Council of any more "Membership Action Plans" (MAPs) to partners seeking to join the alliance. While such a declaration could not tie the hands of future administrations, it would make it harder for one to shift back to a pro-enlargement stance, and it would consolidate the well-known aversion of key NATO allies to further expansion on Russia's periphery.

This concession would credit Russian security interests in two major areas. The first way concerns the Scandinavian neutrals—Finland and Sweden.

These two already have intimate strategic ties to the U.S. and NATO; indeed, some describe them as NATO allies "in all but name."[109] Moscow, no doubt, discerns this practical reality but has clearly warned that their going further by formally joining NATO would be a major provocation.[110] Because many NATO members would welcome them as official allies—if only they would ask for admission—the general U.S. signal that it opposes further MAPs would be a valuable assurance to Russia on this score. At the same time, the administration could confirm the high value of existing U.S. and NATO strategic relations with Sweden and Finland by emphasizing what is already evident: that even as merely "special partners" they contribute more than many NATO allies to U.S. and NATO security priorities.[111]

The second, and more important, way concerns Georgia and Ukraine. For Russia, the tightening of U.S. military alignments against it is most caustic in these two former Soviet republics. Indeed, the nearing prospect that these two neighbors might soon join NATO drove Russian decisions to intervene in them and force facts on the ground to complicate and deter their admission.[112] Here, the general policy against further NATO enlargement will both directly accommodate Russian vital interests *and* improve NATO cohesion by bringing U.S. policy into line with the attitudes of its core allies in Europe.

For over a decade now, those allies have mounted persistent opposition to approving MAPs for Georgia and Ukraine. This emerged at the April 2008 NATO summit in Bucharest, when the George W. Bush administration first pushed for NATO to offer them MAPs. France and Germany blocked it then, but as a concession to the U.S. agreed to a collective statement that NATO would "eventually admit" them. It is likely that this muddled but provocative signal helped to precipitate Russian intervention in Georgia in August 2008.[113] That halted Georgia's progress toward formal membership, for many NATO allies are unwilling to assume the obvious and immediate risks of direct conflict with Russia.[114] Since then, there has been no explicit retraction of NATO's promise to eventually admit Georgia (and probably never will be). But there has neither been any sign of consensus within NATO's ranks to offer it a MAP. At NATO's 2014, 2016, and 2018 summits, France and Germany quashed calls to expedite Georgian membership and insisted that it can become a member only through the MAP-to-accession requirement, ensuring that any NATO member can single-handedly block it.[115] While the Trump administration continued to call for Georgia's prompt accession to NATO, allies like Germany remain opposed.[116]

A parallel pattern has solidified with respect to Ukraine. After Russia's 2014 seizure of Crimea and its deeper intervention in Ukraine's civil war, opposition to admitting it into NATO's ranks intensified, rooted in the well-warranted fear of entrapment in conflict with Russia.[117] That fear extends to concerns about how far NATO should go in developing less formal military ties with Ukraine. This became obvious in 2015 when the Obama administration considered providing Ukraine with defensive lethal weapons. European allies voiced sharp opposition to giving lethal military support to Ukraine under NATO auspices.[118] In sum, a declared end to U.S. support for further MAPs will remove primary points of friction in the U.S.-Russian strategic relationship *and* improve NATO unity by shifting U.S. policy into line with the preferences of its core NATO allies against Georgian and Ukraine membership.

Reduce U.S. Military Ties to Georgia and Ukraine. But if the key to distancing Russia from China is to reduce the profile of U.S. military alignments against Russia, more would have to be done about the substance of Washington's military ties to Georgia and Ukraine. Under the Bush, Obama, and Trump administrations, the U.S. has significantly deepened those military ties—which include training programs led by U.S. military advisors, joint bilateral and multilateral exercises, and arms transfers—mostly on a U.S.-led basis but also under the aegis of NATO's partnership programs.[119] Beyond the nominal goal of preparing them for eventual NATO membership, the U.S. has now openly embraced the more potent aim of improving their "interoperability" for joint fighting against Russian forces. As Assistant Secretary of State A. Wess Mitchell put it to Congress in 2018, "We are building up the means of self-defense for frontier states most directly threatened by Russia militarily: Ukraine and Georgia."[120] In short, even in the absence of a formal NATO collective defense commitment, U.S. policy is overtly to groom Georgia and Ukraine as de facto military allies against Russia.

For Georgia, some of this has come through its special status as a NATO "Enhanced Opportunity Partner," which it received in 2014, and with it, the "Substantial NATO-Georgia Package" to bolster its defense capabilities and interoperability with NATO forces. Over time, this has led to the creation of a NATO-Georgia Joint Training Center in its territory, the integration of Georgian troops in NATO's rapid-reaction "Response Force," the hosting of small numbers of NATO troops in Georgia for joint exercises, and the integration of Georgia into NATO's Black Sea Initiative, a "tailored forward presence" project based in Romania and Bulgaria.[121] Washington also stepped up bilateral measures to deepen military ties with Georgia. In 2016, the Obama administration extended a three-year deal to Tbilisi to upgrade Georgian forces' interoperability with NATO.[122] In 2017, the Trump administration followed up with an agreement to sell Georgia Javelin antitank missiles and provide support and training for their use.[123] NATO allies in Europe, meanwhile, contributed little to this material effort to build up Georgia's military against Russia.[124] And while many have joined in U.S.-led exercises with Georgian forces (which have involved increasing troop levels and sophistication), they have not done so under NATO auspices.[125]

Under Trump, the U.S. also deepened military ties to Ukraine, chiefly bilaterally but also through NATO partnership programs embodied in a 2016 "Comprehensive Assistance Package."[126] Most notably, in 2017, the

U.S. moved ahead with plans to give lethal aid to Ukraine, despite opposition from European allies like Britain, Germany, and France.[127] It transferred to Ukraine portable antitank missiles and support systems and small arms (and Canada moved simultaneously to do the same).[128] In 2019, Washington promised an additional $391 million in military aid to Ukraine, including other lethal weapons systems and support for the Ukrainian navy in the Black Sea. With all of the uproar over the president's subsequent attempt to leverage the release of these funds for his own domestic political purposes, it was clear that the official effort to reinforce Ukraine's military power against Russia commanded broad bipartisan support.[129]

The intensity of U.S. military alignment with Georgia and Ukraine thus entails far more than rhetorical support for their bids to join NATO. A serious attempt to relax tensions with Russia, then, would go beyond the reversal of that rhetoric to include more concrete and immediate steps to unwind the militarization of U.S. ties to those countries. In practice, that would mean stopping further transfers of lethal military hardware, and ramping down U.S.-led multilateral military exercises and training with them. It would also mean additional signals against taking other formal unilateral and multilateral steps to strengthen the alignment, despite Ukraine's and Georgia's recent official efforts to secure such measures.[130] Thus, the administration could indicate that it will not support within NATO a move to upgrade Ukraine's status to "Enhanced Opportunity Partner."[131] Additionally, it could announce that it will not support legislation out of Congress to agree to requests by Ukraine and Georgia to be designated "major non-NATO allies."[132]

In sum, in U.S. military ties to Georgia and Ukraine reside Washington's best options for reducing the counteralignment impulse driving Russia toward China. Moreover, the U.S.'s flexibility to decouple from them will be improved by the fact that core NATO allies (unlike certain peripheral ones) would welcome U.S. retraction of those potentially entrapping forward political and military investments. The U.S. could magnify this advantage by making it clear that curtailing military ties to those countries will be combined with continuing U.S. efforts to bolster NATO's primary collective defense mission for existing members.

Other NATO-Related Measures. Within the NATO context, there are several other steps the U.S. could take to conciliate Russia by signaling military restraint. Some of these would merely confirm existing U.S.-Russia understandings but might have some utility due to the political pressures—in Washington and in some parts of NATO—to go back on those understandings. Reiterating them could thus offer some traction.

First, Washington might reaffirm its intention to conform to the understanding in the 1997 NATO-Russia Founding Act—to avoid permanent stationing of substantial combat forces in the territories of Central and Eastern European NATO allies. Such an affirmation would not contradict the current practice of the U.S. and NATO to maintain "continuous" multilateral force rotations and frequent, complex, defense exercises in those allied territories, but it would defuse calls—from Poland, especially—for the permanent, forward basing of high-end conventional U.S. forces on Russia's flank.[133] This would, of course, carry the stipulation that things would change if Russia began to act more aggressively toward NATO's frontline allies.

Second, Washington could declare its continued intention to limit the mission of its Aegis Ashore Ballistic Missile Defense Systems in Romania and Poland (under construction) to targeting the Iranian missile threat. The more important implication of this would be that the U.S. and NATO—which have considered the option—would refrain from steps to "recalibrate" these systems to shoot at Russian cruise missiles.[134] The less important implication, because the repurposing is far less feasible, would be that the systems would not be converted in some way into an offensive strike capability against Russia.[135] If such assurances are unlikely to allay Russian suspicions, they would have the side benefit of protecting NATO cohesion, because any decision to repurpose those sites requires NATO-wide consensus and will almost certainly face strong internal resistance.

The next two options involve nuclear weapons, where recent developments have made accommodation opportunities quite difficult. Russia's deployment of SSC-8 nuclear cruise missiles in its western areas, coupled with its apparent doctrine to use them to "escalate to deescalate" a conventional clash with NATO, makes it likely that the U.S. will respond by deploying some equivalent new nuclear forces in Europe. The U.S. withdrawal from the 1987 Intermediate Nuclear Forces (INF) Treaty—even if it was driven more by incentives to compete with China than to counter Russian activity—added to that likelihood. Nevertheless, even with renewed U.S.-Russia nuclear strains in Europe, three avenues of accommodation are discernible.

First, Washington could embrace Moscow's offer to adopt a five-year extension of the New START (Strategic Arms Reduction Treaty), which is set to lapse in February 2021. As the last major U.S.-Russia strategic arms control agreement standing—and one that clearly benefits both sides—this is both an important and an easy way to accommodate Russia.[136] Second, Washington could reaffirm that, despite the demise of the INF treaty, it will continue to conform to its commitment (made in the 1997 NATO-Russia Founding Act) not to store or deploy nuclear weapons in the territories of NATO's Eastern allies.[137] Even—or especially—if the administration also claims that this part of the Founding Act has become defunct due to changed strategic circumstances, the signal of intent to continue this "practice" until further notice will offer Russia some assurance, and it holds out the prospect of a larger agreement to restrain nuclear deployments in Europe. Third, along with this, the U.S. could initiate an effort to negotiate a new bilateral treaty with Russia to prevent or limit the forward deployment of intermediate range nuclear missiles in Eastern Europe and in Western Russia.[138]

Actions with Indirect Effects. Finally, there are two avenues of accommodation with Moscow that could energize conflicts of interest between it and China. The first would be the opportunity to conclusively reverse U.S. military alignments in Central Asia that would attend the (perhaps imminent) exit of U.S. and NATO forces from Afghanistan. To support those forces was the main reason the U.S., starting in 2001, built up base arrangements with Central Asia republics. For a time, Moscow even cooperated in this enterprise, but the ensuing competition for influence ultimately added to the deepening distrust between Russia and the U.S. As of 2019, most of these ties were already severed or atrophied; but a clear-cut sign from Washington that such efforts are finished, along with the permanent removal of the U.S.-led forces in Afghanistan, would benefit Russia in an area that touches directly on its vital interests. It might also, as Beebe argues, remove a "unifying factor in cooperation between Russia and China" and "allow the forces of Russian-Chinese rivalry for Central Asian influence gradually to re-emerge."[139]

It may also be possible to promote such indirect effects with measures to ease the flow of Russia's arms trade with India and Vietnam—two of its long-standing customers. U.S. CAATSA (Countering America's Adversaries through Sanctions Act) sanctions, imposed by Congress after Russian interference in the 2016 U.S. election, may constrict this trade by imposing costs on countries that buy Russian weapons. To date, periodic waivers by Congress have shielded India and Vietnam from these penalties. But by carving out these exemptions more robustly, the U.S. government could do three things at once: directly benefit Russia, help to strengthen China's regional adversaries, and aggravate a potential sore spot in Russia-China relations.[140]

Across the spectrum of accommodations to Russia surveyed above, the ones involving NATO enlargement, Georgia, and Ukraine would be the most influential. They would also be the most politically costly, in both domestic and foreign policy arenas. Domestically, the costs will be especially high for an administration operating in a climate of antipathy toward Russia like that aroused by its recent election meddling, and the intensification of bipartisan support for military aid to Ukraine energized by Trump's attempt to twist it for domestic political gain. Any White House successor that pursued a policy of accommodating Russia would face attacks in Congress and public discourse for appeasing Russia and rewarding Putin's pressure tactics. The theoretical framework does not provide purchase over domestic political blowback that makes selective accommodation hard or impossible for a representative government to attempt. But it does posit that potent accommodation is always costly—and because that is so, it predicts that leaders are very likely to attempt it only when perceptions of strategic weight and relative reward power are high. Those expectations suggest two policy logics that might inform an administration's effort to build domestic legitimacy for such a controversial enterprise vis-à-vis Russia.[141]

First, conciliating Russia is a means of strengthening U.S. deterrence of China. To continue escalating confrontation with Russia is to push it further into China's embrace. That will embolden China to expand and challenge U.S. security interests in Asia. Thus, to oppose conciliating Russia implies a willingness to weaken deterrence of China. Second, conciliating Russia is a means to improving the political cohesion of core NATO. The U.S.'s forward military policy toward Georgia and Ukraine creates and exposes rifts within that core. A more politically cohesive NATO—focused on consolidating and defending its present membership—would better restrain Russia from acting against the alliance's central collective defense commitments than one riven by discord over the creeping extension of hazardous, half-hearted ties to nonallies. Moreover, for NATO's core collective defense mission, deterrence of Russia will be improved if Russia is not a strategic ally of China, emboldened by that alliance.

Beyond the domestic costs, a U.S. policy to accommodate Russia, such as that sketched above, would entail significant foreign policy downsides. A rough overview would include the following:[142]

- The risk of encouraging Russia to perceive a general weakening of U.S. resolve, and thus to challenge NATO more directly (e.g., in the Baltics);
- The risk of encouraging China to perceive a general weakening of U.S. resolve, and thus to step up its challenges in Asia;
- The risk of weakening perceptions of U.S. reliability held by its formal allies, in NATO and elsewhere;
- The weakening of the perceived value of NATO partnership status and programs, for other NATO partners participating in them (especially those hoping to convert their partnership status into full membership in the alliance);
- The loss of some leverage to impel Russia to withdraw from captured Georgian and Ukrainian territory, or, more realistically, to settle those conflicts on terms acceptable to Tbilisi and Kiev; and
- The prospect of losing some arm's-length influence over the disposition and transit of energy resources in the Black Sea and Caspian areas, and especially those involving Georgia and Ukraine.

In the scenario laid out above, the calculus for accepting these risks would prioritize the two kinds of offsetting considerations already suggested. It would, above all, take seriously the first-order strategic imperative to balance against China and forefront the strategic gains—in relation to that priority—expected from accommodating Russia. In short, accommodating Russia would improve deterrence and restraint of China in Asia by reducing its chances of forming a strategic alliance with Russia, one that might encourage Russia to provide (and China to expect) support in a U.S-China conflict. The calculus would recognize too that by accommodating Russia in Europe, the U.S. will be better able to concentrate strategic focus and resources on balancing in Asia and even, perhaps, encourage America's most capable European allies to do the same.

The calculus would also include the other ways in which accommodation's effects could mitigate the most salient downside risks outlined above. Thus, the danger of emboldening Russia by weakening its perceptions of U.S. commitment to NATO's core collective defense and deterrence mission would be offset with improved NATO cohesion resulting from bringing U.S. policy into line with its core European allies. Likewise, the danger of emboldening China by suggesting a weakening of general U.S. resolve would be offset by the signaled purpose of reducing tensions in Europe in order to concentrate U.S. balancing efforts (and those of its most capable NATO allies), against China.

Conclusions: Making Selective Accommodation Work

If it is common sense that one should try to split adversaries, much about using accommodation to do it seems unnatural to the cut and thrust of power politics. Most leaders and policy practitioners are, by default, wary and abstemious about rewarding actual or potential adversaries. Certainly, U.S. leaders do not need to be reminded that appeasement may sometimes be interpreted as weakness, incite further demands, and thus undermine deterrence. Nevertheless, such liabilities have not removed accommodation from the toolbox of techniques for influencing potential adversaries, any more than the drawbacks of coercion have made it irrelevant to relations among friends and allies.

The theory of selective accommodation offers no guidance to leaders wishing to accommodate an opponent without running any hazards or costs of doing so. It offers no tricks for those who would like to divide adversaries but are determined, at the same time, to maintain forward positions and inflexible demands against them all, as well as the full confidence of all friends, allies, and others concerned. For policymakers who are, however, powerfully motivated by strategic reasons to try to forestall or unwind an opposing alliance, my theory suggests some basic guidelines. By way of conclusion, I encapsulate them in six general principles.

DO NOT SIMULTANEOUSLY ANTAGONIZE TWO ADVERSARIES

Or, as Luttwak puts it, "It is Geopolitics 101 not to confront both countries at the same time."[143] That is the bedrock premise of selective accommodation. Though other things may encourage opponents to ally against you, nothing does so more surely and deeply than making yourself a common enemy. As Robert Walpole explained to Parliament in 1741, "men easily unite against him whom they have all reason to fear and to hate; by whom they have been greatly injured, and by whom they suspect that no opportunity will be lost of renewing his encroachments."[144] For policymakers and thinkers, this implies two operational corollaries. First, adversaries, potential or actual, must be distinguished and ranked in terms of the dangers they pose to the nation's interest. Here, the tendency to lump adversaries into convenient "bloc" concepts (e.g., "authoritarians," "revisionists," "totalitarians," "Islamo-fascists," etc.) is, as George Kennan reminded us, inimical to such prudential judgments because those concepts obscure meaningful differences in the dangers and ambitions held by adversaries and tend perversely to encourage a one-size-fits-all prescription of simultaneous confrontation.[145] The second corollary is that the weight of confrontation should fall on the *primary* adversary (which should be isolated), not the lesser one (which should be targeted with accommodation). If this seems obvious, policy often gets the proportions backwards, because it is easier—both psychologically and materially—to go down the road of bullying, sanctioning, and isolating the weaker and therefore less menacing adversary.

LOW AIMS AND SMALL GAINS MATTER

Great power alliance competition can be a game of inches in which, as Posen puts it, the "arithmetic of coalitions influences matters great and small." In that context, small alignment changes can have big strategic effects, and it is, as Hartmann observed, sometimes "more important to deny the enemy an ally than to gain an ally oneself."[146] To deny the primary opponent of an ally, all one needs to do is keep the potential ally hedging or neutral. The impact of doing so can be substantial if not always observable: it may cause the adversary to avoid a war it would be willing to risk if more certain of the allied support; it may cause the adversary, should it choose war, to pursue more limited aims; it may weaken the adversary's material capacity to fight; and it may preclude the adversary from using territory that might help it fight more effectively. Besides the potential for such effects, limited alignment changes have two other virtues—they are (relatively) easier and less costly to induce. If accommodating a potential adversary always involves sacrifice, the price is lower when one does not seek to enlist them as allies.

For policy practitioners, there are important implications here. In policy debates over whether to try to divide opponents by accommodating one, there is a tendency for the low aims option to be suppressed by two ways of thinking. The first is an "all-or-nothing" claim: if (or because) the target cannot be induced to "swap sides" (i.e., transformed into an ally), there is nothing to be gained from making concessions.[147] The second is an "all-*and*-nothing" claim: even if the target *could* be "flipped" it will not add appreciably to the power that can be arrayed against the adversary and therefore, again, there is nothing to be gained from accommodating it. Both ways of thinking deflect away from a serious consideration of the potential to achieve less dramatic changes in the target's alignment and the "subtractive" strategic gains that may flow from them.

DO NOT WAIT UNTIL AN OPPOSING ALLIANCE IS CONSOLIDATED, AND CONFRONTATION IMMINENT, BEFORE EXTENDING ACCEPTABLE ACCOMMODATIONS TO THE TARGET

Influential concessions are always costly and politically difficult to make. If some are, for all practical purposes, impossible, others are often more doable, but the natural tendency is to avoid the difficult trade-offs until the situation becomes urgent. This is a setup for failure. The theory of selective accommodation explains why. The doable concessions—those one is willing to make, if necessary—will be less influential once the adversaries close ranks, because the target's costs of altering its alignment will have increased. Concessions that would buy the target's neutrality before it firmly allies with the adversary probably won't after it does. If it would be tolerable to make those concessions once it got to that point, it is better not to wait until it does. Not only does the traction of concessions decline after opponents close ranks, the risks of signaling weakness by making them increase, too. In short, it is easier and less risky to head off an adverse alliance than it is to try to undo and reverse one.

ACCOMMODATE IN AREAS OF ASYMMETRIC INTEREST AND CONTROL

With selective accommodation, one has to give something, somewhere, to get the alignment one wants. What kinds of concessions are most useful? Here, it is best to capitalize on interests and values that matter a lot to the target and less to the divider. These happy "asymmetries of interest" sometimes simply do not exist—the target seeks sacrifices of things that are truly vital to the divider and could be exchanged only by force majeure. Yet often they do, and it is possible to infer them through geopolitical common sense and the target's demands and revealed behavior. But understanding what values the target needs or wants more than you do is necessary but not sufficient. One must also decide which, among those things, can be sacrificed at an acceptable cost. If general policy declarations and grand strategy statements tend to conflate strategic interests of different magnitudes, rendering everything into very important if not vital interests, serious policymakers try to cut through the muddle and make hard trade-offs in allocating resources and effort. But when it comes to making concessions to a potential adversary, the difficulty of the trade-off is especially brutal. The issue is not merely which priorities to shortchange, but which to write off. When everything seems important enough to somehow hold on to, assessments of what is expendable cannot be made in isolation of considerations of the potential return. In making such assessments, then, policymakers must keep in the foreground the strategic motive for selective accommodation and the tally of the target's strategic weight: Would the sacrifice be worth it if it improved the chances of gaining a less dangerous main enemy?

With regard to asymmetries of control, two dimensions are key. First, the concessions a divider offers should concern values over which it exercises prevailing if not unilateral influence. Whether the values are symbolic or material, their disposition should not be subject to a battery of multilateral veto points, or second- and third-order political contingencies that raise real doubts about delivery. This is especially critical if other actors in conflict with the target have declared intentions or obvious incentives to obstruct the improvement in relations the exchange would foster (see below). Second, the divider should emphasize concessions that will be difficult for competitors—trying to shape the target's alignment—to substitute or outbid. Selective accommodation diplomacy usually plays out in a bidding war context: here, potential benefits that are not just highly valued by the target, but also in some sense scarce or hard for others to match, are prime currency.

EXTEND CREDIBLE BARGAINS

The divider's reputation for following through on promises *to the target* will always factor into the credibility of its selective accommodation bids. But beyond that, inducements can be contoured to improve their credibility. First, as is usually the case when incentives are manipulated, greater clarity in specifying rewards makes inducements more credible. Ones that are ambiguously defined or pitched in terms of broad generalities come across as empty promises. And when attempts to clarify them are evaded, targets will suspect an intent to inflate, renege, or play for time. At the very least, they will infer the divider is uncertain about what it can deliver. At any rate, the expected value of inducements is diminished, and influence along with it.

Similarly, the understandable desire to minimize the up-front political costs of conciliating a potential adversary—and to guard against being played for a sucker—by staggering the payoffs and delaying weightier concessions until last can be detrimental to credibility. It is well known that willingness to bear costs for a course of action up-front is a key indicator of determination and commitment; attempting to push off or thin out those costs thus weakens the signal. Of course, in some situations, domestic politics or allied cross-pressures may leave no alternative but to shrink and slow-roll the substance of an accommodation policy, but the toll this takes on the credibility of the approach, and the prospects for its success in a bidding war context, must be recognized.

MANAGE ALLIANCE CONSTRAINTS

When there are large disagreements between a divider and its major allies about the target's strategic weight or whether to conciliate it, a concerted policy of selective accommodation may not be possible, or if it is, it may be so enfeebled that failure in a bidding war is likely. If, in such unfavorable

circumstances, the divider is willing to risk some damage to its alliance relationships and press ahead, two rules for managing around the differences
apply. First, the divider should concentrate on inducements that it can credibly, unilaterally dispose of. Second, and relatedly, the divider should avoid
linking the delivery of those concessions to the development of conditions
that depend on the active cooperation of recalcitrant allies.

When the differences among allies are less sharp, there is more opportunity to apply the traditional techniques of intra-alliance coordination and influence to build an effective concerted approach. Thus, here, consultations,
buttressed by the sharing of intelligence assessments and scenario analyses,
can help to solidify accord around how to rank and differentially approach
potential adversaries. Likewise, gaps in the willingness of allies to contribute to an integrated package of concessions may be bridged, and the value
of the concerted bid enhanced, through the extension of additional assurances and side payments to the allies most critical to the initiative's success.

Even if perceptions and intentions of key allies are largely congruent,
serious coordination is still needed to orchestrate a timely, well-concerted
approach. After all, even with governments acting alone, bureaucratic dis-
connects and dysfunction can produce muddled execution. The rollout of a
concerted accommodation initiative may involve either a single combined
bid or a series of linked steps coming from different allied capitals. Whatever
the form, the arrangement must be crafted to meet the demands of a bidding
war—which requires some flexibility for timely responses to the target's potential counterdemands and outside parties' countervailing bids.

Finally, there remains an important dimension of the problem of selective accommodation that these principles, and the theory that informs
them, do not encompass. As the U.S.-Russia scenario makes clear, not just
the divider's alliance politics but also its domestic politics may obstruct effective execution. Indeed, for some leaders seeking to accommodate an adversary, the alliance constraints inhibiting it may seem small compared to
the those raised by internal opposition, even when there is a compelling
grand strategic interest to do so. As George explained, "The forces of public
opinion, Congress, the media, and powerful interest groups often make
themselves felt in ways that seriously complicate the ability of the president
and his advisers to pursue long-range foreign policy objectives in a coher-
ent, consistent manner." To build the "policy legitimacy" needed to overcome these "complications," George argued that leaders must try to form
a stable national consensus around both the desirability of the long-range
goal and the feasibility of reaching it through the policy in question.[148] My
theory of selective accommodation, because it abstracts away from these
domestic political forces, does not describe or prescribe how they can be
managed. Elements of the theory do, however, suggest the nature of the
case that leaders can make for the desirability and feasibility of selective
accommodation. The desirability of accommodating the target arises from

its strategic weight, and more specifically, from the security and strategic advantages to be gained by isolating the primary adversary. The feasibility of doing it rests on the basic logic of balancing in power politics: while confronting the target will drive it closer to the primary adversary (and thus increases the danger the latter poses), accommodating the target can distance it from the primary adversary and weaken those dangers.

If the problem of policy legitimacy is an important one for those who might wish to put selective accommodation into practice, it is also one that students of the politics of division will do well to study. On that score, I can say no more here than "get to it." But bear in mind that in the realm of great power competition, it is unwise to exaggerate the extent to which domestic politics makes the expedient impossible. Successful attempts to accommodate and detach domestically unpopular adversaries are not confined to the maneuvers of dictators—like Hitler and Stalin—who are untrammeled by internal opposition. Indeed, in the not-too-distant past, even U.S. leaders have found it possible—for grand strategic purposes—to accommodate domestically reviled authoritarian regimes, and have done so successfully. Thus, Franklin D. Roosevelt (in tandem with that ferocious antiappeaser Winston Churchill) conciliated the Fascist Franco regime in World War II, Harry Truman extended advantages to the Communist regime of Tito in Yugoslavia, and Richard Nixon mended fences with Chairman Mao's China. There is no reason to presume that in the great power competition of the twenty-first century the possibility of such maneuvers, and the strategic advantages they may yield, will be put out of reach by the difficult domestic politics that often attend them. Even amid the complications of liberal democratic foreign policymaking, the logic of division in international politics gets a vote and sometimes prevails.

Table 13 Degrees of attemped alignment change*

		Target's Position		
		Fixed	*Hedged*	*Neutral*
Divider's Goal	Realign Target	**High**	**High**	N/A
	Dealign Target	**Medium**	**Medium**	N/A
	Reinforce Target	N/A	**Low**	**Low**

* The three cells denoted N/A are not applicable and logically excluded. To realign a neutral—that is, recruit it as an ally—is a pure alliance-forming move, not an attempt to divide. To dealign a neutral—that is, detach it from an opposing alliance—is a non sequitur. To reinforce a target's fixed position (in an opposing alliance) is antithetical to wedge logic.

Table 14 Overview of case conditions and outcomes

| | | World War I Cases | | | | World War II Cases | | | |
		1. Germany-Japan	2. Germany-U.S.	3. Entente-Ottoman Empire Initiator: Russia	4. Entente-Italy Initiator: Britain	5. Britain & France-Italy Initiator: Britain	6. Germany-USSR	7. Britain & U.S.-Spain Initiator: Britain	8. Germany-Turkey Initiator: Germany
Initiation Conditions	Perceived Strategic Weight of Target	High	High	High	High	High	High	High	Low
	Perceived Reward Power of Divider	Low	High	High	High	High	High	High	High
Contingent Conditions	Attempted Alignment Change	High	Low	Low	High	(a) Low (b) High	Low	Low	High
	Divider's Alliance Constraints	Low	Low	High	High	(a) High (b) High	Low	High	High
	Allied Strategic Consensus	Yes	Yes	No	Yes	(a) Mixed (b) Mixed	Yes	Yes	No
Outcome		Failure	Success	Failure	Success	(a) Failure (b) Failure	Success	Success	Failure

Notes

Introduction

1. On these options, see Claude 1962, 89; Waltz 1979, 118, 156–57; Parent and Rosato 2015; Lobell 2018.

2. The "subversive method"—in which one covertly topples the target government and installs a friendlier one—offers another way; see Duchacek 1960, 377; O'Rourke 2018, 38–39. So does military victory; see Weisiger 2016; Liska 1962, 42–52.

3. On coercive forms, see Izumikawa 2013; Crawford 2011, 161–64; Morgan 2006, 64; Jervis 1997, 245; Snyder 1997, 337; Walt 1987, 19; Snyder and Diesing 1977, 430; Liska 1962, 43–45, 188–90.

4. Including concessions, compensation, and appeasement.

5. Furnishing a unified theory of coercive and accommodative wedge strategies is not my goal. For such work, see Izumikawa 2002; 2013; 2018; Yin 2020.

6. Accommodation "is an act that a state undertakes for the benefit of an actual or potential adversary. It denotes the making of concessions, or the taking of steps that compensate or credit the adversary's interests, for the sake of improving relations or sidestepping conflict" (Crawford 2011, 160). Also see Wolfers 1962, chap. 9; Snyder and Diesing 1977, 243; George 1991, 73–75. The logic of selective accommodation also resides in the notion of "selective surrender," in which states facing general defeat by a coalition offer surrender selectively—to one enemy but not the others—as a way to split the coalition and limit the demands it imposes. See Kecskemeti 1958, esp. 132–33, 153–54.

7. Hartmann 1982, 147.

8. On how wedge strategies fit into the broader sweep of thinking about power politics and balancing dynamics, see Crawford 2008; 2011; 2012; Goddard and Nexon 2016; Nexon 2009; He 2012; Hui 2005.

9. Betts 2014, 23.

10. NSS 2017, 27.

11. DoD 2018, 2. Also see Colby and Mitchell 2020; Kroenig 2020a; Blankenship and Denison 2019; Edelstein 2019; Mazarr et al., 2018.

12. Rapp-Hooper 2020, chap. 5.

13. NSS 2017, 25; Coats 2019, 7; DoD 2018, 2.

14. NSS 2017, 25; Bergerson 2016, 3; also see Blackwill 2020, 4.

15. WTA 2019, 4.

16. Haas 2014, 751–52; Stent 2020.

17. On grand strategy of primacy and deep engagement, see Brooks and Wohlforth 2016; Brooks, Ikenberry, and Wohlforth 2012/13; Posen 2015, chap. 1; Walt 2005. On the circa-2000 variants—"global leadership" and "forward engagement"—see Crawford 2003, 209–11.

18. Recent work covering the range of wedge strategies includes Chai 2020; Cooley and Nexon 2020; Huang 2020; Yin 2020; Scheinmann 2019; Wigell 2019; Taffer 2019; Hager 2017; Wigell and Vihma 2016; Goldstein 2016; Goddard and Nexon 2016; Yoo 2015; Izumikawa 2002; 2013; 2018; Haas 2012a; 2012b; He 2012; Garver and Wang 2010; Nexon 2009; Goddard 2008/09; Hui 2005; Crawford 2003, 28; 2008; 2011; 2012; 2018; Bob 2019, chap. 8.

19. Morgenthau 1959, 134; Liska 1962, 42–60; Modelski 1962, 132; Organski 1968, 278–79; Hartmann 1978, 333–37; Waltz 1979, 118; Snyder 1997, 337–38; Morgan 2006, 64; Betts 2012, 278. For foundational statements, see Machiavelli 1996, bk. 3, chap. 11; Montesquieu 1965, chap. 6.

20. The literature is vast. Recent contributions include Davidson 2020; Henry 2020; Henke 2019; Poast 2019; Resnick 2019; Taliaferro 2019; Krebs and Spindel 2018; Lanoszka 2018; Cha 2016; Kim 2016; Wolford 2015; Johnson 2015b; Weitsman 2004; 2013; Benson 2012; Christensen 2011; Shirkey 2009; Pressman 2008; Bensahel 2007; Press-Barnathan 2000/01; Lake 1999. Classics include Snyder 1997; Schweller 1998; Walt 1987; Waltz 1979; Liska 1962; Morgenthau 1959.

21. See Ripsman and Levy 2008, 155; Kaufman, Little, and Wohlforth, 2007; Morgan 2006, 64; Walt 2002, 140; Rock 2000, 14; Jervis 1997, 188–91; Rosecrance and Lo 1996, 487, 491; Schweller 1998, 78; Snyder and Diesing 1977, 435–36; Liska 1962, 42, 188.

22. Snyder and Diesing 1977, 428–40; Waltz 1979, 164–68; Christensen and Snyder 1990; Walt 1997; 2002; Layne 2009, 10–12; Christensen 1997; 2011; Haas 2014; Resnick 2019; 2010/11; Leeds and Savun 2007; Leeds, Mattes, and Vogel 2009; Dinnerstein 1965; Liska 1962, 103–7; Poast 2019.

23. For alliance reliability research, see Johnson 2015a; Mattes 2012; Leeds, Mattes, and Vogel 2009; Leeds and Savun 2007; Leeds and Anac 2005; Leeds 2003; Leeds, Long, and Mitchell 2000; Bennett 1997; Weitsman 1997; 2003; 2004. Also see Berkowitz 1983; Siverson and King 1980; Holsti, Hopmann, and Sullivan 1973, 16–17.

24. On alliance design, see Poast 2019; Kim 2011; 2016; Beckley 2015; Chiba, Johnson, and Leeds 2015; Johnson 2015a; Rapp-Hooper 2014; 2020, 87–88; Benson 2012. On alliance institutions, see Johnston 2017; Leeds, Mattes, and Vogel 2009; Leeds and Anac 2005; Theis 2009.

25. On the tendency to downplay "inducement and conciliation phenomena" in security research, see Smoke and George 1973, 405; Baldwin 1971; Haass and O'Sullivan 2001, 1. Recent work on such phenomena in security affairs includes Blankenship 2021; Blanchard and Ripsman 2013; Knopf 2012; Nincic 2010; 2011; Davis 2000; Rock 2000; Drezner 1999; Bernauer et al. 1999. Concepts concerning the effective use of economic inducements are well developed in IPE-security work. See, e.g., Blanchard and Ripsman 2013, 17–24; Crumm 1995; Newnham 2002; 2008; Cortright 1997; Drezner 1999; Long 1996. Foundational studies include Hirschmann 1980; Baldwin 1985; Knorr 1975.

26. On inducements in alliance and coalition management, see Blankenship 2021; Henke 2019; Resnick 2019; Johnson 2015b; Wolford 2015; Cooley and Nexon 2013; Poast 2012; Kreps 2011; Pressman 2008; Davis 2008/09; Newnham 2008. Foundational works include Riker 1962; Snyder and Diesing 1977.

27. Snyder 1997, 337; Mandelbaum 1981, 151; Snyder and Diesing 1977, 430. The "dilemma" arises from the fact that trying to reduce the risk of one danger increases the risk of the other.

28. But see Zagare 2012, 87–89.

29. George 1993, 117–18; Smoke 1976; Smoke and George 1973; Byman and Kroenig 2016, 304–5.

30. For examples, see Baldwin 1985; Blanchard and Ripsman 2013; Byman and Waxman 2002; Art and Cronin 2003; Greenhill and Krause 2018.

31. Smoke and George 1973, 403; George 2006, 65. Also see George and Smoke 1974, 616–42; Smoke 1976.

32. George 1993, 20–21; Baldwin 1985, 15–17; Morgan 1977, 78–79, 101–21.

33. The conception of this framework is informed by Alexander George's scheme for building policy-applicable influence theory, which includes an "abstract conceptual model" of

the influence strategy and "conditional generalizations about the strategy." George 2003; George and Bennett 2005.

34. For other work that addresses both conditions that encourage influence attempts and those that promote success or failure, see Chamberlain 2016; Oakes 2012; Greenhill 2010; Kupchan 2010; George 1993.

35. The characteristics of an advantageous reward power position are explained in chapter 1. In brief, they are: the divider can control and, at an acceptable cost, dispose of benefits involving issues that are important to the target, and the benefits cannot easily be substituted or outbid by others.

36. On this point, see Davis 2000, 19; Cortright 1997, 10; Baldwin 1971, 32–33.

37. On this point, see Ikle 1964, 57; Snyder 1997, 337; Holsti 2001, 399.

38. This focus on beliefs about the target's strategic weight locates our approach in a theoretical tradition that sees states' alignment behavior driven by leaders' perceptions of threats and power—rather than "objective" patterns of them. See Ripsman, Taliaferro, and Lobell 2016, 65–66; Snyder 1997, 148–49; Walt 1987; Wohlforth 1987.

39. In case studies, assessing the presence and strength of dividers' beliefs about means helps to establish the strategic context defining the selective accommodation attempt and provides a first-cut account of the divider's inducement options. The reward power position they reflect will be conditioned by other strategic factors—some identified in the theoretical framework, and others case-specific. Thus, leaders may incorrectly judge their reward power options and leverage, and as events play out, may change their beliefs about them; they may also change their beliefs about the target's strategic weight. Such belief changes may also explain why dividers stop or scale back selective accommodation efforts.

40. On forms of multipolar competition and great power diplomacy, see Posen 2009; 2011; Rathbun 2014; Goddard 2018; Shifrinson 2018; Edelstein 2017; 2019; Cooley and Nexon 2020; Kroenig 2020a.

41. "All will try to improve their own coalitions and erode those of others" (Posen 2009, 350). On the return of multipolarity, also see Mearsheimer 2018, 228–29; 2019, 42, 48.

42. Ross 1995.

43. Waltz 1979, 42.

1. The Theory of Selective Accommodation

1. George 1993, 118; George and Bennett 2005, 273.

2. Because initiation of an attempt is a necessary condition for success, initiation conditions are part of the "general logic associated with the successful use" of selective accommodation.

3. George and Bennett 2005, 272, 273, 278.

4. "Conditions that favor success . . . have causal relevance even when, as is often the case, they cannot be regarded as being either necessary or sufficient for a given outcome to occur" (George and Bennett 2005, 281).

5. George and Bennett 2005, 161, 281–82; Davis 2005, 181–82.

6. On how a target's internal political cohesion may affect its alignment mobility, see Scheinmann 2019.

7. George and Bennett 2005, 279–80.

8. Liska 1962, 188–89.

9. On the bidding war in alliance theory, see Riker 1962; Russett 1970, 252; Friedman 1970, 18; Snyder and Diesing 1977, 166, 424; Waltz 1979, 165–66; Snyder 1997, 184–85, 192–98; Morrow 2000, 65–67; Crawford 2003, 41; Zagare 2012, 64–89; Wolford 2015, chap. 3; 2019, 232–33; Blankenship 2021.

10. The bidding war heuristic posited here does not include coercion in the influence/exchange calculus. For a theory that contains it, see Izumikawa 2002; 2018.

11. On these distinctions, see Crawford 2011, 167–75; Davis 2000, 20–21; Rock 2000, 10–12; Resnick 2001, 561–63.

12. Nincic 2010, 180; 2011; Lobell 2011a; Rock 2000, 15; Snyder and Diesing 1977, 303–4. Domestic political shifts that favor compliance may be observed in cases, but are not theorized here.

13. Beyond this primary inducement mechanism, selective accommodation may also divide in two other important ways: first, by weakening common threat perception that otherwise draws one's adversaries together; second, by creating new or aggravating existing conflicts between the target and other(s). Crawford 2011, 166–68.

14. Baldwin 1971, 28–29; Schelling 1963, 177.

15. Liska notes the related risk of encouraging opponents "to elicit gains by alternating in the role of the friendlier adversary" (Liska 1962, 189). Also see Rock 2000, 4; Jervis 1976, 58; Snyder and Diesing 1977, 244; Baldwin 1971, 32.

16. Singer 1963, 423.

17. For a similar concept, see Shifrinson 2018, 25–27.

18. On selective accommodation in a "strategy of coercive isolation," see Crawford 2018.

19. Ripsman and Levy 2008, 156–58.

20. For a sweeping discussion of "domino beliefs," see Jervis 1991. Also see the discussion of "tipping" in Jervis 1997, 150–52.

21. On these features of reward power, see, e.g., Schelling 1989, 115; Grieco and Ikenberry 2003, 192–93; Crumm 1995; Baldwin 1971.

22. In process tracing, one also expects to find evidence that the divider's decision to try accommodation (rather than coercion) reflects a desire to avoid driving adversaries together; see Crawford 2011, 162–63.

23. Nincic 2010, 141.

24. On promises and credibility of inducements, see Singer 1963, 426–27; Schelling 1966, 77; Davis 2000, 17; Art and Greenhill 2018, 22–25.

25. Singer 1963, 421.

26. Morrow 2000; Snyder 1997.

27. On alliance reputations, see Henry 2020; Krebs and Spindel 2018; Mattes 2012; Crescenzi et al., 2012; Miller 2012; Gibler 2008; Mercer 1996; Snyder and Diesing 1977, 432–33.

28. Typically, defected neutrals invoke material and political exigencies or point to treaty loopholes, or to quid pro quos that have not yet been met, and in so doing, keep the embers of alliance commitment alive.

29. For example, see Kissinger 1994, 296.

30. On the framing of dealignment and realignment goals, see Hartmann 1978, 333–37; Liska 1962, 42–60; Snyder and Diesing 1977, 422, 430.

31. On reinforcing influence, see Singer 1963, 421.

32. The logic of these basic distinctions yields analytical expectations that go beyond the simple level of difficulty. For example, inducements that fall below the target's articulated demands are *especially* unlikely to work when tethered to an ambitious realignment goal. Similarly, the rewards a target demanded to remain neutral will be insufficient to dealign it after it has joined an alliance.

33. Likewise, intra-alliance politics can diminish the credibility and effectiveness of coercive diplomacy. Byman and Waxman 2002, 158–71; Christensen 2011.

34. When alliance constraints are low, selective accommodation's prospects hinge on conditions contained in the core theory—i.e., the quality of the divider's reward power relative to its alignment goals and competition.

35. Snyder 1997, 31; Snyder and Diesing 1977, 146; Friedman 1970, 10; Morgenthau 1959, 190. For elaborations see Cha 2016; Christensen 2011. For a challenge see Resnick 2019, 32–45.

36. For recent work on such alliances, see Pressman 2008; Yarhi-Milo, Lanoszka, and Cooper 2016; Resnick 2019. Also see Handel 1990, 121–48; Rothstein 1968.

37. Because both relative capabilities and dependency are key ingredients in these distinctions, I do not operationalize this factor with a priori measures tied to numerical indices. Instead, I code this dimension of alliance ties (and also the dimension of stakes in the relationship with the target), inductively in each case, drawing on secondary histories and official documents, looking at perceptions of relative capabilities, the presence or absence of "great power" status, and the nature of mutual (or nonreciprocal) obligations and expectations.

38. Divergent estimates of the costs of compromise can also inhibit cooperation on an accommodation policy. However, analytically, these are subsumed by level of consensus on strategic weight. When consensus is low, allied perceptions of low benefits and high compromise costs will track each other. As allies' perceptions of strategic weight converge at a high level, differences in their compromise costs diminish in significance.

39. On the importance of such side payments in the "alliance game" of forming a common policy toward a potential adversary, see Snyder and Diesing 1977, 106, 129–32, 145, 147.

40. Case 5 (Britain, France-Italy) is divided into two distinct attempts, because the alignment change goal changed in 1939 (after Italy made a formal military alliance with Germany).

41. If a divider attempts selective accommodation when its motivation is high but it perceives a lack of relative reward power, it may persist in a long-shot effort. If a divider attempts selective accommodation when it perceives its relative reward power strength is high but its motivation is low, then it will be likely to drop the effort (or lower its goals) if parleys reveal that success can be gotten only at high cost. Case 1 fits the first pattern, Case 8 fits the second.

42. In all three Low constraint case studies, there is also allied strategic consensus. This is consistent with the theory's expectation that when there are low constraints, the divider's allies' positions will conform to its preferences.

43. Wolfers 1962, 13; Lobell 2011b; Lobell, Ripsman, and Taliaferro 2009, 282; Taliaferro, Ripsman, and Lobell 2012, 23–24.

44. Waltz 1979; Snyder 1997; Posen 2011.

45. Haas 2014.

46. Haas (2014, 730) codes the pre–World War I system as ideologically bipolar, "divided between liberal (Britain and France) and authoritarian (Russia, Germany, and Austria-Hungary) great powers." But this leaves out the Ottoman Empire, which, along with Italy, was an important player in the alliance competition early in the war. On the Ottoman Empire's ideological distinctiveness, see Derengil 1998.

47. However, as Haas (2014) explains, when states' ranking of ideological and power threats do match up, alliance balancing will be most efficient and tight.

48. On descriptive inference, see Gerring 2004, 347.

49. On within-case methods, see George and Bennett 2005, chaps. 9, 10; Davis 2005, 175–81; Gerring 2007, chap. 7; Mahoney 2015; Lorentzen, Fravel, and Paine 2017.

50. George and Bennett 2005, 252; Tarrow 2010; Slater and Ziblatt 2013.

51. George and Bennett 2005, chap. 3.

2. Germany Fails to Detach Japan, 1915–16

1. Process tracing in this case quotes extensively from translated excerpts of official documents. These are mostly drawn from secondary historical accounts that are heavily based on archival and published documents. For German documents, these include Engram 1976; Ikle 1965;and Farrar 1978 (Fischer 1967 also quotes German documents, but does not cite them). For Japanese documents, these include Ikle 1965; Dickinson 1999; 2003; and Nish 1977. *Diplomacy of Japan, 1894–1922* (DJ) provides both commentary and lengthy extracts of Japanese documents, translated from the Japanese Foreign Ministry's *Nihon Gaiko Bunsho* (Japanese diplomatic documents). For Russian documents, these include Berton 1956; Saveliev and Pestushko 2001.

2. On Japan's entry in to the war, see DJ, 35–59; Sochi 2015; Dickinson 2003; Nish 1988; 1995; Lowe 1969.

3. The conditions in the case are coded as follows: German perceptions of Japan's strategic weight—High; German perceptions of relative reward power—Low; Attempted alignment change—High; Germany's alliance constraints—Low; Outcome—Failure.

4. Engram 1976, 144.

5. Ikle 1965, 63. On the Entente's futile efforts to convince Japan to send troops to Europe, see DJ, 207–12.

6. Ikle 1965, 65; Engram 1976, 142.
7. Engram 1976, 126.
8. Engram 1976, 237.
9. Engram 1976, 160; also see 228.
10. Engram 1976, 147.
11. Engram 1976, 177. Also see Fischer 1967, 230, 228.
12. Engram 1976, 142.
13. Engram 1976, 146.
14. Fischer 1967, 231; Engram 1976, 185, 196.
15. Ikle 1965, 65. Russian leaders had similar assessments of the importance of Japanese arms; see Berton 1956, 92–93. On the significance of Japanese military supplies to Russia, also see Dickinson 2003, 302.
16. Engram 1976, 122, 225.
17. Engram 1976, 197.
18. Fischer 1967, 228; Engram 1976, 128, 227.
19. Engram 1976, 132.
20. Engram 1976, 144.
21. Engram 1976, 109. Bethmann "could contemplate renunciation of Kiachow in the belief that the leased territory was of the utmost importance for Japan's ambitions in Asia" (Engram 1976, 133).
22. Ikle 1965, 63.
23. Engram 1976, 180.
24. Ikle 1965, 65.
25. Engram 1976, 148.
26. On the Entente's no-separate-peace agreement, see Rapp-Hooper 2014.
27. Engram 1976, 119.
28. Engram 1976, 198.
29. Engram 1976, 208.
30. Nish 1977, 95.
31. Sochi 2015, 38.
32. Dickinson 2003, 307–9.
33. Engram 1976, 119. On Japan's twenty-one demands, see Crawford 2018, 234–35.
34. Concerning Japan's alignment decisions in 1915–16, the primary decision makers were the foreign ministers and the elder statesmen (genro), who expressed the priorities of the military elite. The prime minister, Ōkuma Shigenobu, and the wider cabinet routinely deferred to the foreign ministers' agenda, except when it conflicted with strong genro preferences. Three different foreign ministers—Katō Takaaki, Ōkuma Shigenobu, and Ishii Kikujirō (hereafter Katō, Ōkuma, and Ishii)—handled Germany's 1915–16 probes for separate peace. Ōkuma was cabinet premier throughout the duration, which covered two ministries. Katō, who was foreign minister during the first government, was driven out when the cabinet dissolved in late July 1915. Then Ōkuma reformed the cabinet and assumed the foreign minister's portfolio until Ishii took over in October 1915, remaining in that role until October 1916. See Dickinson 2003, 306–9; Sochi 2015, 41; Nish 1977, 110.
35. Nish 1977, 95; Dickinson 2003, 306–11; Stevenson 2004, 88–89; Sochi 2015, 37.
36. Royama 1973, 18, 23; Dickinson 2003, 306–9.
37. Ikle 1965, 64.
38. Engram 1976, 112.
39. Engram 1976, 142–43, 184–85, 232.
40. Fischer 1967, 229.
41. Fischer 1967, 230.
42. Engram 1976, 135.
43. Ikle 1965, 64.
44. Engram 1976, 225.
45. Engram 1976, 111.
46. Engram 1976, 118.

47. The Gorlice-Tarnów offensive was the "big strategic story of 1915" (Stevenson 2004, 125). By September, German and Austrian forces had "overrun the whole of Russian Poland and Lithuania. . . . The Russians' casualties totaled perhaps 1.4 million and their armies retreated some 300 miles." It was "one of the most decisive battles of the entire First World War [and] for Russia it was the beginning of the end" (Afflerbach 2014, 248).

48. Farrar 1978, 22; 1998, 32. Also see Stevenson 2004, 104, 113; Shanafelt 1985, 83.

49. Engram 1976, 123.

50. Engram 1976, 120.

51. Engram 1976, 132.

52. Engram 1976, 131; Ikle 1965, 65.

53. DJ, 96–97.

54. Dickinson 1999, 121, 122.

55. Engram 1976, 136; Lowe 1969, 227; Nish 1972, 153.

56. Ikle 1965, 63–64.

57. Engram 1976, 137.

58. Nish 1972, 183.

59. DJ, 179.

60. Berton 1956, 87.

61. Nish 1972, 183; Ikle 1965, 67.

62. DJ, 179–80.

63. Nish 1972, 180.

64. Engram 1976, 119–20.

65. Ikle 1965, 65.

66. Nish 1972, 164.

67. Ikle 1965, 66–67.

68. Farrar 1978, 59–60.

69. Ikle 1965, 68; Engram 1976, 172.

70. Engram 1976, 174.

71. Engram 1976, 172; Ikle 1965, 68.

72. Ikle 1965, 71; Engram 1976, 176.

73. Engram 1976, 177.

74. Engram 1976, 173.

75. Engram 1976, 178–79; Ikle 1965, 68; Farrar 1978, 59–60; Fischer 1967, 230.

76. Engram 1976, 195; Ikle 1965, 73; Farrar 1978, 60. In exchange for Tsingtao and the Pacific islands, Tokyo would need to: (1) immediately stop supplying Germany's enemies; (2) mediate peace with Russia along specific lines; (3) provide financial compensation for territories traded; (3) protect and promote German economic interests in China; (4) promise to join a defensive alliance against Britain and France after the war; (6) and disclaim interest in the Dutch East Indies (Engram 1976, 188–89).

77. Ikle 1965, 69–70.

78. Ikle 1965, 73.

79. Farrar 1978, 60.

80. Nish 1972, 183.

81. Engram 1976, 201. In February 1917, Bethmann likewise noted: "The Japanese would like to compromise us again in order to make their allies, and perhaps America, more compliant toward their desiderata" (Engram 1976, 226; Ikle 1965, 76).

82. Berton 1956, 118–19.

83. Dickinson 1999, 145–46; Nish 1972, 175.

84. Berton 1956, 204n1.

85. On the genro's role, see Berton 1956, 151–52.

86. On these negotiations, see Berton 1956, chaps. 4–5; Dickinson 1999, 145–51.

87. Dickinson 1999, 139.

88. Berton 1956, 153, 161, 169; Dickinson 1999, 144.

89. DJ, 226; Berton 1956, 128.

90. Ikle 1965, 70; Nish 1977, 110–11; Saveliev and Pestushko 2001, 20–24.

91. For further detail on the public and secret conventions, see DJ, 272–74; Berton 1956, 201–2.
92. Nish 1972, 176; Berton 1956, 216.
93. On "binding" efforts in response to wedge strategies, see Izumikawa 2018.

3. Germany Keeps the United States Neutral, 1914–16

1. The conditions in the case are coded as follows: German perceptions of U.S. strategic weight—High; German perceptions of relative reward power—High; Attempted alignment change—Low; Germany's alliance constraints—Low; Outcome—Success.
2. Osgood 1953, 184.
3. Farrar 1978, 3.
4. Herwig 1997, 316.
5. Craig 1978, 370.
6. May 1959, 212; Link 1960, 434.
7. May 1959, 208, 220; Jonas 1984, 109.
8. OGD II, 1148.
9. May 1959, 199, 210, 199.
10. OGD II, 1136.
11. May 1959, 210.
12. Link 1960, 434n79; May 1959, 211. In 1916, as ground battles moved in Germany's favor, Falkenhayn shifted away from this concern around the effects of U.S. intervention on other neutrals. But in the March 1916 *Sussex* crisis, key Navy officials surprisingly rallied to support it. Doerries 1989, 119–20.
13. Link's paraphrase (1960, 552).
14. OGD II, 1157. Also see 1177–79.
15. OGD II, 1148.
16. OGD II, 1111.
17. PWW 34, 372.
18. Link 1960, 327.
19. OGD II, 1168.
20. FRUS, Lansing Papers, I, no. 524, 555.
21. OGD II, 977.
22. OGD II, 1136.
23. On U.S. gains from wartime neutral trade more generally, see Gholz and Press 2001, 24–41; Buehrig 1955, 87, 97–100.
24. PWW 34, 275.
25. On German perceptions that U.S. gains from munitions and other military-related exports to Allies were enhanced by restrictions on U-boat warfare, see Birnbaum 1958, 39–46; OGD II, 1185.
26. For example, Helfferich: "The reactions of the U-boat war from the political and economic standpoint must not be underestimated. . . . A break with the United States and war with the United States would be unavoidable" (OGD II, 1157).
27. On Wilson's peace moves, see Buehrig 1955, 229–67; Link 1960, 191–231; Birnbaum 1958; May 1959, 347–83.
28. May 1959, 388.
29. OGD II, 982.
30. On U.S. conflicts with Britain, see May 1959, 325–46; Link 1960, 170–90.
31. Link 1960, 451–53.
32. Link 1960, 413.
33. OGD II, 1291; Link 1964, 235. In May 1916, Bernstorff noted to Bethmann his "feeling of hope . . . because the peace movement is gaining strength every day." "Whenever you hear an American talking about the President," wrote he wrote to Jagow, "irrespective of whether he is blaming him or praising him, his comments invariably end with the remark: 'He kept us out of the war'" (OGD II, 1295, 1301).

34. OGD II, 1195.
35. OGD II, 1304.
36. FRUS, 1914, supplement, 547–51.
37. FRUS, Lansing Papers I, 290–91.
38. May 1959, chap. 9; Cooper 2003, 418; Link 1960; 1964.
39. Warner 2002.
40. OGD II, 974.
41. FRUS, 1916, supplement, no. 342; OGD II, no. 7, 975.
42. OGD II, 979.
43. Schroeder 2007, 20.
44. An interesting example of Austrian support for Germany's efforts to accommodate the U.S. appeared with the sinking of the Italian liner *Ancona*, which occurred in November 1915, after Germany had pledged to stop attacking civilian liners. The attacker was an overzealous German submarine sailing under an Austrian flag. In order to deflect blame from Germany and support Bethmann's efforts to conciliate the U.S., Vienna agreed to accept responsibility. Doerries 1989, 118–19; FRUS, 1915, supplement, no. 909, 656–58.
45. Link 1964, 182. For Bethmann's description of these allied concerns, see OGD II, 1133–34.
46. Link 1964, 259.
47. OGD II, 1160; also see May 1959, 396n25, 244.
48. Stone 1983, 25. As Bethmann noted on 10 December: "Our allies have not only complied, but are urgently requesting that the plan be carried out" (OGD II, 1072).
49. Herwig 1997, 317.
50. On the German decision to initiate U-boat warfare against Britain, see Birnbaum 1958, 22–24.
51. FRUS, 1915, supplement, 99.
52. Link 1960, 355, 330–31.
53. Link 1960, 355–56, 398.
54. Birnbaum 1958, 31.
55. Birnbaum 1958, 27.
56. PWW 33, 530–32; FRUS, 1915, supplement, 393–96; 436–38; 480–82. As Wilson put the idea to the cabinet while formulating the note, if there was another German act in violation of principle of visit and search, "then we must consider that an unfriendly act" (PWW 33, 536–37).
57. May 1959, 155–56.
58. Smith 1966, 119.
59. Birnbaum 1958, 32.
60. Link 1960, 399–400; Birnbaum 1958, 34.
61. FRUS, 1915, supplement, 463–66.
62. Link 1964, 454; FRUS, 1915, supplement, 493.
63. Link 1960, 569.
64. Link 1960, 573.
65. FRUS, 1915, supplement, no. 758, 525–26.
66. FRUS, 1915, supplement, no. 759, 526; no. 760, 526–27.
67. Link 1960, 573.
68. On this meeting, see FRUS, 1915, supplement, no. 762; Link 1960, 575–77; May 1959, 219–22.
69. Link 1960, 576.
70. Bethmann quoted in Link 1960, 572.
71. May 1959, 220. Two days later, in a letter to Admiral Bachmann, Falkenhayn insisted that "open partisanship of the United States against us ... must be prevented at all costs." He emphasized the ripple effects of such a development: "Our situation is so serious that it would be irresponsible to make it worse. An open allying of the United States on the side of our enemies would mean just such a worsening, and a very serious worsening indeed. Aside from all the immediate effects on public opinion in Germany and on our economic life during the war and afterward, it would bring a chilling of our relations with all the states that have so far been

neutral—Holland, Sweden, Denmark, Switzerland, Bulgaria, Greece, and Rumania. In order to break this war of exhaustion, we need the help of the neutrals" (Link 1960, 575n76).

72. May 1959, 222; Link 1960, 581; Birnbaum 1958, 35.

73. Link 1960, 574–77, 579.

74. May 1959, 223, 222, 220; Birnbaum 1958, 34–35.

75. Link 1960, 577n80, emphasis in original.

76. PWW 34, 436, emphasis in original; FRUS, 1915, supplement, no. 767, 530–31. Link 1960, 583–84.

77. Link 1960, 585.

78. Link 1960, 666. The U.S. ambassador to Germany cabled back to Washington that Chief of the Admiralty Holtzendorff (who replaced Bachmann, whom Wilhelm had fired) had confirmed that the "Naval Department was now in complete accord with general Government and that instructions given to submarines were strict and would be carried out" (FRUS, 1915, supplement, 553).

79. FRUS, 1915, supplement, no. 820, 560.

80. May 1959, 227; Link 1960, 667.

81. Stevenson 2004, 82.

82. FRUS, 1916, supplement, no. 224, 163–65, 181.

83. Link 1964, 158, 88, 156.

84. May 1959, 228, 235–37.

85. Link 1964, 154–58, 163–64; FRUS, 1916, supplement, 170, 172.

86. Link 1964, 165.

87. OGD II, 1287.

88. Link 1964, 166, emphasis in original.

89. OGD II, 1147.

90. OGD II, 1135–36.

91. OGD II, 1140. FRUS, 1916, supplement, 186, 198. Link 1964, 165.

92. Birnbaum 1958, 70.

93. FRUS, 1916, supplement, 215–23.

94. FRUS, 1916, supplement, 232–34.

95. FRUS, 1916, supplement, 252.

96. Link 1964, 265.

97. Birnbaum 1958, 82–87.

98. Link 1964, 268, emphasis in original.

99. Link 1964, 268.

100. FRUS, 1916, supplement, no. 337, 258–60; PWW 36, 626.

101. FRUS, 1916, supplement, 265–66.

102. As Stevenson (2004, 83), puts it, Wilson "again compelled the U-boats to suspend their sinkings."

103. OGD II, 1117–28.

104. Birnbaum 1958, 137–44; May 1959, 277–301; FRUS, 1916, supplement, no. 386, 291–92.

105. FRUS, 1916, supplement, nos. 388, 390.

106. FRUS, 1916, supplement, nos. 390, 391, 392, 393, 394, 396, 398.

107. The exception, strangely enough, was Falkenhayn, who in January 1917 now claimed that "he did not believe the U.S. would, in the face of German toughness, actively enter the European conflict, and he added his opinion that America would hardly be able to muster enough troops in time anyway" (Doerries 1978, 35n41).

108. OGD II, 1200.

109. May 1959, 414.

110. Ikle 1971, 44.

111. OGD II, 1319; Doerries 1989, 209.

112. Doerries, 1989, 192.

113. May 1959, 200; Ikle 1971, 45. As Ikle points out, the German military chiefs' analysis failed to consider the effect U.S. intervention would have on Britain's resolve to keep fighting, even as losses mounted (46–47).

114. Herwig 1997, 312; Birnbaum 1958, 56.
115. Birnbaum 1958, 51.
116. Herwig 1997, 315.
117. The army elites "felt certain that the United States did not have sufficient combat forces to enter the war. Even if Washington should succeed in raising a modern army . . . the American war material and troops would be intercepted by the German submarines" (Doerries 1980, 9).
118. OGD II, 1152.
119. All quotes from Herwig 1997, 315.
120. May 1959, 294; Ikle 1971, 44.
121. Herwig 1997, 315. As Wilhelm put it in March 1917, "Once and for all, an *end* to negotiations with America. If Wilson wants war, let him make it, and let him then have it" (OGD II, 1336, emphasis in original).
122. Cooper 2003, 426.
123. PWW 33, 505, emphasis in original; Link 1960, 442.
124. PWW 34, 8–9.
125. Link 1960, 446n118.
126. Link 1964, 261.
127. FRUS, 1916, supplement, 232–37.
128. PWW 36, 446.
129. FRUS, Lansing Papers I, 555–59.
130. Wilson's Address to Congress, PWW 36, 506–10; Link 1964, 253–64; May 1959, 194.
131. PWW 36, 597.
132. PWW 34, 290, 299, 318–19, emphasis added.
133. PWW 36, 373, 389, 405, 421.
134. Mearsheimer 2001, 253–54; Morgenthau 1950, 848.
135. Jackson 2012, 466. In the same spirit, see Osgood 1953, 191, 223, 252–54.
136. Jackson 2012, 483.
137. Link 1965, 411–12.
138. Cooper 2003, 222.
139. Thompson 2002, 143.
140. Osgood 1953, 191, 207.
141. Cooper 2003, 425, 424.
142. Thompson 1985, 338.
143. Even those historians who do see consideration of larger balance of power concerns at work in Lansing's and House's advocacy of intervention note that Wilson himself was *not* driven to war in 1917 by the perception that Germany was on the brink of victory and thus posed an acute danger to U.S. security. See May 1959, 437; Smith 1965, 82.
144. Link 1965, 411–12.
145. PWW 41, 438.
146. PWW 41, 138.

4. The Entente Fails to Keep Turkey Neutral, 1914

1. The conditions in the case are coded as follows: Initiator—Russia; Russian perceptions of Turkey's strategic weight—High; Russian perceptions of relative reward power—High; Attempted alignment change—High; Entente alliance constraints—High; Allied Strategic Consensus—No; Outcome—Failure.
2. Bobroff 2006, 97.
3. Howard 1931, 91.
4. Bobroff 2006, 97. As the British military attaché in Constantinople observed, if German warships united with the Turkish navy, "control of the Black Sea would pass to Turkey . . . and this, in turn, might help to determine the attitude of Bulgaria and Roumania" (Miller 1997, 295).

5. Cunningham (1993, 244), writes: "The greatest initiative from the side of the Entente came from Russia, who saw most clearly what loss of the Straits to German control implied."

6. Howard 1931, 98; Albertini 1957, 619.

7. BDFA, II, H, 1, no. 90.

8. Kurat 1967, 292–93.

9. Grey 1925, 170.

10. Miller 1997, 279–82; Heller 1983, 134, 137; Grey 1925, 172.

11. Grey 1925, 172.

12. Quoted in Miller 1997, 311.

13. DD 1915, no. 32.

14. Quoted in Miller 1997, 291.

15. BDFA, II, H, 1, no. 101.

16. CMD 7628, nos. 20, 21; DD 1915, no. 4.

17. CMD 7628, no. 27.

18. Miller 1997, 278.

19. CMD 7628, no. 17.

20. CMD 7628, no. 21.

21. Miller 1997, 276.

22. DD 1915, no. 34; CMD 7628, nos. 21, 28.

23. DD 1915, nos. 30, 54; CMD 7628, no. 24.

24. DD 1915, nos. 48, 31, 33, 34, 41; CMD 7628, nos. 28, 76, 77; BDFA, II, H, 1, no. 236.

25. BDFA, II, H, 1, nos. 97, 101.

26. CMD 7628, no. 77.

27. CMD 7628, no. 24.

28. BDFA, II, H, 1, no. 83; Grey 1925, 173.

29. See esp. BD, X, I, 901–2.

30. Quoted in Heller 1983, 63. On Turkey's proposal, see BD, IX, appendix IV; GD, no. 30.

31. BDFA, II, H, 1, no. 69; also see no. 90.

32. Bobroff 2006, 97, 100.

33. Bobroff 2006, 101.

34. Grey 1925, 165; Howard 1931, 92.

35. BDFA, II, H, 1, no. 236.

36. Quoted in Miller 1997, 226.

37. Hale 2000, 14; Trumpener 1968, 12.

38. Miller 1997, 195.

39. In July 1914, Jagow wrote, "Turkey in her present state could assume no other position than that of swinging like a pendulum between the powers, eventually joining the stronger and more successful group" (quoted in Miller 1997, 208). Also see Kurat 1967, 296.

40. Stevenson 2004, 89.

41. Howard 1931, 92.

42. Fulton 1984, 161.

43. Weitsman 2003, 99, 108.

44. McMeekin 2011, 105.

45. Sazonov 1928, 227.

46. Stone 2007, 15.

47. Rice 1974, 350–51.

48. Heller 1983, 123; also see Rice 1974, 328.

49. Rice 1974, 328.

50. Rice 1974, 330; Cunningham 1993, 245. A British naval officer serving in the blockade outside the Dardanelles in September wrote, "It seems awfully stupid to allow the Turks to go on shilly shallying like this; but I suppose our Govt have enough to do without worrying about a small country who can't do us much damage" (Miller 1997, 307–8).

51. Miller 1997, 295.

52. GD, no. 117

53. On 18 July, Wangenheim had cabled Berlin, "Turkey is today without any question worthless as an ally. She would only be a burden to her associates, without being able to offer them the slightest advantage" (GD, no. 71; Miller 1997, 209).

54. GD, no. 141.

55. GD, no. 149. Howard 1931, 84.

56. GD, nos. 285, 320.

57. Kurat 1967, 299.

58. CMD 7628, nos. 1, 4.

59. Miller 1997, 219–24.

60. GD, no. 733; Trumpener 1968, 16.

61. GD, nos. 836, 662.

62. CMD 7628, nos. 3, 14, 18; DD 1915, nos. 7, 9, 25; GD, no. 836.

63. GD, no. 795; Yasamee 1995, 230.

64. Writes Albertini (1957, 617): "It is well known that not all members of the Turkish Government were in favour of making war on Russia and that those suspected of sympathies with the Entente were only told of the [German] alliance after it was signed. But even those who favoured the alliance seemed half to regret having bound themselves to Germany."

65. GD, no. 775.

66. Trumpener 1968, 28; Kurat 1967, 300; Howard 1931, 406n14.

67. Kurat 1967, 301; GD, nos. 726, 733.

68. Miller 1997, 259–73; Howard 1931, 95; DD 1915, no. 27.

69. Aksakal 2008, 123; Trumpener 2003, 349.

70. Howard 1931, 96–102; Smith, 69–76; Albertini 1957, 618–20.

71. Howard 1931, 97.

72. Bobroff 2006, 101; Miller 1997, 235; Yasamee 1995, 243n47; Gottlieb 1957, 38–39; Smith, 69–70; Trumpener 1968, 24–25.

73. BD, XI, no. 564; Aksakal 2008, 110; Bobroff 2006, 102; Miller 1997, 230; Fulton 1984, 161; Howard 1931, 411n83; Silberstein 1970, 78.

74. Aksakal 2008, 112, 114.

75. DD 1915, no. 44.

76. Bobroff 2006, 102.

77. Cunningham 1993, 244. Also see Bobroff 2006, 106.

78. Howard 1931, 93.

79. Rice 1974, 422n51.

80. Howard 1931, 99.

81. Bobroff 2006, 104; Trumpener 2003, 347.

82. BDFA, II, H, 1, nos. 76, 83, 92. Also see Grey 1925, 173; Bobroff 2006, 106; Gottlieb 1957, 56n2; Smith 1956, 72.

83. Aksakal 2008, 132; Bobroff 2006, 105–6; Howard 1931, 100; Smith 1956, 75.

84. BDFA, II, H, 1, nos. 69, 80. Also see Aksakal 2008, 131; Bobroff 2006, 104; Howard 1931, 100; Miller 1997, 295.

85. Bobroff 2006, 106; Gottlieb 1957, 55; CMD 7628, nos. 17, 21.

86. DD 1915, no. 30; Howard 1931, 101.

87. DD 1915, no. 32; BDFA, II, H, 1, no. 82.

88. Smith 1956, 74. See BDFA, II, H, 1, nos. 201, 209.

89. BDFA, II, H, 1, no. 90; also see nos. 91, 173, 176, 182, 183, 185, 189, 199, 233, 236.

90. Bobroff 2006, 106. Bobroff explains: "Russia had the least to lose from an end to the capitulatory system, since its economic penetration of the Ottoman empire had been so shallow. Great Britain and France had much more to lose" (106). Also see Gottlieb 1957, 41.

91. DD 1915, no. 31; Bobroff 2006, 106.

92. CMD 7628, no. 27. Wrote Mallet: "There is a sharp struggle going on between Minister of Marine and German party on one side, and Moderates on the other" (BDFA, II, H, 1, no. 89). Also see nos. 173, 182, 197.

93. CMD 7628, no. 24.

94. Writes Kurat (1967, 315): "Had Britain and France given material guarantees to Turkey against Russia and Greece . . . the Porte would have exercised a neutrality as recommended by the western powers, allowing freedom of passage in the Straits."

95. BDFA, II, H, 1, no. 92. As Strachan (2002, 675) sums it, "Thus Britain, for all its apparent desire to restrict the war and to ensure Turkey's continued neutrality, made, in furtherance of that policy, not a single concession of any real significance to Turkey."

96. CMD 7628, no. 28, emphasis added; DD 1915, no. 33.

97. CMD 7628, no. 34.

98. Bobroff 2006, 106; Gottlieb 1957, 56.

99. Emin 1930, 71; Gottlieb 1957, 38–39; Yasamee 1995, 243; Bobroff 2006, 106.

100. Howard 1931, 105–6.

101. Bobroff 2006, 103.

102. DD 1915, no. 34.

103. DD 1915, nos. 34, 35; Aksakal 2008, 131; Bobroff 2006, 106; Smith 1956, 73.

104. Smith 1956, 75.

105. DD 1915, no. 52.

106. Aksakal 2008, 136–37.

107. Bobroff 2006, 107; Gottlieb 1957, 109; Smith 1956, 75.

108. DD 1915, nos. 41–43.

109. CMD 7628, 69, 70.

110. DD 1915, no. 51; Silberstein 1970, 80; Akasal 2008, 115n87.

111. DD 1915, nos. 48, 54, 55, 56, 61, 63, 65, 74.

112. Akasal 2011, 201. Also see Silberstein 1970, 81.

113. Yasamee 1995, 248. Miller 1997, 315–16.

114. DD 1915, nos. 47, 66, 75, 76, 83, 86; BDFA, II, H, 1, nos. 202, 208.

115. CMD 7628, no. 77; BDFA, II, H, 1, no. 176.

116. Trumpener 1968, 47; DD 1915, nos. 67–70.

117. Trumpener 1968, 32, 53, 56–57; 2003, 341–42, 347, 349, 350–51, 352; Kurat 1967, 299–300; Yasamee 1995, 242, 245, 251, 253.

118. Yasamee 1995, 247.

119. Emin 1930, 70, 71. Also see Bobroff 2006, 106.

120. Rice 1974, 333.

121. DD 1915, nos. 86, 88; Aksakal 2008, 172–73.

122. CMD 7628, 134. As late as October 22, Djemal and interior minister Talaat Pasha assured the British and French ambassadors that neutrality would be maintained (164). On 27 October, Mallet reported that "a majority of the [CUP] are . . . said to be against war, and are showing considerable opposition to the scheme" (169).

123. Aksakal 2008, 171–72; Trumpener 1968, 50–51; CMD 7628, nos. 131, 157, 162.

124. CMD 7628, nos. 170, 177, 178.

125. Zeman 1971, 60; Gottlieb 1957; Emin 1930, 71, 75. In relation to the influence of the Liman von Sanders mission, it is worth noting that on July 31, the German ambassador reported to Berlin that the colonel himself doubted that Ottomans would declare for Central powers (GD, no. 517). The fact that a British officer was in a similar position of influence vis-à-vis the Ottoman navy also, logically, implies that the von Sanders mission was not a controlling factor. Well into September, German officials worried that the Porte might decide to send the German advisors home in order to conciliate the Entente powers.

126. Akasal 2008; Akmese 2005, 162, 184; Trumpener 1968, 12–20; 2003, 341–44; Trumperner 1962; Yasamee 1995, 232, 258.

127. See Akasal 2008, 113–16, 120–25, 137–41; Trumpener 1962, 371; Yasamee 1995, 253.

128. Karsh and Karsh 1999, 123; Albertini 1957, 618.

129. Trumpener makes the best argument that Turkey's declared neutrality was both a ruse to cover its military preparations and a way to enhance bargaining leverage with Germany. His evidence for this is that Enver revealed the talks with Entente to Berlin, "albeit with some delay" (1968, 25; 2003, 347n34; also Karsh and Karsh 1999, 125). Had Turkey remained neutral, the efforts of Enver and others in the Ottoman cabinet to reassure the Central powers of Turkey's

ultimate commitment, while seeking additional increments of material support to support mobilization, would be interpreted as a clever strategy to string along Berlin and extract maximum resources from it in order to subsidize what was intended ultimately to be a policy of armed neutrality (for references to such motives, see Akasal 2008, 114, 123, 138, 141; Trumpener 1968, 29, 49–50). In this scenario, the fact that Enver informed the Germans that the Porte was also negotiating with the Entente would not count as evidence of the intimacy of Enver's commitment to Germany but rather as another clever Turkish move to play off both sides (for earlier examples interpreted in just such terms, see Trumpener 1968, 20; Akasal 2008, 112).

130. Trumpener 1968, 32, 53, 56–57; 2003, 341–42, 347, 349, 350–52; Kurat 1967, 299–300; Yasamee 1995, 242, 245, 247, 251, 253.

131. Yasamee 1995, 233; Fulton, 1984, 161.

132. Quoted in Heller 1983, 63. On Turkey's proposal, see BD, IX, appendix IV; GD, no. 30.

133. BD, IX, 779–81; X, I, 901–2. Heller 1983, 80.

134. Kurat 1967, 294.

135. Trumpener 2003, 344; Miller 1997, 205; Fulton 1984, 161; Howard 1931, 73.

136. Emin 1930, 71; Gottlieb 1957, 38–39; Yasamee 1995, 243; Bobroff 2006, 106.

5. The Entente Realigns Italy, 1915

1. The case conditions are coded as follows: Initiator—Britain; British perceptions of Italy's strategic weight—High; British perceptions of relative reward power—High; Attempted alignment change—High; Entente alliance constraints—High; Allied Strategic Consensus—Yes; Outcome—Success.

2. Lowe 1969, 544; Renzi 1987, 197.

3. Quoted in Renzi 1987, 197.

4. Gottlieb 1957, 320; BDFA, II, H, 1, no. 490.

5. Valiani 1966; Mulligan 2014, 101–4; Renzi 1987, chap. 10.

6. Quoted in Lowe 1969, 535.

7. BDFA, II, H, 1, nos. 120, 127.

8. BDFA, II, H, 1, nos. 191, 179; also see nos. 187, 191.

9. BDFA, II, H, 1, no. 223. Since "October Rome had made no secret of the fact that if anything would precipitate Italian intervention it would be Allied success in the Balkans" (Lowe 1969, 540).

10. Quoted in Gottlieb 1957, 314.

11. Renzi 1987, 198.

12. BDFA, II, H, 1, no. 484.

13. Gottlieb 1957, 325, 317.

14. BDFA, II, H, 1, no. 488.

15. Gottlieb 1957, 317, 323.

16. BDFA, II, H, 1, no. 179; Renzi 1987, 118.

17. BDFA, II, H, 1, no. 191.

18. Renzi 1987, 216. The British had initially offered 50 million, with one-third collateral in Italian gold shipped to London. Sonnino negotiated the principal up to 60 million, and the gold collateral down to one-sixth.

19. Gottlieb 1957, 231–33.

20. BDFA, II, H, 1, no. 330.

21. BDFA, II, H, 1, no. 425.

22. Snyder 1997, 212–14; GDD, chap. 4.

23. Palumbo 1979, 348, 355.

24. Renzi 1987, 11–12.

25. Joll and Martel 2007, 76; Morgenthau 1967, 349.

26. DDAHI, nos. 2, 9, 15.

27. DDAHI, no. 22; also see nos. 16, 17, 26, 27.

28. Valiani 1966.

29. Renzi 1966, 655; du Quenoy 2003, 410.
30. BDFA, II, H, 1, no. 491.
31. BDFA, II, H, 1, no. 491. Also see Lowe 1969, 541–42; Gottlieb 1957, 317.
32. BDFA, II, H, 1, no. 492.
33. Lowe 1969, 534.
34. BDFA, II, H, 1, no. 490. Quoted in Grey 1925, vol. 2, 206.
35. BDFA, II, H, 1, no. 497. Two days later, Sazonov gave a note to the British and French ambassadors that stated: "Advantages which the three Allied Powers might grant to Italy in exchange for her co-operation should be in proportion to degree of military and political support which they might derive therefrom. Promises which Powers were ready to make to Italy six months ago would have to be revised and made to conform to actual situation" (no. 501).
36. Du Quenoy 2003, 410.
37. Lowe 1969, 534.
38. BDFA, II, H, 1, no. 14. Also see Lowe 1969, 534; du Quenoy 2003, 410–13; Rezni 1966, 654.
39. BDFA, II, H, 1, nos. 11, 23, 28, 33.
40. Quoted in Gottlieb 1957, 199.
41. BDFA, II, H, 1, no. 382.
42. Gottlieb 1957, 314.
43. Gottlieb 1957, 236.
44. BDFA, II, H, 1, nos. 225, 228. Also see Lowe 1969, 538.
45. BDFA, II, H, 1, nos. 72, 109, 191; Lowe 1969, 539.
46. BDFA, II, H, 1, no. 383.
47. Valiani 1966; Mulligan 2014, 101–4; DDAHI; AHM 1915.
48. DDAHI, no. 42; BDFA, II, H, 1, no. 509.
49. DDAHI, nos. 33, 90.
50. DDAHI, no. 41.
51. Valiani 1966, 124.
52. DDAHI, no. 99. Also see Mulligan 2014, 102–3.
53. DDAHI, no. 106.
54. Renzi 1987, 198–99.
55. BDFA, II, H, 1, no. 416.
56. See, e.g., Sazonov's comments to Buchanan (BDFA, II, H, 1, no. 482).
57. Renzi 1987, 202–3.
58. Valiani 1966, 128; DDAHI, no. 115; AHM 1915, 9.
59. Valiani 1966, 128–29; BDFA, II, H, 1, no. 557; AHM 1915, 9.
60. Lowe 1969, 541; Hamilton and Herwig 2003, 382.
61. Renzi 1970, 18.
62. Fulton 1996, 162–63.
63. Renzi 1970, 18n91.
64. Lowe 1969, 544, 547.
65. The Anglo-Franco concession on the Straits is a crucial element in the pattern of coordination, for it indicates that the eventual agreement was not simply a matter of Britain and France demanding Russian acquiescence to their strategic preference and priorities: Russia's flexibility on the Adriatic was, ultimately, propelled by both increased perceptions of Italy's strategic value and side payments by its principal allies.
66. Lowe 1969, 542.
67. Britain and Russia also had conflicting interests in the question; see du Quenoy 2003.
68. Renzi 1987, 206.
69. Quoted in Gottlieb 1957, 348. Also see Lowe 1969, 547; Stevenson 2004, 91.
70. Quoted in du Quenoy 2003, 432.
71. Stevenson 2004, 91.
72. Renzi 1987, 208.
73. Renzi 1987, 210.
74. Hamilton and Herwig 2003, 383. Writes Renzi (1987, 241): "When the King, Salandra, and Sonnino authorized the signature of the Pact of London there could have been no doubt in

their minds: The vast majority of Italians would have stayed [their] hand had a plebiscite been held on the issue of war and peace. . . . As April drew to a close neither Salandra, Sonnino, nor the King were certain that they could effect Italian intervention as promised in London."
75. Renzi 1987, 234.
76. De Grand 1971, 408.
77. Renzi 1987, 240.
78. Renzi 1987, 247. Also see Procacci 1995, 6; De Grand 1971, 400.
79. Renzi 1987, 251; Sullivan 1996, 334.
80. Renzi 1987, 218.
81. Renzi 1987, 241, 226.
82. Renzi 1987, 250.
83. Mack Smith 1997, 266.
84. Hamilton and Herwig 2003, 384.
85. Williamson and May 2007, 373; Hamilton and Herwig 2003, 370, 374; Bosworth 1979, 397; Renzi 1987, 23.
86. See, e.g., French 1986, 78.
87. Schelling 1966, 71–78; Art and Greenhill 2018, 17–19.
88. Stevenson 2004, 91.
89. Weitsman 2003.
90. Stevenson 2004, 92; Kogan 1963, 33.
91. De Grand 1971, 397.
92. Bosworth 1979, 182; Sullivan 1996, 327.

6. Britain and France Fail to Neutralize Italy, 1936–40

1. The conditions in the case are coded as follows: Initiator—Britain; British perceptions of Italy's strategic weight—High; British perceptions of relative reward power—High; Attempted alignment change—(a) Low, (b) High; Alliance constraints—(a) High, (b) High; Allied Strategic Consensus—(a) Mixed, (b) Mixed; Outcome—(a) Failure, (b) Failure.
2. Churchill recollected: "Those of us who saw in Hitler's Germany a danger, not only to peace but to survival, dreaded th[e] movement of a first-class Power, as Italy was then rated, from our side to the other" (Churchill 1948, 167).
3. Seton-Watson 1983, 275; DBFP, 2, XVII, no. 527. Likewise, in 1938, the Joint Planning Sub-Committee of the cabinet's Committee of Imperial Defence wrote of the potential for war with Germany that "it is probable . . . that Germany would be reluctant to embark upon such a war without some prior assurance of support from Italy" (CID 1938, 66).
4. In December 1937, the chiefs of staff warned: "We cannot foresee the time when our defense forces will be strong enough to safeguard our territory, trade and vital interests against Germany, Italy and Japan simultaneously." In September 1938, the Joint Planning Committee of the Chiefs of Staff warned: "War against Japan, Germany and Italy simultaneously in 1938 is a commitment which neither the present nor projected strength of our defence forces is designed to meet, even if we are in alliance with France and Russia" (both quoted in Murray 1979, 43). Also see Watt 1975, 293.
5. Thomas 1996, 215.
6. Salerno 2002, 67, 69.
7. Stafford 1983, 82.
8. DBFP, 2, XVII, no. 462.
9. DBFP, 3, VII, no. 308.
10. Thomas 1996, 211.
11. Mack Smith 1983, 265.
12. Thomas 1996, 215, 213, 215; Watt 1975, 282, 290; Toscano 1967, 394.
13. DBFP, 3, I, no. 164, 222. Likewise, in September 1938, Neville Henderson, the British ambassador to Germany, wrote, "Italy's attitude might be decisive for Hitler, if he is bent on war or is really contemplating making it" (DBFP, 3, II, no. 772, 240).

14. Watt 1975, 285.
15. Stafford 1983, 82; DBFP, 3, III, no. 285, 252–53.
16. DBFP, 3, III, nos. 331, 643.
17. Stafford 1983, 78.
18. DBFP, 3, III, no. 285, 252–53.
19. Salerno 1997, 66.
20. Shorrock 1988, 207.
21. Young 1984, 87.
22. DBFP, 3, III, no. 479.
23. DBFP, 3, III, nos. 474, 471.
24. DBFP, 3, III, no. 479.
25. Watt 1975, 293.
26. DBFP, 3, III, no. 325, 287.
27. Salerno 1997, 73–74.
28. Salerno 1997, 89, 97, emphasis in original. Also see Jervis 1997, 221.
29. Neave-Hill 1975, 346.
30. Such happened in April 1938 Anglo-Franco naval war planning talks. The French wanted the talks to prepare for an allied war against both Italy and Germany. Britain agreed to the talks, but stipulated that "Germany alone is to be assumed as the aggressor." The French "reluctantly accepted the British terms" (Salerno 1997, 81–82).
31. Morewood 1989, 173.
32. Haraszti 1974; Watt 1956. As Mussolini said in November 1935, "The Stresa front had been based on the common recognition of a German danger, but now England had cracked the Stresa front through and through" (BDFA, II, F, 11, no. 59, 102).
33. DBFP, 2, XIV, no. 90; Parker 1974; Robertson 1975.
34. DBFP, 2, XIV, nos. 429, 498, 554.
35. Watt 1975, 279; DBFP, 2, XIV, nos. 301, 308.
36. Thomas 1996, 100.
37. Seton Watson 1983, 272–75; Shorrock 1988, 201; DBFP, 2, XVII, nos. 376, 410, 415, 440.
38. Arielli 2010, chap. 4.
39. Salerno 1997, 73; 2002, 46.
40. DBFP, 2, XVII, nos. 447, 451, 460.
41. DBFP, 2, XVII, no. 462.
42. Thomas 1996, 97–98, 108.
43. Shorrock 1988, 202–3; Seton Watson 1983, 274.
44. Duroselle 2004, 254; DBFP, 2, XVII, nos. 462, 494.
45. Seton Watson 1983, 275; DBFP, 2, XVII, no 526.
46. DBFP, 2, XVII, no. 527, emphasis in original. On 1 January, the deputy undersecretary of the Foreign Office, Orme Sargent, likewise minuted: "So that we lose no opportunity of reaping the practical benefits in the realm of international policy of the Anglo-Italian détente which we have now reached . . . one precaution will be very necessary, and that is that in all comments that we make or that the British press makes *there should be no suggestion that our object in reaching this détente is to 'detach' Italy from Germany*" (DBFP, 2, XVII, no. 527; emphasis added). In subsequent parliamentary debates over the Gentleman's Agreement and its successor the Easter Accords, Chamberlain's government did *not* rebut anti-appeasement attacks by invoking the policy's wedge logic (although critics did, before shooting it down). Hansard 1938.
47. Seton Watson 1983, 275; Salerno 1997, 73–74.
48. Watt 1975, 278; Toscano 1970, 413.
49. Thomas 1996, 214–15.
50. Thomas 1996, 231.
51. Mills 1993.
52. Shorrock 1988, 213.
53. Salerno 2002, 33; Guillen 1998, 158.
54. DGFP, D, I, no. 17.
55. Watt 1975, 282.

56. Hefler 2018.
57. Seton Watson 1983, 276–77.
58. Shorrock 1988, 218, 216, 220; Renouvin 1975, 295; Duroselle 2004, 266.
59. Salerno 2002, 51.
60. Salerno 2002, 41; Strang 1999, 173; Ciano 1953, 87–90; DGFP, C, IV, nos. 485, 486.
61. Seton Watson 1983, 277; Shorrock 1988, 219; Lowe and Marzari 1975, 292.
62. Lowe and Marzari 1975, 310; Salerno 2002, 52.
63. On the provisions of the Easter Accords, see DBFP, 3, III, no. 367; Cmd. 5726; Hansard 1938.
64. Seton Watson 1983, 227; Salerno 2002, 55.
65. Lowe and Marzari 1975, 310.
66. DBFP, 3, I, no. 164, 208.
67. Weizsäcker 1951, 183.
68. Ciano 1953, 112.
69. Toscano 1967, 13. Also see Lowe and Marzari 1975, 292, 308.
70. Watt 1960, 534; Watt 1975, 283. But see Shorrock 1988, 229.
71. Salerno 2002, 55; Shorrock 1988; Strang 1999, 181–82.
72. Guillen 1998, 158.
73. DBFP, 3, III, nos. 471, 490.
74. Lowe and Marzari 1975, 312; Shorrock 1988, 230–32; Salerno 2002, 58–59; Watt 1975, 283.
75. Ciano 1953, 135, 145. Also see Toscano 1967, 36, 40.
76. Salerno 2002, 67, 69.
77. Strang 1999, 163–65.
78. Salerno 2002, 66–67; Mallett 2003, 189–90.
79. Ciano 1953, 163, 165, 168, 172. Also see Strang 1999, 182.
80. Ciano 1953, 168; Toscano 1967, 57, 42, 49.
81. DBFP, 3, III, no. 355, 379.
82. Watt 1975 284; Shorrock 1988, 235.
83. Lowe and Marzari 1975, 319.
84. DGFP, D, IV, no. 400.
85. Ciano 1953, 185.
86. Ciano 1953, 186–87.
87. Stafford 1983, 71; Schmitt 1955, 160.
88. Lowe and Marzari 1975, 319; Ciano 1953, 185, 191; DGFP, D, IV, no. 404.
89. Toscano 1967, 60. Also see Ciano 1953, 185.
90. DBFP, 3, III, nos. 285, 367; Cmd. 5923.
91. Shorrock 1988, 235.
92. On the speech, see DGFP, D, IV, 412; DBFP, 3, III, no. 461.
93. Watt 1975, 284; DBFP, 3, III, no. 469, 473.
94. Stafford 1983, 68.
95. Shorrock 1988, 246.
96. Salerno 2002, 84, 85–86; Stafford 1983, 75.
97. On the Chamberlain-Halifax mission's agenda, see DBFP 3, III, no. 600; DGFP, D, IV, no. 435; Ciano 1945, 10–12.
98. Renouvin 1975, 295; DBFP, 3, III, no. 490.
99. Schmitt 1955, 160; DGFP, D, IV, nos. 421, 422.
100. DGFP, D, IV, nos. 455, 459, 461, 462.
101. Toscano 1967, 168, 169–74; Salerno 2002, 114. Also see Seton Watson 1983, 278.
102. Ciano 1945, 47–48; Shorrock 1988, 256–57.
103. Toscano 1967, 174, 170; Ciano 1945, 46; DGFP, D, VI, nos. 15, 38, 45.
104. Seton Watson 1983, 278; Toscano 1967, 177n17; Shorrock 1988, 257.
105. Toscano 1967, 175–76; Ciano 1945, 43–48.
106. Toscano 1967, 179–80.
107. DGFP, D, VI, no. 55. Also see no. 100; Ciano 1945, 49.
108. Bell 1996, 221.

109. Salerno 2002, 109.
110. Shorrock 1988, 259; Salerno 2002, 112–13.
111. Salerno 2002, 116–17.
112. DBFP, 3, V, nos. 298, 570; Ciano 1945, 72.
113. Salerno 2002, 119; DBFP, 3, V, nos. 76, 78.
114. Shorrock 1988, 264–66; Toscano 1967, 176; DBFP, 3, V, nos. 132, 214, 228, 238, 328.
115. Toscano 1967, 177n17.
116. Ciano 1945, 72.
117. Watt 1975, 290; Toscano 1967, 269n149; DBFP, 3, V, nos. 369, 370; Ciano 1945, 75.
118. Salerno 2002, 130; Toscano 1967, 177n17.
119. Shorrock 1988, 266.
120. Watt 1975, 290. Also see Salerno 2002, 124.
121. DGFP, D, VI, nos. 369, 370, 371, 386, 426.
122. DBFP, 3, V, no. 238. Also see 235.
123. DBFP, 3, V, no. 570, 612–13; Watt 1975, 290.
124. DBFP, 3, V, no. 570, 614.
125. DGFP, D, VI, no. 426.
126. On 29 August 1939, in the Polish crisis, Halifax recognized that this issue complicated British efforts to induce Italy to stay neutral: "We are seeking to bribe Signor Mussolini away from his loyalty to his German ally, when the ink is scarcely dry on Count Ciano's signature" (DBFP, 3, VII, no. 480).
127. DBFP, 3, V, no. 653. Also see nos. 651, 652. After that, Ciano privately pronounced the Easter Accords "dead" (Ciano 1945, 89). Also see DGFP, D, VI, no. 456.
128. DBFP, 3, V, no. 708; DBFP, 3, VI, no. 10; Ciano 1945, 95–96.
129. DBFP, 3, VI, no. 317.
130. DBFP, 3, VI, no. 326. On British pressures, also see Watt 1975, 202; Duroselle 2004, 345–46; Salerno 2002, 139–40; Stafford 1984, 56.
131. Salerno 2002, 125, 131–36.
132. Schmitt 1955, 162–63; Ciano 1945, 108–11.
133. Knox 1982, 44.
134. DGFP, D, VII, nos. 43, 47; Schmitt 1955, 165; Ciano 1945, 118–19.
135. Ciano 1945, 120–25; Mallett 2003, 205–7; Salerno 2002, 134–36.
136. Schmitt 1955, 166; Ciano 1945, 127; Stafford 1984, 58–78; DGFP, D, VII, no. 98.
137. DGFP, D, VII, no. 271, emphasis in original.
138. DGFP, D, VII, nos. 277, 282, 301, 307, 308; Ciano 1945, 128–130; Watt 1960, 539; Sullivan 2007, 124.
139. DGFP, D, VII, nos. 307, 341, 349.
140. DGFP, D, VII, no. 317; Schmitt 1955, 166. Also see 349.
141. To the German ambassador, he declared he would "carry out the Fuhrer's requests one hundred percent." To Hitler, directly, he wrote: "The world does not and will not know before the outbreak of hostilities what the attitude of Italy is, and will learn instead that Italy has concentrated her forces toward the frontiers of the great democracies" (DGFP, D, VII, nos. 349, 350).
142. Stafford 1984, 58.
143. Imlay 2003, 44–48.
144. DBFP, 3, VII, nos. 151, 201, 344.
145. DBFP, 3, VII, no. 276; also nos. 319, 465, 585.
146. DBFP, 3, VII, no. 621, 160. It is likely that Ciano covertly sent a similar assurance to London as early as 22 August (Ciano 1945, 135, 126; Knox 1982, 43; Mack Smith 1983, 264). Also see Gin 2014, 995, 997.
147. As Halifax put it to the French ambassador, their shared goal was to "in any way" encourage "Italy to sit more loosely to her Axis commitments" (DBFP, 3, VII, no. 308). The secretary general of the French Foreign Ministry proposed a more "far reaching policy designed to detach [Italy] ultimately from Germany" (DBFB 3, VII, no. 496).
148. Lowe and Marzari 1975, 359. Notes Schreiber (1995, 36): because "there was certainly far reaching agreement among allied political and military leaders that every effort should be

made to keep Mussolini from entering the war on Hitler's side[,] Italy was . . . benevolently treated."

149. Shorrock 1988, 272; DBFP, 3, VII, nos. 692, 697.

150. Salerno 2002, 157–59.

151. Shorrock 1988, 273–74; Schreiber 1995, 36; Gin 2014, 998.

152. Mallet 1997; Woodward 1970, 22.

153. Mallet 1997, 149–52; Salerno 2002, 162–63; Lowe and Marzari 1975, 360.

154. Umbreit 1991a, 305. Also see DBFP, 3, VI, no. 258; Schreiber 1995.

155. Sullivan 2007, 125; Watt 1960, 541.

156. In response, Italy covertly explored the possibility of forming and leading a bloc of Balkan neutrals (Marzari 1970).

157. Ciano 1939; 1945, 176, 179.

158. Cliadakis 1974, 177–78; DGFP, D, VIII, no. 504.

159. Umbreit 1991a, 305; Watt 1960, 541–42; Knox 1982, 59–67; Lowe and Marzari 1975, 350; Shorrock 1988, 277.

160. Shorrock 1988, 278; Lowe and Marzari 1975, 359.

161. Salerno 2002, 158.

162. Woodward 1970, 147–48; DGFP, D, VIII, nos. 599, 634; Ciano 1945, 209–10; Salerno 2002, 165; Mallet 1997, 155–56; Schreiber 1995, 39; Knox 1982, 69–74; Lowe and Mazari 1975, 362.

163. Woodward 1970, 151–54; DGFP, D, VIII, nos. 647, 652.

164. Sullivan 2007, 125.

165. Ciano 1945, 223; Woodward 1970, 149.

166. Knox 1982, 46; Cliadakis 1974, 180; Shorrock 1988, 278.

167. Ciano 1945, 230.

168. Umbreit 1991a, 306; Salerno 2002, 184; Ciano 1945, 232–34.

169. Schreiber 1995, 46–47; Knox 1982, 94–95.

170. Ciano 1945, 237.

171. Shorrock 1988, 274; Kershaw 2007, 151; Schreiber 1995, 13; Umbreit 1991a, 308.

172. Cliadakis 1974, 181.

173. Cliadakis 1974, 180.

174. DGFP, D, IX, nos. 339, 340, 342; Ciano 1945, 244–45, 251, 255.

175. Mallet 1997, 158; Schreiber 1995, 104; Shorrock 1988, 281–84.

176. Ciano 1945, 249.

177. Lowe and Marzari 1975, 223; Salerno 2002, 13; Mack Smith 1969, 463; Mallet 2003, 149; and, in the same spirit, Davidson 2002, 148–50. By contrast, Toscano (1970, 198–200) argues that it was not until late March 1939 that there was no turning back for Mussolini. And Shorrock (1988, 264) argues that "even as late as April [1939] . . . Mussolini had made no irrevocable commitment to the Axis."

178. Mallet 2003, 149, 164.

179. Cliadakis 1974, 175; FRUS, 1940, I, no. 28, 32, 104. Also see Gin 2014, 1005–8.

180. Ciano 1945, 230. Also see 224, 220.

181. Mallet (2003, 219–20) implies that Mussolini would have gone to war in June 1940 regardless of the course of events in the Battle of France, but does not address the question directly.

182. Lowe and Marzari 1975, 315; Seton-Watson 1983, 279; Gin 2014, 1005–13.

183. DGFP, D, VII, nos. 301, 271.

184. Ciano 1939, 13; Cliadakis 1974, 177–78; Schreiber 1995, 23. In his diary for 17 December, Ciano wrote: "If it had previously been difficult to get Italy to enter the war on Germany's side, this is impossible now they [Italians] understand the profound truth and background . . . that Germany betrayed us twice." On 19 December, he described the speech as giving notice of the "funeral of the Axis" (Ciano 1945, 176, 185).

185. DGFP, D, VIII, no. 504, 605. Mussolini's letter also proposed that Hitler should reconstitute the "Polish state under the German aegis," because that would help "resolve the war and constitute a condition sufficient for peace." And then he warned that any "further step in your relations with Moscow would have catastrophic repercussions in Italy."

186. Sullivan 2007, 125. Also see Mack Smith 2000, 200; Ciano 1945, 191; Weizsäcker 1951, 222; Gin 2014, 1005.

187. On Mussolini's repeated efforts to avert, through mediation, a German attack against Poland, and then in the west, see Schmitt 1955, 165–67; Cliadakis 1974, 175–76; Watt 1960, 541–42; Sullivan 2007, 123–24; Gin 2014, 1005–6; Ciano 1945, 134–37.

188. On these lines, see Shorrock 1988, 273–74.

189. Haas 2003; 2005; 2014.

190. Sullivan 1998, 86–88; Cassels 1983, 262.

191. Haas 2003, 53, 72–73.

192. Schreiber 1995, 39. For a different critique of the ideology argument, see Davidson 2002, 156–57.

193. Watt 1960, 522.

194. Mussolini declared to Ciano: "If they hope to move the frontier post one single yard, they must learn that it cannot be done without the most bitter war in which I shall combine the whole world into a coalition against Germanism. And we shall crush Germany for at least two centuries" (Ciano 1953, 105–6).

195. "I [am] completely disgusted with the Germans," he wrote, "with their leader, with their way of doing things. They have betrayed us and lied to us. . . . They are traitors and we must not have any scruples in ditching them. . . . The Italian people do not want to fight alongside Germany in order to give it that power with which one day it will threaten us. I no longer have doubts about the Germans. Tomorrow it will be Hungary's turn, then ours. . . . The Germans are treacherous and deceitful. Any kind of alliance with them becomes a bad alliance" (Ciano 1945, August 13, 14, 27).

7. Germany Divides the USSR from Britain and France, 1939

1. Weinberg 1980, 629.

2. Weizsäcker 1951, 187, 200.

3. Kissinger 1994, 348–49. Also see Kennan 1961, 328.

4. Weizsäcker explained on 22 August 1939: "We had to dispel the Soviet Government's feeling of being menaced in the event of a German-Polish conflict. The best means of doing this was to continue in concrete form the talks on a non-aggression pact to the point now reached. We thus at the same time realized our original aim of hampering the Anglo-French encirclement negotiations in Moscow" (DGFP, D, VII, no. 180).

5. In May 1939, the German Foreign Office informed the German ambassador in Moscow, "We are of the opinion here that the English-Russian combination certainly will not be easy to prevent" (NSR).

6. The conditions in the case are coded as follows: German perceptions of USSR's strategic weight—High; German perceptions of relative reward power—High; Attempted alignment change—Low; Germany's alliance constraints—Low; Outcome—Success.

7. Neilson 2009, 293, 276.

8. Toscano 1967, 55.

9. NSR, 10. Also see NSR, 11; Ciano 1945, 73–74.

10. Weizsäcker 1951, 186.

11. Messerschmidt 1998, 702.

12. Paraphrase by Weinberg 1980, 611.

13. DGFP, D, VII, appendix I, 22 August 1939, 559.

14. Messerschmidt 1998, 706.

15. Messerschmidt 1998, 703.

16. Crawford 2018, 239–40.

17. Robertson 1963, 181.

18. Overy 2009, 22; DGFP, D, VII, nos. 43, 47; Ciano 1945, 119.

19. DGFP, D, VI, no. 433.

20. Kennan 1961, 309.

21. DGFP, D, VI, no. 211; Toscano 1970, 62.
22. Messerschmidt 1998, 703. Also see Weinberg 1980, 628, 631.
23. Paraphrase by Weinberg 1980, 611. DGFP, D, VII, nos. 192, 193; DBFP, 3, VII, no. 314. Also see Robertson 1963, 176, 180; Powell 2006, 196.
24. Weizsäcker 1951, 203; Robertson 1963, 343, 177.
25. DGFP, D, VII, no. 43; Robertson 1963, 177.
26. Poole 1946–47, 142.
27. NSR, 9.
28. On trade negotiations before August 1939, see Newnham 2002, 93–102; Ericson 1998.
29. DGFP, D, IV, no. 211.
30. DGFP, D, VI, no. 437, emphasis in original.
31. E.g., see NSR, no. 1.
32. Ericson 1998, 265, 270. On the German side, there was a reciprocal demand for agricultural and raw materials that the Soviets were well positioned to exchange: manganese, wolfram, oil, grain, soybeans.
33. Ericson 1998, 270.
34. DGFP, D, VII, no. 700.
35. Ericson 1998, 271. Also see Kotkin 2017, 661.
36. Molotov speech, 31 August 1939, BDFA, II, A, 15, no. 111, 147.
37. DGFP, D, VI, nos. 486, 520.
38. DGFP, D, VII, appendix I, 14 August 1939, 553.
39. NSR, 9.
40. DGFP, D, VII, no. 715.
41. DGFP, D, VI, no. 760.
42. DGFP, D, VI, no. 776; DGFP, D, VII, no. 61.
43. DGFP, D, VII, no. 70.
44. DGFP, D, VII, nos. 75, 79.
45. DGFP, D, VII, appendix I, 22 August 1939.
46. As Ribbentrop wrote in retrospect: "The Anglo-French policy of encirclement against Germany [had] been so greatly intensified" that Germany "had been forced to take desperate measures . . . to neutralize the Soviet Union quickly by concluding the nonaggression pact" (Hosoya 1976, 192).
47. DGFP, D, VI, no. 211.
48. Toscano 1970, 62; Weizsäcker 1974, 186–87.
49. Toscano 1970, 65.
50. DBFP, D, VI, no. 437.
51. Hilger and Meyer 1953, 298–99.
52. Weinberg 1972, 24. Also see Moorhouse 2014, 29.
53. DGFP, D, VI, no. 211. Also see DGFP, D, VII, no. 271.
54. Toscano 1967, 311, 313.
55. Toscano 1967, 291.
56. DGFP, D, VI, no. 523.
57. DGFP, D, VI, no. 569.
58. Sullivan 2002, 132–33; Petracchi 1997.
59. Sullivan 2002, 133.
60. Petracchi 1997, 506. Also see DGFP, D, VI, nos. 211, 341, 523, 536; DGFP, D, VII, no. 79.
61. Petracchi 1997, 506–7.
62. Weinberg 1980, 565–66.
63. Krebs 1997, 542.
64. NSR, 18.
65. Weinberg 1980, 601–2, 630; Messerschmidt 1998, 708; Ikle 1956, 132–34.
66. Weinberg 1980, 629.
67. Moorhouse 2014, 31.
68. Thornton 1964, 6, 7, 10.
69. Garver 2003, 197.

70. Tinch 1951; Coox 1990.
71. Watt 1957, 157.
72. Carr 1964, 87.
73. Beloff 1949, 214–18.
74. Toscano 1967, 46n75, 53.
75. BDFA, II, A, 15, no. 40; Resis 2000, 35–36; Pons 2002, 150.
76. Layne 2008, 397–437; Ripsman and Levy 2008, 148–81.
77. Haas 2014, 715–53.
78. Neilson 1993, 215–16, 283; Herndon 1983, 305–11. But see Kahn 2013.
79. DBFP, 3, V, nos. 16, 44, 53, 57, 59, 61, 66, 10, 101–3, 128, 136.
80. DBFP, 3, V, nos. 166, 170, 176.
81. SPE, nos. 108, 123; DBFP, 3, IV, no. X; DGFP, D, VI, no. 75.
82. DBFP, 3, IV, nos. 433, 461; SPE, nos. 116, 121, 122.
83. DBFP, 3, V, nos. 1, 3, 37, 40, 42, 170.
84. Kahn 2013, 734–35; Manne 1974, 12; Herndon 1983, 309.
85. SPE, no. 135; DBFP, 3, V, nos. 201, 670.
86. SPE, no. 155; Roberts 1996, 390.
87. DBFP, 3, V, no. 42.
88. DGFP, D, VI, no. 185; SPE, no. 159.
89. Resis 2000, 56n73; Kotkin 2017, 636.
90. DBFP, 3, V, no. 166.
91. DBFP, 3, V, no. 201; SPE, no. 171; Kotkin 2017, 621.
92. Resis 2000, 46.
93. Pons 2002, 158.
94. SPE, no. 172; DBFP, 3, V, nos. 305, 312, 316, 318, 327, 344, 350, 397, 433, 436, 441, 481, 494, 520, 539, 548, 550, 554, 589.
95. DBFP, 3, V, nos. 608–9, 624.
96. Neilson 1993, 218; 2009, 292–93; Imlay 2003, 98; Herndon 1983, 310; Manne 1974, 22–23; Kahn 2013, 736–37.
97. Neilson 2009, 295.
98. Manne 1974, 26.
99. DBFP, 3, V, nos. 401, 436, 546, 730.
100. Fleischhauer 1997, 35; DBFP, 3, V, nos. 527, 530, 670, 689, 730; DBFP, 3, VI, nos. 38, 42, 60, 69, 139, 193.
101. DBFP, 3, V, nos. 634, 648; SPE, nos. 227, 229, 230.
102. For British concessions to Soviet demands over the alliance's political terms, see DBFP, 3, VI, nos. 89, 94, 112, 113, 127, 135, 151, 171, 185, 199, 251–53, 290, 298, 329.
103. Weinberg 1972, 22–23; 1980, 568.
104. NSR, 1–2; Handel 1981, 105–6.
105. NSR, 2.
106. Weinberg 1972, 25.
107. Hilger and Meyer 1953, 293–95; Ericson 1998, 270.
108. DGFP, D, VI, no. 424.
109. Toscano 1967, 300, 359n63.
110. Weizsäcker's words, NSR, 13–14.
111. DGFP, D, VI, 460.
112. Weinberg 1972, 28.
113. Weinberg 1972, 28.
114. Weinberg 1972, 31.
115. NSR, 13–14; DGFP, D, VI, no. 451.
116. SPE, no. 232.
117. Ericson 1998, 271. Also see Weinberg 1972, 34–38; Handel 1981, 113–15.
118. NSR, 34.
119. NSR, 36.
120. DGFP, D, VI, no. 574.

121. Weizsäcker 1951, 199. Also see Hilger and Meyer 1953, 298.
122. NSR, 37–39; Roberts 1995, 84.
123. NSR, 40; also see 36, 41. German officials understood that Baltic guarantees was a key concern for Moscow in its negotiations with Britain and France. DGFP, D, VI, no. 486; DGFP, D, VII, appendix I, 19 August 1939, 553.
124. Weizsäcker 1974, 181. Also see Weinberg 1980, 608; Fleischhauer 1997, 40.
125. Fleischhauer 1997, 36.
126. Uldricks (2009, 75) argues that this has become clear with recent "greater availability of Soviet documents."
127. SPE, nos. 317, 318; DBFP, 3, VII, nos. 2, 34.
128. DBFP, 3, VII, nos. 19, 22, 26, 29, 30, 39, 52, 60, 70, 87, 88; SPE, nos. 326, 333–36.
129. NSR, 50.
130. DGFP, D, VII, nos. 70, 79.
131. DGFP, D, VII, nos. 75, 92, 105.
132. DBFP, 3, VII, no. 105.
133. DGFP, D, VII, nos. 142, 159; DBFP, 3, VII, no. 153.
134. For the nonaggression pact and secret protocol, see DGFP, D, VII, nos. 228, 229.
135. Weizsäcker 1951, 200.
136. Weinberg 1980, 629.
137. DIA 1939–1946, 4–5.
138. Uldricks 2009, 70; Haslam 1992, 133; Weinberg 1980, 606; Crawford 2012, 262–63.
139. Vladimir Pozniakov, who researched the archives of Soviet military intelligence, writes: "'Most of all . . . the Kremlin feared the prospect of joint action against the USSR by Germany and Japan" (Pozniakov 2000, 224–26).
140. Weinberg 1980, 616.
141. Messerschmidt 1990, 703–6; Weizsäcker 1951, 157, 181.
142. On propelling factors in qualitative analysis, see Copeland 2015, 72–73.
143. For a good summary of Stalin's retrospective explanations of his calculations in August 1939, which were given after the German invasion of the USSR, see Roberts 2002, 93–99.
144. On ideological inhibitions, see Moorhouse 2014, 32; Steiner 2011, 737; Shaw 2003; Carley 1993, 332; 1999. The most compelling assessment of the impact of the ideological factor is found in Haas 2003, 73–74; 2005, 134–35. The claim that British dilatoriness—induced by ideology—caused the alliance talks to fail is rebutted by Strang 2008, 513–14. Also see Roberts 2006, 31.
145. Roberts 2006, 34. The claim tracks almost exactly Soviet propaganda after the fact, which placed all blame on Britain and France. Molotov's 1 September 1939 speech to the Soviet Supreme Council denounced the Allies' "extreme dilatoriness" and "unserious attitude toward the negotiations" (BDFA, II, A, 15, no. 111, 146).
146. See Uldricks 2009, 71, which reviews recent works in Russian historiography that take this line. Also see Uldricks 2012, 169; Roberts 2006, 34. The original rendition was Voroshilov's: "The military conversations with England and France were not broken off because the U.S.S.R. had concluded a non-aggression pact with Germany; on the contrary, the U.S.S.R. concluded that pact because, among other things, the military conversations with England and France had reached a deadlock as the result of insurmountable differences of opinion" (*Izvestiya* interview of Soviet Commissar for War Kliment Voroshilov, 27 August 1939, BDFA, II, A, 15, no. 109, 142).
147. See Resis 2000, 47; Roberts 1996, 399; Strang 2006, 17.
148. DBFP, 3, VI, nos. 253, 298 (esp. p. 335), 342, 378–79, 414, 429, 435, 473–74, 483, 493, 497.
149. DBFP, 3, VI, nos. 414, 416, 494.
150. DBFP, 3, VII, nos. 512, 525, 527.
151. Roberts 2006, 33.
152. Kotkin 2017, 636, emphasis in the original, 640, 643.
153. Roberts 2006, 31; Carr 1949, 102–3.
154. Pons 2002.
155. Strang 2008; Moorhouse 2014, 26–27; Schweller 1998, 167.
156. Ikle 1964, 55–56.

157. Kotkin 2017, 621.
158. DBFP, 3, VI, nos. 73, 69, 89, 103; SPE, no. 330.
159. Carr 1949, 104.
160. On this point, also see Haas 2012c, 284, 304.
161. Weizsäcker 1951, 186.
162. Haslam 1997, 787.
163. Kotkin 2017, 675.
164. Kissinger 1994, 337; Fleischhauer 1997, 37.
165. Roberts 2006, 32.
166. For example, Moorhouse 2014, 34; Haas 2012c, 304. On the Soviet leaders' distrust of Hitler, see Kotkin 2017, 681–82; Roberts 1992, 61–66.
167. Haslam 1997, 787; Manne 1981, 97.
168. Gorodetsky 1999, 7; Fleischhauer 1997, 39.
169. On the ideological conflict, see Moorhouse 2014, 15–18.
170. Moorhouse 2014, 31.
171. Weizsäcker 1951, 187.
172. Kotkin 2017, 673.
173. Haas 2003, 74.
174. Haas 2014.

8. Britain and the United States Neutralize Spain, 1940–41

1. Colvin 1950, 21. Also see Leitz 2001, 114; Neumann 1946, 275.
2. For overviews, see Stone 2005; Woodward 1970, 433–52; Feis 1966; Puzzo 1962; Fox 1959, chap. 6; Duff 1956, 256–85; Langer and Gleason 1953, 60–64.
3. The case conditions are coded as follows: Initiator—Britain; British perceptions of Spain's strategic weight—High; British perceptions of relative reward power—High; Attempted alignment change—Low; Alliance constraints—High; Allied Strategic Consensus—Yes; Outcome—Success.
4. CID 1939. How much strategic weight they attributed to Spain is indicated by how they compared it to the Soviet Union: if the latter would otherwise stay neutral, then "from the military point of view, the advantages of an alliance with Russia would not offset the disadvantages of the open hostility of Spain" (CID 1939).
5. Thus, in November 1940, Churchill wrote FDR: "The occupation by Germany of both sides of the Straits would be a grievous addition to our naval strain, already severe" (Loewenheim, Langley, and Jonas 1975, 121). Also see Sherwood 1948, 316.
6. Churchill 1949, 460.
7. Smyth 1986, 122–23.
8. Smyth 1986, 61; Feis 1966, 50.
9. BDFA, III, F, 13, 95. For Hoare's similar summation of the policy logic to Halifax, see 105.
10. BDFA, III, F, 13, 109.
11. Loewenheim, Langley, and Jonas 1975, 121.
12. BDFA, III, F, 13, 141.
13. In September, Suñer informed Ribbentrop that Hoare had "intimated" that "England would be prepared to see to it that after the war French Morocco would be ceded to Spain" (DGFP, D, XI, no. 97, 167).
14. Smyth 1986, 44.
15. BDFA, III, F, 13, 98.
16. BDFA, III, F, 13, 131.
17. As Franco's military chief of staff put it to Hitler on 16 June 1940, Spain was "fully and entirely in sympathy with Germany" because it was "fighting against the same enemies who had opposed Spain in the Civil War" (DGFP, D, IX, no. 456, 585). Or, as Franco put it to Hitler in October 1940, "Spain has in every moment felt herself at one with the Axis. . . . A profound unity has arisen among them" (SGA, no. 8).

18. Haas 2003, 35.
19. Pike 1982, 371; Smyth 1986, 33.
20. BDFA, III, F, 13, 142; also see 93. In Suñer's own words, see DGFP, D, XI, nos. 63, 707.
21. Preston 1990, 53, 55.
22. As Suñer explained to Ribbentrop in January 1941 (DGFP, D, XI, no. 707, 1189).
23. Smyth 1986, 86; SGA, no. 4. On Gibraltar, also see BDFA, III, F, 13, 83–84; DGFP, D, IX, nos. 456, 586; DIHGF, 286.
24. Germany expended 500 million reichsmarks in the civil war, and Italy expended 700 million reichsmarks (Detwiler 1971, 57n6).
25. Puzzo 1962, 206.
26. Preston 1990, 52.
27. Puzzo 1962, 209.
28. DGFP, D, IX, no. 129, 191.
29. DGFP D, IX, no. 423; Hernández-Sandoica and Moradiellos 2002, 251; Preston 1990, 59.
30. DGFP, D, IX, 488. Simultaneously, Madrid sought, to no avail, British help in extracting from collapsing France Spanish-claimed territory in Morocco (BDFA, III, F, 13, 92).
31. SGA, no. 2.
32. Schreiber 1995, 184–86.
33. Smyth 1986, 48.
34. On these points, see Umbreit 1991b, 411; Burdick 1968, chap. 1; Goda 1999.
35. Leitz 1996, 186; Burdick 1968, 25–26; Schreiber 1995, 200–245.
36. Detwiler 1971, 41; also see Smyth 1986, 41.
37. Burdick 1968, 30.
38. DGFP, D, X, no. 274.
39. DGFP, D, X, nos. 313, 369.
40. DGFP, D, X, no. 346; Burdick 1968, 41.
41. Puzzo 1962, 223; Burdick 1968, 42.
42. Burdick 1968, 43.
43. Kershaw 2007, 210.
44. FRUS 1940, II, 832.
45. Loewenheim, Langley, and Jonas 1975, 121.
46. Hull 1948, 1187.
47. Overy 1995, 15. On U.S. policy toward Spain early in the war, see Buchanan 2013, chap. 3.
48. Stoller 2000, 28.
49. FRUS 1940, II, 850.
50. Stoller 2000, 30–31.
51. Churchill 1949, 23–24.
52. In June 1940, FDR wrote to Churchill, "As naval people, you and I fully appreciate that the vital strength of the Fleet and command of the seas mean, in the long run, the saving of the democracy" (Sherwood 1948, 148).
53. Conn and Fairchild 1960, 7–9.
54. Conn and Fairchild 1960, 26.
55. Conn and Fairchild 1960, 32.
56. On the corresponding development of German ambitions, see Goda 1998b.
57. "May 1941: Fireside Chat 17: On an Unlimited National Emergency," Miller Center, University of Virginia, https://millercenter.org/the-presidency/presidential-speeches/may-27-1941-fireside-chat-17-unlimited-national-emergency.
58. Conn and Fairchild 1960, 36. The connection of U.S. security to British survival had been emphasized in the "Stark Memorandum" of October 1940, which first articulated the grand strategic concept of focusing U.S. war effort on "Germany first" (Stoller 2000, 32).
59. Langer and Gleason 1952, 775–76.
60. Sherwood 1948, 136–37.
61. Watson 1950, 117–18.
62. Langer and Gleason 1953, 177; Watson 1950, 117.
63. Watson 1950, 118.

64. Sherwood 1948, 296.
65. Loewenheim, Langley, and Jonas 1975, 140–41.
66. Smyth 1999, 204.
67. Detwiler 1971, 52. Likewise, see Preston 1990, 52; 1992, 16; Leitz 2001, 114.
68. Hernández-Sandoica and Moradiellos 2002, 247. Smyth (1986, 64) describes "the tenor of British blockade and economic policy in general" as "predominantly conciliatory rather than coercive."
69. Smyth 1986, 47.
70. Smyth 1986, 49–50. Also see DGFP, D, XI, no. 97, 167.
71. Goda 1998a, 179, and n79.
72. Smyth 1986, 59.
73. Puzzo 1962, 218; Detwiler 1971 42.
74. On the oil embargo, and latter supply, see Caruana and Rockman 2006, 21, 38, 40; Smyth 1986, 61; Leitz 1998.
75. Langer and Gleason 1952, 741. Also see Schreiber 1995, 149.
76. Smyth 1986, 61; Feis 1966, 50.
77. Smyth 1986, 63. Says Feis (1966, 52) about the importance of this agreement: "The opposite course, a refusal to permit Spain to secure oil, might quite possibly have caused the Spanish government to come to terms with Germany."
78. DGFP, D, XI, no. 63, 89; no. 67, 99.
79. Feis 1966, 61–62.
80. SGA, no. 4.
81. Suñer claimed later that if Hitler had agreed to guarantee Spain's territorial claims in North Africa, Spain would have entered war at this time (Smyth 1986, 87).
82. DGFP, D, XI, no. 63, 89. Halder recorded in his diary at this time (14 September 1940) that Hitler's approach was to make promises to meet all of Spain's requests in exchange for its war effort, "regardless of whether they could be kept or not" (Burdick 1968, 43n17).
83. According to Leitz, the only concrete German action on this score was a contract to provide 20,000 tons of wheat and 10,000 tons of rye by March 1944. Of this, only 397 tons had reached Spain by February 1941 (Leitz 1996, 127n5).
84. SGA, no. 4. The next day, Suñer met with Ribbentrop, repeating that Spain was "now willing to join the fight in spite of [economic] difficulties in proportion to the support that could be given her in augmenting her inadequate supplies," but she wanted in return "all of French Morocco in her hands" (DGFP, D, XI, no. 63, 83, 85).
85. Hitler promised "to provide economic help to the greatest extent possible for Germany herself," but that assistance could "only be of an emergency or temporary nature" (DGFP, D, XI, no. 70, 106–7).
86. SGA, no. 5.
87. Smyth 1986, 93.
88. DGFP, D, XI, no. 116, 200.
89. Hitler expressed willingness to forego bases in French Morocco if Spain would cede to German control a Canary island. Hitler's major concern was defending the Continent from the emerging Atlantic alliance (DGFP, D, XI, 250).
90. Puzzo 1962, 227; Schreiber 1995, 190.
91. SGA, no. 7.
92. FRUS 1940, II, 821–23; Woodward 1970, 499; Reynolds 1981, 186–87.
93. See SGA, no. 8; DGFP D, XI, no. 222; Burdick 1968, 50–53; Colvin 1950; Preston 1992.
94. Franco told Hitler that the specifics of German promises of economic assistance should be "enshrined . . . in a protocol" (Preston 1992, 6).
95. Leitz 1996, 132.
96. Detwiler 1971, 43. Hitler floated a formula by which French concessions to Spain would be offset by transfers of conquered British colonies.
97. DGFP, D, XI, no. 221, 377–79.
98. Schreiber 1995, 193.
99. Rich 1973, 165, 171.

100. BDFA, III, F, 13, 147.
101. Quoted in Preston 1992, 13.
102. Franco letter quoted in Goda 1998a, 181. The letter was not found in the German archives after the war, and no record of it was ever released by Madrid. The only version of it appears in Suñer's second volume of memoirs, published in 1977. The actual letter did lead Halder to record this in his diary on 4 November 1940: "Franco has promised that he would seriously carry out the verbal agreements—viz, that he would enter the war on our side" (DGFP, D, XI, no. 273, 452). Also see Burdick 1968, 63; Preston 1990, 69.
103. On 9 November, Suñer received the final version of the secret protocol, and apparently signed it (DGFP, D, XI, nos. 294, 312). See also 244, 466; Schreiber 1995, 193.
104. BDFA, III, F, 13, 156, 158.
105. Woodward 1970, 440.
106. FRUS 1940, II, 827.
107. Feis 1966, 99.
108. FRUS 1940, II, 828–29.
109. FRUS 1940, II, 832; Woodward 1970, 441.
110. FRUS 1940, II, 833.
111. FRUS 1940, II, 836.
112. FRUS 1940, II, 839.
113. FRUS 1940, II, 838.
114. Loewenheim, Langley, and Jonas 1975, 121; Woodward 1970, 441–42.
115. DGFP, D, XI, no. 294, 478–79.
116. DGFP, D, XI, no. 352, 600.
117. DGFP, D, XI, no. 352, 605–6.
118. DGFP, D, XI, no. 357, 623.
119. Preston 1990, 69.
120. BDFA, III, F, 13, 165.
121. Burdick 1968, 66; DGFP, D, XI, no. 414.
122. Burdick 1968, 66; DGFP, D, XI, no. 420.
123. Burdick 1968, 98.
124. FRUS 1940, II, 839–41.
125. FRUS 1940, II, 844.
126. BDFA, III, F, 13, 168; Leitz 1996, 141n61.
127. BDFA, III, F, 13, 170.
128. Burdick 1968, 99.
129. BDFA, III, F, 13, 173–74; Leitz 1996, 142.
130. SGA, no. 11.
131. DGFP, D, XI, no. 476, 816.
132. DGFP, D, XI, no. 479, 824n2. "The scarcity of foodstuffs," wrote Stohrer, "has really become quite disastrous in recent weeks" (825).
133. DGFP, D, XI, no. 476, 817; Burdick 1968, 104.
134. FRUS 1940, II, 847; Feis 1966, 106; Stone 2005, 157.
135. FRUS 1940, II, 848–50. Hull wrote in late December, "The whole question of assistance to Spain is based on our policy of furnishing all possible assistance short of war to Great Britain in her defense against aggression" (851–52). Also see Langer and Gleason 1953, 84.
136. FRUS 1940, II, 854.
137. Smyth 1986, 137–38, 169, 174; Stone 2005, 158.
138. DGFP D, XI, nos. 677, 695.
139. DGFP, D, XI, no. 682, 1157, emphasis in original; no. 702, 1184.
140. DGFP, D, XI, no. 707.
141. SGA, no. 12.
142. Burdick 1968, 119.
143. DGFP, D, XII, no. 46; Leitz 1996, 136–38.
144. On why Hitler did not just invade Spain and take Gibraltar at this time, see Rich 1973, 75–176; Burdick 1968, 97–130 (esp. 115–16, 122, 124); Leitz 2001, 126–27.

145. Stone 2005, 159.
146. Writes Feis: "Spain had [then] been permitted freely to supply itself with all [U.S.] products not in short supply, including ordinary grades of oil. The only limits to this economic transfusion had been the lack of dollars and the British blockade" (Feis 1966, 138).
147. On the role of the Spanish "Blue Division" on the eastern front, see Saenz-Frances 2009, 84–100.
148. Woodward 1970, 452.
149. Feis 1966, 142.
150. Sherwood 1948, 304.
151. Feis 1966, 14.
152. Trevor Roper 1981, 360, 362.
153. Detwiler 1971, 53. Also see Colvin 1950, 21.
154. Rather than greed, fear and distrust of Hitler also might have fed a determination to stay out: if Spain joined the Axis and let German forces into Spain, and Germany won the war, Hitler might make Spain a vassal state. I am grateful to a reviewer for noting this.
155. See Hernández-Sandoica and Moradiellos 2002, 242; Leitz 2001, 114n2; Pike 1982; Preston 1990, 56; 1992.
156. Schweller 2006; Taliaferro 2006.
157. For contemporary judgments along these lines, see Smyth 1986, 32; BDFA, III, F, 13, nos. 8, 37, 73, 77, 113–14, 129; DGFP, D, X, no. 355; XI, nos. 335, 497, 677. For a starkly pessimistic internal report to Franco and his associates in September 1940, see DIHGF, no. 88.
158. See Smyth 1986, chap. 3.
159. Feis 1966, 28–29.
160. For examples, see Smyth 1986, 90–91; Pike 1982, 379; Goda 1998a, 181.
161. Goda 1998a, 181; Burdick 1986, 63; Preston 1990, 69; DGFP, D, XI, no. 273, 452.
162. Burdick 1968, 66; DGFP, D, XI, no. 414.
163. Burdick 1968, 66; DGFP, D, XI, no. 420.

9. Germany Fails to Realign Turkey, 1941

1. The case conditions are coded as follows: Initiator—Germany; German perceptions of Turkey's strategic weight—Low; German perceptions of relative reward power—High; Attempted alignment change—High; Alliance constraints—High; Allied Strategic Consensus—No; Outcome—Failure.
2. Flacker 1998, 216.
3. Nicosia 2015, 154–60.
4. DGFP, D, XII, no. 133.
5. Schwantiz 2004; Flacker 1998.
6. Roth 2004, 198.
7. Umbreit 1991b, 408–15; Rich 1973, 165.
8. DGFP, D, XII, nos. 299, 415.
9. DGFP, D, XII, no. 543.
10. More generally, it would erode British morale and prestige. As Ribbentrop explained to Mussolini and Ciano on 3 June 1941, "From a propaganda point of view, the conclusion of an agreement [with Turkey] would . . . be a heavy blow to England, because Turkey was the only country that England still boasted as an ally" (DGFP, D, XII, no. 584).
11. DGFP, D, VII, no. 208 (359).
12. DGFP, D, VII, no. 303.
13. DGFP, D, XII, no. 514.
14. DGFP, D, XII, no. 404.
15. DGFP, D, XII, no. 514
16. DGFP, D, XII, no, 538.
17. DGFP, D, XII, no. 514 (814, 816).

18. DGFP, D, XII, no. 303.
19. DGFP, D, XII, no. 538.
20. DGFP, D, XII, no. 523 (829n4).
21. Schonherr 1997, 481–84.
22. Woodward 1970, 24; Schreiber 1995, 154–55.
23. See chapter 6.
24. Woodward 1970, 24.
25. Shields 2011, 44.
26. Hale 2000, 67; Trask 1971, 234–35.
27. Woodward 1970, 27.
28. Woodward 1970, 25; Schreiber 1995, 157. For the key provision, see DGFP, D, XII, no. 523, n4.
29. Millman 1998, 198.
30. Hale 2000, 84; Millman 1998, 231; Schreiber 1995, 153.
31. Weber 1979, 45.
32. Weber 1979, 47–48.
33. Schreiber 1995, 156; Woodward 1970, 245–47.
34. Woodward 1970, 503.
35. Millman 1998, 371–73.
36. Weber 1979, 51.
37. Weber 1979, 52; Weisband 1973, 103; Schreiber 1995, 159–60.
38. Schonherr 1997, 489–90; Woodward 1970, 512–14, 523–24; BDFA, III, B, 1, nos. 73 (160), 79 (164), 80 (165).
39. Derengil 1989, 112; Woodward 1970, 513.
40. On these motivations to bandwagon, see Walt 1987; Schweller 1998.
41. Weber 1979, 60.
42. DGFP, D, XI, nos. 436, 443.
43. On Spain, see chapter 8.
44. DGFP, D, XII, nos. 113, 119.
45. DGFP, D, XII, no. 303 (505).
46. DGFP, D, XII, nos. 514 (816–17), 522 (828).
47. DGFP, D, X, nos. 200, 370; Nicosia 2015, 145–46; Schreiber 1995, 178.
48. Schreiber 1995, 176–77; DGFP, D, X, no. 370.
49. Weber 1979, 13.
50. For Ribbentrop's concerns on this score, see DGFP, D, XII, nos. 555, 607.
51. On Japan's "Pan-Asianism" and geopolitical ambitions in the Islamic world, see Esenbel 2004; Aydin 2008.
52. Weber 1979, 97–98; DGFP, D, XII, no. 78.
53. Flacker 1998, 224.
54. Schreiber 1995, 176.
55. Ciano 1945, 368, 370.
56. DGFP, D, XII, no. 177.
57. DGFP, D, VII, no. 208 (359).
58. DGFP, D, XII, no. 523, 829n4.
59. DGFP, D, XII nos. 529 (836), 538 (849).
60. DGFP, D, XII, no. 566 (913).
61. Millman 1995, 492.
62. DGFP, D, XII, no. 531 (840).
63. DGFP, D, XII, no. 566 (913-14).
64. DGFP, D, XII, no. 837.
65. DGFP, D, XII, nos. 837, 849.
66. DGFP, D, XII, no. 303 (504-505) and n5.
67. DGFP, D, XII, no. 514 (813).
68. DGFP, D, XII, no. 514 (814).

69. DGFP, D, XII, no. 514 (814, 817).
70. DGFP, D, XII, no. 514 (817).
71. DGFP, D, XII, nos. 529 (836), 538 (850).
72. DGFP, D, XII, no. 529 (837).
73. DGFP, D, XII, no. 545.
74. DGFP, D, XII, nos. 545, 555.
75. DGFP, D, XII, no. 555 (886). NB: In the 1923 Treaty of Lausanne, Turkey gave up territory in Bulgaria, the Aegean (the Dodecanese Islands), and Iraq and Syria, among other things.
76. DGFP, D, XII, no. 566.
77. At the same time, the Turks refused to give the British a formal commitment that they would *not* allow German transport to Syria. Derengil 1989, 125.
78. DGFP, D, XII, nos. 545, 555, 565.
79. DGFP, D, XII, no. 555.
80. DGFP, D, XII, no 556.
81. DGFP, D, XII, no. 584 (947); Ciano 1945, 361.
82. On 18 June, Ribbentrop telephoned Ciano with a report on the just signed German-Turkish friendship treaty; Ciano, in his diary, counted it as good news that the agreement had "no secret protocols." Italy had no reason to worry about an arms transport protocol: the relief, then, was likely over the matters in the other protocol—territorial compensation for Turkey. Ciano 1945, 367.
83. DGFP, D, XII, no. 602 (976); Derengil 1989, 125.
84. Millman 1995, 502.
85. Hirszowicz 1966, 181.
86. DGFP, D, XII, no. 133 (239).
87. DGFP, D, XII, no. 559.
88. DGFP, D, XII, no. 633.
89. DGFP, D, XII, no. 555 (886).
90. DGFP, D, XII, nos. 602 (976), 607 (986).
91. Hirszowicz 1966, 138; DGFP, D, XII, nos. 413, 415.
92. Hirszowicz 1966, 147; DGFP, D, XII, nos. 435, 436, 528.
93. Hirszowicz 1966, 151.
94. DGFP, D, XII, no. 577.
95. DGFP, D, XII, no. 582.
96. Weber 1979, 96–97.
97. DGFP, D, XII, no. 555 (885).
98. DGFP, D, XII, no. 565 (912).
99. DGFP, D, XII, no. 588 (955); also no. 582.
100. DGFP, D, XII, no. 623 (1022). For Papen's reply, see no. 625 (1024).
101. DGFP, D, XII, no. 625 (1024n5).
102. DGFP, D, XII, no. 607 (985).
103. DGFP, D, XII, no. 648.
104. Woodward 1970, 583–84.
105. For versions of this interpretation, see Fox 1959, 27–30; Weisband 1973, 41–43; Derengil 1989, 120–22, 125. Weisband's larger theme is that the first and most important tenet of Kemalism was anti-"revisionist-expansionism" (1973, 7–20). He asserts that İnönü was "as little interested in gaining ground as in losing some" (43). In respect to the May–June 1941 negotiations, he cites some of the relevant German documents and Papen's memoires, but, inexplicably, does not discuss the contents that reveal the Turkish leaders' bids for territory (4–43n29). For another view of the competing accounts, see Hale 2000, 88.
106. Derengil 1989, 121.
107. Millman 1995, 502.
108. Derengil 1989, 121–22.

10. When Does Selective Accommodation Work?

1. Six of the eight cases conform to the pattern of strong means and motive beliefs—the combination of conditions that makes attempts "likely." The two nonconforming cases (1 and 8)—were "unlikely" attempts because *either* motivation or means beliefs were weak. Within those cases, there was process tracing evidence consistent with expectations about how the two weak/strong patterns of beliefs might influence behavior.

2. On paired comparisons, see Tarrow 2010; Slater and Ziblatt 2013; George and Bennett 2005, 252.

3. The observed outcomes in this pair were also likely influenced by factors picked up in the initiation condition of perceived reward power—which is not reflected in the table. With Japan, recall, the biggest rewards that Berlin could immediately offer were recognition of gains Japan had already captured. And the ones it dangled as possible future payoffs, Tokyo manipulated to extract more plausible and immediate concessions from its Entente partners. With the U.S., German concessions—in the form of restraints of submarine anticommerce warfare—provided immediate and tangible benefits to Washington that would otherwise be hard and very costly for it to obtain.

4. We focus on the initial phase in this case because in it, the degree of attempted alignment change closely matches that of the other paired case.

5. Also, the primary inducements the Entente and Germany tried to use to manipulate their targets' alignments were similar in nature and strength. The dividers offered territorial gains to be captured from their enemies (i.e., the targets' allies), either directly or swapped from gains earmarked for other members of the divider's coalition. Thus, in 1915 the Entente lured Italy with promised gains in Austro-Hungarian and Ottoman territories. And in 1941, Germany tried to lure Turkey with promised gains in Iraq (then under British control), as well as real estate in the Levant.

6. An important difference between the two cases is found in the initiation conditions. In the second case, recall, German leaders did not perceive Turkey to have high strategic weight. This, as argued earlier, encouraged Berlin to drop the attempt once the high costs of Turkey's demands—vis-à-vis Germany's alliance ties—were made clear.

11. Selective Accommodation in Great Power Competition and U.S. Grand Strategy

1. Liff 2018; Garver and Wang 2010.

2. On deep engagement, see Brooks and Wohlforth 2016; Brooks, Ikenberry, and Wohlforth 2012/13.

3. The DoD's 2018 *National Defense Strategy* seeks explicitly to "strengthen" and "expand Indo-Pacific alliances and partnerships" (DOD 2018, 9). Also see DOD 2019; MacDonald and Parent 2019.

4. NSS 2017, 25.

5. Scobell 2018; Goldstein 2013.

6. On China's escalation tendencies, see Fravel 2008, 27–35; Hyer 2015, 255; Rapp-Hooper 2016.

7. Fravel 2008, 6–9, 18; Hyer 2015, 13–14, 265–66; Gilboy and Heginbotham 2012, 87.

8. I exclude South Korea from the possibilities. The reason is the ROK's lack of strategic weight in this contingency. Although Seoul has a strong army and navy for its size, it is obvious that these capabilities are—and will remain—concentrated on North Korea, by far the most significant threat to South Korean security. For this reason, a South Korean opt-out of a Southeast Asia crisis would be likely, irrespective of any Chinese bid to elicit that response.

9. Liff 2018, 147–48; Oros 2017, 82–83; Fravel 2008, 316–17.

10. Liff 2018, 148; Oros 2017.

11. For a recent example, see Liff 2018, 147. Also see Izumikawa 2018.

12. But see Taffer 2019, who argues that in 2010–14, China tried coercively to distance the U.S. from Japan.

13. Garver 2016, 57.
14. Ganguly 2015.
15. Pant 2016, 45.
16. Hagerty 2016, 145.
17. Quoted in Hagerty 2016, 145.
18. Hagerty 2016, 153; Mohan 2013, 79; Chaudhuri 2016, 27–34.
19. Ali 2018.
20. DOD 2019, 34.
21. WH 2020.
22. Granados 2018; Blank et al. 2015.
23. Pant and Rej 2018, 48; Pant 2016, 137–38, 144; Blank et al. 2015.
24. Singh 2016, 36–40; de Saint-Mezard 2016, 345; Mohan 2013, 30.
25. Collin 2019, 19; Pant and Rej 2018, 48; Blank et al. 2015.
26. Pant 2016, 139; Singh 2016, 36–40; Collin 2019, 18–20. A signal of this appeared in June 2017 when, after a Modi-Trump summit, the U.S. and Indian governments issued a joint statement urging all South China Sea countries to support freedom of navigation in the area. That general call was pointed against China—the only challenger to freedom of navigation in the South China Sea (Pant and Rej 2018, 48).
27. The U.S. National Intelligence Council report *Global Trends 2025: A Transformed World* described India as a "rising heavyweight" and projected that by 2025 it would be one of the four most influential powers in the system, behind the U.S., China, and the EU (NIC 2008). Also see Mishra 2013, 113, 119; Rehman 2009, 131; Das 2016.
28. Brewster (2016, 6–7) notes: "The Indian Ocean is the one area in which India holds a clear military advantage over China." Also see Menon 2016, 47; Saalman 2014, 140.
29. Brewster 2013, 130, 127. Also see Collin 2019, 14–15. On India's continuing buildup in the Andaman and Nicobar Islands, see Baruah 2018.
30. Saalman 2014, 140; Baruah 2018.
31. Brewster 2016, 4.
32. Saalman 2014, 142, 146, 142, 145; Pu 2018, 64. Also see Collin 2019, 18–20; Garver 2016, 59.
33. India's naval strategy designates the Strait of Malacca and the principal international sea lines crossing the Indian Ocean as "primary" areas of interest, and the South and East China Seas and the Western Pacific region as areas of "secondary interest" (Collin 2019, 7).
34. Joshi and Pant 2015, 316.
35. Joshi and Pant 2015, 317–18.
36. Singh 2019; Pant 2016, 147; de Saint-Mezard 2016, 339; Singh 2013, 167–68; Ladwig 2009, 95.
37. Singapore, for example, "has positioned itself as the hub of India's . . . strategic relationships in South-east Asia," while for India, "access to Singapore's port and air facilities" enhances its ability in a crisis "to control the Malacca Strait and project power into the South China Sea" (Brewster 2013, 136, 138). India and Singapore have conducted joint naval exercises annually since 2000; many were in the South China Sea (Collin 2013, 293). The 2011 exercises covered both the Malacca Strait and the South China Sea (Williams 2013, 271). On Indian naval cooperation with Vietnam and the Philippines, see Blank et al. 2015, 136; Mohan 2013, 30; Brewster 2013, 140–41; Williams 2013, 274.
38. Singh 2019.
39. Smith 2014, 128.
40. Such Indian reaction was, for example, expected following the June 2020 Galwan Valley border clash near Askai Chin: Pokharel and Spindle 2020.
41. Hagerty 2013, 133; Blackwill and Tellis 2019, 180; Lalwani and Byrne 2019, 53–54; Tellis 2020.
42. Hyer 2015, passim. Fravel 2008, 18–19, 62; but note that Fravel finds that internal insecurity has been a stronger catalyst for Chinese border compromises than external incentives to divide adversaries (60–62). Also see Yoo 2015.
43. Garver and Wang 2010, 238.
44. Rehman 2009, 128, 139. Likewise, see Hyer 2015, 65.

45. Shankar 2018, 41–42; Mastro and Tarapore 2017.
46. Fang 2014, 123.
47. Fang 2014, 106–7, 10, 87, 91.
48. Fang 2014, 108; Hyer 2015, 57–58.
49. Shankar 2018, 33; Fravel 2008, 41–69.
50. Shankar 2018, 33; Hyer 2015, 53.
51. Consistent with this proposition, Fravel (2008, 58) found that China has generally been more willing to compromise over "low value" contested borderlands than in disputes over offshore islands or homeland areas.
52. Hyer 2015, 58.
53. Kondapolli 2016, 99.
54. Fang 2014, 108; Kondapolli 2016, 99.
55. Pardesi 2016, 182–83; Fang 2014, 108.
56. Hyer 2015, 50, 54, 57.
57. Fang 2014, 114–15.
58. Hyer 2015, 61–62.
59. Collin 2019.
60. Ladwig 2009, 88; Brewster 2016, 4–5; Ji 2016, 12–15; Garver 2016, 54–60; Medcalf 2016, 63–64.
61. MEA-GI 2018; Khurana 2016.
62. Malik 2003, 5.
63. Hyer 2015, 119.
64. Fang 2014, 129.
65. Fang 2014, 135.
66. Fang 2014, 142, 135.
67. Hussain 2016, 135.
68. Yousafzai 2016.
69. Hussain 2016, 134.
70. Lalwani and Byrne 2019; Blackwill and Tellis 2019.
71. Allison 2019.
72. Wolff 2015, 1110.
73. On alliance spirals, see Snyder 1971, 70–71; 1984, 461–62, 468–70; 1997, 194–95, 339–44; Snyder and Diesing 1977, 164, 421, 423–24.
74. As U.S. Defense Secretary James Mattis put it in September 2018, "I see little in the long term that aligns Russia and China" (quoted in Gabuev 2018, 1). Also see Kroenig 2020a, 188; Kroenig 2020b; Stokes and Smith 2020; Aron 2019; Carafano 2019. For theoretical accounts of drivers of a Sino-Russian alliance, see Ross 2019; Hancock and Lobell 2010.
75. There is also a tendency of U.S. policymakers to "deny the trade-off" of an expanding alliance system—that it is itself a driver of Russia-China alignment—and to see, instead, their growing cohesion as a result of other forces, and U.S. alliances as offering "leverage" against it. See, e.g., Stokes 2017; Stokes and Smith 2020; Kroenig 2020b; Colby and Mitchell 2020.
76. For a broader discussion, see Korolev 2018b, 890–98.
77. Mitchell and Grygiel 2016, 2.
78. Brooks and Wohlforth 2015/16, 46.
79. Ross 2018; Layne 2018; Heginbotham et al. 2015; Posen 2009; 2011; NIC 2012. For the counterview, see Beckley 2018; Brooks and Wohlforth 2016.
80. Brooks and Wohlforth 2015/16, 46; 2016, 136.
81. Montgomery 2014, 125. On China's local balancing against U.S. naval power in East Asia, see Ross 2018.
82. Indeed, some alliances that consolidate against a common adversary are germinated by "complementary" local interest. Morgenthau 1959, 188; Jervis 1997, 214, 245–53; Snyder 1997.
83. Also, with both Moscow's and Beijing's brands of "authoritarian capitalism" well entrenched, there is no meaningful ideological difference that would stand in the way of a closer relationship (Haas 2014; also see Kroenig 2020a).
84. WTA 2019, 4, 24.

85. Including mechanisms for military-to-military consultations, and military technical cooperation; regular joint military exercises on land and sea; and intermilitary confidence building measures (Korolev 2018a, 5–14). According to Trenin (2019c), the two militaries are "taking part in joint training; making their weapons systems more compatible; and syncing their communications, logistics, tacts, and military doctrines." Also see Gabuev 2018; Wishnick 2015.

86. Korolev (2018a, 15) sums it: "The China-Russia military partnership is solid and comprehensive. It is also highly institutionalized and shows an upward incremental trend. The two countries view themselves as great powers and share hostility toward American hegemony in world politics. Hence, China-Russia military relations are not ad hoc but rather strategic." Also see Stent 2020; Weitz 2019; Trenin 2019a; 2019b; 2019c; Gady 2019.

87. Gady 2019; Trenin 2019b.

88. Miller and Hardy-Chartrand 2019.

89. Makela 2019; Trenin 2019c.

90. Weitz 2019, 11. Also see Goldstein 2020.

91. Trenin 2019c.

92. Weitz 2019, 12. Also see Gady 2019.

93. Weitz 2019, 15–16.

94. Mastro (2019) argues that the trend of increasing Russian military alignment with China will "complicate the U.S. ability to defend its partners and allies in Asia" by creating greater risks in U.S. military responses to Chinese ambitions.

95. Kendall-Taylor and Shullman 2019, 1. Also see Colby and Mitchell 2020, 129; Stent 2020; Stokes and Smith 2020; Mastro 2019; Weitz 2019, 18; Trenin 2019c; Miller and Hardy-Chartrand 2019; Stokes 2017.

96. But see Blackwill 2020, 35-36; Graham 2019, 142–45; Westad 2019, 95; Kendall-Taylor and Shullman 2019; Luttwak 2017; Wolff 2017, 86–88; Wolf 2014. Stokes and Smith 2020, and Kroenig 2020b, dismiss the option of accommodating Russia to detach it from China, but do not consider in detail what that might entail.

97. DOD 2018, 4, 8–9. Also see DOD 2019; Colby and Mitchell 2020; O'Hanlon 2019, 194–95.

98. This reflects a long-standing, bipartisan preference among U.S. political and military leaders and within the foreign and security policy bureaucracy (Walt 2018; Porter 2018).

99. Mearsheimer 2019, 50.

100. For proposals along these lines, see Wolf 2014; Wolff 2017, 86–88; Bandow 2017; Luttwak 2017; Kendall-Taylor and Shullman 2019; Blackwill 2020.

101. Santora 2020. Also see Coats 2019, 5–6; DOD 2019, 7–8; OSD 2019, 1–2.

102. Thus, in January 2020, Secretary of Defense Mark Esper stated that the U.S. needed to "make this leap into great power competition with Russia and China—China principally" (Esper 2020); also see Blackwill 2020.

103. This is a major assumption because U.S. policy practitioners—even as they concede the importance of not doing things that drive Russia and China together—tend to deny cause-effect linkage between the action of expanding U.S. military alignments in Europe and the reaction of undesirable Russian behavior—whether that be intervention in Georgia or Ukraine, or closer military cooperation with China. Also see Glaser 2019, 83, 85–86.

104. It is important to be clear about this goal, for two reasons. First, some critics of accommodating Russia to detach it from China argue that there is nothing to gain from it because Russia does not have enough power to contribute to U.S. balancing efforts against China (see, e.g., Carafano 2019; Stokes 2017, 2–3). Second, it implies a less costly level of accommodation than would be needed to flip Russia against China—which might require a major U.S. decoupling from NATO. On why Russia cannot directly contribute to balancing against China in Asia, see Ross 2019.

105. MNDRP 2018; Wezeman and Kuimova 2018, 8–10.

106. Wolff 2017, 82.

107. Also see Graham 2019; Kupchan 2019; Luttwak 2017.

108. Goldgeier 1999; Asmus 2002.

109. Kupchan 2017a.

110. Lemon 2018; O'Dwyer 2017.

111. Dahl 2018, 132.
112. Wolff 2015, 1109–10; 2017, 81–83; Mearsheimer 2014.
113. Driscoll and Maliniak 2016; Cooley and Nexon 2016.
114. CRS 2019a, 10–11.
115. Emmott and Siebold 2015. The insistence on "MAP as an integral part of the process" leading to Georgia's accession was reiterated at the NATO 2016 and 2018 summits. See NATO 2016; 2018.
116. In August 2018, German chancellor Angela Merkel stated, "I do not see Georgia's prompt accession to NATO, this is the position of Germany" (France24 2018).
117. CRS 2019b, 38. French prime minister François Fillon declared that letting Ukraine join NATO was "not a good answer to the balance of power within Europe and between Europe and Russia" (Taylor 2014). In 2015, French president François Hollande stated publicly that membership for Ukraine was "undesirable. . . . We must state it clearly, we should tell other countries the truth, including what we are not ready to accept. This is the position of France" (Carpenter 2018). In 2016, at the NATO Warsaw Summit, German foreign minister Frank-Walter Steinmeier stated, "I see a partner relationship between Ukraine and NATO, but not membership" (Carpenter 2018).
118. As the German defense minister told reporters: "More weapons in this area will not bring us closer to a solution." Even the British defense secretary held to that line (Croft and Alexander 2015).
119. CRS 2019a, 16–18; Kuimova and Wezeman 2018, 9–10; CRS 2019b, 30–32.
120. Mitchell 2018; CRS 2019a, 17, 83n.
121. Kuimova and Wezeman 2018, 5–6; CRS 2019a, 10.
122. CRS 2019a, 17.
123. CRS 2019a, 17.
124. Socor 2018.
125. Kuimova and Wezeman 2018, 9–10.
126. CRS 2019b, 30–32, 38.
127. Kupchan 2017b.
128. CRS 2019b, 31, 158n; Rogin 2017.
129. Pinkham 2019.
130. CRS 2019a, 9; 2019b, 38.
131. As proposed by Vershbow 2018.
132. On recent efforts along these lines, see Gould 2019; Abrahamyan 2019; Ukrinform 2017.
133. CRS 2019c, 2; MNDRP 2018.
134. Barnes 2019.
135. Axe 2019; Barnes 2019.
136. Albright and Ivanov 2020.
137. Moniz and Nunn 2019, 156.
138. Moniz and Nunn 2019, 159.
139. Beebe 2019, 173.
140. Kendall-Taylor and Shullman 2019, 4.
141. On the need for domestic legitimacy in U.S. foreign policy, see George 2006; Caldwell 2009.
142. On this, also see Wolff 2017, 86–87.
143. Luttwak 2017, 8.
144. Quoted in Schuman 1933, 58
145. There is no better example of the tendency than President Truman's argument that "there is isn't any difference in totalitarian states. I don't care what you call them—you call them Nazi, Communist or Fascist, or Franco, or anything else—they are all alike" (Gaddis 2005, 64). For the most recent and trenchant expression of the tendency, see Kroenig 2020a. For Kennan's critique, see 41–45, 64–69. Also see Walt 2002, 147–48; Dobbins, Shatz, and Wyne 2019.
146. Posen 2011, 337; Hartmann 1982, 147.
147. Stokes and Smith 2020, 146.
148. George 2006, 16–17.

References

Primary Sources

AHM 1915. Austro-Hungarian Monarchy. 1915. *Italy on the Path of War*. Vienna: Imperial and Royal Austro-Hungarian Ministry of Foreign War.

BD. *British Documents on the Origins of the War, 1898–1914*. Edited by G. P. Gooch and Harold Temperly. Vols. IX, X, XI. London: Her Majesty's Stationary Office.

BDFA. *British Documents on Foreign Affairs: Reports and Papers from the Foreign Office. Confidential Print*. Frederick, MD: University Publications of America.

   Part II, From the First to the Second World War. Series A, The Soviet Union, 1917–1939. Vol. 15, *The Soviet Union, January 1939–September 1939*. Edited by D. Cameron Watt. 1986.

   Part II, From the First to the Second World War. Series F, Europe, 1919–1939. Vol. 11, *Southern Europe: Italy*. Edited by Christopher Seton-Watson. 1992.

   Part II, From the First to the Second World War. Series H, The First World War, 1914–1918. Vol. 1, *The Allied and Neutral Powers: Diplomacy and War Aims, I: August 1914–July 1915*. Edited by David Stevenson. 1989.

   Part III, From 1940 through 1945. Series B, Near and Middle East. Vol. 1, *Turkey, January 1940–March 1939*. Edited by Malcolm Yapp. 1997.

   Part III, From 1940 through 1945. Series F, Europe. Vol. 13, *Spain, Portugal and Switzerland, January 1940–December 1941*. Edited by Denis Smyth. 1998.

Ciano, Galeazzo. 1939. "Count Ciano's Speech of December 16, 1939." *Bulletin of International News* 16 (26): 11–14.

CID (Committee of Imperial Defence). 1938. "Appreciation for a European War: Political Setting." Committee of Imperial Defence, Joint Planning Sub-Committee. Memoranda JP 332 - JP 335, CAB 55/14/3, Annex, Memo 334, 65–72.

CID (Committee of Imperial Defence). 1939. "Balance of Strategical Value in War as between Spain as an Enemy and Russia as an Ally." Committee of Imperial Defence, Chiefs of Staff Sub-Committee. CAB 24/286/5.

CMD 7628. White Paper, Miscellaneous, No. 13. Correspondence Respecting Events Leading to the Rupture of Relations with Turkey. Presented to both Houses of Parliament by Command of His Majesty, November 1914, Cmd 7628. London: His Majesty's Stationary Office. 1914.

CMD 5923. Declaration by the Government of the United Kingdom and Italy Bringing into Force Protocol of April 16, 1938 and Annexed Agreements and Declarations. British Parliamentary Papers, 1938–1939, *Treaty Series* no. 6 (1939), Cmd 5923. London: His Majesty's Stationary Office. 1914.

CMD 5726. Agreement between the United Kingdom and Italy. British Parliamentary Papers, *Treaty Series* no. 31 (1938), Cmd 5726. London: His Majesty's Stationary Office. 1914.

Coats, Dan. 2019. Remarks as Prepared for Delivery by the Honorable Dan Coats, Director of National Intelligence, Opening Statement, Annual Threat Assessment, January 29.

CRS (Congressional Research Service). 2019a. "Georgia: Background and U.S. Policy." CRS Report No. R45307. April 1. Washington, DC: Congressional Research Service.

CRS (Congressional Research Service). 2019b. "Ukraine: Background and U.S. Policy." CRS Report No. R45008. September 19. Washington, DC: Congressional Research Service.

CRS (Congressional Research Service). 2019c. "U.S. Military Presence in Poland." CRS Report No. 7-5700. August 1. Washington, DC: Congressional Research Service.

DBFP. *Documents on British Foreign Policy*. London: Her Majesty's Stationary Office.
Series 2, Vols. 14, 17.
Series 3, Vols. 1, 3–7.

DD. Sazonov, Sergei. 1915. *Diplomatic Documents: Negotiations Covering the Period from August 1 to November 1, 1914, Preceding the War with Turkey*. St. Petersburg: Imperial Russian Ministry of Foreign Affairs.

DDAHI. Austro-Hungarian Monarchy. 1915. *Diplomatic Documents Concerning the Relations of Austria-Hungary with Italy: From July 20th, 1914 to May 23rd, 1915*. Vienna: Imperial and Royal Austro-Hungarian Ministry of Foreign Affairs.

DGFP. U.S. Department of State. *Documents on German Foreign Policy, 1918–1945*. Washington, DC: Government Printing Office.
Series C, Vol. IV.
Series D, Vols. I, IV, VI–XII.

DIA 1939–1946. Toynbee, Arnold, ed. 1951. *Documents on International Affairs, 1939–1946*. Vol. 1, *March–September 1939*. London: Oxford University Press., 1951.

DIHGF. Fundación Nacional Francisco Franco. 1992. *Documentos Inéditos para la Historia del Generalísimo Franco*. Vol. 2. Madrid: Fundación Nacional Francisco Franco.

DJ. Kajima, Morinosuke, ed. and trans. 1980. *Diplomacy of Japan, 1894–1922*. Vol. 3, *First World War, Paris Peace Conference, Washington Conference*. Tokyo: Kajima Institute of International Peace.

DOD (U.S. Department of Defense). 2018. *Summary of the National Defense Strategy of the United States of America: Sharpening the American Military's Competitive Edge*. Washington, DC: U.S. Department of Defense.

DOD (U.S. Department of Defense). 2019. *Indo-Pacific Strategy Report: Preparedness, Partnerships, and Promoting a Networked Region*. Washington, DC: U.S. Department of Defense.

Esper, Mark. 2020. "Maintaining the U.S. National Security Innovation Base." Keynote Address by Mark T. Esper, U.S. Secretary of Defense. January 24, Center for Strategic and International Studies, Washington DC.

FRUS. U.S. Department of State. *Foreign Relations of the United States*. Washington, DC: Government Printing Office.
Lansing Papers, Vol. I.
1914, Supplement.
1915, Supplement.
1916, Supplement.
1940, Vol. II.

GD. Max Monteglas, Max, Walter Schucking, and Karl Kautsky, eds. 1924. *Outbreak of the World War: German Documents*. New York: Oxford University Press.

GDD. Dugdale, E. T. S., ed. 1928. *German Diplomatic Documents, 1871–1914*. Vol. 2. London: Methuen.

Hansard 1938. *Hansard Parliamentary Debates*. Anglo Italian Agreement. HC Deb 02 May 1938, Vol. 335: 533–669.

Mitchell 2018. U.S. Senate Foreign Relations Committee, Subcommittee on Europe and Regional Security Cooperation. 2018. Testimony of Assistant Secretary A. Wess Mitchell, Bureau of European and Eurasian Affairs.; U.S. Policy in Europe Hearing, June 26. Washington, DC: Government Printing Office.

MNDRP (Ministry of National Defense, Republic of Poland). 2018. *Proposal for a U.S Permanent Presence in Poland*. Warsaw: Ministry of National Defense, Republic of Poland.

NATO. 2016. "Joint Statement of the NATO-Georgia Commission at the Level of Foreign Ministers." July 8, Warsaw. https://www.nato.int/cps/en/natohq/official _texts_133175.htm.

NATO. 2018. "NATO-Georgia Commission Declaration at the Brussels Summit." July 12, Brussels. https://www.nato.int/cps/en/natohq/official_texts_156627 .htm?selectedLocale=en.

NIC (National Intelligence Council). 2008. *Global Trends 2025: A Transformed World*. Washington, DC: Office of the Director of National Intelligence.

NIC (National Intelligence Council). 2012. *Global Trends 2030: Alternative Worlds*. Washington, DC: Office of the Director of National Intelligence.

NSR. Sontag, Raymond J., and James Stuart Beddie, eds. 1948. *Nazi-Soviet Relations 1939–1941: Documents from the Archives of the German Foreign Office*. Washington, DC: Department of State.

NSS. White House. 2017. *National Security Strategy of the United States of America*. December, Washington, DC. https://www.whitehouse.gov/wp-content/uploads /2017/12/NSS-Final-12-18-2017-0905.pdf.

OGD. Carnegie Endowment for International Peace, trans. 1923. *Official German Documents Relating to the World War*. Vol. 2.New York: Oxford University Press.

OSD (Office of the Secretary of Defense). 2019. *Annual Report to Congress: Military and Security Developments Involving the People's Republic of China 2018*. May 28.

PWW. Link, Arthur, ed. 1980–1983. *The Papers of Woodrow Wilson*. Vols. 33–41. Princeton, NJ: Princeton University Press..

SGA. U.S. Department of State. 1948. *The Spanish Government and the Axis*. Washington, DC: U.S. Department of State.

SPE. Gromyko, A. A., A. N. Grylev, I. N. Zemskov, S. P. Kozyrev, B. Y. Sipols, V. M. Falin, M. A. Kharlamov, V. M. Khvostov, eds. 1976. *Soviet Peace Efforts on the Eve of World War II (September 1938–August 1939): Documents and Records*. Moscow: Progress Publishers.

WH (White House). 2020. "Joint Statement: Vision and Principles for the United States–India Comprehensive Global Strategic Partnership." February 25, Washington, DC. https://www.whitehouse.gov/briefings-statements/joint-statement-vision-principles-united-states-india-comprehensive-global-strategic-partnership/.

WTA. U.S. Senate Select Committee on Intelligence. 2019. *Worldwide Threat Assessment of the U.S. Intelligence Community*. January 29. Washington, DC: Government Printing Office.

Secondary Sources

Abrahamyan, Eduard. 2019. "Can Major Non-NATO Ally Status Temporarily Solve Georgia's Security Dilemma?" *New Eastern Europe*, February 5. https://neweasterneurope.eu/2019/02/05/can-major-non-nato-ally-status-temporarily-solve-georgias-security-dilemma/.

Afflerbach, Holger. 2014. "The Eastern Front." In *The Cambridge History of the First World War: Global War*, edited by J. Winter, vol. 1, 234–265. Cambridge: Cambridge University Press.

Akmese, Handan Nezir. 2005. *The Birth of Modern Turkey: The Ottoman Military and the March to World War I*. London: I. B. Tauris.

Aksakal, Mustafa. 2008. *The Ottoman Road to War: The Ottoman Empire and the First World War*. Cambridge: Cambridge University Press.

Aksakal, Mustafa. 2011. "The Limits of Diplomacy: The Ottoman Empire and the First World War." *Foreign Policy Analysis* 7 (2):197–204. doi:10.1111/j.1743-8594.2011.00132.x.

Albertini, Luigi. 1957. *The Origins of the War of 1914*. Vol. 3. London: Oxford University Press.

Albright, Madeleine, and Igor Ivanov. 2020. "A Plea to Save the Last Nuclear Arms Treaty." *New York Times*, February 10. https://www.nytimes.com/2020/02/10/opinion/albright-ivanov-nuclear-treaty.html.

Ali, Idrees. 2018. "In a Symbolic Nod to India, U.S. Pacific Command Changes Name." Reuters, May 30. https://www.reuters.com/article/us-usa-defense-india/in-symbolic-nod-to-india-us-pacific-command-changes-name-idUSKCN1IV2Q2.

Allison, Graham. 2019. "China and Russia: A Strategic Alliance in the Making." *National Interest*, December 14. https://nationalinterest.org/feature/china-and-russia-strategic-alliance-making-38727.

Arielli, Nir. 2010. *Fascist Italy and the Middle East, 1933–40*. New York: Palgrave Macmillan.

Aron, Leon. 2019. "Are Russia and China Really Forming an Alliance?: The Evidence Is Less Than Impressive." *Foreign Affairs*, April 4. https://www.foreignaffairs.com/articles/china/2019-04-04/are-russia-and-china-really-forming-alliance.

Art, Robert J., and Patrick M. Cronin. 2003. *The United States and Coercive Diplomacy*. Washington, DC: United States Institute of Peace.

Art, Robert J., and Kelly M. Greenhill. 2018. "Coercion: An Analytical Overview." In *Coercion: The Power to Hurt in International Politics*, edited by Kelly M. Greenhill and Peter Krause, 3–32. New York: Oxford University Press.

Asmus, Ronald D. 2002. *Opening NATO's Door: How the Alliance Remade Itself for a New Era*. New York: Columbia University Press.

Axe, David. 2019. "Why Russia Is Angry at America's Missile Defense Systems." *National Interest*, October 22. https://nationalinterest.org/blog/buzz/why-russia-angry-americas-missile-defense-systems-90111.

Aydin, Cemil. 2008. "Japan's Pan-Asianism and the Legitimacy of Imperial World Order, 1931–1945." *Asia-Pacific Journal* 6 (3): 1–33.

Baldwin, David A. 1971. "The Power of Positive Sanctions." *World Politics* 24 (1): 19–38. doi:10.2307/2009705.

Baldwin, David A. 1985. *Economic Statecraft*. Princeton, NJ: Princeton University Press.

Bandow, Doug. 2017. "A Nixon Strategy to Break the Russia-China Axis." *National Interest*, January 4. https://nationalinterest.org/blog/the-skeptics/nixon-strategy-break-the-russia-china-axis-18946.

Barnes, Julian. 2019. "NATO Considers Missile Defense Upgrade, Risking Further Tensions with Russia." *New York Times*, July 5. https://www.nytimes.com/2019/07/05/world/europe/nato-nuclear-missile-defenses-russia.html.

Baruah, Darshana M. 2018. "The Andaman and Nicobar Islands: India's Eastern Anchor in a Changing Indo-Pacific." *War on the Rocks*, March 21. https://warontherocks.com/2018/03/the-andaman-and-nicobar-islands-indias-eastern-anchor-in-a-changing-indo-pacific/.

Beckley, Michael. 2015. "The Myth of Entangling Alliances: Reassessing the Security Risks of U.S. Defense Pacts." *International Security* 39 (4): 7–48. doi:10.1162/ISEC_a_00197.

Beckley, Michael. 2018. *Unrivaled: Why America Will Remain the World's Sole Superpower*. Ithaca, NY: Cornell University Press.

Beebe, George. 2019. *The Russia Trap: How Our Shadow War with Russia Could Spiral into Nuclear Catastrophe*. New York: Thomas Dunne Books.

Bell, P. M. H. 1996. *France and Britain, 1900–1940*. London: Longman.

Beloff, Max. 1949. *The Foreign Policy of Soviet Russia, 1929–1941*. Vol. 2. New York: Oxford University Press.

Bennett, D. Scott. 1997. "Testing Alternative Models of Alliance Duration: 1816–1984." *American Journal of Political Science* 41 (3): 846–878. doi:10.2307/2111677.

Bensahel, Nora. 2007. "International Alliances and Military Effectiveness: Fighting alongside Allies and Partners." In *Creating Military Power: The Sources of Military Effectiveness*, edited by Risa A. Brooks and Elizabeth A. Stanley, 186–206. Palo Alto, CA: Stanford University Press.

Benson, Brett. 2012. *Constructing International Security: Alliances, Deterrence, and Moral Hazard*. New York: Cambridge University Press.

Bergerson, Kristien. 2016. "China's Efforts to Counter U.S. Forward Presence in the Asia Pacific." U.S.-China Economic and Security Review Commission, Washington, DC, March 15.

Berkowitz, Bruce D. 1983. "Realignment in International Treaty Organizations." *International Studies Quarterly* 27 (1): 77–96. doi:10.2307/2600620.

Bernauer, Thomas, Dieter Ruloff, Charles W. Kegley, and Donald J. Puchala. 1999. *The Politics of Positive Incentives in Arms Control*. Columbia: University of South Carolina Press.

Berton, Peter. A. 1956. "The Secret Russo-Japanese Alliance of 1916." PhD diss., Columbia University.

Betts, Richard. 2012. *American Force: Dangers, Delusions, and Dilemmas in National Security*. New York: Columbia University Press.

Betts, Richard. 2014. "Pick Your Battles: Ending America's Era of Permanent War." *Foreign Affairs* 93 (6): 15–24.

Birnbaum, K. E. 1958. *Peace Moves and U-Boat Warfare*. Stockholm: Almqvist and Wiksell.

Blackwill, Robert D. 2020. *Implementing Grand Strategy Toward China: Twenty-Two U.S. Policy Prescriptions*. Council Special Report no. 85 (January). New York: Council on Foreign Relations.

Blackwill, Robert D., and Ashley Tellis. 2019. "The India Dividend: New Delhi Remains Washington's Best Hope in Asia." *Foreign Affairs* 95 (5): 173–183.

Blanchard, Jean-Marc, and Norrin Ripsman. 2013. *Economic Statecraft and Foreign Policy: Sanctions, Incentives, and Target State Calculations*. London: Routledge.

Blank, Jonah, Jennifer D. P. Moroney, Angel Rabasa, and Bonny Lin. 2015. *Look East, Cross Black Waters: India's Interests in Southeast Asia*. RR-1021-AF. Washington, DC: Rand.

Blankenship, Brian. 2021. "Promises under Pressure: Statements of Reassurance in U.S. Alliances." International Studies Quarterly, forthcoming.

Blankenship, Brian, and Benjamin Denison. 2019. "Is America Prepared for Great-Power Competition?" *Survival* 61 (5): 43–64. doi:10.1080/00396338.2019.1662134.

Bob, Clifford. 2019. *Rights as Weapons: Instruments of Conflict, Tools of Power*. Princeton, NJ: Princeton University Press.

Bobroff, Ronald. 2006. *Roads to Glory: Late Imperial Russia and the Turkish Straits*. London: I. B. Tauris.

Bosworth, R. J. B. 1979. *Italy, the Least of the Great Powers*. London: Cambridge University Press.

Brewster, David. 2013. "India's Defence Strategy and the India-ASEAN Relationship." In *India-ASEAN Defence Relations*, edited by Ajaya Kumar Das, 124–145. Singapore: S. Rajaratnam School of International Studies.

Brewster, David. 2016. "India and China at Sea." *Asia Policy* 22 (July): 4–10.

Brooks, Stephen G., G. John Ikenberry, and William C. Wohlforth. 2012/13. "Don't Come Home America: The Case against Retrenchment." *International Security* 37 (3): 7–51. doi:10.1162/ISEC_a_00107.

Brooks, Stephen G., and William C. Wohlforth. 2015/16. "The Rise and Fall of the Great Powers in the Twenty-First Century." *International Security* 40 (3): 7–53. doi:10.1162/ISEC_a_00225.

Brooks, Stephen G., and William C. Wohlforth. 2016. *America Abroad: The United States' Global Role in the 21st Century*. Oxford: Oxford University Press.

Buchanan, Andrew. 2013. *America's Grand Strategy in the Mediterranean in World War II*. Cambridge: Cambridge University Press.

Buehrig, Edward H. 1955. *Woodrow Wilson and the Balance of Power*. Bloomington: Indiana University Press.

Burdick, Charles B. 1968. *Germany's Military Strategy and Spain in World War II.* Syracuse, NY: Syracuse University Press.

Burns, William J. 2019. "How the U.S.-Russian Relationship Went Bad." *The Atlantic,* March 8. https://www.theatlantic.com/magazine/archive/2019/04/william -j-burns-putin-russia/583255/.

Byman, Daniel, and Matthew Kroenig. 2016. "Reaching beyond the Ivory Tower: A How-To Manual." *Security Studies* 25 (2): 289–319. doi:10.1080/09636412.2016 .1171969.

Byman, Daniel, and Matthew Waxman. 2002. *Dynamics of Coercion.* New York: Cambridge University Press.

Caldwell, Dan. 2009. "The Legitimation of the Nixon-Kissinger Grand Design and Grand Strategy." *Diplomatic History* 33 (4): 633–653. doi:10.1111/j.1467-7709 .2009.00801.x.

Carafano, James Jay. 2019. "Why the China-Russia Alliance Won't Last." Commentary/Defense, The Heritage Foundation, August 7. https://www.heritage .org/defense/commentary/why-the-china-russia-alliance-wont-last.

Caraley, Michael J. 1999. *1939: The Alliance That Never Was and the Coming of World War II.* Chicago: Ivan Dee.

Carley, Michael J. 1993. "End of the 'Low, Dishonest Decade': Failure of the Anglo-Franco-Soviet Alliance in 1939." *Europe-Asia Studies* 45 (2): 303–341.

Carpenter, Ted Galen. 2018. "Poking the Russian Bear with the NATO Umbrella." *American Conservative,* October 23. https://www.theamericanconservative.com /articles/poking-the-russian-bear-with-the-nato-umbrella/.

Carr, Edward Hallet. 1949. "From Munich to Moscow. II." *Soviet Studies* 1 (2): 93–105.

Carr, Edward Hallet. 1964. *The Twenty Years' Crisis.* 2nd ed. New York: Harper & Row.

Caruana, Leonard, and Hugh Rockman. 2006. "An Elephant in the Garden: The Allies, Spain, and Oil in World War II." National Bureau of Economic Research Working Paper 12228, Cambridge, MA.

Cassels, Alan. 1983. "Was There a Fascist Foreign Policy? Tradition and Novelty." *International History Review* 5 (2): 254–268.

Cha, Victor. 2016. *Powerplay: The Origins of the American Alliance System in Asia.* Princeton, NJ: Princeton University Press.

Chai, Tommy Sheng Hao. 2020. "How China Attempts to Drive a Wedge in the U.S.-Australia Alliance." *Australian Journal of International Affairs.* doi:10.1080/10357 718.2020.1721432.

Chamberlain, Diane Pfundstein. 2016. *Cheap Threats: Why the United States Struggles to Coerce Weak States.* Washington, DC: Georgetown University Press.

Chaudhuri, Pramit Pal. 2016. "New Delhi at Sea: The China Factor in the Indian Ocean Policy of the Modi and Singh Governments." *Asia Policy* 22 (July): 27–34.

Chiba, Daina, Jesse C. Johnson, and Brett Ashley Leeds. 2015. "Careful Commitments: Democratic States and Alliance Design." *Journal of Politics* 77 (4): 968–982. doi:10.1086/682074.

Christensen, Thomas J. 1997. "Perceptions and Alliances in Europe, 1865–1940." *International Organization* 51 (1): 65–97. doi:10.1162/002081897550302.

Christensen, Thomas J. 2011. *Worse Than a Monolith: Alliance Politics and Problems of Coercive Diplomacy in Asia*. Princeton, NJ: Princeton University Press.

Christensen, Thomas J., and Jack Snyder. 1990. "Chain Gangs and Passed Bucks: Predicting Alliance Patterns in Multipolarity." *International Organization* 44 (2): 137–168. doi:10.1017/S0020818300035232.

Churchill, Winston. 1948. *The Second World War*. Vol. 1, *The Gathering Storm*. New York: Houghton Mifflin.

Churchill, Winston. 1949. *The Second World War*. Vol. 2, *Their Finest Hour*. New York: Houghton Mifflin.

Ciano, Galeazzo. 1945. *The Ciano Diaries, 1939–1943*. New York: Doubleday.

Ciano, Galeazzo. 1953. *Ciano's Hidden Diary, 1937–1938*. New York: Dutton.

Claude, Inis. 1962. *Power and International Relations*. New York: Random House.

Cliadakis, H. 1974. "Neutrality and War in Italian Policy, 1939–1940." *Journal of Contemporary History* 9 (3): 171–190. doi:10.1177/002200947400900307.

Colby, Elbridge A., and A. Wess Mitchell. 2020. "The Age of Great Power Competition: How the Trump Administration Refashioned American Strategy." *Foreign Affairs* 99 (1): 118–130.

Collin, Koh Swee Lean. 2013. "ASEAN Perspectives on Naval Cooperation with India." In *India-ASEAN Defence Relations*, edited by Ajaya Kumar Das, 281–312. Singapore: S. Rajaratnam School of International Studies.

Collin, Koh Swee Lean. 2019. "China-India Rivalry at Sea: Capability, Trends and Challenges." *Asian Security* 15 (1): 5–24. doi:10.1080/14799855.2019.1539820.

Colvin, Ian. 1950. "The Hendaye Tapestry: Hitler and Spain." *The National and English Review*, June, 21.

Conn, Stetson, and Byron Fairchild. 1960. *The Framework of Hemisphere Defense*. Washington, DC: Government Printing Office.

Cooley, Alexander, and Daniel Nexon. 2013. "The Empire Will Compensate You: The Structural Dynamics of the U.S. Overseas Basing Network." *Perspectives on Politics* 11 (4): 1034–1049. doi:10.1017/S1537592713002818.

Cooley, Alexander, and Daniel Nexon. 2016. "Interpersonal Networks and International Security: US-Georgia Relations during the Bush Administration." In *The New Power Politics: Networks and Transnational Security Governance*, edited by Deborah Avant and Oliver Westerwinter, 74–103. New York: Oxford University Press.

Cooley, Alexander, and Daniel Nexon. 2020. *Exit from Hegemony: The Unraveling of the American Global Order*. New York: Oxford University Press.

Cooper, John M. 2003. "The United States." In *The Origins of World War I*, edited by Richard F. Hamilton and Holger Herwig, 415–442. Cambridge: Cambridge University Press.

Coox, Alvin. 1990. *Nomonhan: Japan against Russia, 1939*. Palo Alto, CA: Stanford University Press.

Copeland, Dale. 2015. *Economic Interdependence and War*. Princeton, NJ: Princeton University Press.

Cortright, David. 1997. *The Price of Peace*. Lanham, MD: Rowman & Littlefield.

Craig, Gordon. 1978. *Germany, 1866–1945*. Oxford: Oxford University Press.

Crawford, Timothy W. 2003. *Pivotal Deterrence: Third-Party Statecraft and the Pursuit of Peace*. Ithaca, NY: Cornell University Press.

Crawford, Timothy W. 2008. "Wedge Strategy, Balancing, and the Deviant Case of Spain, 1940–41." *Security Studies* 17 (1): 1–38. doi:10.1080/09636410801894126.

Crawford, Timothy W. 2011. "Preventing Enemy Coalitions: How Wedge Strategies Shape Power Politics." *International Security* 35 (4): 155–189. doi:10.1162/ISEC_a_00036.

Crawford, Timothy W. 2012. "Powers of Division: From the Anti-Comintern to the Nazi-Soviet and Japanese-Soviet Pacts, 1936–1941." In *The Challenge of Grand Strategy: The Great Powers and the Broken Balance between the World Wars*, edited by Jeffrey Taliaferro, Steven Lobell, and Norrin Ripsman, 246–278. Cambridge: Cambridge University Press.

Crawford, Timothy W. 2014. "The Alliance Politics of Concerted Accommodation: Entente Bargaining and Italian and Ottoman Interventions in the First World War." *Security Studies* 23 (1): 113–147. doi:10.1080/09636412.2014.874177.

Crawford, Timothy W. 2018. "The Strategy of Coercive Isolation." In *Coercion: The Power to Hurt in International Politics*, edited by Kelly M. Greenhill and Peter Krause, 228–250. New York: Oxford University Press.

Crescenzi, Mark, Jacob Kathman, Katja Kleinberg, and Reed Wood. 2012. "Reliability, Reputation, and Alliance Formation." *International Studies Quarterly* 56 (2): 259–275. doi:10.1111/j.1468-2478.2011.00711.x.

Croft, Adrian, and David Alexander. 2015. "European Defence Ministers Oppose Sending Weapons." Reuters, February 5. https://www.reuters.com/article/us-ukraine-crisis-nato-weapons-idUSKBN0L91SR20150205.

Crumm, Eileen. 1995. "The Value of Economic Incentives in International Relations." *Journal of Peace Research* 32 (3): 313–330. doi:10.1177/0022343395032003005.

Cunningham, A. 1993. "The Wrong Horse? Anglo-Ottoman Relations before the First World War." In *Eastern Questions in the Nineteenth Century: Collected Essays, Volume 2*, edited by E. Ingram, 226–248. London: Frank Cass.

Dahl, Ann-Sofie. 2018. "Sweden and Finland: Partnership in Lieu of Membership." In *Strategic Challenges of the Baltic Sea Region*, edited by Ann-Sofie Dahl, 129–140. Washington, DC: Georgetown University Press.

Das, Ajaya Kumar. 2016. "Can India Balance between China and America?" *National Interest*, May 10. https://nationalinterest.org/feature/can-india-balance-between-china-america-16137.

Davidson, Jason. 2002. "The Roots of Revisionism: Fascist Italy." *Security Studies* 11 (4): 125–159. doi.org/10.1080/714005356.

Davidson, Jason. 2020. *America's Entangling Alliances: 1778 to the Present*. Washington, DC. Georgetown University Press.

Davis, Christina. 2008/09. "Linkage Diplomacy: Economic and Security Bargaining in the Anglo-Japanese Alliance, 1902–1923." *International Security* 33 (3): 143–179. doi:10.1162/isec.2009.33.3.143.

Davis, James W. 2000. *Threats and Promises: The Pursuit of International Influence*. Baltimore: Johns Hopkins University Press.

Davis, James W. 2005. *Terms of Inquiry: On the Theory and Practice of Political Science*. Baltimore: Johns Hopkins University Press.

De Grand, A. J. 1971. "The Italian Nationalist Association in the Period of Italian Neutrality, August 1914–May 1915." *Journal of Modern History* 43 (3): 394–412. doi:10.1086/240649.

De Saint-Mezard, Isabelle. 2016. "India and Southeast Asia: Whither India's Strategic Engagement with ASEAN?" In *Engaging the World: Indian Foreign Policy since 1947*, edited by Sumit Ganguly, 326–351. New York: Oxford University Press.

Derengil, Selim. 1989. *Turkish Foreign Policy during the Second World War.* Cambridge: Cambridge University Press.

Derengil, Selim. 1998. *The Well-Protected Domains: Ideology and Legitimation of Power in the Ottoman Empire, 1876–1909.* London: Palgrave Macmillan.

Detwiler, Donald S. 1971. "Spain and the Axis during World War II." *Review of Politics* 33 (1): 36–53. doi:10.1017/S0034670500025377.

Dickinson, Frederick R. 1999. *War and National Reinvention: Japan in the Great War, 1914–1919.* Cambridge, MA: Harvard University Press.

Dickinson, Frederick R. 2003. "Japan." In *The Origins of World War I,* edited by Richard F. Hamilton and Holger Herwig, 300–336. Cambridge: Cambridge University Press.

Dinnerstein, Herbert S. 1965. "The Transformation of Alliance Systems." *American Political Science Review* 59 (3): 589–601. doi:10.2307/1953170.

Dobbins, James, Howard Shatz, and Ali Wyne. 2019. "A Warming Trend in China-Russia Relations." *The Rand Blog,* April 18. https://www.rand.org/blog/2019/04/a-warming-trend-in-china-russia-relations.html.

Doerries, Reinhard. 1978. "Imperial Berlin and Washington: New Light on Germany's Foreign Policy and America's Entry into World War I." *Central European History* 11 (1): 23–49.

Doerries, Reinhard. 1980. "The Politics of Irresponsibility: Imperial Germany's Defiance of the United States Neutrality during World War I." In *Germany and America: Essays on Problems of International Relations and Immigration,* edited by Hans L. Trefousse, 3–20. New York: Brooklyn College Press, 1980.

Doerries, Reinhard. 1989. *Imperial Challenge.* Chapel Hill: University of North Carolina Press.

Drezner, Daniel. 1999. "The Trouble with Carrots: Transaction Costs, Conflict Expectations, and Economic Inducements." *Security Studies* 9 (1–2): 188–218. doi:10.1080/09636419908429399.

Driscoll, Jesse, and Daniel Maliniak. 2016. "With Friends Like These: Brinkmanship and Chain-Ganging in Russia's Near Abroad." *Security Studies* 25 (4): 585–607. doi:10.1080/09636412.2016.1220208.

Duchacek, Ivo. 1960. *Conflict and Cooperation among Nations.* New York: Holt.

Duff, Katharine. 1956. "Spain between the Allies and the Axis." In *Survey of International Affairs, 1939–1946,.* Vol. 7, *The War and the Neutrals,* edited by Arnold Toynbee and Veronica M. Toynbee, 256–285. London: Oxford University Press.

Du Quenoy, Paul. 2003. "With Allies Like These, Who Needs Enemies? Russia and the Problem of Italian Entry into World War I." *Canadian Slavonic Papers* 45 (3–4): 409–440.

Duroselle, J. B. 2004. *France and the Nazi Threat.* New York: Enigma Books.

Earle, Edward Meade. 1966. *Turkey, the Great Powers, and the Bagdad Railway.* New York: Russell and Russell.

Edelstein, David M. 2017. *Over the Horizon: Time, Uncertainty, and the Rise of Great Powers.* Ithaca, New York: Cornell University Press.

Edelstein, David M. 2019. "The Persistence of Great Power Politics." *Texas National Security Review* 2 (2): 116-20.

Emin, Ahmed. 1930. *Turkey in the World War.* New Haven CT: Yale University Press.

Emmott, Robin, and Sabine Siebold. 2015. "NATO Split on Message to Send Georgia on Membership Hopes." Reuters, November 27. https://www.reuters.com

/article/us-nato-georgia/nato-split-on-message-to-send-georgia-on-member
ship-hopes-idUSKBN0TG1HP20151127.

Engram, J. H. 1976. "Partner or Peril: Japan in German Foreign Policy and Diplomacy, 1914–1920." PhD diss., Washington State University.

Ericson, Edward E. 1998. "Karl Schurre and the Evolution of Nazi-Soviet Relations,
1936–1941." *German Studies Review* 21 (2): 263–283.

Esenbel, Selcuk. 2004. "Japan's Global Claim to Asia and the World of Islam: Transnational Nationalism and World Power." *American Historical Review* 109 (4):
1140–1170. doi:10.1086/ahr/109.4.1140.

Fang, Tien-sze. 2014. *Asymmetrical Threat Perception in India-China Relations*. New
Delhi: Oxford University Press.

Farrar, L. L. 1978. *Divide and Conquer: German Efforts to Conclude a Separate Peace,
1914–1918*. Boulder, CO: East European Monographs.

Farrar, L. L. 1998. "The Strategy of the Central Powers, 1914–1917." In *World War I:
A History*, edited by Hew Strachan, 26–38. New York: Oxford University Press.

Feis, Herbert. 1966. *The Spanish Story: Franco and the Nations at War*. New York:
Norton.

Fischer, Fritz. 1967. *Germany's Aims in the First World War*. New York, Norton.

Flacker, Edgar. 1998. "Fritz Grobba and Nazi Germany's Middle Eastern Policy
1933–1942." PhD diss., London School of Economics and Political Science, University of London.

Fleischhauer, Ingeborg. 1997. "Soviet Foreign Policy and the Origins of the Hitler-
Stalin Pact." In *From Peace to War: Germany, Soviet Russia and the World, 1939–1941*,
edited by Bernd Wegner, 27–46. Providence, RI: Berghahn Books.

Fox, Annette Baker. 1959. *The Power of Small States*. New York: Columbia University Press.

France24. 2018. "No Fast-Track NATO Membership for Georgia: Merkel." France24,
August 24. https://www.france24.com/en/20180824-no-fast-track-nato-member
ship-georgia-merkel.

Fravel, M. Taylor. 2008. *Strong Borders, Secure Nation: Cooperation and Conflict in China's Territorial Disputes*. Princeton, NJ: Princeton University Press.

French, David. 1986. *British Strategy and War Aims, 1914–1916*. London: Allen &
Unwin.

Friedman, Julian. 1970. "Alliance in International Politics." In *Alliance in International Politics*, edited by Julian R. Friedman, Christopher Bladen, and Steven
Rosen, 3–32. Boston: Allyn & Bacon.

Fulton, L. Bruce. 1984. "France and the End of the Ottoman Empire." In *The Great
Powers and the End of the Ottoman Empire*, edited by Marian Kent, 141–171. London: Frank Cass.

Gabuev, Alexander. 2018. "Why Russia and China Are Strengthening Security Ties."
Foreign Affairs, September 24. https://www.foreignaffairs.com/articles/china
/2018-09-24/why-russia-and-china-are-strengthening-security-ties.

Gaddis, John Lewis. 2005. *Strategies of Containment: A Critical Appraisal of American
National Security Policy during the Cold War*. New York: Oxford University Press.

Gady, Franz-Stefan. 2019. "Why the West Should Not Underestimate China-Russia
Military Ties." *EastWest Institute*, January 30. https://www.eastwest.ngo/idea/why
-west-should-not-underestimate-china-russia-military-ties.

Ganguly, Sumit. 2015. *Indian Foreign Policy*. New York: Oxford University Press.

Ganguly, Sumit, and S. Paul Kapur. 2017. "Is India Starting to Flex Its Military Muscles?" *Foreign Policy*, October 17. https://foreignpolicy.com/2017/10/17/is-india-starting-to-flex-its-military-muscles/.

Garver, John. 2003. "China." In *The Origins of World War Two: The Debate Continues*, edited by Robert Boyce and Joseph A. Maiolo, 190–204. New York: Palgrave Macmillan.

Garver, John W. 2016. "Diverging Perceptions of China's Emergence as an Indian Ocean Power." *Asia Policy* 22 (July): 56–60.

Garver, John W., and Fei-Ling Wang. 2010. "China's Anti-encirclement Struggle." *Asian Security* 6 (3): 238–261. doi:10.1080/14799855.2010.507412.

George, Alexander. 1991. *Forceful Persuasion: Coercive Diplomacy as an Alternative to War*. Washington, DC: United States Institute of Peace Press.

George, Alexander. 1993. *Bridging the Gap: Theory and Practice in Foreign Policy*. Washington, DC: United States Institute of Peace Press.

George, Alexander. 2003. "The Need for Influence Theory and Actor-Specific Behavioral Models of Adversaries." *Comparative Strategy* 22 (5): 463–487. doi:10.1080/01495930390256527.

George, Alexander. 2006. *On Foreign Policy: Unfinished Business*. Boulder, CO: Paradigm Publishers.

George, Alexander, and Andrew Bennett. 2005. *Case Studies and Theory Development in the Social Sciences*. Cambridge, MA: MIT Press.

George, Alexander, and Richard Smoke. 1974. *Deterrence in American Foreign Policy*. New York: Columbia University Press.

Gerring, John. 2004. "What Is a Case Study and What Is It Good For?" *American Political Science Review* 98 (2): 341–354. doi:10.1017/S0003055404001182.

Gerring, John. 2007. *Case Study Research: Principles and Practices*. Cambridge: Cambridge University Press.

Gholz, Eugene, and Daryl Press. 2001. "The Effects of Wars on Neutral Countries." *Security Studies* 10 (4): 1–57. doi:10.1080/09636410108429444.

Gholz, Eugene, Daryl Press, and Harvey Sapolsky. 1997. "Come Home, America: The Strategy of Restraint in the Face of Temptation." *International Security* 21 (4): 5–48.

Gibler, Douglas. 2008. "The Costs of Reneging: Reputation and Alliance Formation." *Journal of Conflict Resolution* 52 (3): 426–454. doi:10.1177/0022002707310003.

Gilboy, George J., and Eric Heginbotham. 2012. *Chinese and Indian Strategic Behavior: Growing Power and Alarm*. Cambridge: Cambridge University Press.

Gin, Emilio. 2014. "Speak of War and Prepare for Peace: Rome, 10 June 1940." *Nuova Rivista Storica* 98 (3): 991–1013.

Glaser, Charles. 2019. "A Flawed Framework: Why the Liberal International Order Concept Is Misguided." *International Security* 43 (4): 51–87. doi:10.1162/ISEC_a_00343.

Goda, Norman J. W. 1998a. "Franco's Bid for Empire: Spain, Germany, and the Western Mediterranean in World War II." *Mediterranean Historical Review* 13 (1–2): 168–194.

Goda, Norman J. W. 1998b. *Tomorrow the World: Hitler, Northwest Africa, and the Path toward America*. College Station: Texas A&M University Press.

Goda, Norman J. W. 1999. "Germany's Conception of Spain's Strategic Importance, 1940–1941." In *Spain in an International Context, 1936–1959*, edited by Christian Leitz and David Joseph Dunthorn, 129–148. New York: Berghan Books.

Goddard, Stacie. 2008/09. "When Right Makes Might: How Prussia Overturned the European Balance of Power." *International Security* 33 (3): 110–142. doi:10.1162/isec.2009.33.3.110.

Goddard, Stacie E. 2018. *When Right Makes Might: Rising Powers and World Order.* Ithaca, NY: Cornell University Press.

Goddard, Stacie, and Daniel Nexon. 2016. "The Dynamics of Global Power Politics." *Journal of Global Security Studies* 1 (1): 4–18. doi:10.1093/jogss/ogv007.

Goldgeier, James M. 1999. *Not Whether but When: The U.S. Decision to Enlarge NATO.* Washington, DC: Brookings Institution Press.

Goldstein, Avery. 2013. "First Things First: The Pressing Danger of Crisis Instability in U.S.-China Relations." *International Security* 37 (4): 49–89. doi:10.1162/ISEC_a_00114.

Goldstein, Lyle. 2016. "Does China Think America Is Using a 'Wedge Strategy'?" *National Interest,* July 27. https://nationalinterest.org/feature/does-china-think-america-using-wedge-strategy-17152.

Goldstein, Lyle. 2020. "China Is Prepared to Reap the Strategic Rewards of Its Relationship with Russia." *National Interest,* February 29. https://nationalinte rest.org/feature/china-prepared-reap-strategic-rewards-its-relationship-russia-128037.

Gorodetsky, Gabriel. 1999. *Grand Delusion: Stalin and the German Invasion of Russia.* New Haven, CT: Yale University Press.

Gottlieb, W. W. 1957. *Studies in Secret Diplomacy during the First World War.* London: Allen & Unwin.

Gould, Joe. 2019. "Key US Lawmakers Want to Give Ukraine Anti-ship and Anti-aircraft Missiles to Counter Russia." *Defense News,* May 31. https://www.defensenews.com/global/europe/2019/05/31/key-us-lawmakers-want-to-give-ukraine-anti-ship-and-anti-aircraft-missiles-to-counter-russia/.

Graham, Thomas. 2019. "Let Russia Be Russia: The Case for a More Pragmatic Approach to Moscow." *Foreign Affairs* 98 (6): 134–147.

Granados, Ulises. 2018. "India's Approaches to the South China Sea: Priorities and Balances." *Asia and the Pacific Policy Studies* 5 (1): 122–137. doi:10.1002/app5.223.

Greenhill, Kelly. 2010. *Weapons of Mass Migration.* Ithaca, NY: Cornell University Press.

Greenhill, Kelly M., and Peter Krause. 2018. *Coercion: The Power to Hurt in International Politics.* New York: Oxford University Press.

Grey, Viscount of Fallodon. 1925. *Twenty-Five Years: 1892–1916.* Vol. 2. New York: Frederick Stokes.

Grieco, Joseph M., and G. John Ikenberry. 2003. *State Power and World Markets: The International Political Economy.* New York: Norton.

Guillen, Peter. 1998. "Franco-Italian Relations in Flux." In *French Foreign and Defense Policy, 1918–1940: The Decline and Fall of a Great Power,* edited by Robert Boyce, 148–162. London: Routledge.

Haas, Mark L. 2003. "Ideology and Alliances: British and French External Balancing Decisions in the 1930s." *Security Studies* 12 (4): 34–79. doi:10.1080/09636410390447626.

Haas, Mark L. 2005. *Ideological Origins of Great Power Politics.* Ithaca, NY: Cornell University Press.

Haas, Mark L. 2012a. *The Clash of Ideologies: Middle Eastern Politics and American Security.* New York: Oxford University Press.

Haas, Mark L. 2012b. "Missed Ideological Opportunities and George W. Bush's Middle Eastern Policy." *Security Studies* 21 (3): 416–454. doi:10.1080/09636412.2 012.706499.

Haas, Mark L. 2012c. "Soviet Grand Strategy in the Interwar Years: Ideology as Realpolitik." In *The Challenge of Grand Strategy: The Great Powers and the Broken Balance between the World Wars*, edited by Jeffrey Taliaferro, Norrin Ripsman, and Steven Lobell, 279–307. Cambridge: Cambridge University Press.

Haas, Mark L. 2014. "Ideological Polarity and Balancing in Great Power Politics." *Security Studies* 23 (4): 715–753. doi:10.1080/09636412.2014.964991.

Haass, Richard, and Meghan L. O'Sullivan. 2001. *Honey and Vinegar: Incentives, Sanctions, and Foreign Policy.* Washington, DC: Brookings Institution Press.

Hager, Robert. 2017. "The Laughing Third Man in a Fight: Stalin's Use of the Wedge Strategy." *Communist and Post-Communist Studies* 50:15–27. doi:10.1016/j. postcomstud.2016.11.002.

Hagerty, Devin T. 2016. "The Indo-US Entente: Committed Relationship or 'Friends with Benefits'?" In *Engaging the World: Indian Foreign Policy since 1947*, edited by Sumit Ganguly, 133–166. New York: Oxford University Press.

Hale, William. 2000. *Turkish Foreign Policy, 1774–2000.* London: Frank Cass.

Hamilton, Richard F., and Holger Herwig. 2003. "Italy." In *The Origins of World War I*, edited by Richard F. Hamilton and Holger Herwig, 356–387. Cambridge: Cambridge University Press.

Hancock, Kathleen J., and Steven E. Lobell. 2010. "Realism and the Changing International System: Will China and Russia Challenge the Status Quo?" *China and Eurasia Forum Quarterly* 8 (4): 143–165.

Handel, Michael. 1981. *The Diplomacy of Surprise: Hitler, Nixon, Sadat.* Cambridge, MA: Harvard Center for International Affairs.

Handel, Michael. 1990. *Weak States in the International System.* London: Frank Cass.

Haraszti, Eva H. 1974. *Treaty Breakers or "Realpoliker": The Anglo-German Naval Agreement of June 1935.* Budapest: Harald Bolt Verlag, Académia Kiadó.

Hartmann, Frederick H. 1978. *The Relations of Nations.* 5th ed. New York: Macmillan.

Hartmann, Frederick H. 1982. *The Conservation of Enemies.* Westport, CT: Greenwood Press.

Haslam, Jonathan. 1992. *The Soviet Union and the Threat from the East, 1933–1941.* Pittsburgh, PA: University of Pittsburgh Press.

Haslam, Jonathan. 1997. "Soviet-German Relations and the Origins of the Second World War: The Jury Is Still Out." *Journal of Modern History* 69 (4): 785–797. doi:10.1086/245594.

He, Kai. 2012. "Undermining Adversaries: Unipolarity, Threat Perception, and Negative Balancing Strategies after the Cold War." *Security Studies* 21 (2): 154–191. doi:10.1080/09636412.2012.679201.

Hefler, H. Matthew. 2018. "In the Way: Intelligence, Eden, and British Foreign Policy towards Italy, 1937–38." *Intelligence and National Security* 33 (6): 875–893. doi: 10.1080/02684527.2018.1444433.

Heginbotham, Eric, et al. 2015. *The U.S.-China Military Scorecard: Forces, Geography, and the Evolving Balance of Power, 1996–2017.* Washington, DC: Rand.

Heller, Joseph. 1983. *British Policy towards the Ottoman Empire, 1908–1914*. London: Frank Cass.

Henke, Marina E. 2019. *Constructing Allied Cooperation: Diplomacy, Payments, and Power in Multilateral Military Coalitions*. Ithaca, NY: Cornell University Press.

Henry, Iain. 2020. "What Allies Want: Reconsidering Loyalty, Reliability, and Alliance Interdependence." *International Security* 44 (4): 45–83. doi.org/10.1162/ISEC_a_00375

Hernández-Sandoica, Elena, and Enrique Moradiellos. 2002. "Spain and the Second World War, 1939–1945." In *European Neutrals and Non-belligerents during the Second World War*, edited by Neville Wylie, 341–267. Cambridge: Cambridge University Press.

Herndon, James S. 1983. "British Perceptions of Soviet Military Capability, 1935–9." In *The Fascist Challenge and the Policy of Appeasement*, edited by W. J. Momsen and L. Kettenacker, 297–319. London: George Allen & Unwin.

Herwig, Holger. 1997. *The First World War: Germany and Austria-Hungary, 1914–1918*. New York: Arnold.

Hilger, Gustav, and Alfred G. Meyer. 1953. *Incompatible Allies: A Memoire-History of German-Soviet Relations, 1918–1941*. New York: Macmillan.

Hirschmann, Albert O. 1980. *National Power and the Structure of Foreign Trade*. Berkeley: University of California Press.

Hirszowicz, Lukasz. 1966. *The Third Reich and the Arab East*. London: Routledge & Kegan Paul.

Holsti, Ole R. 2001. "Alliances: Political." In *International Encyclopedia of the Social and Behavioral Sciences*, edited by Neil J. Smelser and Paul B. Bates, 397–401. Oxford: Pergamon.

Holsti, Ole R., P. Terrence Hopmann, and John D. Sullivan. 1973. *Unity and Disintegration in International Alliances: Comparative Studies*. New York: John Wiley & Sons.

Hosoya, Chihiro. 1976. "The Tripartite Pact, 1939–1940." In *Deterrent Diplomacy: Japan, Germany, and the USSR, 1935–1940*, edited by James W. Morley, 191–258. New York: Columbia University Press.

Howard, Harry N. 1931. *The Partition of Turkey: A Diplomatic History, 1913–1923*. Norman: University of Oklahoma Press.

Huang, Yuxing. 2020. "An Interdependence Theory of Wedge Strategies." *Chinese Journal of International Politics* 13 (2): 253–286. doi.org/10.1093/cjip/poaa004.

Hui, Victoria Tin-bor. 2005. *War and State Formation in Ancient China and Early Modern Europe*. Cambridge: Cambridge University Press.

Hull, Cordell. 1948. *The Memoirs of Cordell Hull*. Vol. 2. New York: Macmillan, 1948.

Hussain, Syed Rifaat. 2016. "Sino-Pakistan Ties: Trust, Cooperation, and Consolidation." In *The New Great Game: China and South and Central Asia in the Era of Reform*, edited by Thomas Fingar, 116–146. Palo Alto, CA: Stanford University Press.

Hyer, Eric. 2015. *The Pragmatic Dragon: China's Grand Strategy and Boundary Settlements*. Vancouver: University of British Columbia Press.

Ikle, Frank W. 1956. *German-Japanese Relations, 1936–1940*. New York: Bookman Associates.

Ikle, Frank W. 1965. "Japanese-German Peace Negotiations during World War I." *American Historical Review* 71 (1): 62–76. doi:10.1086/ahr/71.1.62.

Ikle, Fred C. 1964. *How Nations Negotiate*. New York: Praeger.

Ikle, Fred C. 1971. *Every War Must End*. New York: Columbia University Press.

Imlay, Talbot. 2003. *Facing the Second World War: Strategy, Politics, and Economics in Britain and France*. Oxford: Oxford University Press.

Izumikawa, Yasuhiro. 2002. "United We Stand, Divided They Fall: Use of Coercion and Rewards as Alliance Balancing Strategy." PhD diss., Georgetown University.

Izumikawa, Yasuhiro. 2013. "Theorizing Wedge Strategies in Alliance Politics," *Security Studies* 22 (3): 498–531. doi:10.1080/09636412.2013.816121.

Izumikawa, Yasuhiro. 2018. "Binding Strategies in Alliance Politics: The Soviet-Japanese-U.S. Diplomatic Tug of War in the Mid-1950s." *International Studies Quarterly* 62 (1): 108–120. doi:10.1093/isq/sqx070.

Jackson, Galen. 2012. "The Offshore Balancing Thesis Reconsidered: Realism, the Balance of Power in Europe, and America's Decision for War in 1917." *Security Studies* 21 (3): 455–489. doi:10.1080/09636412.2012.706502.

Jervis, Robert. 1976. *Perception and Misperception in International Politics*. Princeton, NJ: Princeton University Press.

Jervis, Robert. 1991. "Domino Beliefs and Strategic Behavior." In *Dominos and Bandwagons: Strategic Beliefs and Great Power Competition in the Eurasian Rimland*, edited by Robert Jervis and Jack Snyder, 20–50. New York: Oxford University Press.

Jervis, Robert. 1997. *System Effects: Complexity in Political and Social Life*. Princeton, NJ: Princeton University Press.

Ji, You. 2016. "China's Emerging Indo-Pacific Naval Strategy." *Asia Policy* 22 (July): 11–19.

Johnson, Jesse C. 2015a. "Alliance Treaty Obligations and War Intervention." *Conflict Management and Peace Science* 35 (5): 455–468. doi:10.1177/0738894215577557.

Johnson, Jesse C. 2015b. "The Costs of Security: Foreign Policy Concessions and Military Alliances." *Journal of Peace Research* 52 (5): 665–679. doi:10.1177/0022343314565434.

Johnston, Seth A. 2017. *How NATO Adapts: Strategy and Organization in the Atlantic Alliance since 1950*. Baltimore: Johns Hopkins University Press.

Joll, James, and Gordon Martel. 2007. *The Origins of the First World War*. 3rd ed. Harlow, UK: Pearson Longman.

Jonas, Manfred. 1984. *The United States and Germany: A Diplomatic History*. Ithaca, NY: Cornell University Press.

Joshi, Yogesh, and Harsh Pant. 2015. "Indo-Japanese Strategic Partnership and Power Transition in Asia." *India Review* 14 (3): 312–329. doi:10.1080/14736489.2015.1066215.

Kahn, Martin. 2013. "British Intelligence on Soviet War Potential in 1939." *Intelligence and National Security* 28 (5): 717–747. doi:10.1080/02684527.2012.748369.

Karsh, Efraim, and Inari Karsh. 1999. *Empires of the Sand: The Struggle for Mastery in the Middle East, 1789–1923*. Cambridge, MA: Harvard University Press.

Kaufman, Stuart, Richard Little, and William Wohlforth. 2007. *Balance of Power in World History*. London: Palgrave Macmillan.

Kecskemeti, Paul. 1958. *Strategic Surrender: The Politics of Victory and Defeat*. Palo Alto, CA: Stanford University Press.

Kendall-Taylor, Andrea, and David Shullman. 2019. "A Russian-Chinese Partnership Is a Threat to U.S. Interests." *Foreign Affairs*, May 14. https://www.foreign

affairs.com/articles/china/2019-05-14/russian-chinese-partnership-threat-us-interests.

Kennan, George F. 1961. *Russia and the West under Lenin and Stalin*. Boston: Little, Brown.

Kennedy, Ross A. 2001. "Woodrow Wilson, World War I, and an American Conception of National Security." *Diplomatic History* 25 (1): 1–31. doi:10.1111/0145-2096.00247.

Kershaw, Ian. 2007. *Fateful Choices: Ten Decisions That Changed the World, 1940–1941*. New York: Penguin Press.

Khurana, Gurpreet. 2016. "First China-India Maritime Dialogue: Beyond Icebreaking." Center for International Maritime Security (CIMSEC), April 5. http://cimsec.org/first-china-india-maritime-dialogue-beyond-icebreaking/23990.

Kim, Tongfi. 2011. "Why Alliances Entangle but Seldom Entrap States." *Security Studies* 20 (3): 350–377. doi:10.1080/09636412.2011.599201.

Kim, Tongfi. 2016. *The Supply Side of Security: A Market Theory of Military Alliances*. Palo Alto, CA: Stanford University Press.

Kissinger, Henry. 1994. *Diplomacy*. New York: Touchstone.

Knopf, Jeffrey. 2012. *Security Assurances and Nuclear Proliferation*. Palo Alto, CA: Stanford University Press.

Knorr, Klaus. 1975. *The Political Economy of International Relations*. New York: Basic Books.

Knox, Macgregor. 1982. *Mussolini Unleashed, 1939–1941: Politics and Strategy in Fascist Italy's Last War*. Cambridge: Cambridge University Press.

Kogan, Norma. 1963. *The Politics of Italian Foreign Policy*. New York: Praeger.

Kondapolli, Srikanth. 2016. "Perception and Strategic Reality in India-China Relations." In *The New Great Game: China and South and Central Asia in the Era of Reform*, edited by Thomas Fingar, 93–115. Palo Alto, CA: Stanford University Press.

Korolev, Alexander. 2018a. "On the Verge of an Alliance: Contemporary China-Russian Military Cooperation." *Asian Security* 15 (3): 233–252. doi:10.1080/14799855.2018.1463991.

Korolev, Alexander. 2018b. "Theories of Non-balancing and Russia's Foreign Policy." *Journal of Strategic Studies* 41 (6): 887–912. doi:10.1080/01402390.2017.1283614.

Kotkin, Stephen. 2017. *Stalin: Waiting for Hitler, 1929–1941*. New York: Penguin Press.

Krebs, Gerhard. 1997. "Japan and the German-Soviet War." In *From Peace to War: Germany, Soviet Russia and the World, 1939–1941*, edited by Bernd Wegner, 541–560. Providence, RI: Berghahn Books.

Krebs, Ronald R. and Jennifer Spindel. 2018. "Divided Priorities: When and Why Allies Differ Over Military Intervention." *Security Studies* 27 (4): 575–606. doi:10.1080/ 09636412.2018.14836089

Kreps, Sarah. 2011. *Coalitions of Convenience: United States Military Interventions after the Cold War*. New York: Oxford University Press.

Kroenig, Matthew. 2020a. *The Return of Great Power Rivalry: Democracy vs. Autocracy from the Ancient World to the U.S. and China*. Oxford: Oxford University Press.

Kroenig, Matthew. 2020b. "The United States Should Not Align with Russia Against China." *Foreign Policy*, May 13. https://foreignpolicy.com/2020/05/13/united-states-should-not-align-russia-against-china-geopolitical-rivalry-authoritarian-partnership/#.

Kuimova, Alexandra, and Siemon T. Wezeman. 2018. "Georgia and Black Sea Security." SIPRI Background Paper, Stockholm International Peace Research Institute. https://www.sipri.org/sites/default/files/2018-12/bp_1812_black_sea_georgia_0.pdf.

Kupchan, Charles. 2010. *How Enemies Become Friends: The Sources of Stable Peace.* Princeton, NJ: Princeton University Press.

Kupchan, Charles. 2017a. "Is NATO Getting Too Big to Succeed?" *New York Times,* May 25. https://www.nytimes.com/2017/05/25/opinion/nato-russia-donald-trump.html.

Kupchan, Charles. 2017b. "Why Giving Ukraine Lethal Weapons Would Be a Massive Mistake." *Washington Post,* August 7. https://www.washingtonpost.com/news/global-opinions/wp/2017/08/07/why-giving-ukraine-lethal-weapons-would-be-a-massive-mistake/.

Kupchan, Charles. 2019. "NATO Is Thriving in Spite of Trump: Adversity Has Made the Alliance Stronger." *Foreign Affairs,* March 20. https://www.foreignaffairs.com/articles/2019-03-20/nato-thriving-spite-trump.

Kurat, Y. T. 1967. "How Turkey Drifted into World War I." In *Studies in International Diplomacy,* edited by Kenneth Bourne and Donald Cameron Watt, 291–315. London: Longman.

Ladwig, Walter C. 2009. "Delhi's Pacific Ambition: Naval Power, 'Look East,' and India's Emerging Influence in the Asia-Pacific." *Asian Security* 5 (2): 87–113. doi:10.1080/14799850902886476.

Lake, David. 1999. *Entangling Relations: American Foreign Policy in its Century.* Princeton, NJ: Princeton University Press.

Lalwani, Sameer, and Heather Byrne. 2019. "Great Expectations: Asking Too Much of the US-India Strategic Partnership." *Washington Quarterly* 42 (3): 41–64. doi:10.1080/0163660X.2019.1666353.

Langer, William L., and S. Everett Gleason. 1952. *Challenge to Isolation: The World Crisis of 1937–1940 and American Foreign Policy.* New York: Harper & Row.

Langer, William L., and S. Everett Gleason. 1953. *The Undeclared War, 1940–1941.* New York: Harper & Row.

Lanoszka, Alexander. 2018. *Atomic Assurances: The Alliance Politics of Nuclear Proliferation.* Ithaca, NY: Cornell University Press.

Layne, Christopher. 2008. "Security Studies and the Use of History: Neville Chamberlain's Grand Strategy Revisited." *Security Studies* 17 (3): 397–437. doi:10.1080/09636410802319628.

Layne, Christopher. 2009. "America's Middle East Grand Strategy after Iraq: The Moment for Offshore Balancing Has Arrived." *Review of International Studies* 35 (1): 5–25. doi:10.1017/S0260210509008304.

Layne, Christopher. 2018. "The US-China Power Shift and the End of the Pax Americana." *International Affairs* 94 (1): 89–111. doi:10.1093/ia/iix249.

Leeds, Brett Ashley. 1999. "Domestic Political Institutions, Credible Commitments, and International Cooperation." *American Journal of Political Science* 43 (4): 979–1002. doi:10.2307/2991814.

Leeds, Brett Ashley. 2003. "Alliance Reliability in Times of War: Explaining State Decisions to Violate Treaties." *International Organization* 57 (4): 801–827. doi:10.1017/S0020818303574057.

Leeds, Brett Ashley, and Sezi Anac. 2005. "Alliance Institutionalization and Alliance Performance." *International Interactions* 31 (3): 183–202. doi:10.1080/0305062 0500294135.

Leeds, Brett Ashley, Andrew G. Long, and Sara McLaughlin Mitchell. 2000. "Reevaluating Alliance Reliability: Specific Threats, Specific Promises." *Journal of Conflict Resolution* 44 (5): 686–699. doi:10.1177/0022002700044005006.

Leeds, Brett Ashley, Michaela Mattes, and Jeremy S. Vogel. 2009. "Interests, Institutions, and the Reliability of Alliance Commitments." *American Journal of Political Science* 53 (2): 461–476. doi:10.1111/j.1540-5907.2009.00381.x.

Leeds, Brett Ashley, and Burcu Savun. 2007. "Terminating Alliances: Why Do States Abrogate Agreements?" *Journal of Politics* 69 (4): 1118–1132. doi:10.1111/j.1468 -2508.2007.00612.x.

Leitz, Christian. 1996. *Economic Relations between Nazi Germany and Franco's Spain.* Oxford: Clarendon Press, 1996.

Leitz, Christian. 1998. "More Carrot Than Stick: British Economic Warfare and Spain." *Twentieth Century British History* 9 (2): 246–273.

Leitz, Christian. 2001. *Sympathy for the Devil: Neutral Europe and Nazi Germany in World War II.* New York: New York University Press, 2001.

Lemon, Jason. 2018. "Russian Defense Minister Threatens Response If Sweden and Finland Join NATO." *Newsweek*, July 24. https://www.newsweek.com/russian -defense-minister-threatens-response-if-sweden-finland-join-nato-1040806.

Liff, Adam P. 2018. "China and the US Alliance System." *China Quarterly* 233 (March): 137–165. doi:10.1017/S0305741017000601.

Link, Arthur S. 1960. *Wilson: The Struggle for Neutrality, 1914–1915.* Princeton, NJ: Princeton University Press.

Link, Arthur S. 1964. *Wilson: Confusions and Crises, 1915–1916.* Princeton, NJ: Princeton University Press.

Link, Arthur S. 1965. *Wilson: Campaigns for Progressivism and Peace, 1916–1917.* Princeton, NJ: Princeton University Press.

Liska, George. 1962. *Nations in Alliance.* Baltimore: Johns Hopkins University Press.

Lobell, Steven E. 2009. "Threat Assessment, the State, and Foreign Policy: A Neoclassical Realist Model." In *Neoclassical Realism, the State, and Foreign Policy,* edited by Steven E. Lobell, Norrin M. Ripsman, and Jeffrey W. Taliaferro, 42–74. Cambridge: Cambridge University Press.

Lobell, Steven E. 2011a. "Winning Friends and Influencing Enemies among Great Power Rivals: The Case of Washington, Beijing, and Moscow, 1969–1979." *Chinese Journal of International Politics* 4: 205–230. doi:10.1093/cjip/por007.

Lobell, Steven E. 2011b. "Great Powers in a Restrictive International Environment." *International Journal* 66 (2): 335–350. doi:10.1177/002070201106600206.

Lobell, Steven E. 2018. "A Granular Theory of Balancing." *International Studies Quarterly* 62 (3): 593–605. doi:10.1093/isq/sqy011.

Lobell, Steven E., Norrin M. Ripsman, and Jeffrey W. Taliaferro, eds. 2009. *Neoclassical Realism, the State, and Foreign Policy.* Cambridge: Cambridge University Press.

Loewenheim, Francis L., Harold D. Langley, and Manfred Jonas. 1975. *Roosevelt and Churchill: Their Secret Wartime Correspondence.* New York: E. P. Dutton, 1975.

Long, William J. 1996. *Economic Incentives and Bilateral Cooperation.* Ann Arbor: University of Michigan Press.

Lorentzen, Peter, M. Taylor Fravel, and Jack Paine. 2017. "Qualitative Investigation of Theoretical Models: The Value of Process Tracing." *Journal of Theoretical Politics* 29 (3): 467–491. doi:10.1177/0951629816664420.

Lowe, C. J. 1969. "Britain and Italian Intervention, 1914–1915." *Historical Journal* 12 (3): 533–548. doi:10.1017/S0018246X00007275.

Lowe, C. J., and F. Marzari. 1975. *Italian Foreign Policy, 1870–1940*. London: Routledge and Kegan Paul.

Lowe, Peter. 1969. *Great Britain and Japan: A Study of British Far Eastern Policy*. London: Macmillan.

Luttwak, Edward. 2017. "Play Russia against China: 6 Out of the Box Ideas for Trump." *Politico Magazine*, January/February, 8–9. https://www.politico.com/magazine/story/2017/01/outside-the-box-ideas-policies-president-trump-administration-214661.

MacDonald, Paul K., and Joseph M. Parent. 2019. "Trump Didn't Shrink U.S. Military Commitments Abroad—He Expanded Them." *Foreign Affairs*, December 3. https://www.foreignaffairs.com/articles/2019-12-03/trump-didnt-shrink-us-military-commitments-abroad-he-expanded-them.

Machiavelli, Niccolò. 1996. *Discourses on Livy*. Translated by Harvey C. Mansfield and Nathan Tarcov. Chicago: University of Chicago Press.

Mack Smith, Denis. 1969. *Italy: A Modern History*. Ann Arbor: University of Michigan Press.

Mack Smith, Denis. 1983. "Appeasement as a Factor in Mussolini's Foreign Policy." In *The Fascist Challenge and the Policy of Appeasement*, edited by W. J. Momsen and L. Kettenacker, 258–266. London: Allen & Unwin.

Mack Smith, Denis. 1997. *Modern Italy: A Political History*. New Haven, CT: Yale University Press.

Mack Smith, Denis. 2000. "Mussolini: Reservations about Renzo de Felice's Biography." *Modern Italy* 4 (2): 193–210. doi:10.1080/713685676.

Mahoney, James. 2015. "Process Tracing and Historical Explanation." *Security Studies* 24 (2): 200–218. doi:10.1080/09636412.2015.1036610.

Makela, Petri. 2019. "These Are the Military Exercises Russia Will Conduct This Fall." *National Interest*, September 15. https://nationalinterest.org/blog/buzz/these-are-military-exercises-russia-will-conduct-fall-80451.

Malik, Mohan. 2003. "Eyeing the Dragon: India's China Debate." Special Assessment, Asia-Pacific Center for Security Studies, Honolulu, HI.

Mallet, Robert. 1997. "The Anglo-Italian Trade Negotiations, Contraband Control and the Failure to Appease Mussolini, 1939–40." *Diplomacy and Statecraft* 8 (1): 137–167. doi:10.1080/09592299708406033.

Mallett, Robert. 2003. *Mussolini and the Origins of the Second World War*. New York: Palgrave Macmillan.

Mandelbaum, Michael. 1981. *The Nuclear Revolution*. Cambridge: Cambridge University Press.

Manne, Robert. 1974. "The British Decision for Alliance with Russia, May 1939." *Journal of Contemporary History* 9 (3): 3–26. doi:10.1177/002200947400900301.

Manne, Robert. 1981. "Some British Light on the Nazi-Soviet Pact." *European Studies Review* 11:83–102. doi:10.1177/026569148101100104.

Marzari, Frank. 1970. "Projects for an Italian-Led Balkan Bloc of Neutrals, September–December 1939." *Historical Journal* 13 (4): 767–788. doi:10.1017/S0018246X00009493.

Mastro, Oriana Skylar. 2019. "China/Russia Strategic Alliance." *Newt's World,* Westwood One Podcast Network, October27, 9:24–10:12.

Mastro, Oriana Skylar, and Arzan Tarapore. 2017. "Countering Chinese Coercion: The Case of Doklam." *War on the Rocks,* August 29. https://warontherocks.com /2017/08/countering-chinese-coercion-the-case-of-doklam/.

Mattes, Michaela. 2012. "Reputation, Symmetry, and Alliance Design." *International Organization* 66 (4): 679–707. doi:10.1017/S002081831200029X.

May, Ernest R. 1959. *The World War and American Isolation 1914–1917.* Chicago: Quadrangle Books.

Mazarr, Michael J., Jonathan S. Blake, Abigail Casey, Tim McDonald, Stephanie Pezard, and Michael Spirtas. 2018. *Understanding the Emerging Era of International Competition: Theoretical and Historical Perspectives.* RR-2726-AF. Santa Monica, CA: Rand.

McMeekin, Sean. 2011. *The Russian Origins of the First World War.* Cambridge, MA: Harvard University Press.

MEA-GI 2018. "Second India-China Maritime Affairs Dialogue." Ministry of External Affairs, Government of India, July 13. https://www.mea.gov.in/press -releases.htm?dtl/30048/Second+IndiaChina+Maritime+Affairs+Dialogue.

Mearsheimer, John J. 2001. *The Tragedy of Great Power Politics.* New York: Norton.

Mearsheimer, John J. 2014. "Why the Ukraine Crisis is the West's Fault." *Foreign Affairs* 93 (5): 1–12.

Mearsheimer, John J. 2018. *The Great Delusion: Liberal Dreams and International Realities.* New Haven, CT: Yale University Press.

Mearsheimer, John J. 2019. "Bound to Fail: The Rise and Fall of the Liberal International Order." *International Security* 43 (4): 7–50. doi:10.1162/isec_a_00342.

Medcalf, Rory. 2016. "The Western Indo-Pacific: India, China, and the Terms of Engagement." *Asia Policy* 22 (July): 61–67.

Menon, Raja. 2016. "India's Response to China's Naval Presence in the Indian Ocean." *Asia Policy* 22 (July): 41–48.

Mercer, Jonathan. 1996. *Reputation in International Politics.* Ithaca, NY: Cornell University Press.

Messerschmidt, Manfred. 1998. "Foreign Policy and Preparation for War." In *Germany and the Second World War,* vol. 1, *The Build-Up of German Aggression,* edited by the Research Institute for Military History, Freiburg, Germany, 541–717. Oxford: Clarendon Press.

Miller, Geoffrey. 1997. *Straits: British Policy towards the Ottoman Empire and the Origins of the Dardanelles Campaign.* Hull, UK: University of Hull Press.

Miller, Gregory. 2012. *The Shadow of the Past: Reputation and Military Alliances before the First World War.* Ithaca, NY: Cornell University Press.

Miller, J. Bershire, and Benoit Hardy-Chartran. 2019. "Russia and China's Strategic Marriage of Convenience." *National Interest,* August 27. https://nationalinterest .org/feature/russia-and-china%E2%80%99s-strategic-marriage-convenience -76466.

Millman, Brock. 1995. "Turkish Foreign and Strategic Policy, 1934–42." *Middle Eastern Studies* 31 (3): 483–508.

Millman, Brock. 1998. *The Ill-Made Alliance: Anglo-Turkish Relations, 1934–1940.* Montreal: McGill-Queen's University Press.

Mills, W. C. 1993. "The Nyon Conference: Neville Chamberlain, Anthony Eden, and the Appeasement of Italy in 1937." *International History Review* 15 (1): 1–22.

Mishra, Rahul. 2013. "China in India's Southeast Asian Strategy." In *India-ASEAN Defence Relations*, edited by Ajaya Kumar Das, 96–123. Singapore: S. Rajaratnam School of International Studies.

Mitchell, A. Wess, and Jakub Grygiel. 2016. "Predators on the Frontier." *American Interest* 11 (5): 1–10.

Modelski, George. 1962. *A Theory of Foreign Policy*. New York: Praeger.

Mohan, C. Raja. 2013. "An Uncertain Trumpet? India's Role in Southeast Asian Security." In *India-ASEAN Defence Relations*, edited by Ajaya Kumar Das, 8–32. Singapore: S. Rajaratnam School of International Studies.

Moniz, Ernest J., and Sam Nunn. 2019. "The Return of Doomsday: The New Nuclear Arms Race—and How Washington and Moscow Can Stop It." *Foreign Affairs* 98 (5): 150–161.

Montesquieu. 1965. *Considerations on the Causes of the Greatness of the Romans and Their Decline*. Translated and edited by David Lowenthal. New York: Free Press.

Montgomery, Evan Braden. 2014. "Contested Primacy in the Western Pacific: China's Rises and the Future of US Power Projection." *International Security* 38 (4): 115–149. doi:10.1162/ISEC_a_00160.

Moorhouse, Roger. 2014. *The Devils Alliance: Hitler's Pact with Stalin, 1939–41*. London: The Bodley Head.

Morewood, Steven. 1989. "Anglo-Italian Rivalry in the Mediterranean and the Middle East, 1935–1940." In *Paths to War: New Essays on the Origins of the Second World War*, edited by Robert Boyce and Esmonde M. Robertson, 167–198. New York: St. Martin's Press.

Morgan, Patrick. 1977. *Deterrence: A Conceptual Analysis*. Beverly Hills, CA: Sage.

Morgan, Patrick. 2006. *International Security: Problems and Solutions*. Washington, DC: Congressional Quarterly Press.

Morgenthau, Hans J. 1950. "The Mainsprings of American Foreign Policy: The National Interest vs. Moral Abstractions." *American Political Science Review* 44 (4): 833–854. doi:10.2307/1951286.

Morgenthau, Hans J. 1959. "Alliances in Theory and Practice." In *Alliance Policy in the Cold War*, edited by Arnold Wolfers, 184–212. Baltimore: Johns Hopkins University Press.

Morgenthau, Hans J. 1967. *Politics among Nations: The Struggle for Power and Peace*. 3rd ed. New York: Knopf.

Morrow, James D. 2000. "Alliances: Why Write Them Down?" *Annual Review of Political Science* 3 (June): 63–84.

Mulligan, William. 2014. *The Great War for Peace*. New Haven, CT: Yale University Press.

Murray, Williamson. 1979. "The Role of Italy in British Strategy, 1938–1939." *Journal of Royal United Services Institute* 124 (3): 43–49.

Naidu, G. V. C. 2013. "India and the Indian Ocean." In *India-ASEAN Defence Relations*, edited by Ajaya Kumar Das, 236–259. Singapore: S. Rajaratnam School of International Studies.

Neave-Hill, B. R. 1975. "Franco-British Strategic Policy, 1939." In *Les Relations Franco-Britanniques, 1935–1939*, 337–358. Paris: Centre National de la Recherche Scientifique.

Neilson, Keith. 1993. "Pursued by a Bear: British Estimates of Soviet Military Strength and Anglo-Soviet Relations." *Canadian Journal of History* 28 (2): 215–216.

Neilsen, Keith. 2009. *Britain, Soviet Russia and the Collapse of the Versailles Order, 1919–1939*. Cambridge: Cambridge University Press.

Neumann, Sigmund. 1946. *The Future in Perspective*. New York: G. P. Putnam and Sons.

Newnham, Randall. 2002. *Deutsche Mark Diplomacy: Positive Economic Sanctions in German-Russian Relations*. University Park: Pennsylvania State University Press.

Newnham, Randall. 2008. "Coalition of the Bribed and Bullied: U.S. Economic Linkage and the Iraq War Coalition." *International Studies Perspectives* 9 (2): 183–200. doi:10.1111/j.1528-3585.2008.00326.x.

Nexon, Daniel. 2009. "The Balance of Power in the Balance." *World Politics* 61 (2): 330–359. doi:10.1017/S0043887109000124.

Nicosia, Francis R. 2015. *Nazi Germany and the Arab World*. Cambridge: Cambridge University Press.

Nincic, Miroslav. 2010. "Positive Inducements in International Relations." *International Security* 35 (1): 138–183. doi:10.1162/ISEC_a_00006.

Nincic, Miroslav. 2011. *The Logic of Positive Engagement*. Ithaca, NY: Cornell University Press.

Nish, Ian. 1972. *Alliance in Decline*. London: Athlone Press.

Nish, Ian. 1977. *Japanese Foreign Policy, 1869–1942*. London: Routledge and Kegan Paul.

Nish, Ian. 1988. "Japan, 1914–18." In *Military Effectiveness*, vol. 1, *The First World War*, edited by Allan R. Millet and Williamson Murray, 229–248. Boston: Unwin Hyman.

Nish, Ian. 1995. "Japan." In *Decisions for War 1914*, edited by Keith Wilson, 229–268. New York: St. Martin's Press.

Oakes, Amy. 2012. *Diversionary War: Domestic Unrest and International Conflict*. Palo Alto, CA: Stanford University Press.

O'Dwyer, Gerard. 2017. "Russia Promises 'Countermeasures' If Finland Joins NATO." *Defense News*, October 13. https://www.defensenews.com/global/europe/2017/10/13/russia-promises-countermeasures-if-finland-joins-nato/.

O'Hanlon, Michael. 2019. "Can America Still Protect Its Allies? How to Make Deterrence Work." *Foreign Affairs* 98 (5): 193–203.

Oran, B. 2010. *Turkish Foreign Policy, 1919–2006: Facts and Analyses with Documents*. Salt Lake City: University of Utah Press.

Organski, A. F. K. 1968. *World Politics*. New York. Knopf.

Oros, Andrew. 2017. *Japan's Security Renaissance: New Policies and Politics for the Twenty-First Century*. New York: Columbia University Press.

O'Rourke, Lindsay. 2018. *Covert Regime Change: America's Secret Cold War*. Ithaca, NY: Cornell University Press.

Osgood, Robert E. 1953. *Ideals and Self-Interests in America's Foreign Relations*. Chicago: University of Chicago Press.

Overy, Richard. 1995. *Why the Allies Won*. New York: Norton, 1995.

Overy, Richard. 2009. *1939: Countdown to War*. London: Allen Lane.

Palumbo, Michael. 1979. "German-Italian Military Relations on the Eve of World War I." *Central European History* 12:343–371. doi:10.1017/S0008938900022469.

Pant, Harsh. 2016. *Indian Foreign Policy: An Overview*. Manchester: Manchester University Press.

Pant, Harsh V., and Abhijnan Rej. 2018. "Is India Ready for the Indo-Pacific?" *Washington Quarterly* 41 (2): 47–61. doi:10.1080/0163660X.2018.1485403.

Pardesi, Manjeet. 2016. "India's China Policy." In *Engaging the World: Indian Foreign Policy since 1947*, edited by Sumit Ganguly, 167–194. New York: Oxford University Press.

Parent, Joseph M., and Sebastian Rosato. 2015. "Balancing in Realism." *International Security* 40 (2): 51–86. doi:10.1162/ISEC_a_00216.

Parker, R. A. C. 1974. "Great Britain, France and the Ethiopian Crisis, 1935–1936." *English Historical Review* 89 (351): 293–332.

Petracchi, Giorgio. 1997. "Pinochio, the Cat, and the Fox: Italy between Germany and the Soviet Union." In *From Peace to War: Germany, Soviet Russia and the World, 1939–1941*, edited by Bernd Wegner, 499–524. Providence, RI: Berghahn Books.

Pike, David W. 1982. "Franco and the Axis Stigma." *Journal of Contemporary History* 17 (3): 369–480. doi:10.1177/002200948201700301.

Pinkham, Sophie. 2019. "Ukraine Needs More Than Lethal Aid from the United States: It Needs a Partner in Peace." *Foreign Affairs*, November 8. https://www.foreignaffairs.com/articles/ukraine/2019-11-08/ukraine-needs-more-lethal-aid-united-states.

Poast, Paul. 2012. "Does Issue Linkage Work? Evidence from European Alliance Negotiations, 1860–1945." *International Organization* 66 (2): 277–310. doi:10.1017/S0020818312000069.

Poast, Paul. 2019. *Arguing about Alliances: The Art of Agreement in Military-Pact Negotiations*. Ithaca, NY: Cornell University Press.

Pokharel, Krishna and Bill Spindle. 2020. "After China Border Fight, India Likely Weighs Closer U.S. Military Ties." *Wall Street Journal*, June 21. https://www.wsj.com/articles/after-china-border-fight-india-likely-weighs-closer-u-s-military-ties-11592765506

Pons, Silvio. 2002. *Stalin and the Inevitable War*. New York: Routledge.

Poole, DeWitt C. 1946. "Light on Nazi Foreign Policy." *Foreign Affairs* 25 (1): 130–154.

Porter, Patrick. 2018. "Why America's Grand Strategy Has Not Changed: Power, Habit, and the U.S. Foreign Policy Establishment." *International Security* 42 (4): 9–46. doi:10.1162/ISEC_a_00311.

Porter, Patrick. 2019. "Advice for a Dark Age: Managing Great Power Competition." *Washington Quarterly* 42 (1): 7–25. doi:10.1080/0163660X.2019.1590079.

Posen, Barry. 1984. *The Sources of Military Doctrine*. Ithaca, NY: Cornell University Press.

Posen, Barry. 2009. "Emerging Multipolarity: Why Should We Care?" *Current History* 108 (721): 347–352.

Posen, Barry. 2011. "From Unipolarity to Multipolarity: Transition in Sight?" In *International Relations Theory and the Consequences of Unipolarity*, edited by G. John Ikenberry, Michael Mastanduno, and William C. Wohlforth, 317–341. Cambridge: Cambridge University Press.

Posen, Barry. 2014. *Restraint: A New Foundation for U.S. Grand Strategy*. Ithaca, NY: Cornell University Press.

Powell, Robert. 2006. "War as a Commitment Problem." *International Organization* 60 (Winter): 169–203. doi:10.1017/S0020818306060061.

Pozniakov, Vladimir. 2000. "The Enemy at the Gates: Soviet Military Intelligence in the Inter-War Period and Its Forecasts of Future War, 1921–41." In *Russia in the*

Age of Wars, 1914–1945, edited by Silvio Pons and Andrea Romano, 224–226. Milan: Feltrinelli.

Press-Barnathan, Galia. 2000/01. "The Lure of Regional Security Arrangements: The United States and Regional Security Cooperation in Asia and Europe." *Security Studies* 10 (2): 49–97. doi:10.1080/09636410008429430.

Pressman, Jeremy. 2008. *Warring Friends: Alliance Restraint in International Politics*. Ithaca, NY: Cornell University Press.

Preston, Paul. 1990. *The Politics of Revenge: Fascism and the Military in Twentieth-Century Spain*. London: Unwin-Hyman.

Preston, Paul. 1992. "Franco and Hitler: The Myth of Hendaye 1940." *Contemporary European History* 1 (1): 1–16. doi:10.1017/S0960777300005038.

Procacci, Giovanni. 1995. "A 'Latecomer' in War: The Case of Italy." In *Authority, Identity, and the Social History of the Great War*, edited by Frans Coetzee and Marilyn Shevin-Coetzee, 3–28. Providence, RI: Berghahn Books.

Pu, Xiaoyu. 2018. "Asymmetrical Competitors: Status Concerns and the China-India Rivalry." In *The China-India Rivalry in the Globalization Era*, edited by T. V. Paul, 55–74. Washington, DC: Georgetown University Press.

Puzzo, Dante. 1962. *Spain and the Great Powers, 1936–1941*. New York: Columbia University Press.

Rapp-Hooper, Mira. 2014. "Ambivalent Albion, Ambitious Ally: Britain's Decision for No Separate Peace in 1914." *Security Studies* 23 (4): 814–844. doi:10.1080/096 36412.2014.965002.

Rapp-Hooper, Mira. 2016. "China's Short-Term Victory in the South China Sea and Its Long-Term Problem." *Foreign Affairs*, March 21. https://www.foreignaffairs .com/articles/china/2016-03-21/chinas-short-term-victory-south-china-sea.

Rapp-Hooper, Mira. 2020. *Shields of the Republic: The Triumph and Peril of America's Alliances*. Cambridge, MA: Harvard University Press.

Rathbun, Brian C. 2014. *Diplomacy's Value: Creating Security in 1920s Europe and the Contemporary Middle East*. Ithaca, NY: Cornell University Press.

Rehman, Iskander. 2009. "Keeping the Dragon at Bay: India's Counter-Containment of China in Asia." *Asian Security* 5 (2): 114–143. doi:10.1080/14799850902885114.

Renouvin, Pierre. 1975. "Les Relations de la Grand-Bretagne et de la France avec L'Italie en 1938–1939." In *Les Relations Franco-Britanniques, 1935–1939*, 295–315. Paris: Centre National de la Recherche Scientifique.

Renzi, William. 1966. "The Russian Foreign Office and Italy's Entrance into the Great War, 1914–1915: A Study in Wartime Diplomacy." *The Historian* 28 (4): 648–668.

Renzi, William. 1970. "Great Britain, Russia, and the Straits, 1914–1915." *Journal of Modern History* 40 (1): 1–20. doi:10.1086/240513.

Renzi, William. 1987. *In the Shadow of the Sword: Italy's Neutrality and Entrance into the Great War, 1914–1915*. New York: Peter Lang.

Resis, Albert. 2000. "The Fall of Litvinov: Harbinger of the German-Soviet Non-aggression Pact." *Europe-Asia Studies* 52 (1): 35–56. doi:10.1080/09668130098253.

Resnick, Evan N. 2001. "Defining Engagement." *Journal of International Affairs* 54 (2): 551–566.

Resnick, Evan N. 2010/11. "Strange Bedfellows: U.S. Bargaining Behavior with Allies of Convenience." *International Security* 35 (3): 144–184. doi:10.1162/ISEC_a_00026.

Resnick, Evan N. 2019. *Allies of Convenience: A Theory of Bargaining in U.S. Foreign Policy*. New York: Columbia University Press.

Reynolds, David. 1981. *The Creation of the Anglo-American Alliance, 1937–41: A Study in Competitive Cooperation*. Chapel Hill: University of North Carolina Press.

Rice, E. H. 1974. "British Policy in Turkey 1908–1914." PhD diss., University of Toronto.

Rich, Norman. 1973. *Hitler's War Aims: Ideology, the Nazi State, and the Course of Expansion*. Vol. 1. London: Andre Deutsch.

Rich, Norman. 1992. *Great Power Diplomacy, 1814–1914*. New York: McGraw Hill.

Riker, William H. 1962. *The Theory of Political Coalitions*. New Haven, CT: Yale University Press.

Ripsman, Norrin M., and Jack S. Levy. 2008. "Wishful Thinking or Buying Time? The Virtues of British Appeasement in the 1930s." *International Security* 33 (2): 148–181. doi:10.1162/isec.2008.33.2.148.

Ripsman, Norrin M., Jeffrey W. Taliaferro, and Steven E. Lobell. 2016. *Neoclassical Realist Theory of International Politics*. New York: Oxford University Press.

Roberts, Geoffrey. 1992. "The Soviet Decision for a Pact with Nazi Germany." *Soviet Studies* 44 (1): 57–78.

Roberts, Geoffrey. 1995. *The Soviet Union and the Origins of the Second World War*. London: Macmillan.

Roberts, Geoffrey. 1996. "The Alliance that Failed: Moscow and the Triple Alliance Negotiations, 1939." *European History Quarterly* 26 (3): 383–414. doi:10.1177/026569149602600303.

Roberts, Geoffrey. 2002. "Stalin, the Pact with Nazi Germany, and the Origins of Postwar Soviet Diplomatic Historiography." *Journal of Cold War Studies* 4 (4): 93–103. doi:10.1162/15203970260209527.

Roberts, Geoffrey. 2006. *Stalin's Wars*. New Haven, CT: Yale University Press.

Robertson, Esmonde M. 1963. *Hitler's Pre-war Policy and Military Plans, 1933–1939*. London: Longman.

Robertson, James C. 1975. "The Hoare-Laval Plan." *Journal of Contemporary History* 10 (3): 433–464. doi:10.1177/002200947501000304.

Rock, Stephen. 2000. *Appeasement in International Politics*. Lexington: University Press of Kentucky.

Rogin, Josh. 2017. "Trump Administration Approves Lethal Arms Sales to Ukraine." *Washington Post*, December 20. https://www.washingtonpost.com/news/josh-rogin/wp/2017/12/20/trump-administration-approves-lethal-arms-sales-to-ukraine/.

Rosecrance, Richard, and Chih-Ching Lo. 1996. "Balancing, Stability, and War: The Mysterious Case of the Napoleonic International System." *International Studies Quarterly* 40 (4): 479–500. doi:10.2307/2600888.

Ross, Robert. 1995. *Negotiating Cooperation: The United States and China, 1969–1989*. Palo Alto, CA: Stanford University Press.

Ross, Robert. 2018. "Troubled Waters." *National Interest* 155 (May/June): 53–61.

Ross, Robert S. 2019. "Sino-Russian Relations: The False Promise of Russian Balancing." *International Politics*, first online, September 13. doi:10.1057/s41311-019-00192-w.

Roth, Karl Heinz. 2004. "Berlin-Ankara-Baghdad: Franz von Papen and German Middle East Policy during the Second World War." In *Germany and the Middle East, 1871–1945*, edited by Wolfgang G. Schwanitz, 181–214. Princeton, NJ: Markus Wiener.

Rothstein, Robert L. 1968. *Alliances and Small Powers*. New York: Columbia University Press.

Royama, Masamichi. 1973. *Foreign Policy of Japan: 1914–1939*. Westport, CT: Greenwood Press.

Russett, Bruce. 1970. "Components of an Operational Theory of Alliance Formation." In *Alliance in International Politics*, edited by Julian Friedman, Christopher Bladen, and Steven Rosen, 238–259. Boston: Allyn & Bacon.

Saalman, Lora. 2014. "Fractured Mirrors: Chinese Views on Indian Deterrence at Sea." In *Maritime Security in the Indo-Pacific: Perspectives from China, India, and the United States*, edited by Mohan Malik, 137–154. Lanham, MD: Rowman & Littlefield.

Saenze-Frances, Emillio. 2009. *Entre la Antorcha y la Esvastica: Franco en la Encrucijada de la Segunda Guerra Mundial*. Madrid: Actas Editorial.

Salerno, Reynolds. 1997. "The French Navy and Appeasement of Italy, 1937–9." *English Historical Review* 112 (445): 66–104. doi:10.1093/ehr/CXII.445.66.

Salerno, Reynolds. 2002. *Vital Crossroads: Mediterranean Origins of the Second World War, 1935–1940*. Ithaca, NY: Cornell University Press.

Santora, Marc. 2020. "Pompeo Calls China's Ruling Party 'Central Threat of Our Times.'" *New York Times*, January 31, A4.

Saveliev, Igor R., and Uri S. Pestushko. 2001. "Dangerous Rapprochement: Russia and Japan in the First World War, 1914–1916." *Acta Slavonica Japonica* 18:19–41.

Sazonov, Serge. *Fateful Years, 1909–1916*. New York: Frederick A. Stokes Co.

Scheinmann, Gabriel. 2019. "Competing for Allies: How, When, and Why States Flip Alliances." In *Ironclad: Forging a New Future for America's Alliances*, edited by Michael J. Green, 183–192. Lanham, MD: Rowman & Littlefield.

Schelling, Thomas C. 1963. *The Strategy of Conflict*. Cambridge, MA: Harvard University Press.

Schelling, Thomas C. 1966. *Arms and Influence*. New Haven, CT: Yale University Press.

Schelling, Thomas C. 1989. "Promises." *Negotiation Journal* 5 (2): 113–118. doi:10.1111/j.1571-9979.1989.tb00504.x.

Schmitt, Bernadotte E. 1955. "Italian Diplomacy 1939–1941." *Journal of Modern History* 27 (2): 159–168. doi:10.1086/237784.

Schonherr, Klaus. 1997. "Neutrality, 'Non-belligerence,' or War: Turkey and the European Powers' Conflict of Interests." In *From Peace to War: Germany, Soviet Russia and the World, 1939–1941*, edited by Bernd Wegner, 481–498. Providence, RI: Berghahn Books.

Schreiber, Gerhard. 1995. "Political and Military Developments in the Mediterranean Area, 1939–1940." In *Germany and the Second World War*, vol. 3, edited by the Research Institute for Military History, Freiburg, Germany, 5–278. Oxford: Clarendon Press.

Schroeder, Paul. 2007. "Stealing Horses to Great Applause." In *An Improbable War*, edited by Holger Afflerbach and David Stevenson, 17–42. New York: Berghahn Books.

Schuman, Frederick L. 1933. *International Politics: An Introduction to the Western State System*. New York: Mc-Graw Hill.

Schwantiz, Wolfgang. G. 2004. "The Jinee and the Magic Bottle: Fritz Grobba and the German Middle Eastern Policy, 1900–1945." In *Germany and the Middle East,*

1871–1945, edited by Wolfgang G. Schwanitz, 86–117. Princeton, NJ: Markus Wiener.

Schweller, Randall L. 1998. *Deadly Imbalances: Tripolarity and Hitler's Strategy of World Conquest.* New York: Columbia University Press.

Schweller, Randall L. 2006. *Unanswered Threats: Political Constraints on the Balance of Power.* Princeton, NJ: Princeton University Press.

Scobell, Andrew. 2018. "The South China Sea and U.S. China Rivalry." *Political Science Quarterly* 133 (2): 199–224.

Seton-Watson, Christopher. 1983. "The Anglo-Italian Gentleman's Agreement of January 1937 and Its Aftermath." In *The Fascist Challenge and the Policy of Appeasement*, edited by W. J. Momsen and L. Kettenacker, 267–283. London: George Allen & Unwin.

Shanafelt, G. 1985. *The Secret Enemy: Austria-Hungary and the German Alliance, 1914–1918.* Boulder, CO: East European Monographs.

Shankar, Mahesh. 2018. "Territory and the India-China Competition." In *The China-India Rivalry in the Globalization Era*, edited by T. V. Paul, 27–54. Washington, DC: Georgetown University Press.

Shaw, Louise Grace. 2003. *The British Political Elite and the Soviet Union, 1937–1939.* New York: Routledge.

Sherwood, Robert E. 1948. *The White House Papers of Harry L. Hopkins.* Vol. 1. London: Eyre and Spottiswoode.

Shields, Sarah D. 2011. *Fezzes in the River: Identity Politics and European Diplomacy in the Middle East on the Eve of World War II.* New York: Oxford University Press.

Shifrinson, Joshua R. Itzkowitz. 2018. *Rising Titans, Falling Giants: How Great Powers Exploit Power Shifts.* Ithaca, NY: Cornell University Press.

Shirkey, Zachary. 2009. *Is This a Private Fight or Can Anybody Join?* Burlington, VT: Ashgate.

Shorrock, William. 1988. *From Ally to Enemy: The Enigma of Fascist Italy in French Diplomacy, 1920–1940.* Kent, OH: Kent State University Press.

Silberstein, Gerard E. 1970. *Troubled Alliance: German-Austrian Relations, 1914–1917.* Lexington: University Press of Kentucky.

Singer, J. D. 1963. "Inter-Nation Influence: A Formal Model." *American Political Science Review* 57 (2): 420–430. doi:10.2307/1952832.

Singh, Abhiji. 2016. "India's Strategic Imperatives in the Asian Commons." *Asia Policy* 22 (July): 35–40.

Singh, Bilveer. 2013. "ASEAN's Defence Strategy: Betwixt Vocabulary and Actions." In *India-ASEAN Defence Relations*, edited by Ajaya Kumar Das, 146–167. Singapore: S. Rajaratnam School of International Studies.

Singh, Sinderpal. 2019. "The Dilemmas of Regional States: How Southeast Asian States View and Respond to India-China Maritime Competition." *Asian Security* 15 (1): 44–59. doi:10.1080/14799855.2019.1539819.

Siverson, Randolph M., and Joel King. 1980. "Attributes of National Alliance Membership and War Participation, 1815–1965." *American Journal of Political Science* 24 (1): 1–15.

Slater, Dan, and Daniel Ziblatt. 2013. "The Enduring Indispensability of Controlled Comparison." *Comparative Political Studies* 46 (1): 1301–1327. doi:10.1177/0010414012472469.

Smith, Clarence Jay. 1956. *The Russian Struggle for Power, 1914–1917*. New York: Philosophical Library.

Smith, Daniel M. 1965. *The Great Departure: The United States and World War I, 1914–1920*. New York: John Wiley & Sons.

Smith, Daniel M. 1966. *American Intervention, 1917*. Boston: Houghton Mifflin.

Smith, Jeff M. 2014. "Traditional Maritime Challenges." In *Maritime Security in the Indo-Pacific: Perspectives from China, India, and the United States*, edited by Mohan Malik, 121–136. Lanham, MD: Rowman & Littlefield.

Smoke, Richard. 1976. "Theory for and about Policy." In *In Search of Global Patterns*, edited by James N. Rosenau, 185–191. New York: Free Press.

Smoke, Richard, and Alexander George. 1973. "Theory for Policy in International Affairs." *Policy Sciences* 4:387–413.

Smyth, Denis. 1986. *Diplomacy and Strategy of Survival: British Policy and Franco's Spain, 1940–41*. Cambridge: Cambridge University Press.

Smyth, Denis. 1999. "Franco and the Allies in the Second World War." In *Spain and the Great Powers in the Twentieth Century*, edited by Sebastian Balfour and Paul Preston, 185–209. London: Routledge.

Snyder, Glenn H. 1971. "Prisoner's Dilemma and Chicken Models in International Politics." *International Studies Quarterly* 15 (1): 66–103. doi.org/10.2307/3013593.

Snyder, Glenn H. 1997. *Alliance Politics*. Ithaca, NY: Cornell University Press.

Snyder, Glenn H., and Paul Diesing. 1977. *Conflict among Nations: Bargaining, Decision Making, and System Structure in International Crises*. Princeton, NJ: Princeton University Press.

Sochi, Naraoka. 2015. "Japan's First World War–Era Diplomacy, 1914–15." In *Japan and the Great War*, edited by Oliviero Frattolillo and Antony Best, 36–50. New York: Palgrave Macmillan.

Socor, Vladimir. 2018. "The United States Does the Heavy Lifting for NATO in Georgia." *Eurasia Daily Monitor* 15 (119). https://jamestown.org/program/the-united-states-does-the-heavy-lifting-for-nato-in-georgia/.

Stafford, Paul. 1983. "The Chamberlain-Halifax Visit to Rome: A Reappraisal." *English Historical Review* 98 (386): 61–100. doi:10.1093/ehr/XCVIII.CCCLXXXVI.61.

Stafford, Paul. 1984. "The French Government and the Danzig Crisis: The Italian Dimension." *International History Review* 6 (1): 49–87.

Steiner, Zara. 2011. *The Triumph of the Dark: European International History 1933–1939*. Oxford: Oxford University Press.

Stent, Angela. 2020. "Russia and China: Axis of Revisionists?" Global China Report, Brookings Institution, Washington, DC. https://www.brookings.edu/research/russia-and-china-axis-of-revisionists/.

Stevenson, David. 2004. *Cataclysm: The First World War as Political Tragedy*. New York: Basic Books.

Stokes, Jacob. 2017. "Russia and China's Enduring Alliance: A Reverse Nixon Strategy Won't Work." *Foreign Affairs*, February 22. https://www.foreignaffairs.com/articles/china/2017-02-22/russia-and-china-s-enduring-alliance.

Stokes, Jacob, and Julianne Smith. 2020. "Facing Down the Sino-Russian Entente." *Washington Quarterly* 43 (2): 137–156. doi.org/10.1080/0163660X.2020.1771048

Stoller, Mark A. 2000. *Allies and Adversaries: The Joint Chiefs of Staff, the Grand Alliance, and U.S. Strategy in World War II*. Chapel Hill: University of North Carolina Press.

Stone, Glyn A. 2005. *Spain, Portugal and the Great Powers, 1931–1941.* New York: Palgrave Macmillan.

Stone, Norman. 1983. "The Austro-German Alliance, 1914–18." In *Coalition Warfare: An Uneasy Accord,* edited by Keith Nielsen and Roy Prete, 17–28. Ontario: Wilfred Laurier University Press.

Stone, Norman. 2007. *World War One: A Short History.* New York: Basic Books.

Strachan, Hew. 2004. *The First World War.* Vol. 1, *To Arms.* Oxford: Oxford University Press.

Strang, G. Bruce. 1999. "War and Peace: Mussolini's Road to Munich." *Diplomacy and Statecraft* 10 (2–3): 160–190. doi:10.1080/09592299908406128.

Strang, G. Bruce. 2006. "John Bull in Search of a Suitable Russia: British Foreign Policy and the Failure of the Anglo-French-Soviet Alliance Negotiations." *Canadian Journal of History* 41 (1): 47–84.

Strang, G. Bruce. 2008. "The Spirit of Ulysses? Ideology and British Appeasement in the 1930s." *Diplomacy and Statecraft* 19 (3): 513–514. doi:10.1080/09592290802344970.

Sullivan, Brian. 1996. "The Strategy of the Decisive Weight: Italy 1882–1922." In *The Making of Strategy: Rulers, States, and War,* edited by Williamson Murray, MacGregor Knox, and Alvin Bernstein, 307–339. Cambridge: Cambridge University Press.

Sullivan, Brian. 1998. "From Little Brother to Senior Partner: Fascist Italian Perceptions of the Nazis and of Hitler's Regime, 1930–1936." *Intelligence and National Security* 13 (1): 85–108. doi:10.1080/02684529808432464.

Sullivan, Brian. 2002. "Where One Man and Only One Man, Led: Italy's Path from Non-alignment to Non-belligerency to War, 1937–1940." In *European Neutrals and Non-belligerents during the Second World War,* edited by Neville Wylie, 119–149. Cambridge: Cambridge University Press.

Sullivan, Brian R. 2007. "The Path Marked Out by History: The German-Italian Alliance, 1939–1943." In *Hitler and His Allies in World War II,* edited by Jonathan R. Adelman, 116–132. London: Routledge.

Taffer, Andrew D. 2019. "Threat and Opportunity: Chinese Wedging in the Senkaku/Diaoyu Dispute." *Asian Security,* online, February, 1–21. doi:10.1080/14799855.2019.1567493.

Taliaferro, Jeffrey W. 2006. "State Building for Future Wars: Neoclassical Realism and the Resource-Extractive State." *Security Studies* 15 (3): 464–495. doi:10.1080/09636410601028370.

Taliaferro, Jeffrey W. 2019. *Defending Frenemies: Alliance Politics and Nuclear Nonproliferation in US Foreign Policy.* New York: Oxford University Press.

Taliaferro, Jeffrey W., Norrin M. Ripsman, and Steven E. Lobell. 2012. *The Challenge of Grand Strategy: The Great Powers and the Broken Balance between the World Wars.* New York: Cambridge University Press.

Tamkin, N. 2009. *Britain, Turkey and the Soviet Union, 1940–45: Strategy, Diplomacy and Intelligence in the Eastern Mediterranean.* London: Palgrave Macmillan.

Tarrow, Sidney. 2010. "The Strategy of Paired Comparison." *Comparative Political Studies* 43 (2): 230–259. doi:10.1177/0010414009350044.

Taylor, Adam. 2014. "That Time Ukraine Tried to Join NATO—and NATO Said No." *Washington Post,* September 4. https://www.washingtonpost.com/news

/worldviews/wp/2014/09/04/that-time-ukraine-tried-to-join-nato-and-nato
-said-no/.

Tellis, Ashley J. 2020. "The Surprising Success of the U.S.-India Partnership." *Foreign Affairs*, February 20. https://www.foreignaffairs.com/articles/india/2020
-02-20/surprising-success-us-indian-partnership.

Theis, Wallace. 2009. *Why NATO Endures*. Cambridge: Cambridge University Press.

Thomas, Martin. 1996. *Britain, France and Appeasement*. Oxford: Berg.

Thompson, J. A. 1985. "Woodrow Wilson and World War I: A Reappraisal." *Journal of American Studies* 19 (3): 325–348. doi:10.1017/S0021875800015310.

Thompson, J. A. 2002. *Woodrow Wilson*. London: Routledge.

Thornton, Sandra Winterberger. 1964. "The Soviet Union and Japan, 1939–1941." PhD diss., Georgetown University.

Tinch, Clark W. 1951. "Quasi-War between Japan and the USSR, 1937–1939." *World Politics* 3 (2): 174–199. doi:10.2307/2008951.

Toscano, Mario. 1967. *The Origins of the Pact of Steel*. Baltimore: Johns Hopkins University Press.

Toscano, Mario. 1970. *Designs in Diplomacy: Pages from European Diplomatic History*. Baltimore: Johns Hopkins University Press.

Trask, R. 1971. *The United States Response to Turkish Nationalism and Reform, 1914–1939*. Minneapolis: University of Minnesota Press.

Trenin, Dmitri. 2019a. "China, Russia, and the United States Contest a New World Order." *East Asia Forum*, May 7. https://www.eastasiaforum.org/2019/05/05
/china-russia-and-the-united-states-contest-a-new-world-order/.

Trenin, Dmitri. 2019b. "US Obsession with Containment Driving China and Russia Closer." *Global Times*, July 31. http://www.globaltimes.cn/content/1159900
.shtml.

Trenin, Dmitri. 2019c. "How Cozy Is Russia and China's Military Relationship?" *Carnegie Moscow Center Q&A*, November 19. https://carnegie.ru/2019/11/19
/how-cozy-is-russia-and-china-s-military-relationship-pub-80363.

Trevor Roper, Hugh. 1981. "History and Imagination." In *History and Imagination: Essays in Honor of H. R. Trevor Roper*, edited by Hugh Lloyd-Jones, Valerie Pearl, and Blair Worden, 356–369. London: Duckworth.

Trumpener, Ulrich. 1962. "Turkey's Entry into World War I: An Assessment of Responsibilities." *Journal of Modern History* 34 (4): 369–380.

Trumpener, Ulrich. 1968. *Germany and the Ottoman Empire, 1914–1918*. Princeton, NJ: Princeton University Press.

Trumpener, Ulrich. 2003. "The Ottoman Empire." In *The Origins of World War I*, edited by Richard F. Hamilton and Holger Herwig, 337–355. Cambridge: Cambridge University Press.

Ukrinform. 2017. "Ukraine Asks U.S. for Status as Major Non-NATO Ally." *Ukrainian Weekly*, March 31. http://www.ukrweekly.com/uwwp/ukraine-asks-u-s-for
-status-as-major-non-nato-ally/.

Uldricks, Teddy J. 2009. "War, Politics, and Memory: Russian Historians Reevaluate the Origins of World War II." *History and Memory* 21 (2): 60–82. doi:10.1353/
ham.0.0021.

Uldricks, Teddy J. 2012. "The Impossible Alliance: Strategy and Reliability in the Triple Entente Negotiations of 1939." In *Pacts and Alliances in History: Diplomatic*

Strategy and the Politics of Coalitions, edited by Melissa P. Yeager and Charles Carter, 154–169. London: I.B. Tauris.

Umbreit, Hans. 1991a. "The Battle for Hegemony in Western Europe." In *Germany and the Second World War*, vol. 2, edited by the Research Institute for Military History, Freiburg, Germany, 227–316. Oxford: Clarendon Press.

Umbreit, Hans. 1991b. "The Return to an Indirect Strategy against Britain." In *Germany and the Second World War*, vol. 2, edited by the Research Institute for Military History, Freiburg, Germany, 408–15. Oxford: Clarendon Press.

Valiani, Leo. 1966. "Italian-Austro Hungarian Negotiations, 1914–1915." *Journal of Contemporary History* 1 (3): 113–136. doi:10.1177/002200946600100306.

Vershbow, Alexander. 2018. "NATO Can Help Itself by Pulling Closer to Ukraine Now." *RealClearWorld*, June 19. https://www.realclearworld.com/articles/2018/06/19/nato_can_help_itself_by_pulling_ukraine_closer_now_112829.html.

Walt, Stephen. 1987. *The Origins of Alliances*. Ithaca, NY: Cornell University Press.

Walt, Stephen. 1997. "Why Alliances Endure or Collapse." *Survival* 39 (1): 156–179. doi:10.1080/00396339708442901.

Walt, Stephen. 2002. "Keeping the World 'Off-Balance': Self-Restraint and U.S. Foreign Policy." In *America Unrivaled: The Future of the Balance of Power*, edited by G. John Ikenberry, 121–152. Ithaca, NY: Cornell University Press.

Walt, Stephen. 2005. *Taming American Power: The Global Response to U.S. Primacy*. New York: Norton.

Walt, Stephen. 2018. *The Hell of Good Intentions: America's Foreign Policy Elite and the Decline of U.S. Primacy*. New York: Farrar, Straus, and Giroux.

Waltz, Kenneth N. 1979. *Theory of International Politics*. New York: McGraw-Hill.

Warner, Geoffrey. 1974. *Iraq and Syria, 1941*. London: Davis Poytor.

Warner, Michael. 2002. "The Kaiser Sows Destruction: Protecting the Homeland the First Time Around." *Studies in Intelligence* 46 (1): 3–9.

Watson, Mark S. 1950. *Chief of Staff: Prewar Plans and Preparations*. Washington, DC: Government Printing Office.

Watt, D. C. 1956. "The Anglo-German Naval Agreement of 1935: An Interim Judgment." *Journal of Modern History* 28 (2): 155–175. doi:10.1086/237885.

Watt, D. C. 1957. "An Earlier Model for the Pact of Steel." *International Affairs* 33 (2): 185–197. doi:10.2307/2608855.

Watt, D. C. 1960. "The Rome-Berlin Axis, 1936–1940: Myth and Reality." *Review of Politics* 22 (4): 519–554. doi:10.1017/S0034670500004095.

Watt, D. C. 1975. "Britain, France, and the Italian Problem, 1937–1939." In *Les Relations Franco-Britanniques, 1935–1939*, 277–294. Paris: Centre National de la Recherche Scientifique.

Weber, Frank W. 1979. *Germany, Britain, and the Quest for a Turkish Alliance in the Second World War*. Columbia: University of Missouri Press.

Weinberg, Gerald. 1972. *Germany and the Soviet Union*. Leiden: E. J. Brill.

Weinberg, Gerald. 1980. *Foreign Policy of Hitler's Germany*. Vol. 2. Chicago: University of Chicago Press.

Weisband, Edward. 1973. *Turkish Foreign Policy, 1943–1945*. Princeton, NJ: Princeton University Press.

Weisiger, Alex. 2016. "Exiting the Coalition: When Do States Abandon Coalition Partners during War?" *International Studies Quarterly* 61 (3): 753–765. doi:10.1093/isq/sqw029.

Weitsman, Patricia. 1997. "Intimate Enemies: The Politics of Peacetime Alliances." *Security Studies* 7 (1): 156–193. doi:10.1080/09636419708429337.

Weitsman, Patricia. 2003. "Alliance Cohesion and Coalition Warfare: The Central Powers and Triple Entente." *Security Studies* 12 (3): 79–113. doi:10.1080/09636410390443062.

Weitsman, Patricia. 2004. *Dangerous Alliances: Proponents of Peace, Weapons of War.* Palo Alto, CA: Stanford University Press.

Weitsman, Patricia. 2013. *Waging War: Alliances, Coalitions, and Institutions of Interstate Violence.* Palo Alto, CA: Stanford University Press.

Weitz, Richard. 2019. *The Expanding China-Russia Defense Partnership.* Washington, DC: Hudson Institute.

Weizsäcker, Ernst von. 1951. *The Memoirs of Ernst von Weizsäcker.* Translated by John Andrews. Chicago: Henry Regnery.

Weizsäcker, Ernst von. 1974. *Die Weizsäcker-Papiere 1933–1950.* Edited by Leonidas E. Hill. Frankfurt, Germany: Propyläen Verlag.

Westad, Odd Arne. 2019. "The Sources of Chinese Conduct: Are Washington and Beijing Fighting a New Cold War?" *Foreign Affairs* 98 (5): 86–95.

Wezeman, Siemon T., and Alexandra Kuimova. 2018. "Romania and Black Sea Security." SIPRI Background Paper, Stockholm International Peace Research Institute.

Wigell, Mikael. 2019. "Hybrid Interference as a Wedge Strategy: A Theory of External Interference in Liberal Democracy." *International Affairs* 95 (2): 255–275. doi:10.1093/ia/iiz018.

Wigell, Mikael, and Antto Vihma. 2016. "Geopolitics versus Geoeconomics: The Case of Russia's Geostrategy and Its Effects on the EU." *International Affairs* 92 (3): 605–627. doi:10.1111/1468-2346.12600.

Williams, Lawrence Prabhakar. 2013. "India's Expanded Maritime Mandala: Naval Intent and Strategy in Southeast Asia." In *India-ASEAN Defence Relations,* edited by Ajaya Kumar Das, 260–280. Singapore: S. Rajaratnam School of International Studies.

Williamson, Samuel R., and Ernest R. May. 2007. "An Identity of Opinion: Historians and July 1914." *Journal of Modern History* 79 (2): 335–387. doi:10.1086/519317.

Wishnick, Elizabeth. 2015. "Russia and China Go Sailing: Superpower on Display in the Eastern Mediterranean." *Foreign Affairs,* May 25. https://www.foreignaffairs.com/articles/china/2015-05-26/russia-and-china-go-sailing.

Wohlforth, William. 1987. "The Perception of Power: Russia in the Pre-1914 Balance." *World Politics* 39 (3): 353–381. doi:10.2307/2010224.

Wolf, Albert B. 2014. "Drive a Wedge between Russia and China." *National Interest,* April 4. https://nationalinterest.org/commentary/drive-wedge-between-russia-china-10189.

Wolfers, Arnold 1962. *Discord and Collaboration: Essays on International Politics.* Baltimore: Johns Hopkins University Press.

Wolff, Andrew T. 2015. "The Future of NATO Enlargement after the Ukraine Crisis." *International Affairs* 91 (5): 1103–1121. doi:10.1111/1468-2346.12400.

Wolff, Andrew T. 2017. "NATO's Enlargement Policy to Ukraine and Beyond: Prospects and Options." In *NATO's Return to Europe: Engaging Ukraine, Russia, and Beyond,* edited by Rebecca R. Moore and Damon Coletta, 71–96. Washington, DC: Georgetown University Press.

Wolford, Scott. 2015. *The Politics of Military Coalitions*. Cambridge: Cambridge University Press.

Wolford, Scott. 2019. *The Politics of the First World War: A Course in Game Theory and International Security*. Cambridge: Cambridge University Press.

Woodward, Llewellyn. 1970. *British Foreign Policy in the Second World War*. Vol. 1. London: H. M. Stationary Office.

Yarhi-Milo, Keren, Alexander Lanoszka, and Zack Cooper. 2016. "To Arm or to Ally? The Patron's Dilemma and the Strategic Logic of Arms Transfers and Alliances." *International Security* 41 (2): 90–139. doi:10.1162/ISEC_a_00250.

Yasamee, F. A. K. 1995. "Ottoman Empire." In *Decisions for War 1914*, edited by Keith Wilson, 229–269. New York: St. Martin's Press.

Yin, Chengzhi. 2020. "Accommodation or Coercion: China's Choices of Alliance Balancing Strategies." PhD diss., Boston College.

Yoo, H. J. 2015. "China's Friendly Offensive toward Japan in the 1950s: The Theory of Wedge Strategies and International Relations." *Asian Perspective* 39 (1): 1–26. doi:10.1353/apr.2015.0007.

Young, Robert. 1984. "Soldiers and Diplomats: The French Embassy and Franco-Italian Relations, 1935–6." *Journal of Strategic Studies* 7 (1): 74–91. doi:10.1080/01402398408437177.

Yousafzai, Fawad. 2016. "China to Build Mega Oil Pipeline from Gwadar to Kashgar." *The Nation* (Pakistan), June 13. http://nation.com.pk/national/13-Jun-2016/china-to-build-mega-oil-pipeline-from-gwadar-to-kashgar.

Zagare, Frank. 2012. *The Games of July: Explaining the Great War*. Ann Arbor: University of Michigan Press.

Zeman, Z. A. B. 1971. *A Diplomatic History of the First World War*. London: Weidenfeld & Nicolson.

Index

Page numbers in italic refer to tables.